WATCHING WALTER CRONKITE

Austin Kutscher has written a memoir that not only delights in the '60s suburbia, but also brings thoughtful insight to the current mind-set of the Baby Boomer Generation.

Ed Harris, Actor/Director

As a historian, I took special interest in Ken's take on the major events of the 1960's. He touches on almost all of them, but thankfully he isn't a Zelig or even a Forrest Gump. *Watching Walter Cronkite* is a coming-of-age memoir to which high school and college students can readily relate. It is a narrative that a skilled teacher can use in an American History or American Studies course.

Eric Rothschild, Retired Chairman of History Department of Scarsdale High School and 1990-91 Distinguished Social Studies Educator of New York State

As a Marine infantry officer during the 1968 Tet Offensive and a veteran who experienced the effect that Walter Cronkite's nightly news reports had on the public's attitude towards the war and its warriors, I was deeply moved by reading Dr. Kutscher's *Watching Walter Cronkite*—a "coming-of-age" memoir that reads like a novel and provides a poignant "flashback" of the decades that largely shaped the world we live in today. And as a retired secondary school administrator, I highly recommend this book for educators who want a valuable resource to help students understand the complexities that face all Americans during this most tumultuous period in American history.

Nicholas S. Romanetz, Colonel USMCR (Ret)

WATCHING WALTER CRONKITE

Reflections on Growing Up in the 1950s and 1960s

by

Austin Ken Kutscher, M.D.

Aunt Ken Kutscher

Gordian Knot Books

An Imprint of Richard Altschuler & Associates, Inc.

New York

Watching Walter Cronkite: Reflections of Growing Up in the 1950s and 1960s. Copyright© 2009 by Austin Ken Kutscher. For information contact the publisher, Richard Altschuler & Associates, Inc., at 100 West 57th Street, New York, NY 10019, RAltschuler@rcn.com or (212) 397-7233.

www.watchingwaltercronkite.com

Library of Congress Control Number: 2009922289

CIP data for this book are available from the Library of Congress

Hardcover ISBN: 978-1-884092-81-7

Softcover ISBN: 978-1-884092-80-0

First Printing

Printed in the United States of America

Acknowledgements

Acknowledging all of the people who have helped with my memoir would require a list of all of the people who made the 60s what they were. However, on a personal level, without Mary Ellen and my families and our friends—there wouldn't be much to tell.

It was only with the encouragement and support of my wife Mary Ellen that I was able to even begin this project, let alone bring it to fruition. Many hours of writing, research, and editing were undertaken with her comforting presence. But most importantly, she provided the inspiration to give our story its soul. Thank you from the bottom of my heart!

Of course, along the way there were many readers who felt strongly that I should continue my efforts to bring my book to print. My oldest friends, Barbara and Laird Coates, stepped aside from their professional editorial careers to help direct my writing. My editors, Richard and Jane Altschuler, were instrumental in helping to bring my project to its publication.

Nick Romanetz, Colonel, USMCR (Ret) read and edited my manuscript when it was titled *1969* and it was through our discussions that I came to realize the importance that Walter Cronkite had on the perceptions of our generation. And thus the change of the title to *Watching Walter Cronkite*. My high school history teacher, Eric Rothschild, came out of "retirement" to read and edit my manuscript, as we met to relieve our times together forty years ago.

For my Mom and my Dad—through our happiness and our sadness, I only wish you were here together to share our love.

And finally, to my daughter, Jannie, and Mary Ellen's son, Philip, thank you for letting me share your parents' story.

Dedication

This book is dedicated to the members of the Class of 1969 and their colleagues who died in Vietnam serving their government. May their sacrifices never be forgotten.

"If the reader prefers, this book may be regarded as fiction. But there is always the chance that such a book of fiction may throw some light on what has been written as fact."

Ernest Hemingway, A Moveable Feast—Preface

mem-oir / noun

A record of events written by a person having intimate knowledge of them and based on personal observation.

Random House Unabridged Dictionary

The memories here are my own, and I apologize for any discrepancies between those of my family and friends. Although historical references are all factual, on a personal level some names and events were slightly altered to protect the "guilty." The innocent need no such protection.

Foreword

The phone rang. "Mr. Rothschild," a deep voice asked. "Do you remember me?" I did, of course. Ken Kutscher, Class of '69 and his younger brother, Martin, Class of '73, were strong students. And now, nearly forty years after his graduation from Scarsdale High School, Ken wanted me to read and comment on his *magnum opus*, a memoir set in the 1960s. I told him to email it to me and that I'd think about it and would call him after the weekend.

Initially, I wasn't overjoyed at Ken's offer. My past experiences with memoirs were mixed at best. A few years ago, Arthur Schlesinger, Jr. signed off on a memoir that among other things, reviewed all the movies he had seen while he was waiting out the entry of the U.S. into World War II. Other than a few movie buffs, I wondered who would care. To be charitable, after the *Age of Jackson, The Imperial Presidency,* and Schlesinger's multi-volume *Age of Roosevelt,* almost any prose would prove disappointing.

A few years earlier, David McCullough's glorious biography of Harry Truman, had led me to revisit our 33rd president, his memoirs, and especially his defense of his actions in firing General Douglas MacArthur. As I let these memoirs wash over me, I wondered whether only the ruminations of men and women of power would capture my interest. As a high school teacher with nearly forty years in the classroom, I knew instinctively that was absolutely the wrong message to give my students. Remember, these are adolescents. They are the center of the world, at least to them. Who speaks for them?

I had a half answer, and it wasn't exactly a memoir. It was the *Roots* phenomenon of the mid-1970s. Jim Dyer, a friend of mine from college, had helped finance the publication of *Roots* in his job at the Carnegie Foundation. For part of a year, I had the opportunity of seeing the impact of Alex Haley's brainchild up close, including listening to the prisoners in the Greenhaven Penitentiary hear Haley talk about the moment when he realized that the Griot who was telling the history of his people was describing the moment that they were taken away to a distant land. This was the true beginning of the story that has led us to the historic election and inauguration of Barack Obama four decades after Ken's story left off.

Over that long weekend, I did more than think about Ken's four hundred page memoir. I started to read it. Miraculously, I think, Ken had managed to capture the two strands of writing that earlier memoirs had too often missed. Years earlier, as his teacher, I knew next to nothing about his real life. I knew that his mother had died but had nary a hint that his father had remarried and at his step-mother's insistence, had taken the family to Scarsdale. In reading about the life of this young man, I found myself caring about him. I also found myself angry at his father (for reasons I won't go into here) and curious about his love interest. We also shared an interest in sports.

AS a historian, I took special interest in Ken's take on the major events of the 1960s. He touches on almost all of them, but thankfully he isn't a Zelig or even a Forrest Gump. The result is a narrative that a skilled teacher can use in an American History or American Studies class.

By Sunday evening, I had finished reading *Watching Walter Cronkite*. My call to Ken that evening was a request. "Could I read his memoir again?"

Eric Rothschild, Retired Chairman of the History Department of Scarsdale High School and the 1990-91 Distinguished Social Studies Educator of New York State. He now has the honor of being the Historian of the Village of Scarsdale, New York.

PROLOGUE

November 5, 2008, 1 a.m.

"WOW! What a nite! Obama wins! Hope u were watching! Luv ya, DAD"

In this era of texting, IM, and YouTube, everything is here, now, truncated down into its minimalist form.

But here's what I really wanted to tell my daughter Jannie, as my wife Mary and I watched President-elect Barack Obama during his victory speech at Grant Park in Chicago a few hours ago. I could not help but reflect back to a time 40 years ago in that same Grant Park, when all was not so celebratory. The United States was in a state of turmoil as my generation was protesting against our government's involvement in Vietnam and the discrimination of the blacks and poor in the cities and throughout the South. How far we have come—and how far we have to go!

Jannie was just 13 when our country and our sense of safety and security were violated on September 11, 2001. That day was much the same as a week 39 years earlier. Our country was on the brink of a nuclear war, when Russia supplied nuclear missiles to Cuba, only 90 miles away from our border. Our citizens came together, prayed together, and were united in purpose. Everyone who watched television or kept up with the news will always remember where they were and what they were doing when mankind's existence was threatened.

But for those of us who grew up during the 1960s, this sense of unity and cohesiveness would soon dissolve. For sure, we all remembered where we were when John Kennedy, Martin Luther King, Jr., and Robert Kennedy were assassinated. And who could forget watching Walter Cronkite on the CBS Evening News keeping us spellbound during the historic space flights of Alan Shepard, John Glenn, and Apollo XI.

What was so different about the years following my 13th birthday compared to Jannie's teenage years, however, was the division amongst our citizens of different ages and socio-economic and racial backgrounds. Mary and I were members of the high school classes of 1968and 1969. We had lived through the '50s, much as Jannie had lived through the '90s, playing baseball and tag, certain we were protected from the outside world by our families. But our innocence was shattered— not by the fear of terrorism but by the threat of nuclear weapons. And although, much as with Iraq today, we were fighting a controversial war in Vietnam in the '60s, there was no such respect for our soldiers as heroes.

Our memories of growing up during that decade, especially the year 1969, have taken on mystical feelings. Despite the "miracles" of Neil Armstrong's walk on the Moon and the New York Mets' World Series victory, the '60s were more about who and what we left behind—in the jungles of Vietnam, in America's inner cities, on the Moon, and in our private lives.

The '60s transformed into the '70s, as I went to medical school, and then in the '80s respectability and responsibility became paramount, as I became a cardiologist and a parent. Then, in the 1990s, when I was also Mayor of Flemington, New Jersey, I stood before our Vietnam Vets and their families, during the opening Memorial Service at the "Moving Vietnam Wall." As I nervously began to speak, I was overwhelmed by a deep-seated conflict and guilt. Although I felt I had righteously protested an immoral war, I also know that I had cowardly avoided the draft and the "killing fields," by virtue of my student 2S deferment. That day, even after all of those years, I was humbled standing before these heroes, who had made such a big sacrifice for our country. How could I make them understand why we had marched against the war and now, somehow, ask for their forgiveness, so I that I could honor them? Would they understand? Could Jannie understand?

Now, on this election night, as Mary and I watched Senator Obama assume the baton of national leadership after listening to Senator John McCain (former POW of the Vietnam War and hero of the Vietnam Vets) give his moving concession speech, we wondered, "Could there be healing now?"

The only thing missing on the television tonight, as we tuned out the "talking heads," so full of their self-importance, was a voice filled with intelligence but tempered by humility. We kept channel surfing, as we watched the commentators on CNN or Fox or CBS drone on, as they micro-analyzed the votes cast. Who was Jannie watching in her dorm? I only fantasized that, instead of Jannie being 90 miles away at college, she was sitting with us in our living room watching Walter Cronkite—the most respected voice on TV, and perhaps in the entire nation—during the years Mary and I came of age.

But reality hit as I remembered that my daughter was all "grown up" now, a college junior, an eaglet spreading her wings. And Mary and I are now the senior generation—with no parents for us to text messages of love.

"Obama rules! Everyone says hi! Luv 2 u and Mary! Jannie"

Then the Obama girls came out onto the platform with their mom to join their dad. Martin Luther King's words, spoken back in August 1963, had come true: "I have a dream that my four little children will one day live in a nation where they will not be judged by the color of their skin but by the content of their character."

The Obama girls' beaming faces reminded me of our days when I took off my cardiologist hat and, as mayor, walked down Main Street during the Memorial Day parades, with Jannie at my side as the "Little Mayor," smiling and waving at the crowds.

I remembered back to another night over seven years ago, before 9/11, when Jannie was still innocent and I discovered that, as Ricky Ricardo would so often say to Lucy, "You've got some 'splaining to do."

That was June 8, 2001.

"Daaad, you promised me you'd help me with a topic for my paper. Somehow it's got to be about China." Even as Jannie sat down quietly next to us, I could sense the beginning of a tear, the held back sob. And then, almost as an afterthought, she said, "And it's due tomorrow!" We didn't call her "DQ"—"Drama Queen"—for no reason.

What parent hasn't heard those dreaded words? At least Jannie hadn't waited until the library was closed to blurt out her confession. I started to relive the painful memories of both my junior high school study habits and my parents' futile attempts to "comfort me," as they asked:

"Austin, why didn't you start working on this earlier?"

Now I was the benign, comforting parent. "Jannie, don't worry. We'll get through this together. Let's go find some books."

Jannie raced us upstairs to the history section. She was a freshman in high school and, although she was diligent about studying her Torah portion from "The Book of Numbers" for her upcoming Bat Mitzvah, she was much more interested in her teen boy bands, N'Sync and the Backstreet Boys, and her horse than in world history. And she had finally outgrown her "Beanie Babies." No more early morning standing on line by her parents to procure the latest bear or lion or shaggy dog!

Even then, I didn't see much of her parents in her face, but she was the spitting image of my mother, in a picture I found of her when she was Jannie's age. Jannie, however, is neither from my mom's generation nor from mine. Her T-shirt was stenciled "American Eagle" as opposed to having an embroidered French Lacoste alligator. She was dressed in jeans with just a mild flair—not baggy like the pants some of the boys her age wore, two sizes too large, sagging halfway down their butts, with their boxer shorts the only thing keeping them from perpetually "mooning" the world. And they were certainly not like the skin-tight, hip-hugger, bell-bottom jeans my girlfriends wore in the late '60s, which were meant to signify a sexual freedom that has re-emerged in the shape of "hooking up" and having sex with friends. As the fear of AIDS has diminished because of new anti-viral drugs that have continued to appear, I live with parental dread about the sexual expectations of a generation where the most famous advertising slogan is "Just Do It."

As we reached the stacks, I realized that to Jannie this was still just a school assignment. To me, it was a flashback.

"How about getting out some books on Red China and Russia and writing about the Cold War and the Red Menace?" My old days as a political science major at Columbia College were emerging.

I thought about Mao and the Cultural Revolution, about Chiang Kai-shek and Taiwan, about the "two Chinas," one "free," one "Red," about all the books I had read, highlighting entire paragraphs in yellow marker. I remembered the all-nighters I had pulled, typing up my college term papers. Now, of course, I couldn't remember any details about them.

I had become a cardiologist, and although I was not a neurologist, I believed the brain could only retain a certain amount of information. My memory bank was overloaded with information about drugs and disease processes, and I'd had to jettison so much information from my hard drive. Any computer geek could've told me that.

"Dad, the paper is due in 12 hours!"

Jannie's panic recreated in my mind my own recurrent adolescent nightmare. Feelings of remorse for not starting my paper earlier would escalate into full-blown desperation—another late night was looming ahead to finish my book report! Would my mom get up early in the morning to help edit my paper? Would I have enough time to rewrite my report legibly?

I tried to connect with what was going on in my mind and life when I was Jannie's age, in 1964. My mom was still alive. We were still a family tightly rotating around her center, a gyroscope spinning steadily on its vertical axis. But off in the not-so-distant world the Beatles sang of revolution, of drugs, of escape. The nightly news was beginning to show the horrors of the Vietnam War. I awaited my transformation into maturity and independence.

By the summer of 1969, the impact of the war in that small Southeast Asian country, so far away, with so many lives sacrificed and destroyed, had far reaching implications, as our country also tried to come to grips with our own racial and economic inequalities. These experiences have long been ingrained in the minds of my generation, including those who fought and did not fight; they are part of our permanent hard drives that just cannot be replaced by another CD.

I wondered, "Where will Jannie be four years from now?"

Jannie had never lived through a war—neither "cold" nor with "warm," living, human bodies. She didn't know the fear of nuclear annihilation, of the threats of the Russians and Chinese to wipe out democracy. In this new millennium, Russia and Red China, no longer our evil enemies, were now economically intertwined with us, as Communism merged with Capitalism.

"Why don't you write about China and Vietnam, about the Chinese invasion of Vietnam in the late 1970s?"

"Dad, what are you talking about? I don't get it." Jannie's eyes filled with real tears.

I knew I had to explain. "Jannie, take a deep breath."

But how do you tell your 13-year-old daughter in five minutes the background and substance of a history that was the center of your universe as a high school and college student—the exact period of her life she was now entering? She had seen a little of the Vietnam War on the reruns of the "Wonder Years," a television series about growing up in the early '70s, but her generation was oblivious to the issues that had consumed those of us who had come of age in the 1960s.

"Jannie, how do I begin?"

"Just make it short, Dad, I don't have all night."

"Jannie, Vietnam was a country divided. In the North, it was Communist; in the South, there was an attempt at democracy, corrupt as it was. The United States was afraid that if the Communist armies of the North took over the South, there would be a 'Domino Effect'."

"Dad, wait, you're going too fast. What's a Domino Effect?"

"You know, like when you put all the dominoes in a curving row, and then knock the first one over and watch all of the rest go down."

"Yeah, we did that in third grade."

"Anyway, we were afraid that if the Communists took over Vietnam, they would take over all of Southeast Asia. So we fought there for

20 years, first with just money and some military advisors but then, finally, in the last 10 years, we sent over 600,000 soldiers and lost over 55,000 men and women."

"But who won, Dad?"

"Well, there were lots of us high school and college kids along with some grownups here in the U.S. who were very upset with what was going on. There were lots of meetings and marches, and in the end we had our own civil unrest as our generation protested loudly, and at times violently, saying that this was a bad war, an immoral war. As the North Vietnamese continued to show that they weren't going to give up on their Civil War, the U.S. decided to withdraw our army and let the South Vietnamese fight their own battles. But in reality, we ended up abandoning Vietnam, knowing we couldn't win the war, and knowing that the South couldn't defend itself without us. And when North Vietnam invaded South Vietnam after we left, our new president at the time, Gerald Ford, refused to get our soldiers involved again, to lose any more men or women in a hopeless cause. So all of Vietnam became Communist."

"So did the 'dominoes' fall?"

"No."

"So what does that have to do with China?"

"Well, after all of the fighting, after the Vietnamese had kicked us out, China tried to invade them five years later—and as your friends would say, the Vietnamese 'kicked their butts,' and kept them out, just like they did to the French and to us."

It was obvious, at least to me, that Ho Chi Minh and his freedom fighters were more Vietnamese than they were Communist!

"Well, I guess it wasn't like the Desert Storm War, Dad! Remember, I still have my General Schwarzkopf baseball card. We didn't lose that war, did we?"

"No, Jannie. Maybe we learned our lesson to get out quickly and not get stuck in someone else's business."

"T.M.I. [Too Much Information] Dad. Just help me get the books so I can start working." Jannie was tired. She was beat. Ah, I could see the teenage years ahead. But she was my daughter.

Figuring this should be easy, we scanned the racks for a book covering the history of Vietnam after the United States withdrew in defeat in 1975. Publication dates of 1974, 1975, 1976, 1982 . . . all books written solely from the American perspective. Then there was nothing. Twenty years of barren literary efforts. It was as if Vietnam was forgotten, only existing in the minds and hearts and various injured or missing body parts of those soldiers who lived through the hell of their tour of duty. No wonder we lost the war—even the revisionist historians still didn't look at the war from the Southeast Asians' perspective!

Then I found it!

"Jannie, this is it. We finally hit gold. This book has everything you need summarized in 20 pages."

Fodor's Guide to Vietnam. The only book in the Hunterdon County Library that discussed what had transpired during the 20 years after our generation was "defined." Vietnam had become a footnote in our history.

As we climbed back down the stairs, Jannie started reading her books. Meanwhile, I started killing time looking through *The New York Times* microfilm. I was trying to find the write-up of the first baseball game that I remembered going to with my family. I knew it was in 1958, after the National League intra-city rivals, the New York Giants and the Brooklyn Dodgers, had abandoned their fans for the glitz and revenues of California. My dad must have been pretty angry with his heroes as he took us to see the Baltimore Orioles play the hated American League dominators at Yankee Stadium.

But first I took a side trip down memory lane to the microfilm of May 29, 1951—my birthday—to see what happened that day. It was only six years since World War II had ended with the Allied victory over the German Nazis and Italian Fascists and the dropping of the atomic bomb over Hiroshima and Nagasaki. It was only six years since the end of Hitler's genocide of six million Jews. And there had been only six years of healing and rebuilding Europe as the Cold War escalated with the Communist threat to annihilate the Free World.

Years ago, *The Times* had advertised laminated copies of the front page from a reader's birthday. It occurred to me, however, that what I really wanted to read was the issue dated May 30, 1951, because that contained the news of what had happened on the day I was born—what crises occurred, what happened to our troops in Korea, and what Cold War event occurred. That issue also contained news of Willie Mays' exploits early in his rookie season with the Giants, when he was a struggling colored player breaking into a profession that was only slightly behind the United States Armed Forces in ending segregation. Luckily for Willie, New York was the melting pot where he could easily assimilate, much as Vietnam, on a more tragic level, was the cauldron where the lower class (and occasionally middle class) blacks and whites of our generation were left to be burned, toasted, and congealed together.

I fast-forwarded the tape to one other date in New York Giant history—October 1951, the famous (or infamous) day of Bobby Thomson's pennant winning home run. I had heard Russ Hodges, the Giant's radio announcer, call of the game (recorded for eternity) by a Brooklyn Dodger fan): "THE GIANTS WIN THE PENNANT, THE GIANTS WIN THE PENNANT! AND THEY'RE GOING CRAZY!"

Later, as I was writing this book, trying to connect to my past, to have my dad connect to his past, I asked him where he was that day, three months after I was born.

"I was in my dental office," he laughed, "with a patient in the chair. The radio was on. It was a lost cause. The Giants were down by two runs in the ninth inning, one man out and two men on base when Bobby Thomson hit his home run to win the playoff. I left my patient and went out to the waiting room and kissed my secretary!" She was probably the only other woman he had kissed in his life at that time, except for my mom (and I suppose my grandmother).

That night, as I tried to center the microfilm tape, which contained a whole month of the Earth's history on celluloid no larger than a can of tuna fish, to read about "The Shot Heard Round the World," I saw the description of the first Hydrogen Bomb exploded by the Soviet Union! That marked the beginning of Soviet catch-up in the Cold War, which would accelerate into their superiority in the race for space—a competition that would pervade the first 18 years of my life. Other articles described the trial of Julius and Ethel Rosenberg, who were found guilty of spying for the Communists and sentenced to death. Ads were promoting J.D. Salinger's new book, *The Catcher in the Rye,* along with a new movie starring Ronald Reagan, "Bedtime for Bonzo."

It was "History's Timeline": Democracy battling Communism, defining Superman's mission on Earth—"Defending truth, justice and the American way"—along with coming-of-age books and baseball. These were the parallel threads that wove the fabric of my existence. They rarely crossed paths, but at times flowed so close as to have an effect on each other, altering the direction of my future. And for my wife, Mary, these threads wove a fabric much more flamboyant, much more colorful. She was the Catholic girl gone rebellious, while I remained the good Jewish boy, afraid to go bad! But it was still our families, the looms for these fabrics, who were probably the ultimate determinants of the ongoing procession of our lives.

The yins and yangs of family: parents striving to protect their children as their children are yearning to spread their wings. My mom had died in 1966 when I was 14. She wasn't around to guide me, to help me grow up, mature, escape, become my own person. But I could still feel her gravitational pull teaching me her precepts of goodness. Could I keep Jannie in my gravitational forces, even as she was spiraling away? Could I teach her to love and respect her fellow man as my mom had taught me?

GENESIS

THE FIELD OF DREAMS

June, 1958

First grade is a wonderful time in school if you are not a problem child. Our teacher, Mrs. Plum, was kind and motherly, her black hair carefully straightened, framing her dark brown face. It was the end of academic innocence for me, as by second-grade my classmates were already being labeled "special" or "average." (In those days, we didn't classify students as "ADHD.") It was also an era when the outside world did not intrude upon our lives. How could a six-year-old understand nuclear annihilation or Communism, let alone his own parents' problems and angst?

It was only on the playground that we understood competition. Not yet ready to play baseball, we enjoyed playing kickball. We learned the fundamentals of hits, runs, and, unfortunately, errors and outs. When I was the captain, I tried to pick Ellis, a short black boy, wearing thick glasses, his curly black hair closely cropped, because he could kick the ball the farthest. No one dared call him "four-eyes." My best friend, George, a real brain but uncoordinated, a prototype for the phrase "White Men Can't Jump," would always yell, "Pick me! Pick me!" as the tears ran down his cheeks, because he didn't get chosen until there were only girls left. And, even then, several of the more mature girls had already been asked to join my team, which was an even greater insult to his impending manhood. Oh how I wished that my favorite Mouseketeer, Annette Funicello, were in my class. Her short, curly, black hair, heavy eyebrows, and playful innocence would be such an asset to our team. She already had a uniform—with "ANNETTE" in bold across the front of her white pullover. Her Mouseketeer hat was a little unusual for the ball field, but it would do. Instead, there was George—but even his new, blue Keds sneakers didn't help.

"Why do I always get picked last?" George moaned. He trudged over to our side of the field, his head down, as if the world had just come to an end.

It was the mid-'50s, and we were living in the suburbs of New Jersey. We didn't know black from white. We all studied together and played on the ball field together. Sure, we knew we weren't all equal, but still everyone deserved a chance. That's why we let George play on the team—even if it was in right field.

"Because you stink at kickball!" I was brutally honest. "You throw and kick like a girl." I'd hear these words ring again in my ears in later life, when I was unceremoniously informed, after the first tryout for the high school basketball team, that I would have the rest of the day off to finish studying for my math test.

What words of sympathy did I know at age six? We didn't understand diplomacy any more than did Nikita Khrushchev. And the 12-Step-Programs, the Serenity Prayer—"God, grant me the serenity to accept the things I cannot change, the courage to change the things I can, and the wisdom to know the difference"—had not yet infiltrated down into the Stelton Elementary School.

But at least in first grade I was still considered a student athlete. I dreamed of playing baseball in the Big Leagues. I just needed a little more skill, which I was sure I would learn from watching my first live baseball game. So, on the Saturday night before we were to see this life-expanding event, I had my bath, put on my baseball "PJs," and went to bed early. Everything was lined up for the game tomorrow—my brother Harlan's hand-me-down jeans with shortened cuffs and my sneakers, clean shirt, and blue baseball cap. I figured if I fell asleep early, then Sunday morning would come sooner and we would all be on our way to New York City. I had seen the World Series game last year on television, with players in their baggy woolen uniforms, pitchers and catchers, batters and infielders, all against a background of a wide-open, black and white outfield and scoreboard. It was something like the field with the backstop at our school, only the bleachers were a little bigger and the grass wasn't green.

My mom told me we would be leaving at 11 a.m. to make the 40 mile adventurous trip from Edison, New Jersey, to Yankee Stadium. To say that I can recall the exact details of my inner and outer child's enthusiasm would be absurd, but given my subsequent behavior over the years, I am sure I was up at 6 a.m., and dressed and ready to go at 6:10. My patience started to wear thin, so I called my dog, Fuzzer, a black Cocker Spaniel who was my best pal. But on this morning, she looked up from her bed, stretched, wagged her tail, yawned, and went back to sleep. Even though I had told her the night before what we were doing, I guess she was unimpressed—after all, we didn't buy her a ticket! My brothers, Harlan—eight years old and lucky enough to have his own bedroom because of childhood asthma—and Marty—three years my junior, with whom I was condemned to share a bedroom until I went off to college— were still asleep.

On the way to the bathroom, my gait closer to stomping than to tiptoeing, I passed my parents' bedroom. The door was closed but I listened and heard their rhythmic breathing, still peacefully sleeping. I knocked on the door quietly.

"Austin, give us ten more minutes."

It seemed to take my mom and dad forever to get up that morning. It was like watching grass grow. But, finally, they were up, dressed, and in the kitchen. My mom was wearing a blue blouse with frills, a black skirt hemmed below the knees, stockings, and sturdy black shoes. Her hair was brown, neatly permed, and combed back off her forehead. She was a woman of stature, tall for her time at 5'-7". Although she would never be skinny, having "large bones," full hips, and a well- proportioned torso, she was pretty, if not beautiful, easy to look at, with her fair complexion and striking blue eyes.

She stood fixing our food for the day trip. In those days, before corporate greed, you were allowed to bring your own food into the stadium. Her dad had been a *Maitre D'* at a leading New York City restaurant during both the "Roaring '20s" and Depression of the '30s, so she had once known good food. Unfortunately, her life had turned tragic at 14 when her mother died of breast cancer, and her father went to jail as the "fall guy" for tax evasion by the owners of the restaurant. She was brought up on Riverside Drive by her Aunt Hilda and Uncle Alan, lived with her cousins, Harriet and Bruce, and attended Richmond High School and then Hunter College, a fellow "alum" of Humphrey Bogart's flame, Lauren Bacall.

She was putting together the "staple"—bologna on white (we were a Wonder Bread family), with a little Hellmann's mayonnaise. No Kraft's Miracle Whip for my mom! She believed in the commercial jingle "Bring out the Hellmann's and bring out the best." If we were lucky, we would get two slices of that Red Dye #2- colored meat product, with the crust cut off the edges of the bread. PB & J was the other staple, but she knew we'd get peanuts at the game. There were no juice boxes in those days; instead, she mixed orange Kool-Aid in a thermos bottle.

My dad was already preparing for the worst. You could tell from looking at him that he wasn't hip like my friends' dads. He had grown up in Staten Island, the younger of two sons of a not-so-prominent New York City attorney and a Jewish, Texan "debutante." He was born with a congenital hip disorder that limited his athleticism and enhanced his being a "mama's boy." His father had died when he was 14, just like my mom's mom, and he felt no pressure to follow in his footsteps as an attorney. Today (or any other day, for that matter) he was no Humphrey Bogart, as he was predictably dressed in his baggy pants, probably from a worn-out suit, along with a white dress shirt, tie, and black shoes. His pens were in the plastic pen-holder in his shirt pocket, along with a few note pads held in place by his tie clasp. Medium height and medium build, with short, wavy, brown hair greased back over his head, unfashionable tortoise shell glasses, and my Jewish nose, his face predicted how I might look 40 years later, if I wasn't careful.

"Helene, make sure you put in extra sandwiches and juice. What if the game goes into extra innings and they run out of food at the stadium?"

"Don't worry, Bill, they don't look like they're going to starve to death." My mom, a saint in my eyes except for the days when she would wash my mouth out with Ivory soap when I talked back to her, continued packing the lunch. She knew full well that we would be stuffed after the peanuts and hotdogs we would insist upon eating.

"Well, don't forget to bring that dental journal for me to read in between games." His obsession for not wasting time was, unfortunately, being ingrained into my character at that time.

"Of course, Bill."

That was settled, as usual, with Dad having the last word and Mom smart enough to know that her devotion to him exceeded any need to correct his incorrigible behavior. After all, she had married my father, her high school sweetheart, and would follow and work with him wherever his professional dreams would carry him. It was her responsibility to smooth the way, as her three boys were brought along. We were hardly as transient as army brats but still moved so often that we saw a new part of metropolitan New York every five years.

She met my dad when she was "Sweet 16" on the day he came with a friend to visit her sister, and they fell instantly in love. They dated while my dad went through dental school at Columbia University (having passed up an opportunity to go to Tufts Medical School in respect to her Christian Science background). By the end of World War II, they were married. Three boys later, our family surfaced in central New Jersey, my dad leaving his lucrative dental practice and fifth-floor apartment on Fifth Avenue, along with our summer home in Sharon, Connecticut, with all of the potential for a life of urban splendor, to join Squibb Pharmaceuticals as a drug researcher. He achieved, among other things, a significant pay cut, but also developed Kenalog with orabase, a great treatment for oral canker sores that is still used today. Instead of sirloin steaks when we went out for dinner on special occasions, we got chopped sirloin at the new drive-in restaurant with Golden Arches up the road (12 cents for a hamburger, 15 cents for a cheeseburger, and 12 cents for fries or a coke—the original ½-dollar meal); and my mom, instead of being a homemaker, became his executive secretary, as he now was the Editor of *The Journal of Dental Pharmacology and Therapeutics*.

Instead of prime real estate in New York, we moved into a new development where our house was one of the first to be occupied in the typical '50s look-alike community. The only difference among houses was the color of the shutters and whether the garage was on the left side or the right. Our mansion was the last on the block, a split-level, white with blue shutters. The farmland it was built on was barren of landscaping or trees. Behind our house was scrub, with the New York-Washington railroad tracks about ½ mile away, delineating any growth potential for our suburb. What irony that we were two miles from the military base Camp Kilmer, named after Joyce Kilmer, author of:

"I think that I shall never see

A poem lovely as a tree"

Mr. Kilmer certainly had not traveled down our road recently. Even Camp Kilmer was pretty empty now, its rows of barracks, which had only 12 years ago been full of recruits being trained to fight during World War II, now used for YMCA camp sleepovers. The camp was a fitting spot for the beginning of the Nuclear Age, devoid of significant animal life or vegetation. It seemed we wouldn't need soldiers to kill anymore—nuclear weapons would make them obsolete.

My new neighborhood lacked any other sense of history—no nooks, crannies, ghosts in the house, trees to climb outside. When I drove by my old house years later to show Jannie where I had grown up, the only change was the maturity of the trees, which now reached the half-century mark, similar in age to myself. One small oak, which I protected from the gardeners when it was just a little sprout, was now maturing nicely, coming into its own, just as I was reaching the peak of my career. It had a bright future of becoming a model for Joyce Kilmer, bigger and stronger.

As we grew, so had the weeping willow, which also served as third base for our sandlot field. So had the small evergreen that stood as second base, right across our property line. First base never changed—it was the tree trunk stripped barren, its gnarled wood now standing upright into the sky, ready to transmit telephone and power amperages to our homes. It was here that we had honed our baseball skills, pre-Little League era. Our uniforms were jeans, horizontal, pinstriped polo shirts, white socks, and black Keds sneakers. Only the hats gave each of us individuality. Mine was the blue Braves hat with the "M" on it, for Milwaukee. I was Eddie Mathews, All-Star third baseman—except when they needed me to pitch or play outfield. We were men for all seasons.

But today I was looking forward to the real thing, real uniforms, real grass, and real dirt.

Finally, we piled out to the car, me leading the way. I'd seen us waste enough time!

Marty yelled. "Where's my Pinky?" His little pink bear, which he took everywhere, had not been packed.

As he ran back into the house to get him, Dad yelled, "OK boys, get in the car while we are waiting for Marty and Mom." And then he said with added enthusiasm, which many years later was mimicked on TV advertisements for Disney World, "We're going to a ballgame!"

Our gray '57 Chevy station wagon with tailfins and air conditioning was fully loaded. The only thing missing was a partition for the back seat to keep us brothers from attacking each other. Harlan had to be kept up front or else there would have been a riot. In the meantime, all the food was on the center seat between Marty and me—a blueprint for the Berlin Wall of New Jersey.

As we finally got our ticket to get on the New Jersey Turnpike, the noise started, as a whisper, then escalated to a general whine:

"Are we there yet?"

"Be careful, Dad. Don't drive too fast. Otherwise the "Highway Patrol" will hunt you down."

"Yeah, Dad, I can just see Broderick Crawford coming up to the window, his pistol drawn, ready to arrest you."

"Enough, boys, just let your dad drive," Mom begged. "He has a hard enough time without your encouragement."

"Can I have a sandwich?"

"I need to go to the bathroom."

"I can't hold it anymore. Can we pull over to the side of the road?"

"Dad, Harlan made a stinky smell!"

"No, Austin, it's not Harlan. It's just New Jersey."

Harlan turned and stuck his tongue out at me as we passed by the natural gas tanks and factories, with their sulfa exhausts, near Newark Airport.

We drove across the George Washington Bridge, the upper and only deck, as "Martha" (the lower deck) had not yet been built, past Columbia-Presbyterian Medical Center, where my dad taught part-time in the dental school, and then down the Major Deegan Expressway. There, in the distance, was not just one but two sporting edifices: to the east of the East River, Yankee Stadium, and to the west of the river, built on Coogan's Bluff in Harlem, the Polo Grounds, which up until last year was the home of his Giants. I felt the car being steered towards the Polo Grounds by an invisible force, mournful and desolate, the spirit of my dad's favorite player, Mel Ott, casting a spell over us. But Mel Ott had become an announcer for the Detroit Tigers, and the Giants were now even more remote in California. And we were following the line of cars into the nearest parking lot to Yankee Stadium.

I was the first out of the car, the door almost taken off as the car behind us suddenly pulled in beside us.

"Austin, be careful. We've got plenty of time,"

"Look at all those people up ahead. We'll never get in. Hurry!"

Of course, all of my prodding wouldn't get us anywhere fast, no matter how far I ran in advance, because of my dad's congenital hip problem. And no one would hear me anyway, as the elevated subway rattled by and screeched to a halt.

We approached the stadium. I stopped. I looked from right to left and then behind us. I started crying.

"What's wrong, Austin? Did you forget something?" My mom had a look of non-understanding. She could usually discern what was wrong with her middle son, but now she was dumbfounded.

"Dad drove us to the wrong place! This isn't a baseball field! It's a building! Where is the grass? Where are all of the players? Where is everyone sitting?" I was inconsolable.

I guess my mom and dad smiled at each other, as parents do who love their children's innocence and humorous mistakes.

"Don't worry, Austin," my dad intoned in a serious voice that belied his amusement. "We know what we are doing. Just trust us."

I was six and I still trusted my parents fully—it would take eight or nine years before I would know more than them! And although I still had tears in my eyes, I followed them through the turnstiles, getting stuck between the metal prongs as I tried to squeeze through with my mom. I held on to my ticket with both hands, not wanting to lose it, initially refusing to surrender it, until I was assured by the nice man in the blue uniform that I would get half of it back once I went in.

At first I walked slowly up the ramps, then ran out ahead of everyone, out into the concourse—with concession stands, the aroma of hot dogs, men yelling "Programs! Get your Programs!" and finally dashed through the portal to the field!

What a beautiful sight. I was speechless. A rare occurrence for me or any six-year-old.

That it was already the third inning was a fact missed by me. I was mesmerized by the green grass mowed in a criss-cross pattern, the mass of people in the stands, and, most of all, by the white ball and the players with their easy, graceful, innate motion of throwing, hitting, running, catching. Other than remembering a third baseman by the name of Brooks Robinson, my recall of the game is what you would expect from a preteen. And for years I remembered that day—hearing vendors stride through the park yelling "Peanuts!" "Hot dogs!" "Cracker Jacks!" and "Hey, get your cobia." I would wander through supermarkets, scanning the shelves and refrigerated areas for "cobia." Only later in life, as I began to drink Rheingold and Ballantine, did I realize that they were yelling "get your cold beer!"

We left in the middle of the second game, with Marty and Harlan asleep. Despite my complaint that they were still playing, we headed back to the car and were soon on our way back into Manhattan. As my dad's other passion was Chinese food, he, alone among us, didn't stuff himself on hot dogs and peanuts, but instead waited to go to Ruby Foo's at 125st and Broadway, right below the elevated IRT #7. In the '50s, this was still an area of Harlem that was safe to park and walk at night. "The best Chinese food in Manhattan" was how my father described his favorite restaurant. And so a day that started in New Jersey ended five blocks from Columbia University, where so much was to happen 11 years later. Ruby Foo's was no longer at that site when I was at Columbia, as it had long succumbed to changes for the worse in that neighborhood. And while food was paramount on my dad's mind that night in 1958, it would be the farthest thing from my mind when I returned to that area as a college freshman.

I don't have any souvenirs of that day at the ballpark, just my memories. I can recreate what actually happened on the field that day by my research tonight—if I can find the article in *The New York Times* describing when the Yankees and Orioles played a double-header in the early summer of 1958. But the only way to bring some sense of what happened in a bigger picture—as I grew up, as my mom died, as the world teetered on the brink of destruction, as generations fought generations, as I became who I am today—is to research the rest of the microfilms, not only from *The Times* but also from my own personal "files."

SPACE—THE EARLY SETTLEMENT—WAGON HO

Sputnik, the Russian satellite, had been launched on October 4, 1957, to the consternation of Dwight "Ike" Eisenhower, 5-Star Army General and World War II hero, former Columbia University president, and now the overwhelming choice of Americans as he served his second term as president of the United States. Although the '50s represented "family values" for "middle America," with "Leave it to Beaver" and "Our Miss Brooks" along with "The Howdy Doody Show" as tranquilizers for this decade, it was also a time of desegregation of the schools and the advancement of the Civil Rights Movement in the South, with repercussions for the cities of the North to follow in the next decade. But one had only to watch the McCarthy Hearings in the mid-'50s to realize that the real perceived threat to the "American Way of Life" was Communism. And Sputnik clearly showed that the United States was lagging behind in the race for space—and, with that, the fear that he who owned space would ultimately control the arms race. I wasn't there in "Ike's" cabinet meetings, but I cannot imagine he was too pleased as he saw the strategic balance falter, with the Red, White and Blue falling behind.

December 6, 1957 (not that 1958 was that much better!)

When you're in second grade, your life still revolves in a tight spiral around the center of your family and your own personal universe. And now, so many years later, my memories of the early space launches are of vague images on our Sylvania black and white television console or through my parents' conversations. When I asked my wife, Mary, what she recalled, it was not only much more first-hand, for she had grown up in Florida, but also much more imaginative, as her seven-year-old universe was already expanding, albeit imperceptibly to her dysfunctional family, beyond the pull of her mother and father and sister, to a circumference beyond mine.

"Come on Mary, time to get up, the rockets are being launched again this morning." Mother was dressed in the best beach fashion: white blouse tied at the waist, Capri pants down to mid-calf, and pink sandals. She seemed so pretty to Mary, with her perfect complexion, her brown hair pulled back in a ponytail.

"Oh boy! Lots of noise and smoke." Mary was wearing her new jeans and a pink, striped blouse. Her red Keds sneakers matched the outfit. Her hair was blonde and cut in a tomboy fashion, meaning it was shaped by cutting her hair around the mixing bowl her mother placed over her head.

Over the past year, Mary had gone with her parents and younger sister Kate ("Katrina" in her later sophisticated years) to the beach two miles from Cape Canaveral to watch those big sticks fly through the sky and hear the loud "boom" that occurred about ten seconds after lift-off, as the speed of sound caused a de-synchronization of the visual and auditory senses (much like watching the singing of "The Star Spangled Banner" on the video screen at a baseball game). These beaches were usually inhabited by the bird-watchers, but these were really big birds, without wings!

"Today's important, Mary. This one's different," Mary's Mom, Ellen, proclaimed. "They're going to throw a ball into space and watch it fly around the world over and over again."

"Will it ever come down, Dad?" Mary asked.

"Won't it get lonely up there, Mommy?" Kate started to cry. She was only three, only half Mary's age and half Mary's maturity.

"Don't worry, President Eisenhower will be sending up plenty more for him to play with."

As for it coming down, it was a question better left unanswered. Only a month ago, Mary heard her parents talking about the Russian dog, Laika, who was in space on Sputnik II. They didn't have the heart to tell her that the Russians didn't have any way to bring the dog back down to Earth safely and that the poor mongrel had died in space.

"But what if a fly got caught inside it—how'll it survive?" Kate was determined to have an answer.

"Kate, the ball's only the size of a grapefruit," her Dad reassured her. He inhaled his Chesterfield deeply. He didn't know yet what R.J. Reynolds knew—that every puff he took was making cancer cells grow in his lungs.

"Maybe it'll be a mosquito and it will die a slow death." Mary was always so reassuring.

By 9 a.m. the beach was filled with the bird and the BIRD watchers. Their binoculars were focused on Vanguard, which was ready to be launched. Even several soldiers on leave were standing next to Mary, their eyes focused upwards, under their crew cut hair, in their pressed khaki pants and shirts, collars loosened, nametags over their left breast pockets.

"We have to succeed," Dad's voice was suddenly serious. "Otherwise, we'll be so far behind in the arms race—and we'll lose the Cold War."

Mary didn't understand. She'd watched men run on their legs around the track during the Olympics on television the year before. But she'd never seen them run on their arms. Maybe it was like in the circus, where all of the clowns stood on their heads and walked around. But they were funny. Why were her parents so worried now?

And why the "Cold" War? It was hot down here in Florida. She'd only seen snow in pictures, although once she had tasted a snowflake while visiting her Grammy in Virginia. "Mom, do they throw snow balls at each other during the Cold War?"

"That's a good one, Mary. Someday, we'll explain."

At 11 a.m. they were still standing, watching, waiting.

"I wish I was back at the park, Mom. You could push me on the swing and make me go higher and higher, until I swung all the way around."

"That'd be dangerous, Mary."

"Please, Mom, can we go back later—you can push me all the way and I can fly off the seat like an astro, astro…"

"… naut. No, Mary that would really be dangerous."

"Aw, Mom, you're just afraid I'd fly away from you."

Kate screamed, as she jumped up and down in her short, yellow dress, her legs tightly held together.

"What is it?"

"I have to go potty. Now!"

"Kate, just go behind those bushes! No one's watching—they are all looking at the rocket."

As Kate ran back into the bushes, a loud, thunderous noise arose from the Cape, as the rocket started to lift off. Mom grabbed Mary's hand.

And then, over it fell, at first slowly, then, gathering momentum, it tumbled over onto its side, flames and smoke surrounding the launch pad.

It was quiet at first, then everyone was aghast, and the people were in tears, they couldn't stop talking. "It's the end of the world!" "We'll be eating Russian herring for dinner." And "Russia's dominance is insurmountable."

Only in the United States would the public have scrutinized such a debacle. The openness of democracy led to ridicule by our free press.

"Kaputnik." *The Washington Daily Express.*

"Flopnick." *The Chicago Sun Times.*

May 29, 1959

My eighth birthday. Second grade was almost a memory. As I watched the sunrise outside of my window, I wondered how much longer would I have to wait until I went into my parents' room to awaken them to get my presents? Marty was still asleep—4½-years-old and still not in school. Harlan was in the next room, his tenth birthday just weeks away. But we were all excited because my parents always gave gifts to the other brothers on each of our birthdays. I guess they wanted us all to feel special, although it sort of made the birthday boy feel a little less special.

As I got up to go to the bathroom, I walked by their door, making as much noise as I could without being accused of deliberately awaking them. Peeking into their room, I saw my presents on their ottoman next to the window.

As I came back towards my room, I thought I perceived a slight change in my mom's position—a very good sign—so I knocked.

"Is that the birthday boy?" my mom answered.

"Yessireebob." And I charged into the room, jumping into the bed, arriving at the same time as Fuzzer.

"Can I open my presents now? Can I? Can I?" I was still in my pajamas—one piece, red, with pictures of dogs, and the "trap door" in the back for a "number 2."

"First we have to get Harlan and Marty up, then we'll have breakfast and then, maybe we can open up the gifts." My dad was winking at my mom.

"Austin, just let us get our robes on. You can open grandma's gift while we're getting ready. Then we'll eat and come on back up."

I opened the package, ripping off the ribbon, and found a blue sweater.

"It's nice." An understatement. But what else was I expecting?

"It'll keep you warm during the fall when you go out to play."

I looked anxiously at the other presents, all nicely wrapped.

"Go wake up Harlan and Marty and you can open one more gift before breakfast." Dad was a real softy.

I raced back into the other bedrooms. "Wake up, Harlan! Wake up, Marty! It's time for presents!"

Finally, we all traipsed down in our PJs and robes. Mom poured the cereal—Special K for her, as she was watching her diet, and Kellogg's Corn Flakes for the rest of us. Dad was a dentist, so we were deprived children—no Frosted Flakes, no "Tony the Tiger" for us. She went out the back door and took out the two glass quarts of milk in the silver box with "Edison Dairy" written on it. It was still cold, as the milkman had only arrived 30 minutes ago. (Sorry, no milkman jokes, this was a serious morning.) And today, there was a special treat—orange juice!

My dad had the newspaper spread out before him.

"It's my birthday. I get the comics first!" On this day alone, Harlan wouldn't get away with his claim of seniority. As I reached to prop open the comics, my eye caught sight of the front page, with pictures of the first Americans in space—"Able" and "Baker"—two monkeys, looking none too excited about the prospect of space travel.

"I hear they are looking for a dog to send up in space," Harlan interjected. "There were some military men around here yesterday taking a look at Fuzzer."

"Nooo! They can't take Fuzzer. Just because Harlan has allergies to him, he still belongs to me. Dad, please don't let them take Fuzzer." I grasped my dog and held on to him for dear life.

"Don't worry, we won't let him go—he's too valuable as a watch dog here."

"Yeah, and if he peed up there in outer space it would rain on your head, Austin," Harlan so helpfully intoned.

As we shoveled our cereal into our mouths, slurping down the milk left in the bowl, Harlan started reading the cereal box, trying to figure out the riddle "What has two hands but no fingers?" I often wondered later in life how many hours we spent reading the drivel on the corn flakes boxes. What a major potential for propaganda the box represented— "Wheaties, The Breakfast of Champions!" (The answer to the riddle, by the way, is a clock, for those of you of riddle ignorance.)

I was jealous of Harlan. I could read about Dick and Jane and Spot, but I couldn't read the entire box yet, let alone adventure books about travelers in space. But I did like the toys they advertised. For five box tops (only three more to go) and ten cents, I could get my spy ring, with decoder and magnifying glass. My dad thought it was a Communist plot to get me to eat more cereal and finish the box earlier. But it was not until several years later when Post Grape Nuts (where are the grapes, anyway?) put baseball cards on the boxes that I would begin to eat like a champion. Even then, my mom would scream when she found a box half full of cereal with the cards cut out of the box, and only the wax paper separating the cereal from being scattered all over the floor.

Finally, breakfast was over and we went bounding up the stairs into my parents' room. "Slowly, Austin, open the packages one at a time."

I know my parents got pleasure out of watching me open my gifts. They lived for each other and for their kids (except for my dad's work, which at times took overwhelming precedence). Today was their day of satisfaction as they watched their seven . . . I mean eight-year-old scream with joy, as I opened my Roy Rogers gun and holster. As it turned out, these were the last weapons of mass destruction that we banditos were to own—not because of pointing the guns at each other and shooting bullets, but because we were continually imitating the Lone Ranger, who would knock out his foes with the butt of his gun.

I found my last gift—a box 14 inches long and 4 inches wide. As I opened it, my eyes lit up. It was an entire box of Topps' 1959 Baseball cards. There were 36 beautifully wrapped wax packages, each with a piece of gum (that my father wouldn't let me chew—"You'll get cavities!") and beautiful, crisp cards. Each pack sold for a nickel, but now I hoped I could put together a whole series.

I knew which card I wanted as I opened the first pack, but on top was a picture of Ozzie Virgil, attired in a Tigers' uniform, in an oval orange colored frame. Ozzie Virgil . . . his claim-to-fame was unknown to me, as the first black player on the Detroit Tigers.

As I would reflect back in later years, it was inevitable that, in 1967, Detroit would follow the violent blueprint of the 1965 Los Angeles Watts riots, ten years after Rosa Parks' refusal to give up her seat to a white person led to Martin Luther King's non-violent boycott of the public bus lines in Montgomery, Alabama; and 11 years after the Tigers became the second to last (penultimate for any English majors reading this book) major league team to become integrated. It wouldn't be until Willie Horton, the Tigers' star black left fielder, went back to his home street that the riots began to be quelled. And healing wouldn't occur until the following year, when black and white baseball fans came together at Tiger Stadium to root their team on to a World Series victory.

Of course, I didn't understand all this stuff about integration. We were unaware of what was going on in the rest of the country, where, because of the 1954 Supreme Court decision, Brown vs. Board of Education, separate but equal education was now "legally unconstitutional." Only in Arkansas did a defiant Governor Orville Faubus call out the National Guard to obstruct federal orders to integrate the public schools, forcing President Eisenhower to send in the 101st Airborne Division to ensure that the schools would be integrated.

Although my parents weren't activists per se, they knew right from wrong. They had just gotten back from a conference in Miami, where my dad was president of the American Association of Dental Editors. He had walked into the formal dinner with one of his colleagues, a black professor from Tuskegee University, when the *Maitre 'D* stopped them and refused to allow Dad's co-editor to enter. My dad held his ground and threatened to cancel the entire dinner and two-day program unless they were all seated together. He won—*de facto* integrating this Southern hotel!

The one baseball card I wouldn't find was that of Pumpsie Green. That's because his first card wouldn't appear until the following year, six weeks after my eighth birthday, in 1959, when he stepped onto the playing field wearing a Boston Red Sox uniform. Boston—home of the American Revolution, Civil War Abolitionist movement, Harvard University, and John and Bobby Kennedy—had the last major league ball club to be integrated. Boston was as racist a town as Miami, Florida, as racist in its own way as those infamous Southern cities, Selma and Birmingham, Alabama.

I was sorting the cards as I opened them by color—not of the players' skin, but by the background hue. A great way to play "war" later on.

"Austin, don't open them all up at once. Open just a few and save the rest for later." Mom was always the pragmatist, trying to offset our gluttonous urges. After all, my weekly allowance was only a nickel, or one pack of cards. And even with doing household chores such as drying the dishes or walking the dog, I still only got another nickel. I wasn't worrying about saving up for a car for college, or even for a new Schwinn 3-speed bicycle. For me, it was a trip to the local 5 & 10-cent store to get some baseball cards. My mom later told me how the owner of the store said we were the politest children who came to his establishment. She probably couldn't believe what she heard, but I know it made her proud to tell my dad about their wondrous offspring. After all, I was the one they threatened to send to military school to learn discipline. But let's not think about this on my birthday!

Of course, she would also threaten to take away my baseball cards and throw them in the garbage, as so many moms did, albeit innocently during spring cleaning (not to be confused with spring training) after their sons went off to college. And although in my childhood the cards had no inherent monetary value, they did have value on the trading market. Other kids would flip their cards, or play "leaners." I could also play my own version of "war," trying to match teams or colors or positions in a game against myself (thereby protecting my assets.)

As I opened my fifth pack, I was already putting aside the Orioles and Giants cards, saving them, looking for other duplicates that I could either trade or flip. I obviously hadn't learned my lesson from last week in an after school adventure with Mike Weinstein, a fourth-grader in Harlan's class.

"Don't worry, Austin. You can have a couple of practice throws. Let's see who gets closest to the wall. The first three throws won't count."

Mike flipped one and then another card, the first falling at least six inches short of the wall, and the next bouncing off the wall and landing five inches away. Had I been less naïve, I would have known he was conning me, but once I flipped my Joe Adcock and got him two inches from the wall, I was ready.

"Let's go." I was confident.

The first four flips were split, and then I won three in a row. I was beaming.

"Maybe we should stop?" Mike said.

"No, I want to keep going." I was on a roll.

And then I lost track of what I was doing. Time after time I would lose, winning only a token card every fourth or fifth flip.

Suddenly disaster struck. I inadvertently allowed my San Francisco Giants team card—all the players including Willie Mays in an oval against a yellow background—to be lost. I wasn't even aware I had the card with me until I saw it lying face up, covered by Mike's card, inches closer to the wall.

It took me five cards, including three Yankees, to trade with Mike to get it back. It was almost like trading captured spies between the U.S.

and Russia, although somehow I knew I had gotten the worst of it. And that didn't even take into account when my mom found out.

"You were gambling!" she had yelled that day. "No more. If I catch you again, I'll take all of your cards away." Maybe they should have had a 12-Step-Program for us kids: "Flippers Anonymous."

But today, "Just one more pack, Mom. Please."

"Okay, it's your birthday. Here, let me pick one and kiss it for good luck."

She handed me a pack from the bottom of the box. I opened it and let out a yell. There he was, Eddie Mathews, my favorite player, Eddie Mathews of the Milwaukee Braves, third baseman, a perfect card of a man my father's age, against a bright yellow background. His face was tanned, with chiseled features and an evening shadow. I turned the card over slowly, reading the statistics. Bats: Left. Throws: Right. No way. Harlan was a lefty but I was a righty. Stung for a minute, I vowed to become a switch-hitter.

From the corner of my eye, I watched as Marty opened his gift—a double can of Play-Doh. He immediately started molding a Humpty Dumpty, with a dimple for a nose.

Off in his corner, Harlan was breaking the cellophane off of his gift—a new B52 bomber model, complete with Strategic Air Command (SAC) decals and guns and bombs. He took out the shell, put on the wings, and started running around the room "flying" his plane and making bombing noises, as he protected his people from the Russian MIGs that were attacking our imaginary air space. And he ran out of my parents' bedroom with the box in his other hand, determined to finish the project in time to take it to school with him that morning. His Sky King single-engine model plane had been made obsolete.

How I hated to go off to school that morning, but I was determined to show everyone my new baseball cards. I waited until we got off the bus, afraid that Jimmy would grab them with his grimy hands from the seat next to me. After we got to class, I stowed my Superman lunch box in my desk, filled with what I hoped was a birthday surprise, and then I passed a small stack back to George, when the air raid siren went off.

George was also our air raid monitor. It was his job to listen for the bell—three short rings and then three long rings, followed by the wail of the siren.

"Everyone up quickly!" George yelled, trying to act calm and mature, hiding his excitement at being in charge. He leapt to the front of the room, his black pants two inches too short, showing his white socks and black leather shoes, his red and green plaid shirt neatly buttoned to the collar, his hair slicked back with a little dab of BrylCream. "Come on, line up behind me!"

As we weren't at war and none of us had experienced the bombings and the destruction in London 13 years earlier, most of us stood up, giggling and talking. The girls tried to get next to their best friends, jockeying for position next to Sarah Cohen, the most popular girl in the class, whose parents owned a new house with a swimming pool in back.

"Quiet!" Miss Phillips could say one word or give you one glance and you knew you'd better behave. She was older than any of our mothers, and dressed in her mid-calf-length flowered dress, hair pulled back in a bun, she reminded me of my great aunt Mollie, who lived in New York City with her friend, Gert, and their three Siamese cats. None of us understood sex at that time, but even if we did, Miss Phillips would have been considered asexual. What wasn't even considered by our parents was the fear that she could be a homosexual. But 1950s school boards must have thought about appropriate sexual models, or otherwise why weren't there any male kindergarten teachers (at least until Arnold Schwarzenegger came along)?

However, it wasn't worth missing recess playtime by disobeying her. And so we filed out, two abreast, into the hall and took our position, our backs against the drab yellow cinderblock wall, sitting on the old tan and green floor tiles, heads down between our legs, hands over our heads, silent.

I thought about Harlan and his SAC model bomber, and wondered if the real planes were up in the sky protecting us. How safe were we? After all, I had heard a few weeks earlier about how one of our planes, flown by a Francis Powers, had been shot down over Russia, and that Khrushchev had demanded an apology from President Eisenhower.

When our president refused, I heard my dad say he was worried about another war. Where was my dad? What was my mom doing now? If there were really a bomb, would she be okay? Was she down in our basement with Marty and Fuzzer, protected by the concrete foundation?

In retrospect, it was wishful (or ridiculous) for us to really think that we would be protected from a nuclear attack by lining up in our cowering position in the hall. Although we would be able to protect our eyes from flying glass from an explosion, we would still be crushed by the falling building, which in any circumstance would not serve as protection against nuclear fallout, radiation burns, and premature cancer cells.

As the all-clear siren rang, we stood up and straggled back into our rooms. We took for granted that these air raid drills were just drills, but our parents never talked with us about what this all meant. Miss Phillips did get asked questions afterwards, such as "Are the Russians coming here to New Jersey?" "Will we have to eat Russian dressing on our salads in the cafeteria?"

We were reassured with patriotic answers: "We are safe. The United States is the greatest country and we have General Eisenhower to protect us."

But I still had doubts. "Then why are we having these drills? Are we going to die? And who is protecting my Mommy and Daddy?" I wanted so much to bring them to school with me so that we would all be okay. Harlan was here already, and they could bring Marty and Fuzzer with them. (I figured the goldfish would be okay to stay at home. They would just keep swimming around and around in their glass bowl.)

On the surface, Miss Phillips' little hug and reassurance was enough to get me through the day, but I was glad to get on the school bus with Harlan and get home that afternoon. And at dinner my parents reassured me, through my unending wailing.

"Don't worry boys, we are all here together, Mommy and Daddy will protect you. We would never leave you alone or let anything happen to you."

But when I saw a brochure for a bomb shelter in the mail on the hall table, I couldn't sleep in my room for three nights. Instead, I slept on the floor outside their bedroom with Fuzzer, the nightlight from their room steadily reflecting under their closed door, assuring me that all was safe. But still, I dreamed about a dragon chasing me through clouds of dust, fire flaming from its mouth, the darkness being destroyed by the searing red illumination.

I never did tell them why I was lying there, sprawled with my blanket, when my mom got up in the morning to fix breakfast. But this would not be the last time I would find myself outside their bedroom, with two inches of wood all that separated me from crawling into their bed, under the covers, back into the protection of my mom's womb.

Fall, 1960

It had been a good summer. I'd gone to the co-ed YMCA/YWCA camp and had a great time playing softball and swimming. We'd play baseball all afternoon and weekends on the homemade field on our corner lot. And when no one was around, I'd throw the ball up in the air as high as I could, pretending I was Eddie Mathews. Or I'd throw it on a bounce against the back door steps, practicing my backhand pickups of grounders or line drives.

We went to the drive-in movies several times over the summer, Harlan sliding down in the seat so he'd look like he was less than ten years old and get in for free—my parents only unethical action I can remember. While we waited for dusk, we played miniature golf with my mom, although I started crying when I couldn't understand why my score of 38 strokes didn't beat her score of 33 strokes. My parents sat in the car, anticipating movies such as "Ben Hur," starring Charlton Heston, the car speaker attached to our windowsill by a wire, as we'd go to the snack bar and get candy and hot dogs.

It was also my first memory of a presidential election. My parents loved Adlai Stevenson, both in 1952 and in 1956, and they still supported him in 1960. He avoided being a three-time loser to the Republican candidate when the Democrats nominated John Fitzgerald Kennedy, a youthful senator from Massachusetts whose greatest asset other than his wealth was his beautiful wife Jackie. Even if JFK hadn't been my parents' choice in the national election, he would have been mine for the simple reason that we were both born on May 29th. I guess I figured if we had George Washington and Abraham Lincoln's birthdays off as a national holiday, maybe we would get our birthday off also!

This was the year of the first television debates, and my parents made us sit in front of the family television console in the living room to watch as Vice-President Nixon and Senator Kennedy had a series of debates, starting on September 26th. As a nine-year-old, I obviously didn't know what it meant when Nixon accused Kennedy of wanting to spend federal money on education or health care for Senior Citizens. I knew that Nixon had been vice-president and Kennedy only a senator, so that meant Nixon must know more. And I was scared when they talked in such serious tones about the strength of the Soviet Union and the threat of Communism—especially when Kennedy kept talking about how fast Russia's economy was growing and, even more importantly, about the missile gap and the Soviet's winning the war in space. But what I can remember—accentuated by the black and white television imagery—was Nixon in his gray suit, needing a shave, just like my dad did at night, just like Eddie Mathews on his baseball card, while Kennedy looked so handsome in his dark suit, speaking with such authority, just like my fourth-grade teacher, Mrs. Wilson.

Election night was fun for me, as we went over to the Singers' to watch the returns on television. While we waited for the results, we played with Joan Singer's "Magic 8" Ball. We'd ask simple questions, such as, "Will Kennedy Win?" Answer: "You may rely on it." Or "Am I going to get a new bike for Christmas?" Answer: "Reply hazy. Try again." We asked the really important questions about our classmates: "Does George like Theresa?" Answer: "It is decidedly so." But then, "Does Theresa like George?" Answer: "My sources say no." Ah, there was still hope for me, but I didn't dare ask the same question regarding my status.

As the evening progressed, I remember as they added up the states, with New Jersey proudly in my parents' candidate's side; and I was still awake when JFK eked out his victory by only 100,000 votes. But my highlight of the evening was the "spread" that was put out, which included my first taste of smoked salmon and cream cheese. And my parents were so busy arguing over the election that no one noticed when I went back for thirds!

May 5, 1961

After the morning bell and attendance, Mrs. Wilson had us line up in two rows to walk to the gym. Only a week earlier, we were all ready to watch the first American astronaut, Alan Shepard, be launched into outer space, but our mission to the gym was aborted by bad weather in Cape Canaveral, Florida. This morning, however, Mrs. Wilson again told us that all systems were "go" for our journey. We knew this was a special occasion and we took all of the liberties that fourth-graders would take when they knew their teacher was a bit distracted. So we made sure that we lined up next to our buddies, and we whispered as laughter was sprinkled throughout the drab, yellow, cinderblock-lined hallway.

As we entered from the rear of the gym, I waved to Harlan when we passed his sixth grade class. He was busy talking to Amy, and it was not clear to me whether he actually did not see me, whether he was ignoring me, or whether he was embarrassed by me. Whatever, I thought, "he'll get his" at home when I tell Mom. Marty was in kindergarten, and his class was up front. They probably thought they were still watching cartoons! Why were they lucky enough to be up front? Whatever, this was probably the only time all three of us boys were in the same room at school together. We were only missing Mom and Dad.

After we all were in the gym, Mr. Rhodes, our principal, stood and went to the front of the students, standing right in front of the 17-inch, black and white television that had been wheeled into the gym on a stand. It was now showing a rocket standing in solitude in the distance on the launch pad. We could barely make out a small capsule at the top of the rocket, which was still attached to what appeared to be a large ladder.

"Boys and Girls, Attention! How many of you know what is happening today?"

Some of us raised our hands, and then a few more, as their friends whispered in their ears. The rest of the kids were either giggling with each other or just not paying attention.

"Today, America is sending a brave man into outer space. Who knows his name?"

"Superman."

"The Lone Ranger."

"Buffalo Bob"

"Alan Shepard?" a voice whispered from the side.

All were superheroes to us, but at least a few of us knew who would be in the Mercury capsule, Freedom 7.

"Yes, someone has been listening at the dinner table. Mr. Shepard is a hero," Mr. Rhodes continued, "and we should all thank him and pray for him today."

What none of us even dreamed was that our own President Kennedy and our scientists were afraid of what would happen if this rocket exploded with Astronaut Shepard in it. This wasn't the Soviet Union. All 140 million Americans would see him incinerated on television screens—science fiction and horror movies merging with fact.

What we were also too young to appreciate was the importance of this space launch to President Kennedy, during the first four months of his term in office. Just a few weeks before, I had laughed when my parents were talking about some "pigs" that had tried to swim to Cuba. In fact, what was carefully kept from public scrutiny was that on April 17th, 1,700 Cuban exiles, insufficiently supported by the United States, had landed in their homeland in an attempt to overthrow the Castro regime. Only later would the shameful truth come out: The military campaign had ended in utter defeat, with 114 of the counter-revolutionaries dead and another 1,100 taken as prisoners. Our ineffectual involvement was too obvious to cover up, and there had been considerable political embarrassment to Kennedy throughout the world.

I tried to sit next to Theresa Ryan, whom I had a crush on, but there was George next to her, so I ended up squatting Indian-style next to him. This wasn't a time to "jettison" your friends for a girl, so I ignored her and spoke with George about the excitement at hand. He had been addicted to the space program over the past two years, and had a shelf full of model rockets at home that we spent hours gluing together with as much exactitude as the riveters who worked at Cape Canaveral. We put on all of the USA decals and sat in his room practicing liftoffs, making our own sound effects. Every once in a while, we pretended it was a Russian rocket and it would crash on takeoff. We didn't understand all of the details, but we knew the Russians were our enemies, and that they were ahead of us in the "space race," as a man named Yuri Gagarin had orbited the Earth a month earlier and returned safely to his native country.

Ironically, while we children were simulating the "ascent" of these rockets, with their long, sleek cylindrical bodies beneath a small capsule being catapulted into space, our parents and teachers kept from us their fear—the "descent" of the rockets with their massive destructive payloads. And while this Atlas rocket would disintegrate in the atmosphere after sending Alan Shepard on his historic journey—its remnants falling harmlessly into the Atlantic Ocean, followed by the gentle descent of the Mercury capsule beneath its billowing parachute—the real fear for my parents and our teachers was of the widespread destruction that a nuclear warhead attached to a Russian missile would cause as it came down out of space and exploded over our country. For us, it was the adventure of space. For them, the stakes were much higher.

No wonder Mrs. Wilson was so serious as she watched. My dad had asked the night before, while my mom was serving the meatloaf, "What do you think the Russians will write in *Pravda* if the rocket fails?"

Mom answered, "Well I don't know Russian, but I'm sure there will be pictures all over the place. But, of course, if we're successful, there will probably be three lines on page 27."

Mr. Rhodes was standing next to the television, trying to adjust the "rabbit ear" antennae to make the black and white television picture less fuzzy. We could barely make out a map of Florida and the Atlantic Ocean, with a superimposed arc showing the expected pathway of the capsule. Walter Cronkite—the CBS News "anchor"—explained the simulations of the capsule re-entering the atmosphere, with a fiery shower behind it, protected by the heat shield, and finally, the parachutes deploying and the capsule gently landing in the ocean. None of us in the room except, of course, the adults, understood the tension in Washington and at the launch site. They hoped and prayed that this simulation, which we were all viewing on CBS, would actually come true, and that we would begin to make up the ground on the Russians. There were prayers that the mission would be successful and that Alan Shepard would become a national hero.

As my eyes turned back to the television, I thought about Mr. Shepard, up there alone. I wondered how the dogs and monkeys had felt before their flights. I had asked Fuzzer if she would want to go on a flight, but she just sat there and licked my face. I tried explaining to her that she would be on the front page and would get a giant bone when she returned . . . and also movie offers, with titles like "A Dog's Day in Space."

George brought me back to reality. "Wow, look at the size of that rocket," he exclaimed in wonder, "and look at all of the smoke! I hope Smokey the Bear is out there so that no one throws a lit cigarette." But the rocket was still off in the distance. This was not like today's high tech movies, with close-ups and slow motion. No one even thought about a fake transmission, as some would suggest about future space missions. There were too many people watching from the beach a mile away, including journalists from around the world. And no one wanted it to simulate a big budget Hollywood "flop!"

As the countdown continued, the time seemed interminable. Freedom 7 sat on top of the tall Redstone rocket. As Mr. Cronkite described all of the preparations that Alan Shepard had been through, what time he had gotten up, and what he had eaten for breakfast, off to the right several second-graders started hitting each other over a comic book they had brought with them. And Jill and Clara Stone, identical twins in the third grade, were laughing, not paying any attention to the screen, getting the brunt of Miss Phillips' icy stare.

As a first-grader was waving her hands wildly to the teacher, jumping up and down, obviously in need of transportation to the lavatory, what we didn't hear was Alan Shepard's top-secret conversation with Mission Control:

"Man, I got to pee!"

"You what?" Gordon Cooper answered.

"You heard me. I've got to pee. I've been up here forever"

And so, Alan Shepard, as did so many little boys and girls, ended up peeing in his pants, in this case a highly sophisticated space suit.

The countdown was put on delay at T-minus-15 minutes. Of course the announcers could only guess as to what was the problem, as they awaited word from Mission Control. We heard about Alan Shepard's family, saw pictures of his wife, her face lit up with a smile deserving of an Academy Award. What we didn't hear was Alan Shepard's voice:

"Why don't you just fix your little problem and light this candle."

When the countdown continued, it was back to T-minus-35 minutes. It was a new exercise in mathematics. Einstein's Theory of Special Relativity on a fourth grade level. Hadn't we been there before?

"Hey George," I asked, "wouldn't if be awful if Mrs. Wilson said she didn't like our behavior and set the clock back 20 minutes so that we had to sit in class longer?"

"Yeah, it would be like you were farther away from getting to the end than you were an hour ago," he replied. It was our first introduction to the concept of that yearly phenomenon when we all find an extra hour in our lives — Daylight Savings Time.

When the countdown finally resumed, we waited for the dreaded interruption. We all held our breath as the countdown approached ten seconds. Would there be another delay? 9, 8, 7, 6, 5, 4, 3, 2, 1. We were all counting, yelling together. "Ignition!" And then, for an interminable instant, nothing happened. A split- second of doubt. Would it take off? Would it explode? But finally, as the pressure from the rocket's fuel increased, we watched with our very eyes. At 9:34 a.m., "We have liftoff!"

In those few seconds that followed, George and I held each other's hands tightly, afraid to let go. Thelma had her hands over her eyes, afraid to look. The entire student body was transformed from a hoard of school children, previously pushing each other to get that extra territorial inch, into a patriotic army of the future. There was an anticipatory silence in the elementary school gym—only the roar of the rocket from the television set was heard, a grainy black and white picture showing the entire world that we were not afraid. I truly think that everyone of my generation and the generation before me can tell you where they were on three days: Alan Shepard's flight, John Kennedy's assassination, and Neil Armstrong's walk on the Moon.

At first, the rocket moved very slowly, inching up from the launch pad. We watched as it gathered momentum, now assured that it wouldn't fall over on its side. We followed Mercury's trajectory on the television, exuberant each minute there was no unexpected explosion. When the rocket went out of range of the television cameras, there appeared dotted lines, increasing as the route of ascent and descent occurred, all an illusion of technology as the capsule could obviously no longer be seen with the naked eye. As we listened to Walter Cronkite on the television we heard a voice, accompanied by a lot of static. "What a beautiful view." Alan Shepard's first speech from 37 miles into outer space, his capsule having achieved a maximal speed of 5,134 miles per hour. And when several minutes later we heard, "Everything is A-OK," it was as if my mom and dad were there, reassuring me that all would be okay, that we would be safe.

Soon we heard for the first time what was to become the mantra of newscasters regarding re-entry. "The capsule must be at the proper angle so that the heat shield will protect the capsule from burning up." And so we cheered when the first report came that the rescue helicopters sighted the capsule, its parachute open. As reports came in that the capsule had splashed down and was safe, we all clapped and cheered. At Control Center, adults imitated children, jumping up and down, hugging each other, as Shepard boarded the Carrier Lake Champlain II.

George started to jump up and down. "I knew we could do it. That's what I want to be when I grow up. I want to go to the Moon!" Until then, I really hadn't heard of anyone actually planning on sending anyone to the Moon. No, that's not right. I had heard Jackie Gleason tell Audrey Meadows on the "Honeymooners" the week before, "To the Moon, Alice. To the Moon!" I guess she would have company.

On that day, a new brand of heroes was born—men with the "Right Stuff," willing to push the edge of the envelope. Baseball greats such as Mickey Mantle, Willie Mays, and Babe Ruth could all now take a step back. Instead of a baseball uniform, boys now wanted spacesuits for their birthdays.

In all honesty, Shepard's flight paled when viewed next to the Russian achievements, but at least we were in the race, in the arena. Alan Shepard had flown through space, if only for 15 minutes and 22 seconds, going 302 miles. Test pilots, such as Chuck Yeager, had felt contempt for the astronauts, whom they felt were not really in control of the aircraft. But in 15 minutes, Alan Shepard earned more adulation than all the pilots who preceded him, than all of the pilots who died in "perfecting" our advancement in the space program.

As we went back to our classrooms, double file, the lines quickly broke down, as Jimmy, our class clown, started making strange noises meant to suggest ignition and take off, but which quickly degenerated into the sounds a fourth-grader would make to embarrass the little girl sitting next to him, while shrugging his shoulders, implying "It wasn't me, it must have been her." Soon lunch recess was upon us, and out on the playing field we went, once again emulating our favorite baseball players, throwing, running, sliding, getting our clean clothes dirty so that our moms could wash them in 20 Mule Team Borax.

As we got on the school bus that afternoon, I had my heroes on my brain—astronauts, Eddie Mathews, my parents, and my teacher. But then, my heart sank as I saw Mrs. Wilson get into her car, lighting up a cigarette. How could she? I had tried a puff when I was seven, when our babysitter had offered me a drag. I nearly choked to death. And to this day, it is my only puff on a taxable vegetative product. I emulated my parents, who had neither the vice of smoking nor drinking liquor, and who would have qualified as honorary Baptists. Despite the commercials on TV and in magazines showing famous people smoking, I hurt inside to see a hero so human. But at least I had Mr. Shepard.

At home that night, my parents' sense of serenity, that all was right with the world, lasted until Marty spilled his milk all over the linoleum floor. Harlan started talking about forces and speed and impact, and wondered what it was like to be weightless, without gravity. He was acting like a big shot sixth-grader, teaching me as if I didn't already know that. But then Marty started talking about the great cartoons he had seen on the television that morning. We all laughed, but soon talk returned to my dad's work at Squibb, and his concern about a deadline for a research grant that had been missed. The race-for-space crisis was forgotten for at least one evening, as we reverted back to more mundane affairs, such as whether my dad would get FDA approval for his new drug or who would get the extra Twinkie.

In bed that night, Marty asked, "Do you want to go to the Moon?"

"No, I'm going to leave that for George. And besides, Mom would probably make me take you along."

"Don't you want me to come with you? I promise I won't make a mess."

Marty's question went unanswered, as I pretended to be asleep. How could I let on that I was afraid—afraid to be without Mom and Dad, and maybe even my brothers? Who would take care of them, or who would take care of me? Later that night, snuggled under the covers listening through my earplug on my transistor radio to the baseball game being broadcast from Baltimore, the radio signals miraculously bouncing their way off clouds to my house 150 miles away, I heard my mom come in to check on me. I knew she would always be there to love me and to protect me. I wasn't ready to grow up and fly the coop to the Moon.

NASA engineering was still all the rage, taking the United States by storm. George wanted to be an astronaut, but I wanted to be grounded and just build his space ship. However, my attempt at electrical experimentation was fraught with as many problems as early NASA research. For my science project, Harlan had helped me build a miniature Morse Code system, complete with two stations, batteries included, along with the necessary wires, all connected and ready to send and receive top-secret messages. We had set it all up, and I brought it to class on the day my family was embarking on a journey to Boston, Massachusetts, where my dad was one of the speakers at the American Dental Association annual meeting.

I gave George and Mrs. Wilson explicit instructions about how to set up the batteries and wires, impressing the class with my electrical engineering skills, coding ". . . - - - . . ." for "SOS" to Theresa from my unit. And then I left it in their able hands for the class to enjoy as I went to meet Harlan and Marty in the principal's office, where my mom was waiting for us.

We had quite a week in Boston, staying at the Mayflower Hotel, sightseeing with my mom during the day, following the Freedom Trail and seeing Paul Revere's House, Faneuil Hall, and Bunker Hill. It was great spending the day with her, touring houses, buying souvenir replicas of the guns used by the Minutemen, Paul Revere's horse, the U.S.S. Constitution (for Harlan), and the Liberty Bell (oops, wrong city, right war). And best of all—no school!

We didn't see much of my dad, as he was off at the Convention Center going to meetings, giving lectures, presenting his research. And at night, my parents had their social obligations, especially as my dad had the dual role of Squibb researcher and journal editor.

But did we mind? No, because Harlan was old enough to take care of us in our hotel room, and we were able to watch television to our heart's content, as long as we did our assigned reading and homework. But the most memorable part of the trip was that every night we would get dinner to take out from the coffee shop in the lobby: Cheeseburgers and French fries, wrapped in greasy wax paper bags, washed down with a real chocolate milk shake. I couldn't accept McDonald's for weeks after that.

On Monday, I returned to class, expecting to hear the accolades, stories of how the class had becomes experts in Morse code.

"Austin, it didn't work," George blurted.

"What do you mean? It was working when I left"

"You must have done something wrong," he retorted.

I was devastated, rebuked, a failure. Where had I gone wrong? I had disappointed my class, let down the astronauts. We'd never get to the Moon now.

I walked over in tears and looked down.

"George, I told you not to cross the wires."

As I uncrossed the strands and tightened the connections, the telegraph began to work.

I typed quickly, from my memory of Morse code from Boy Scouts.

-- . . --- . - . -- . . . . - . . - . -- . . . . - . .

GEORGE IS STUPID.

But it clearly pointed out how you do have to sweat the small things, that space missions could be aborted, scrubbed, or even worse, end in disaster by simple nuts or bolts or wiring gone wrong. Attention to detail, in school, in driving, and later in medicine, was important. Obsessiveness and compulsiveness would be positive attributes, if they didn't get in the way, if you could still see the forest for the trees. This was a distinction I would have to learn, try to internalize in later years as a physician, to overcome my neurosis about being perfect, about being a superman, a computer, not making mistakes.

Of course, the telegraph fiasco was also the forerunner of what to do in the new millennium when your computer didn't work.

1.) Check the wires to see if they are connected.

2.) Turn it off and then turn it on again.

3.) Kick the damn machine.

A NEW BEGINNING

September 3, 1961

Some days in our lives are memorable because of events occurring in close proximity that affect us and other people. Others are important only to me, a day in my life. On this particular night, I was traveling up the New Jersey Turnpike, my dad driving the 1952 Blue Oldsmobile Sedan, windows open to let in the breeze. It was a car that did not reflect the new sleekness of the later generation of automobiles. And as usual, we were driving in the right hand lane, the new Ford Edsels and Thunderbirds speeding by us on our left. As we drove by those same refineries that expelled such terrible odors we had passed on our trips to New York, Dad commented cheerily, "I'm glad we don't have to make this trip again soon." I only wished he would go a little faster so this trip would "end" sooner.

Harlan and Marty were driving with mom in the '57 Chevy, packed to the "gills" (an appropriate metaphor as the car did have rear fins!) with all of the things we would need until the moving van arrived tomorrow. They were lucky in one respect—their car had air conditioning. And they could keep the windows closed!

Our car was also loaded, but there was still enough room for me to bring my baseball mitt, ball, and bat, along with my baseball cards, all neatly stacked in rubber bands in the Tiparillo Cigar box. Although I had left behind the small dried out branch of our Christmas tree that I had saved from last holiday season (So what if my parents were ecumenical? At least I hadn't named it "Rosebud!"), I had packed my gyroscope and miniature Torah (the Five Books of the Old Testament), which our kindly rabbi in Plainfield had given to me several years ago to comfort and protect me after my parents had dropped me off at Sunday school, "abandoning" me to cry from loneliness among the strange kids in the new temple 20 miles from home. Somewhere packed in my dad's artifacts were the last possessions from his youth, carefully carried from home to home, lost among his files of articles, papers, reprints and research studies. These memories of his childhood that were carefully packed away:

1.) A small stuffed Steiff Terrier;

2.) A few pictures of his Dad; and

3.) A baseball board game he had invented, complete with players' cards, dice, and a baseball diamond, all ready to be patented.

What made this night memorable was not only that we were moving from Highland Park to Tenafly, New Jersey as my dad was leaving Squibb to work full time at the Columbia Dental School. Most importantly, what made it so memorable was that it was just my dad and me, without my mom or brothers, as we listened to the radio broadcast of the New York Yankees and Detroit Tigers baseball game, waiting to hear if Roger Maris would hit another home run to creep closer to Babe Ruth's record of 60 in a season. We were still Baltimore Oriole fans, and we needed the Yankees to lose this game so that our team could make up ground in the pennant race. We had tried to get the Oriole game on the radio from Baltimore. Often, in those days, with fewer radio stations and minimal FM interference, if the atmospheric pressure was just right, I was able to actually hear my team's games from Memorial Stadium. But tonight there was just too much static in the air. We could only hear a few words, and so we were resigned to listening to the hated Yankees. As we listened, my dad talked about watching Mel Ott, his favorite player when he was growing up as a New York Giant fan. My dad's voice quieted as he mourned the loss of his Giants when they left New York in 1957 and how he had bought stock in the Baltimore Orioles, the only publicly owned baseball team, just so he could say he owned a major league baseball club. He didn't own any other stock, just the ten shares at $10 each, but that $100 investment gave him such pleasure. And for me, it gave me the opportunity to idolize a young rookie pitcher, Chuck Estrada, whose career I would follow through the next three decades.

Other than baseball, Dad was "mostly work and a little play." His play, because of his congenital hip problem, had consisted of playing first base on his Curtis High School team in Staten Island. His limited mobility was a forerunner to the hapless New York Mets "Marvelous"

Marv Throneberry. He could play catch with us only if one of us (usually Marty, being the youngest) would stand by him to pick up any errant throws. My dad had great hands (he was a dentist after all), and as long as our throws back to him were on target, he would catch the ball and throw it back with a velocity and height that neither of my brothers could replicate. It was just like playing catch on a ball field built in the middle of the cornfields of Iowa. And it was certainly better than playing solo— the hours spent practicing fielding grounders by throwing the ball against the wall.

That night we talked about baseball. But because he was not around during the afternoons, after school—when our backyard that melded into the empty lots behind us became our "Field of Dreams" minus the corn stalks—he could not be aware of how important sports were in the socialization process for his boys. He had missed seeing us play for hours, three or four boys to a side, mimicking our favorite players. So my dad never saw any of my sensational fielding plays or smashes into the shrubs, with George searching for the ball as I circled the bases.

That night we also reminisced about Fuzzer, whom we had to give away that summer, due to Harlan's allergy to dander, and how she would be up in Connecticut on a farm. I suggested, "Dad, maybe we should send Harlan up to Connecticut instead," to which my father smiled, understanding where I was coming from, but never letting on just how much he was also going to miss Fuzzer. He'd had Cocker Spaniels since he was married to Mom, and he'd suffered as his favorite died in his arms one night after he got home from work. He comforted me by telling me how much fun Fuzzer would have, running around in the fields, and he promised me that I could get a stuffed dog to cuddle in bed with me, which would offer me at least a little solace.

In later years, I would realize that fifth grade was a terrible time to move into a new class. I would no longer be able assume my parents could protect me from my social gaffes. And although we brothers were not FLKs (funny looking kids), I did need braces and I was not likely to be a candidate to be a poster child for a teen idol magazine. I would soon be missing the camaraderie I had in Highland Park with George and Ellis and Theresa, where I was an integral part of the neighborhood gang.

I didn't as yet have the trepidation I would have later that week, of going to school on the first day and having to come to grips with entering a classroom where I was a stranger among previously established friends and cliques. When we'd moved before, when Harlan was going into second grade and I into kindergarten, the adjustments were relatively easy to make, so my parents never fully understood the social difficulties we would encounter.

In the end, we were moving because my dad had always put his intellectual needs before his income. That meant less steak for us and more hamburgers and potatoes. My mom learned how to stretch a chicken for a family of five. She revered (or was it "served"—almost the same letters) her husband. She would even take the pits out of his grapes, as those were the days before genetically engineered pitless green and purple spheres.

So it was of no wonder that she agreed to follow him to a community six miles from the George Washington Bridge. Even though I heard her protest, I now know it really wasn't so bad for my mom. Our new house was only two blocks from where her only sister, Julie, lived. It could have allowed them to reestablish some type of relationship that their five year age difference had forced between them, if Julie had not moved to Chicago the month before we arrived. But her dad, who had remarried about ten years after my grandmother died of breast cancer, was recently divorced, and was moving up from Princeton to live in a rental apartment near by. And as her cousins, Bruce and Lois, and their families lived close by, I think Mom was actually feeling like she was leaving Siberia and coming back to the real world.

At 10:05 p.m. we turned onto Windsor Road, where the trees lining the street were mature enough to qualify for Joyce Kilmer's poem. Then we turned into the driveway to start our new lives in a sturdy, white, Colonial home built in the 1930s. It was two full stories, but as I ran up the stairs, I started crying when I counted the bedrooms—one for my parents, one for Harlan, and the last one for me—and Marty!! I went down to the basement to check out if there was room for a bomb shelter, especially since tensions had now increased with the construction of the Berlin Wall in August.

I was excited but sad—sad for all of the above reasons, but, perhaps most of all, because my hour alone with my dad was up. And although I remember being with him alone on "Gil Hodges Night" in 1962, a great baseball night, we wouldn't talk like this again until my mom got sick with breast cancer in 1965. But this night was perhaps our most honest night together, because as my mom lay dying, he tried to keep the secret of her terminal illness from his children, trying to protect us, forgoing any comfort we might have been able to afford him.

Two days later, after barely beginning to unpack and still not meeting any kids in my neighborhood, I was in Mr. Oren's fifth grade class. He was my first male teacher. Marty was in first grade and Harlan was in junior high school. My mom was waiting for me at home with lunch that day. And my dad was back "home" in New York City, working full time at Columbia University's Dental School.

That night, as I fell asleep without Fuzzer, I thought about my friends I had left behind in Highland Park. They wouldn't be brooding tonight about their new teacher or worried about whether they would be invited to Debbie's birthday party. I had been one of the "Founding Fathers" of our community gang—but now I would have to prove myself to a group of kids who'd grown up together. It couldn't happen instantaneously. There would be no "immaculate reception" for me by my new classmates. So tonight it was only my new stuffed dog, Floppy, held tight to my chest, not moving at all, there to protect me from what would come in the morning.

February 20, 1962

I was not in a gymnasium this time to watch an American being hurled into space. Now we were in the auditorium, squirming in actual seats as we tried to concentrate on the television screen showing John Glenn's liftoff in Freedom 7. Finally, America would be catching up to the Russians. We would actually have an astronaut orbiting the Earth. And unlike Enos the Chimp, who had circled the Earth in the stratosphere in November 1961, John Glenn could actually "fly" his capsule. But we were still a long way from JFK's promise that we would land a man on the Moon by the end of the decade. We still needed to test the effects of space travel. How would weightlessness affect the human body and spirit? Only the tether from the space suit to the capsule would keep the astronauts tied to the "mother ship," as they floated around in outer space without gravitational forces.

There were multiple delays, starting with problems with the fuel tanks, and then another two week delay because of bad weather. Today, while we slept, John Glenn entered the Friendship 7 capsule at 6:03 a.m., only to suffer another 2-hour delay to fix a defective bolt. But after being in the capsule 3 hours and 44 minutes, he lifted off at 9:47. The Atlas rocket performed admirably, unlike at least one of its predecessors, which had blown up at 27,000 feet. But at last Glenn was in orbit, planning a trip of seven go-arounds. Almost five hours later, after traveling 75,679 miles at a maximum speed of 17,544 mph, Glenn brought Friendship 7 down to a safe landing in the Atlantic Ocean. But not before there were multiple misfirings, requiring Glenn to use more fuel and terminate the flight after three orbits; technical difficulties with the yaw system, causing the capsule to have attitude and stabilization malfunctions, requiring Glenn to manually fly his spaceship; "fireflies" flashing by the capsule, causing concern that the heat shield was disintegrating; and, finally, the ultimate fear that the heat shield would come off during reentry, leading to the capsule's burning up, along with our astronaut hero.

By the time John Glenn had landed, I was home. Our class had been let out early so we could watch the landing (or "oceaning," to be more precise) with our families. The principal probably felt we'd be better off viewing a tragedy with our loved ones. Instead, I was home with Marty and my mom. We held hands and cheered, as our hope for the future, our hope to protect us from the Communists, finally emerged from Friendship 7 onto the U.S.S. Noa, telling us, "It was hot in there."

Several days later, there was a tickertape parade in New York and Glenn visited with President Kennedy and his family. He was the All-American Hero. How soon we could forget Alan Shepard!

April 4, 1962

My parents never fully appreciated the importance of my playing sports with classmates. At dinner one night, about a month after we moved, I proudly boasted, "I blocked Eddie's punt and scored a touchdown," only to be told that I couldn't play football anymore because I could get injured. They had no understanding of the impact that their joint parental decision, discussed behind closed doors that night, would have on the already difficult transition I was having in my new school.

I raced up to my room in tears, screaming, "You're the worst parents. No one will play with me. They'll all think I'm a momma's boy." And then I slammed my door shut, jumped onto my bed, and whispered to my dogs. "At least you understand me. I'd never keep you from playing football!" And I held my breath when my mom came up to see me that night, hoping that she'd think I wasn't breathing because I had died. That would show them! But then she stood there for an "eternity," and I couldn't hold it any longer. Then she whispered, "We love you," and turned off the lights.

Everyday that week, I came home from school early, skulking around the house, hoping for the question, "Why are you home so early?" so that I could mutter as I turned away, "Because all of the other boys are playing football and you won't let me." But my mom was smart enough not to ask anything other than, "Can I get you a snack?"

No matter how much I sulked, they just didn't seem to get my message. It didn't even matter when Petey broke his arm sliding down the banister at school later that week.

"See, Dad," I pleaded that night. "It's dangerous going to school. If I can't play football, then I shouldn't be allowed to go to school."

I raced back up to my room before my mom could bring out the Ivory soap!

Thank heaven my dad let me try out for baseball. I didn't make the Majors Division, but as I was practicing with my Intermediate League team, waiting our turn for our team picture on Opening Day, my coach came up to me and asked, "Austin, do you think you could pitch today in relief if I need you?"

"Sure, coach." Why was I so certain? I'd only pitched once in practice the last week, and then only for an inning. What did he see in me that I didn't see in myself?

"Well, why don't you warm up here with Jimmy to get some practice?"

I was flying as I walked over and picked up a scuffed baseball. My white Clinton Inn uniform with the red number 10 on my back was my new suit of honor; my blue cap with a "C" on it was my crown.

"Come on, Jimmy. I need you to catch me."

"Austin, I'm tired."

"Coach said to warm me up."

As Jimmy and I wandered off to the side, I thought about Don Larsen pitching his perfect game in the World Series. That could be me. And then I remembered that screaming Giants announcer, "The Giants Win the Pennant, The Giants Win the Pennant." Ralph Branca had thrown that pitch. That could also be me. And don't forget Ralph Terry against Maz and the Pirates in 1960. Maybe I should just stay in center field.

My control during warm-ups left something to be desired, so I was happy that Charlie was the starting pitcher that afternoon. Dad and Mom were in the bleachers when I came up to the plate for my first official appearance, with men on first and second, two men out. But four pitches later, with only a weak foul ball to my credit, I was walking back to the bench, a strikeout victim. I took the last pitch right down the middle of the plate, as tears welled in my eyes. I could've kicked myself! Why didn't I listen to coach's exhortation to "swing the bat!" I could've been a hero. And when history repeated itself two innings later, it was all my dad could take. He left with my mom, not wanting to watch my painful expression and tears, which were no longer confined to the corner of my eyes. Crybaby and strikeout king! How much more shame could I have before my coach, and worse, my classmates?

But although my dad didn't see me get any hits that day, he did miss my catch in center field. I would be labeled "Good field, No hit." And he wasn't there for my relief-pitching debut—one inning pitched, two runs given up—as our team suffered its first loss. My ERA was an astronomical 18.00. Don't forget to add to my label, "And not much of a pitcher either."

April 13, 1962 (A Friday)

As a fifth-grader, your parents can simply write you a note and pretty much make any excuse for their child to miss school. My excuse was Opening Day for the new New York Mets, the National League expansion team meant to re-kindle the hearts of the disenfranchised New York Giants and Brooklyn Dodgers fans, and my whole family was going to play hooky. The space race was on the back burner, the Cold War was in the oven. Today was about America, about our pastime (notwithstanding Cuba's Fidel Castro), about our team's pennant race.

This morning, however, was going to start with an inventory spelling test. My anxiety level rose each Thursday night before our Friday exam, as I would be under pressure (both internal and external, I am sure) to move up to the highest level—"10"—and then beyond. I couldn't sleep by myself, so I'd plop myself down outside my parents' closed bedroom door, my stuffed dogs "Junior" and "Senior" at my side, curled up in the fetal position, studying my words relentlessly, then putting the list under my pillow, hoping for osmotic learning. Two weeks earlier, I'd been on the edge of "immortality," ready to advance to the extra credit projects, when I misspelled "rhythm" as "rythym" (even now, I am having trouble forcing the computer's spell check to allow me to spell it wrong, as it is underlined in red, glaring out at me, saying, "Are you sure you want to spell it that way?").

Each Friday, after Dad got up to shave, I would climb into their bed and lie with my mom as we went over the list for that level, over and over again, my worries escalating with each misspelled word and easing with each calming rendition of the word by Mom. These were great moments for me, as any moment for a middle child alone with his parent is special and to be guarded. We worked together for about 30 minutes, until it was time to get up and wake the others.

After I was dressed, I'd still run into my mom's room for one last practice session. After making my way downstairs and putting on my coat, I'd give Mom a hug and a kiss.

"I love you, Mom."

"I love you, Austin. Do your best."

Not "Good luck." Luck had nothing to do with success in our family. It was all about hard work. And as long as I did my best, my mom promised she'd be proud of me.

On this day, our work together led to perfection. I spelled all ten words correctly, including "minuscule," "embarrassing," "remedial," and "futile," all of which would fit the talent pool of our new baseball team. By 10 o'clock, my books were packed and I was ready to go. Mr. O. had read Mom's note regarding my early dismissal with mixed reaction, remembering his professional obligation as a teacher while reminiscing about his childhood baseball career. Today, his inner child, joyfully, was there to rescue me. With the envy of all the boys in the class, I proceeded down to the principal's office, where Mom was waiting with Marty and our sweaters and lined jackets. It was a misty and raw morning, the sky steely without benefit of any sun; not much of a day to honor the summer pastime. I know my dad had to use his influence to convince Mom to let us go to Opening Day, telling her, "They won't catch a cold," and answering her concerns about Harlan by scientifically asserting, "Don't worry, the pollen count will be down in the rain."

It was Friday the 13th, an omen of what was to befall our team this inaugural season. My dad, the old Giants fan, had been waiting for baseball to return to his hometown. Although it was obvious during the Mets' first few seasons, when the Los Angeles Dodgers or San Francisco Giants would come back to the Polo Grounds, that there were two sets of fans—one set like me, new fans, the New Breed, without tentacles from the past, rooting for the Mets, and the other set, like the Tories during the American Revolution, still loyal to their Sultans of Swat, Willie Mays and Duke Snider, continuing to live in their past lives.

However, on this day, there weren't really many from either camp, as only 12,000 fans braved the snow flurries and the non-existent traffic jam to see the Mets play the Pittsburgh Pirates. This time, unlike when we drove to Yankee Stadium several years earlier, my dad knew how to get to the stadium. There was no problem finding a parking space today on the winding street behind the stadium.

"Harlan, Austin, Martin, be careful getting out of the car. There is a lot of traffic here. I don't want to take you back to Dad's hospital" Mom was multi-tasking, checking on our safety, and getting all of the food and coats out of the trunk.

"Helene, do you have the tickets?"

"Yes, Dear," suppressing whatever emotion must have built up after all the preparation she had done. "Right here in my pocketbook. Do you want to see them?"

Dad intelligently just said, "You're the best."

And off we went, we four boys and one wife, beginning our trek through the turnstiles and entering into this magical kingdom

The Polo Grounds had the appearance of an elder society lady, with makeup and face-lifts to the tune of $375,000; but it still left it a third cousin to Yankee Stadium. There was red, white, and blue bunting hanging from the box seat railings, proclaiming a special day. But the empty seats throughout the ballpark allowed the sounds of batting practice, and "Hot Dogs, get your Hot Dogs," to echo through the cavernous park as if you were standing on the North Rim of the Grand Canyon. The park would only be full on the days that the Tories came to watch their once-removed heroes. Today, however, rather than signifying a new beginning, it was a study of desolation, of an experiment going bad. The Mets were only 0-1 so far this year, having lost 11-4 in their true first game in St. Louis on April 11, 1962.

I still have my ticket stub and my program from that game, along with the grainy pictures I took with my Brownie camera. So I can recreate the plays whenever I wish. The ticket cost $2.50, the program cost 15 cents, and the yearbook put us back 50 cents. However, today my ticket stub is worth $400, my program the same, and my yearbook would be worth $300, except for the fact that I colored in the cartoon on the front cover. But the memories and the Brownie snapshots are "priceless."

As we watched batting practice, my dad pointed to where the left field stands jetted out over the field. "That's where Bobby Thomson's home run landed, with Andy Pafko watching, hoping that it would fall into his glove instead. And over there, way near the bleachers, 475 feet away, that's where Willie Mays made his miraculous over-the-shoulder catch in the '54 World Series."

But what he didn't talk to me about, which I'm sure was in his mind, was the image of Mel Ott standing in the batter's box, his right leg raised in anticipation of the next pitch, and then pulling the ball deep into the right field stands. My dad was no longer in his research lab or teaching in his classroom, but, rather, watching a game during his teenage years, his idol once again alive and well in New York City.

The Pittsburgh Pirates were introduced first to a smattering of boos. Not even Roberto Clemente was able to attract more than a few cheers, despite our being only blocks away from Spanish Harlem. The Mets were introduced and lined up along the first base line, led by the revival of Casey Stengel, the former Yankee manager, who was hailed with a standing ovation. Casey was to be the drawing card for this new team. All he proved, however, was that whatever ability he had to manage had been made easier by writing out a lineup that included Mickey Mantle, Yogi Berra, and Whitey Ford. There were great cheers for Gil Hodges, the old Brooklyn Dodger and future Mets' manager in 1969, as he limped out onto the playing field, wearing his baggy, flannel, white uniform. But the cheers were then followed by "sounds of indifference" for the rest of the unknown players.

Looking at our roster, the new Mets' fans could be hopeful, with so many stars, so many home runs in the past. All hope was soon put to rest, however, as the ravages of increasing age and delayed reflexes brought reality to our fantasies. As the Mets took the field, the outfield of Richie Ashburn, Frank Thomas, and Gus Bell had an average age of 38—similar to my dad's age! The vast green expanse of the outfield, rimmed by the clay-colored infield and warning track, seemed a potential torture chamber for them. Although there was no question they could beat my dad in a footrace, they certainly didn't deceive anyone when Ashburn and Bell let a routine fly ball drop between them in right center field. Gil Hodges was already out of action with a stiff knee. The Mets did field some real major leaguers that day who were still somewhere near the prime of their career, including Charlie Neal. And players such as Frank Thomas still could hit, knocking out 38 home runs that year. But even if the hitters could still hit, they couldn't run or field.

And then there was the pitching. Oh, the pitching!

Sherman "Roadblock" Jones started the opening game. The name "roadblock" suggested that he could keep runners from advancing around the bases. We groaned as the Pirates scored the first runs, and cheered as the Mets came back. We ate our way through the sandwiches and hot chocolate, and tried to persuade my parents that we needed more.

"Who wants gum?" Mom asked, mimicking the Trident commercial. And of course, it was sugar-free, not the good Double Bubble that we really wanted. At least we didn't have braces yet, which would have meant the absolute end of gum!

"I want some popcorn, please," I pleaded, although what I really wanted was the orange megaphone with the Mets' logo on it that the popcorn came in, so I could yell to the players like the kids next to me. Marty convinced my parents to buy a box of Cracker Jacks, and then started to fight with Harlan over the prize that came with the trusty peanuts and popcorn—in this case, a decal that said "USA."

The seats were cold, the air uncomfortable, and the best way to stay warm was under the blankets that Mom had brought. Bored between innings, I looked around the stadium from our seats on the third base line. Off in the distance was a banner, "Leonia, New Jersey Loves Rod Kanehl." I looked in my program to see whom the fans from my neighboring town were cheering for. There it was on the scorecard: #10, Rod Kanehl. The same number 10 that was on my Little League uniform. And so, as easy as that, Eddie Mathews was out and Rod Kanehl was in as my new idol.

As the game proceeded, the Mets scored a run in the fifth inning on Ashburn's hit. Woeful as it would be this season, the pitching staff actually kept the Pirates, only one season removed from Bill Mazeroski's walk-off ninth inning home run against the Yankees, in check, so that when Frank Thomas hit a home run in the seventh inning, the score was actually tied at 3-3.

But my brothers weren't convinced. Perhaps, in retrospect, they were the brightest.

Marty whined, "I'm so cold. Please let's go."

I countered, "You're such a cry baby. Just cuddle up with Mom."

"Do you want my allergies to get worse?" Harlan always tried to play that trump card.

"Please, let's stay! Please! Please! I want to stay, Helene, please! I'll take us out to dinner when we get home." Dad was on my side! Wow.

And so, a 2-2 tie in the stands was settled by Mom, not a true base-ball fan, but joyfully on the side of tradition that day. And so we stayed, despite Harlan and Marty's fight over the pink cotton candy in the seventh inning. The only ignominy of the day was when Mom made Harlan escort me to the bathroom—something that he would proudly relate to the rest of our extended family whenever we saw them.

But, as we would learn over and over again that year, the "Mutts" would torture their fans, tantalizing them with comebacks only to find a way to lose again, as they did today on the weakness of two wild pitches by rookie pitcher Ray Daviault in the ninth inning. As the Mets went out feebly in the bottom of their ninth, we packed up our goodies, our souvenirs, and our memories. We trudged out into the late afternoon, still dreary, without sun in the sky, with the bunting already beginning to tear loose, but I couldn't wait to come back.

"Can we come back tomorrow? It's Saturday, I don't have school."

"Don't bring me, then. I've got a report due Monday for English," Harlan screamed.

"Mommy, do we have to come back?" Marty started to cry.

I could see I wasn't getting much support from my fraternal end, so I turned to Dad with a mournful look.

"Let's see when the Giants come to town. Helene, why don't we send away for tickets for the doubleheader in June?"

"Thanks, Pop!" I said that day.

And thank you, Dad, for taking me to the Opening Day of the New York Mets. With all of the loss, with all of the pain that I would feel in the next few years, this day remains with me to this moment, the sun forever shining on our family.

Summer of '62

Even if my dad didn't come to any more of my Little League games, I was lucky that we went as a family to four or five games each of the two years that the Mets played in the Polo Grounds—although in retrospect, his explanation that Mets' baseball was played a step above our games was subject to question. Several excursions included double headers, a 12-year-old's delight, but with lots of preparation by mom. I would meticulously keep score in my program, penciling in the line-up, placing the position next to each player, and marking in each little square what each player had done in each inning. "K" meant strike out (lots of them in the Mets' column), "W" a walk, "-" a single, "=" a double, and "6-3" a groundout to the shortstop. And a leading entry for the other team, E-6, meant error, Mets' shortstop. At the end of the game, I would shade in all of the boxes not used. However, with so many Mets' substitutions, pinch hitters, relief pitchers, and names squeezed in-between lines, as neat as I would try to make it, it always came out looking like a kindergarten project.

You can imagine my distress when my dad or my brothers wanted to leave before the end of the game. Whether he had run out of his editorial work that he had brought along to do, or whether my brothers were bored or had upset stomachs, there would be pressure to beat the exiting traffic. Their well-deserved pessimism, that the Mets would always find a way to blow a lead in the ninth inning, or could just never overcome a deficit in the late innings, always conflicted with my desire to stay. After all, it didn't count as my attending a "win" if I didn't see the last out. And what if we were to miss the Mets' improbable ninth inning comeback? Although I am clearly the one who needs long-term psychoanalysis, please just reflect on how those Mets' fans felt who left Shea Stadium in the 10th inning of the sixth game of the 1986 World Series, after missing the miraculous victory as Mookie Wilson's grounder went through Bill Buckner's legs!

Of all of the games that I went to, the only other one I remember clearly was in the late summer of 1962. What possessed my dad to take me to the Polo Grounds on this muggy Friday night in late August, with the Mets far out of first place, was that it was "Gil Hodges Night." There were 39,741 fans who came to pay their respects to a gentleman baseball player who no one on that night would have predicted would lead these Mets out of the desert, where they had wandered in last place for eight years, to the 1969 World Series. Although my dad was a Giant fan when he was growing up, and Mr. Hodges had played for the Dodgers, tonight it was just Dad and me, here to honor a man he considered a true sportsman, even if he was on the opposition.

As we would reminisce later as co-adults, it became clear that our memories of that night are diametrically opposed. I remember having the time of my life, watching Rod Kanehl, my hero, hit a home run off of Don Drysdale, one of the most feared pitchers in baseball. On my right, as I was cheering, was my dad, who was my other hero that night. And on my left were two servicemen in uniform, who were more than willing to entertain me, an impressionable teenager. I was in awe of their stature, brave young men protecting our country and the American way, sporting crew cuts, just like I had, pressed khaki pants and shirts, their collars loosened, their nametags over their left shirt pockets—and they were actually talking to me. I had never met men in uniform before, and I had quite a story to tell Mom when I got home.

Dad recollected differently, because after the pair of seats that were occupied by the servicemen, the tier of seats ended abruptly, with a precipice to the lower stands. To this day, if you ask my him, he doesn't remember the score or the home run—only that every time I stood up to cheer, he was afraid I was going to fall over the edge. That there were two military men ready to protect their fellow countryman was of no solace to my dad.

Dad was always trying to protect his children from what might befall them (or what they might fall off of), but he forgot that at some time every young bird has to attempt to fly on its own. When I played my first Little League game and struck out both times, he refused to come back to any other games. The agony of watching his son's pain at failure was too much for him. But, by avoiding the strikeouts, he would miss my complete game victory as a pitcher, and my inside-the-park home run, which I could share at the moment with my teammates and coaches. He, however, could only share that glorious event in the retelling. For all his fears, for all his missing the pain, he also missed the joy.

As we got ready to follow our Mets to Shea Stadium in April 1964, would he be ready for change, to leave the Polo Grounds behind in rubble, as it was a victim of the wrecking ball to make room for new apartment projects? But more importantly to me, would he be ready for the transformation in his son to puberty and manhood?

But before we could celebrate the 1964 World's Fair, with all of its futuristic exhibits and the opening of Shea Stadium in Flushing, New York, our timeline was shifted by two major events in our country and in the world, which would change our focus from baseball to survival of country and family. Although it was only a ten minute drive, it would be a long way from watching the Mets at the Polo Grounds to the new era beginning at Shea Stadium in 1964.

THE BEGINNING OF THE END

October 21, 1962

It is predictable that I can remember details of the excitement of the Mets' opening game; that exams and book reports are still fresh in my mind; that the first image of a *Playboy* centerfold remains indelibly ingrained in my id; and that I can still hear Stanley Marsh proclaim how big Miss B's bosoms were—my mind still not comprehending what that term described. But the major event of the year, the Cuban Missile Crisis, is only a blur in my "database." What remains is only the psychological devastation that it produced. My mom's cousin Bruce and his wife, Gail, were making plans to drive with their family as far north as they could go, to escape the annihilation that was sure to come. They were carrying a newly purchased rifle with which to defend their family from any other "refugees." We made no such plans to abandon home. That left us to deal with the threat that a nuclear bomb would land on New York City, where my dad was teaching. My mom and my brothers would survive without him, "protected" from the nuclear holocaust six miles away, by crawling under our make-shift bomb shelter (i.e. built-in cabinet in the basement.) That I was so upset of the possibility of being fatherless suggests that I wouldn't have made a good Oedipus.

My relative amnesia of those events, those 13 days, is such that it makes more sense for Mary's story to be told. Although she has told me throughout her reminiscences for this book that her memories for dates and venues often appear to be mildly distorted by her travels through the time warp of the '60s, she seems to remember better this fortnight—probably because her family members were serving in the armed forces in the Caribbean when this occurred. But, then again, as her life had already lost its core—with her mother and father having divorced and remarried, leaving her behind with her grandparents—she was already spinning off at a distance, allowing a perspective different than mine.

Norfolk, Virginia

"Mary, did you do your homework for American History?"

"Yes, Grammie, I finished it last night. I'm so tired of learning about Christopher Columbus and the discovery of America. Is it true that they landed right near us here at Plymouth Rock?"

"So they say, Mary. Get ready for bed and then you can come watch Lawrence Welk with us."

It was Sunday, but Mary had yet to change from her frilly church dress. Her long hair, parted in the center and worn shoulder length, framed her innocent Irish face, masking her childlike beauty. Gramps was reading his paper and Mary had already reached for the comics.

"Let me see . . . I want to read Dick Tracy."

As Mary grabbed the paper out of Gramps' hands, she applied her "silly putty" to the detective's face, and then removed it to show the mirror image to her grandmother. The face was distorted from pulling the putty in all directions.

"Look, Grammie, Dick Tracy's face looks like when we went into the funhouse at the carnival."

Mr. Welk came on the television. Ever since Mary's parents had divorced and she'd come to live with her grandparents in Norfolk, it had become a weekly treat for her to sit with them in the living room and watch the pretty young ladies and handsome men sing beautiful melodies, led by Mr. Welk in his tuxedo, his smile so like that of her Uncle Ben.

As they finished the final songs, and the credits went by, Gramps asked.

"Are you falling asleep, Mary? Why don't you go up to your room and change into your pajamas and come back down to watch the news with us."

"Don't you think she should go to bed? She has school tomorrow, after all."

Mary frowned at her grandmother, who was knitting a sweater, her black reading glasses halfway down her nose. Her long, undyed gray hair was braided around her head, which was appropriate for her sturdy build and broad shoulders. She was sitting in her favorite chair next to the window. Her flowery, green apron covered her housedress, her childhood and youth transformed into a kindly matron. She had been forced back into motherhood, however, with Mary's appearance.

But then Mary cuddled up with her grandfather, gave him a big kiss, whispered into his ear, and ran up to her bedroom.

She saw her favorite doll sitting alone on the bureau. "Does Dolly feel as lonely as I do sometimes?" Mary wondered.

"Dolly, let's get undressed and then we'll go downstairs and watch TV. But first, we have to brush our teeth and then I'll comb your hair." Mary started to laugh as she became a seven-year-old again. There was Dolly, her baby, bald, swathed in her blanket. Mary picked her up, held her closely to her torso, and watched as her plastic eyelids closed. "Come on Dolly, it'll be fun. Maybe Grammie will have some hot chocolate for you and me."

After she changed into her pajamas and changed Dolly into her nightgown, they both went to the top of the stairs.

"We're coming down with our Slinky. Here Dolly, push it down the stairs."

Spider, Mary's cat, stood at the bottom of the stairs, waiting for his dinner as he watched the wire toy climb its way down, accelerating, until it reached the bottom, followed by Mary sliding down on her backside, holding Dolly close to her chest.

"Dolly wants to watch the news with me!" Mary shouted. "She's such a smart doll."

"Mary, where did that beautiful baby come from?" beamed Gramps, as he moved over on the couch to let Mary sit next to him.

"She looked so sad, Gramps. I wanted her to know I still love her."

The news came on and the first story was about a fire in downtown Norfolk.

"I wonder which fire company got there first." Gramps had retired from the department a year ago, but he still kept up with his friends, meeting with the boys every Friday night for a couple of beers at Ryan's. "It looks like they did a good job of containing the fire."

"I bet you'd have done better, Grandpa." Even in his old T-shirt and khaki pants, still smelling of Old Spice shaving lotion, his pipe at his side with its aromatic scent from his Prince Albert tobacco permeating the air, Grandpa still looked like he was ready to answer the siren at a moment's notice. He still maintained his "fighting weight" of 170 pounds, and even the Betty Boop tattoo on his arm belied the fact that he was no longer a young man.

"Maybe, more so in my younger days," he said, as his eyes took on a reminiscent glow. "But now, with all of these young men just out of the Navy applying to the department, they didn't seem to have much use for me anymore."

In the background, the TV voice interjected, "We'll be right back after this commercial interruption." (No, he didn't really say "interruption?")

"Well, now you can just sit around here and drink your Pabst Blue Ribbons and watch the TV," Grandma interjected. "How about you getting up and getting me my cup of tea."

"I'll get it, Grandma. You and grandpa just sit and relax. Dolly and I'll take care of you."

Up she went and put the teapot kettle on the Frigidaire stove. Then she went over to the avocado green Hotpoint refrigerator for another beer for Grandpa.

"You'll wonder where the yellow went, when you brush your teeth with Pepsodent," a voice droned on in the background.

"If I hear another commercial about toothpaste or Fixadent, I'll take out my dentures and thrown them at the TV," Grandma retorted.

"You'd look funny, Grammie. And how'd you eat your steak? I hope they have that Alka Seltzer commercial on later. I like the little singing boy."

They were on a roll now. Grams continued, "The names they have for these products. They have all of these people with college degrees sitting around making up these names while this country goes soft. What kind of job is it to decide on "Lestoil" as a brand? I mean, 'It's so easy when you use Lestoil.' How corny can you get?"

"Yes, but it works, Margaret. What do you use when you clean the floor? You used to use Spic and Span, but now you use Lestoil," Gramps was unrelenting.

"Keep it up, smarty pants, and I'll pour some into a bucket and you can wash the floor tonight. That'll be your Sunday night treat!"

"Ha, Gramps, she got you that time." Mary was so pleased with herself, at least until he replied, "So Mary, I'll let you scrub the corner on your hands and knees!"

"No Gramps, I was just kidding."

"Reports from Oxford, Mississippi, suggest that things are finally settling down on the campus of 'Ole Miss,' as James Meredith attended classes last week as the first Negro student. The federal troops sent by Attorney General Robert Kennedy are finally leaving campus, but only after 160 of them were injured and two people were killed."

"Why don't they want that man to go to school, Gramps?"

"Because some people are prejudiced."

"What's prejudice?"

"It's when you don't like somebody just because they have different skin color or go to a different church," Grams answered.

"But that's not fair. I mean, I play with Nancy all of the time and she has a different color skin and she goes to a different church."

"Mary, that's because we're not prejudiced," Gramps answered. "I've fought fires with white and Negro men, and tried to save the houses of Negro and white families."

"Maybe you should go down to that state and teach 'em, Gramps."

"They might not like it so much, Mary. But at least you know right from wrong."

"And now on the international scene." That voice, deep and sonorous, so serious, hoping for its big break so it could start doing the network news in Richmond, instead of on this military town's local station "There are rumors from unidentified sources that some type of unauthorized Russian military buildup is occurring in Cuba. President Kennedy is meeting with his advisors and is said to be watching the situation carefully. We hope to have more details before we go off the air."

"What do you think is happening, Jimmy?" Grandma asked, her tone changing perceptibly.

"I don't know. I guess the President is worried that Fidel Castro is up to no good again. We can't trust him as long as the Communists remain in power in Cuba."

"Where is Cuba, Gramps?"

"Too close for my liking. It's only 90 miles below the tip of Florida, about 250 miles from where you lived. Not much farther than Washington, DC is from our house. Its capital city is Havana, which used to be a great place to have fun. I remember going there when I was in the Navy. But now, it's Communist and the people are poor and have no freedom. They don't even own their own houses. It's like a little Russia."

"Do the little girls have dolls?"

"Maybe one, if that," answered Grandma.

"And they probably all have long, straggly beards."

"Jimmy, don't scare Mary."

"Grammie, I feel sorry for them. Can we send one of my old dolls to one of the little girls there?"

"Honey, they're our enemies—we can't write or visit them."

"But how can a little girl be our enemy? What's she done wrong? It isn't fair!!"

"Don't worry, honey," Grandpa tried to comfort her. "This Mr. Castro is a bad man and he won't stay in power very long. The Cubans are good people and they'll get tired of him and rebel."

"I doubt it," Grandma interjected. "The Commies have been in power in Russia for 45 years and Khrushchev still rules with an iron hand."

"Maybe we can call a Cuban family on the telephone and tell them we want them to come visit us." Mary was pleading now.

"Mary, that's long distance. And besides, they can't leave. Mr. Castro won't let them go."

"Sort of like the nuns at St. Mary's. They won't even let me leave to go to the bathroom without their permission."

"Don't complain, Mary. Imagine if your entire life was like that."

"And now to the sports. Today, the Washington Redskins, behind the passing of Norm Snead, beat the Philadelphia Eagles. And behind Y. A. Tittle, the ageless quarterback, the New York Giants beat the Detroit Lions."

"Now that's an old man," Gramps was laughing. "And he's still playing with the boys."

"Look at him, Gramps. He's bald and so funny looking. What does Y. A. stand for?"

"Your . . ."

"Stop right there, Jimmy. Watch your tongue."

"Sorry. Mary, he may look old, but boy can he play football. Why, when I was his age, I could climb into buildings with the best of them. I still would, but I'd rather sit home with you on my lap. "

"Thanks, Gramps," Mary whispered as she snuggled close, feeling his warmth as she fell to sleep, Dolly in one arm, feeling protected and far away from danger. For one night, at least, Mary didn't cry herself to sleep remembering the night her mother didn't come home and her father explained that she had gone away on a vacation with Mary's sister Kate. Mary spent the next week curled up in bed at night with her Dad—she in a red "nightie" with blue bears on it, he in his black and red striped pajamas, the smell of Vitalis in his hair and the cleanliness of Ivory soap emanating from his freshly showered body. In her eleven-year-old mind, she was unable to understand why her mom's vacation was taking so long. And then he, too, was gone, and she was here with Grams and Gramps.

October 22, 1962

As Mary came down to dinner, she realized something was very different tonight. There was nothing cooking on the stove or in the oven. The smells of dinner were nowhere in the air.

"That's funny," she thought, "I guess we're going out to eat tonight." But it was Monday, usually chicken night, pan-fried with cornbread and okra. She looked forward to the chicken and cornbread, although the okra was too bitter for her.

"Hey, Gramma. What's for dinner?"

"Shhh, Mary, we're watching the President."

Mr. Kennedy looked so serious as he talked, not like when he was playing with his little children.

". . . Soviet military buildup on the island of Cuba. Within the past week, unmistakable evidence has established the fact that a series of offensive missile sites is now in preparation on that imprisoned island."

"Jimmy, how far are we from Cuba?"

"To halt this offensive buildup, a strict quarantine on all offensive military equipment under shipment to Cuba is being initiated."

"Margaret, isn't Brian down in the Caribbean on his tour of duty?" Grandpa put his arm around Mary as she sat down next to him on the couch, but it was more perfunctory than in the moment.

"It shall be the policy of this nation to regard any nuclear missile launched from Cuba against any nation in the Western Hemisphere as an attack by the Soviet Union on the United States, requiring a full retaliatory response upon the Soviet Union."

"What does this mean?"

"It means that the Cubans have missiles that could attack us and we're ready to go to war with them if they don't get rid of them."

"Will there be shooting?"

"Yes, and planes and bombs and soldiers dying."

"What about my Uncle Brian?"

"That's what we are worried about. He's in the Navy."

"Grandpa, can I write him?"

"Of course."

"Maybe I can call Mommy and tell her to write him also."

"I don't know, Mary. When your mom left to go back down to Florida, Uncle Brian was very angry at her. I don't think he writes his sister anymore."

"I'm scared, Grandpa. Will we be okay? Will Mom be safe? We won't be attacked, will we?"

"Of course not, we are the United States. Our armed forces will protect us." Thank heavens, he thought; she doesn't understand how much danger we are in.

"Well, then, I'm hungry as a horse. I'm gonna ago outside and ride my bike until dinner."

October 23, 1962

Mary was sitting with Dolly watching "McHale's Navy" while her grandfather was sitting in his chair reading the newspaper.

"What's that you're watching, Mary?" Grandma called out from the kitchen.

"It's a funny show about some men in the Navy. Maybe we should call them up and have them come help us in Cuba."

"I don't think so, Mary." Gramps added. It's just a television show with actors. And I don't think its very funny, with everyone so worried about Cuba."

"Jimmy, just let Mary watch her television show. She doesn't need to worry herself sick."

As her grandmother came back into the living room and sat down with her knitting, Mary looked up.

"Grandma, I overheard the nuns talking today. They said the world may come to an end, and all of the sinners have caused this." Mary could barely keep her tears back.

"Mary, don't be so upset. The Pope's trying to help. I read today in the paper that he's trying to negotiate to end the crisis." Grandma tried to pacify the family.

"That's a lot of baloney!" Grandpa wasn't about to let his wife get away with believing that! "The Communists are all atheists. Why should they listen to the Pope? That's like when we tried to negotiate for better working conditions for our firefighters, and the court-appointed arbitrator used to work in the same law firm as the mayor."

"What's an atheist, Grandpa?"

"Someone who doesn't believe in God," Grandma answered before her husband could come up with some inappropriate definition.

"How could someone not believe in God? We pray to him everyday in school and on Sunday. Who else'll forgive us for all of our sins when we are bad?"

"I don't know, Mary. The atheists must be pretty lonely after they die, not being able to go to heaven or hell, according to them," Grandma explained.

"Yeah, but according to the Pope, they'll all go to hell, so I guess it doesn't matter to them," Mary tried to reason it all out in her mind.

"Where did you hear that, Mary?"

"From the nuns, of course. And they said that they're glad that a good Catholic like President Kennedy is there to lead us."

Then Mary started crying inconsolably.

"What's wrong with you?" Grandma wanted to know.

"I'm all to blame. I'm the sinner the nuns were talking about. I caused all of this. I told a lie to the nuns last week in school about my homework and now the world is coming to an end. And it's all my fault."

"Mary, Mary, you're so silly. Come here, let me hug you. Of course you didn't cause this. You're the sweetest girl anyone could ever want. No one would ever hurt you."

Mary thought, "Except for my mother and father," as she recalled images of her father dropping her off at his in-laws, promising to come back to get her with her mother and Kate.

October 25, 1962

"Where're you going, Grandpa?" Mary asked, as she saw him getting into the car when she got home from school.

"I'm going to the store to stock up on some food."

"Can I come with you? I'd like to get some Sugar Pops and some Ovaltine."

"Sure, Mary. But what we really need are some foods we can store down in the basement or take with us in case we have to go to a special place. We'll need evaporated milk, peanut butter, crackers, canned juices, things which don't need to be refrigerated."

"I don't understand, Grandpa. What's happening? We got these instructions in school today to give to you."

"The Russians have threatened to start a nuclear war if we shoot at their boats. Then we'll have to worry that they will attack us."

"Like those drills from elementary school—head down, between my legs. Let me show you," she said, as she dropped to the ground.

"That's okay, Mary. Let's go to the store and you can demonstrate later."

They got into the old Studebaker sedan and drove off, leaving behind their small gray house, neatly painted, with a white picket fence—a throwback to Tom Sawyer's Missouri homestead. The white flagpole stood regally in the front yard, needing someone to climb up top to freshen the paint. Already this morning, Grandpa had proudly raised the flag, bearing the 50 stars and stripes, a display of patriotism that would be repeated in 12 hours, when he proudly lowered the stars and stripes safely back to earth, at dusk.

As they rode in silence to the A&P, Mary's face became distorted with fear. "What happens if we're attacked while I'm at school? Who'll take care of me? What if the bomb drops near you and something happens to you and Grandma? Tell me, Grandpa, tell me."

"Mary, you'll be safe in school. They've set up bomb shelters in the schools. The nuns will watch you till we can get you home."

"But I've seen those big bombs. I've seen pictures of them. I've seen pictures of the peoples' faces. I'm so scared. I'm not going to school anymore. Spider and I are going to be with you forever. That way, if anything bad happens to you, it'll also happen to me."

They pulled into the parking lot. Only there were no places to park. The only other time Mary had seen it this crowded was last winter, when they announced there would be three inches of snow, and everyone was at the store buying bread and milk. But then, everyone was in a cheery mood, with the kids yapping about missing a day of school and going sledding on their garbage can lids. Today, everyone was so serious looking.

Finally, they squeezed into a parking space far away from the entrance to the store.

"We're going to have to walk a bit, sweetie. But, you know what? You can also get a few of your favorite candy bars for later."

"How many can I get, Grandpa? Can I get an extra one for Dolly?"

"Of course, and get a Milky Way for me. Just don't tell Grandma!"

"I'll get the Skippy peanut butter and Welch's grape jelly. I also want some Wonder Bread. You get the Saltine crackers and the orange juice." Mary was already orchestrating the day.

"Not so fast. We work together as a team on this one. The store's too crowded. I don't want to lose you."

"Don't worry Gramps, I'm 12."

"Just the same, you stick with me. Otherwise, I'll make you ride in the shopping cart like a little girl.

"No, that's for babies."

After they had picked up everything they needed, they stood on line at the checkout counter. Mary picked out her magazine with Elvis on the front. And Grandpa picked up *The National Enquirer*, with the lead article "What You Need to Build a Bomb Shelter in Your Backyard."

As they pulled out of the parking lot, Mary poked her grandfather's arm.

"We forgot the powdered water, Gramps!"

"Mary, you're so silly—what would we dilute it with?"

Mary was still deep in thought about how to answer him when Grandpa stopped at a spot overlooking the Chesapeake Bay.

"Mary, I want to show you why you don't need to worry."

He drove down to the navy yard, where the gray destroyers were in various states of readiness.

"This is why we will win. Just look at the size of those boats. I served on that one over there during World War II. And your cousin is trained on the artillery guns over there. Our whole family has its roots down here. We are military, through and through, and proud of it!" he boasted. •

October 27, 1962

"What a great Saturday, Gramps. No school! I can't wait to got outside and play with Sally and Maggie!"

"Not till after breakfast." Grandma knew the necessity of a good, hearty breakfast every day, and Saturday was no exception. "The oatmeal will be ready in a minute."

"Aw, Grams, can't we have something different. I used to have grits all of the time when I was living in Florida. Dad would be sitting there with the newspaper, reading us the comics, while Mom made breakfast. Kate and I would be listening to him read Dick Tracy and Dagwood."

"Well, your mother may have spoiled you by spending 25 minutes cooking grits for your highness, but today, here in Norfolk, we are having good old Irish oatmeal."

"Tomorrow, can we have something special? We haven't had bacon and eggs for the longest time."

"If there is a tomorrow." Gramps was being a little too honest this morning. Mary gave him a quizzical look as she glanced over at *The Washington Post* that he had folded in front of him, as he used the handle of his spoon to stir his coffee, light with sugar. "Just look at these headlines. "US Hints New Action on Cuba." "Reds Speed Build Up of Isle Bases." The Ruskies are just itching for a war with us. But we're ready. Look at those rocket launchers on the Florida Keys. One move by the Reds and that's it for Cuba."

"Uncle Brian is down there on one of those ships, Gramps. He'll never let those enemy boats by."

"It's not only the ships coming in we are worried about, Mary." Grandma's serious tone made both of them stare at her long and hard. "It's the missile bases that they're building in Cuba, ready to fire at us. The President wants them taken apart also."

"I am sure we won't back down. We're the good guys. I heard that on television last night when they showed a picture of Mr. Kennedy."

"Mary, of course our television announcers will always tell the truth while discussing our government. This is America, the land of freedom of speech. That's what makes us so different from the Russians." Grandma believed Walter Cronkite more than she believed the president.

"You and your Walter Cronkite. Give me Huntley and Brinkley any day."

"You can give me Dick Clark and the American Bandstand. That's who I believe."

"Mary, why don't you finish your cereal and see if Maggie wants to play hopscotch with you? You need some fresh air, and the weather may not be so good tomorrow."

"Thanks. I'll go get Spider and then I'll go to Maggie's. Can I bring her back here for lunch?"

"I'll fix some Campbell's chicken soup and Ritz crackers for you. I just have to run to the store to get the milk you and Grandpa forgot to get yesterday."

As Mary went outside, she saw a group of girls from the public school running by.

"Janey! Hi."

"Hi, Mary, do you wanna come with us? We're going to play 'hide and seek' in Becky's yard."

"I better ask my Grammie. I don't want to get in trouble."

"We're just down the street. Just do it."

Her mind went back to Janey's birthday party last week. When they played Pin the Tail on the Donkey, she had been blindfolded and turned around so many times that she ended up putting the ass's tail on the bathroom toilet. "Why do they always blindfold me first?" she wondered, as she struck over and over again at the piñata, never even hitting the treat-filled bag with her weapon. And even though the girls had all laughed with her, she knew they were laughing at her. She had never felt so humiliated, so alone, so ready to lash out at the world.

Mary took one look back at the house, sucked in her fear, and joined the group.

"Let's play hoola hoops. See who can keep it spinning the longest."

"Can I play?" Mary pleaded.

"After I'm done, then you can try."

Mary watched as Becky swirled the bright red plastic hoop around her waist, keeping it above her belt line for as long as she could, until at last it slid down to the asphalt.

"My turn," Mary cried.

"Here, try it."

Mary raised the red hoop over her head and started rotating her body, as the hoop fell quickly to the ground.

"No, Mary. It's all in the hips. Sort of like Elvis."

"Let me try again." She wiggled her hips and got it to stay up for one revolution.

"One more try, please."

"Sure." And she pulled it over her head and there it was. She was getting the hang of it.

"Look, I'm doing it." she screeched, but her friends were through with this game, and were running off to play hide and seek.

"You all hide. I'll find you all." Becky ran to her favorite tree and hid her eyes against the cool bark.

Mary didn't know where to hide. She had never been in this yard before. She saw the porch and crawled under it. She peered out through the grate, the darkness hiding her body from Becky.

After five minutes, Becky had rounded up everyone but Mary. All of the girls were laughing together. "Have they forgotten me?" Mary cried to herself.

"Gotcha!" It was Becky. She had snuck around the back of the porch.

"I saw you all the way." Mary boasted.

"No way, I saw you jump."

"Did not."

"Did."

"You all hide and let me find you." Mary was more confident now.

As she counted to 50 with her eyes closed tightly, Mary heard the scurrying sounds of girls. Their giggles bounced off her ears like underwater sonar.

"47, 48, 49, 50 . . . Ready or not, here I come!"

Mary searched. There was no one to be seen. They had all scattered. She was alone, abandoned. It brought back memories of Mom and Dad and Kate. They all said they'd be back. And they'd lied. As she started to cry, she heard a cough behind a bush. She ran as hard as she could. There was Janey.

"I found you!"

"Not fair, I got dust in my throat."

Then she saw Becky's red sneaker sticking out from behind the garbage can.

"Gotcha!"

"I knew I shouldn't have hid there."

Within the next two minutes, Mary had rounded up the entire group.

"Hey, Mary. You're good. Can you play some more?"

From the distance, "Mary, where are you?"

"Uh oh, that's my Grammie. I better get home."

"See ya tomorrow?"

"I'll ask my Grammie."

As Mary approached her house, she heard her grandfather:

"If there is a tomorrow."

She burst into the house.

"There has to be a tomorrow. Janey and Becky asked me to play with them again."

"Is that where you were? You better get washed up. You're a mess."

In the living room, Grandpa continued to read the paper, oblivious to his wife's efforts to clean up the kitchen before they went out. "I mean it, Margaret, we're on the road to destroying each other. It's not just in Cuba. Look here. Both the U.S. and the Soviets exploded huge hydrogen bombs over the Pacific Ocean yesterday. Just one turn of the winds and the radiation will carry over to Hawaii. No more fresh air here, just cancer producing X-rays. And if that isn't bad enough, here's China invading India."

"It's enough to turn this military wife into a pacifist," Margaret proclaimed. "I just want Mary to have the opportunity to grow into adulthood."

"You better watch yourself, hon. If Joe McCarthy had heard you, he'd have had you before his anti-Communist committee. Around here, 'Better dead than Red' still applies."

"I just don't know. We are the richest country in the world and we still have such violence here. Look it here, 'Smith Gets Life Sentence in Merson Case.' The poor music teacher he killed."

"What makes you think that we're any better than our ancestors? Just because we can prevent polio doesn't make us better than Attila the Hun. Unlike you, I believe in Darwin, evolution, survival of the fittest, descending from the apes."

"Stop with your sacrilege, Jimmy, or I'll have to pray extra long for you tomorrow at church."

Later that night, as Mary was falling asleep, she heard her grandma say,

"Be careful with that rifle, Jimmy. You'll kill yourself with it."

"I'm just getting it ready in case, Margaret."

October 28, 1962

Dinnertime: corned beef and cabbage, Mary's favorite. But her excitement was not about the food. Aunt Kitty was coming for dinner. Aunt Kitty, a lieutenant in the Navy Nursing Corps, was the "bestest." And tonight she arrived carrying a box from Drake's bakery, which made the "tastiest" best cherry pie.

"Hi, Aunt Kitty!" Mary was jumping up and down, hugging her, not letting go of her olive green uniform. She looked so prim and proper, in her stockings, black pumps, and her military hat, which fit so securely on her red, Irish hair.

"Let me sit down first. I have to put these packages in the kitchen. Hello, Dad. Hi, Mom. What can I do to help?"

"Just sit down and take a load off," her mother said. "Johnny, get a couple of beers for you and Kitty, and open one for me. Dinner will be ready as soon as the news is over."

Mary headed straight for Kitty's lap as her aunt plopped herself down into Grandpa's favorite armchair. "What'd you do today, Aunt Kitty?"

After glancing at Mary and smiling at her for a second longer than she needed to simply pacify her niece, Kitty turned to her father.

"You know, Dad, we were all put on active duty and full alert this week. They had us training for emergency evacuation, in case there are Cuban refugees. I load out tomorrow for Miami, ready to go to the Keys at a moment's notice."

Her mother eyed her wearily. "I guess that's better than being shipped over to that awful country in Southeast Asia where the Army was going to send you."

"I don't know. At least in Vietnam I'd be serving a purpose. We were supposed to start up a public health program in the villages, with the hope that they'll see that the Americans are not all 'ugly', that we are their friends. Now I have to go south. God forbid there are nuclear weapons used near Cuba by some hothead. The radiation casualties will be devastating."

"What's radiation?" Mary tried to get Kitty's attention.

"You know, Mary. I know you learned it in school. That's the energy that comes from those big bombs you see on television, the ones that look like big mushrooms. It also can provide energy and cure cancer, but that's not what is worrying us now."

"I know. That's what I am afraid of. I know that Mr. Khrushchev wants to blow us all up."

"Not so fast, sweetie, that's where our Army and Navy and Air Force come in. He's afraid of us. He's afraid of your Uncle Brian and Aunt Kitty."

"Is that true, Aunt Kitty? Will you beat him up?'

"I'll try, my pretty, I'll try."

As the cuckoo clock struck "VII," Jimmy got up and turned up the news.

Walter Cronkite was speaking in the background, with pictures on the screen of ships floating in the Caribbean, at a standoff. The Russian boats were at a safe distance from the American fleet, not attempting to run the blockade.

"I wonder which ship Brian is on," Kitty thought out loud, glancing at his picture on the mantelpiece. He had a serious face, crew cut hair, pressed khaki shirt, collar loosened, and nametag above his left shirt pocket. "They have really made it difficult to communicate with our soldiers down there, even one military person to another. I'm sure Brian is OK, but he has to be a little scared."

"If I know your brother, he's out on the deck, binoculars on those Ruskies, smoking his Camels, pretending he's blowing smoke in their faces." Grandma was just a little proud of her middle son.

"Do we have to wait for the end of the news before dinner? I'm hungry."

"Mary, I want to watch the sports, and then we can eat."

"Father, you are so inconsiderate. Come on Mary. Let him watch his stupid sports and you and I can go outside."

"Oh boy. Wait a minute. Grandpa, isn't that the old football player we saw last week? Y. A. something. Look, he's still bald. He looks like Mr. Khrushchev."

"Unfortunately for our Redskins, he plays football better than Mr. Khrushchev. And he doesn't take his shoes off during a discussion. Uh oh, I think we lost to his Giants. But I want to see anyway."

When Kitty and Mary got outside, Kitty slipped a cigarette out of her package of Salems, carefully opening the top of the box to avoid crushing the filter. She motioned to Mary to get inside her red Oldsmobile convertible, a pair of dice hanging off the rearview mirror. She turned on the radio, and they listened to Peter, Paul and Mary singing about "Puff the Magic Dragon." She struck a match and put the cigarette to her lips, slowly lighting it and inhaling deeply.

"Do you want a puff?" Kitty asked jokingly, knowing that the puff they were singing about had a little more of a jolt.

"Won't I go to hell, Kitty?"

"No, Mary, this is not a mortal sin. And if it is, you can join me in that fiery inferno. It will just make you feel like you're a grownup. With all that is happening in the world, you can't be a baby anymore."

Mary took her first puff and coughed in Kitty's face. Kitty laughed, "Don't worry, that's what happened to me with my first smoke. You'll get used to them."

"You won't tell Grandma, will you?"

"Not if you don't tell her about my new boyfriend, Jeffrey Michaels."

"Why, isn't he Catholic?"

"No, of course he's Catholic."

"Is he in the Army?"

"No, silly, he's based here in the Navy."

"Then, I don't see the problem. He's a Navy man, like Grandpa, and he's a Catholic. What else could they want?"

"He's a Negro."

"Is he a good kisser?"

"Of course."

"Then that's all that matters! I promise I won't tell."

Five minutes later, they were on their way inside, giggling like a gaggle of geese, chewing away on their Juicy Fruit gum.

"Sit down, Kitty. There is a special announcement from the President's office." And with that, Grandma and Grandpa sat down together on the couch, with Mary and Kitty sitting side by side, crammed into the overstuffed chair.

Mr. Cronkite was at his broadcast desk, lights shining on him, carefully announcing the success of brinkmanship diplomacy and repeating, slowly, the President's words to Mr. Khrushchev, "We step back from danger," in response to the Communist leader's announcement that the Soviet Union would dismantle its missiles in Cuba.

Kitty stood up and cheered. Grandma and Grandpa hugged each other.

There would be no war tomorrow. No heroism in the trenches. No "Better dead than Red." And Castro and his fellow Cubans could still keep playing America's game, baseball.

"Now we can breathe again. I've never been so scared in all my life," Grammie said. Now we can get rid of all of those cans of sardines you bought in case we need to run to the shelter."

"I don't know," Gramps winked at Mary, "I kind of liked the idea of peanut butter and sardine sandwiches."

"I think I just lost my appetite for dinner," Kitty said with a laugh. "Mary, just go get me a beer. And while you are at it, get one for yourself. It's time you learned to grow up."

Grandma scowled, but Grandpa answered:"Wait, Kitty, I'm going to break out the Middleton's Irish whiskey. It's time for a celebration."

"Don't you two dare corrupt our innocent child," grandma scolded her husband and daughter. "You two drink all you want. I'm just gonna keep Mary close by my side. It's still time for her to be a child."

After dinner, they all sat satiated, even Kitty, who ate when she realized she needed something to accompany the beer and whiskey. They tried to focus on Lawrence Welk, listening to a Spanish lullaby. They watched "The Ed Sullivan Show," with its circus acts and magicians. They laughed as they watched the Alka Seltzer commercial, with the fat man's stomach shaking with the jackhammer, as "plop, plop, fizz, fizz" played in the background. And Mary lay with her grandfather in his arms and Spider in her arms. She fell asleep dreaming of a dog she had once owned when she was in Florida, a little white and brown shih-tzu named Max, licking her face until he felt tired and fell asleep in her arms.

Grandpa slowly carried Mary up the stairs and laid her in her bed, carefully pulling up the covers. He slowly climbed down the stairs with a slight limp caused by arthritis, from carrying equipment up and down burning buildings. He stepped outside, walked over to the flagpoles, and slowly pulled the rope down until the flags of the United States and of Virginia were safely in his hands. He carefully folded them and put them away until tomorrow, when he would rise as the sun came up, and again salute his wonderful state and country.

October 28, 1962

After dinner and the President's announcement, we sat on the floor in my parents' room in Tenafly, New Jersey, watching police officers Toody and Muldoon drive around on the television screen in "Car 54." We were finally able to laugh again, for the first time in a week, as their theme song—"There's a traffic jam in Harlem that's backed up to Jackson Heights, there's a scout troop short a child, Khrushchev's due at Idlewild, Car 54 where are you?"—came on the air.

My parents firmly believed that we either watched television as a family or it was a waste of time. And this was one of the few television shows we were allowed. Their three sons would sit together on the floor while my parents lay on their bed as we watched "Bonanza" on our new color television, spending half the show trying to adjust the colors to make Hoss Cartwright's oval face have any semblance of flesh tones. Only "Walt Disney's Wonderful World of Color," with its spectacular peacock, escaped our criticism. But my favorite was "The Ed Sullivan Show"— especially if he had the talking mouse, Topo Gigio, who would always say, "kissa me goodnight, Eddie." And, of course, the Mets were permitted, occasionally also broadcast in color, with the grass too green, and the infield dirt and the players' faces also tinted green, at least until my father demanded we turn another error-filled game off to prevent his "ulcer" from acting up. But no daytime soap operas or kids shows like "Soupy Sales." Worst of all was that corruption of American teenagers, "Dick Clark's American Bandstand." I guess they'd forgotten when Harlan had been on "The Howdy Doody Show" in the "Peanut Gallery."

But, after the shows were over, after Harlan and Marty were in bed, the crisis averted but still lingering in my mind, I laid outside my parents' room, holding my stuffed dogs close to my chest, and dreaming of Fuzzer licking my face until she tired of the salt and fell asleep in my arms.

As Mary and I slept that night in homes 300 miles from each other, unknown to each other, we were both comforted by the love of family. But at the same time, the orbits of our lives continued to change, the gravitational forces of our centers pulled by such different stars. While I would be spinning in a tight circumference around my center, my family, Mary's life was an expanding, elliptical spiral, tilted from abandonment by her parents at the age of six. She couldn't figure out what had happened to them. She didn't comprehend that they had met at a U.S.O.

dance—her mom a Navy nurse, her father a journalist—and fell in love during the end of the war; or that they conceived two babies together (or, perhaps, only one) until her mom's roving eye led to her abandoning Mary and her sister, Kate, and then, without explanation, her dad also abandoning her. At times, as when she fell asleep with her grandfather, she was close to family and Earth—only to then be launched out into space, propelled by her Aunt Kitty, escaping what was all too real to her, what was all too missing. She wished she was back in the playground, pumping her legs wildly, getting the swing to go higher and higher, until she could defy gravity and escape from her reality, away from the negative "Gs" of her mother and father, so far away from her.

I was like Alan Shepard, like a New York City pigeon, flapping my wings in the sky, but unable to go to far from base. Mary was a young Neil Armstrong, preparing to "soar like an eagle," leaving the Earth's gravitational pull to establish her own life, her own lunar colony.

IT'S JUST ANOTHER DAY OF MY LIFE

May 1963

The day, like the date, is unimportant. I obviously cannot remember the details, and even what follows is just a compilation of the events of the days of the month. It's nearing the end of sixth grade. Spring is merging into summer. I still had a report on Colombia, for our World Civilization class, which was due the following morning.

I got up early and crawled out into the hall so that I could turn on the light without awakening Marty. I checked out the agriculture of Colombia, taking notes from my encyclopedias and almanacs. My mom and dad were just getting up as I closed my notebook and curled up outside their room for five more minutes of sleep. After my dad got out of bed to shower, I knocked on their bedroom door.

"Who is it?" As if my mom didn't know.

"Can I come in, Mom?"

"Ok, but just for a minute. Then I have to go downstairs and fix breakfast."

I had only gotten a few minutes of snuggle time when I heard those dreaded words from my dad, as he emerged from the bathroom, towel around his torso.

"Up and at 'em, big boy. Give me a few minutes with your mom and then we'll meet you downstairs."

I reluctantly took my cue and left, taking a few minutes to go to the bathroom and then brush my teeth, my dad's admonishments about cavities ever on my mind. By the time I was dressed and ready, Mom was downstairs, still in her bathrobe and slippers, getting the cereal boxes down from the cabinet, along with the bowls and spoons, sugar, and milk.

Harlan beat me downstairs and grabbed the Cocoa Puffs. I got the Frosted Flakes, which my dad finally allowed in a moment of weakness. And Marty arrived a few minutes later, opening a new box of Kix. We were a "multi-lingual" cereal family.

As we were chomping away, slurping up the milk, she made Harlan his bologna on rye with mayonnaise, wrapping his sandwich carefully in wax paper.

"Harlan, here's an extra quarter so you can buy milk and a Hostess Twinkie. Just make sure you bring the change home."

"Thanks, Mom."

My dad arrived and my mom put his toast out, spread carefully with strawberry jam. Finally, she got to sit down and carefully measured and poured out a ½-cup of Special K, adding a quarter teaspoon of sugar and skim milk. She was on a perpetual diet, even though she probably only weighed five pounds more than she did in high school.

"Austin, did you finish all of your homework?"

"Yes, Mommy."

"Then what were you doing this morning?"

"It's for my report due tomorrow."

"I've told you not to wait until the last minute."

"I'm sorry, Mom."

"No going out to play softball this afternoon until the report is done."

"Mom, we're having our final game this afternoon," I whined.

"Can't he play, Helene?" My dad was pleading my case.

"Austin, you'd better come home straight from school over lunch. I'll make you a sandwich and then you can study for the rest of the time."

"I'll run right home, Mom. Thanks, Dad."

At noon the lunch bell rang. I was first in line for the students who could go home for lunch. I had my notebook in hand as I ran down the stairs, out to the playground, ignoring the kids playing. I ran the two blocks home and charged into the house. My mom was still in the office, typing away at a manuscript.

"Austin, I'll be done in ten minutes. I didn't expect you home so soon. Why don't you go upstairs and start writing your report?"

"I'm hungry, Mom."

"Lunch'll be ready soon enough."

After 15 minutes, I came back downstairs. Mom was in the kitchen, standing by the sink in her dress work clothes — black skirt, white blouse, stockings, and comfortable shoes — fixing a salad for both of us: lettuce, tomatoes, and carrots.

"Let me do the cucumbers," I begged.

"Just be careful you don't slice your finger off."

Finally, we sat down to eat, just the two of us. Mom poured her diet Metrical French dressing on the salads—not much taste. And we had Metrical biscuits, which barely had more taste than Fuzzer's dog biscuits.

"How was school this morning?"

"Everything's fine, Mom."

"Just make sure you finish your paper in time so I can help you edit it."

"What are we having for dinner?"

"I don't know. Why don't we go shopping after school and you can help me pick something out."

"Mom, I'm playing baseball, don't you remember."

"Sorry, Austin. I was just thinking about the paper I was typing for your dad."

"Well, I hope we have Swanson's Chicken TV dinners. We haven't had them in a while."

"Sounds good to me."

"Can you pick up some Pillsbury biscuits also?"

"Now you're really pushing it. Anyway, I'll try. And tomorrow after school, I've got to take you all for haircuts. Don't let me forget."

By 12:50, it was time to go. I was dreading leaving and held onto her hug for just a second longer.

"Love you, Mom."

"Love you, Austin."

That afternoon actually wasn't so bad as it was our final assembly of the year. Our class was putting on the play "Our Town." I'd helped with the scenery, but I wasn't one of the actors, so I got to watch the abbreviated version that was produced by Mrs. B.

The first act was pretty boring, what with the Stage Manager intro-ducing all of the parents and children of Grover's Corner, New Hamp-shire. We watched them in their morning activities, which were not much different than what I had just left.

But during the third act, even as the third-graders and fourth-graders began to fidget, I found myself wanting to cry. Poor Emily dies during childbirth and is in heaven. Despite what all of the family members al-ready in heaven tell her, she decides that she wants to have the experi-ence of living a day of her life, of going back, of watching herself as she lives/lived the days of her life.

"Don't do it, Emily," Mrs. Gibbs warns.

"But I won't live over a sad day. I'll choose a happy one," Emily re-sponds.

But as the day goes on, Emily realizes, "Oh Mama, just look at me one minute as though you really saw me. . . .

I can't go on. Oh! Oh! It goes so fast. We don't have time to look at one another. I didn't realize. So all that was going on and we never no-ticed. . . .

Oh, Earth, you're too wonderful for anyone to realize you. Does any human being ever realize life while they live it—every, every minute?"

I remember I hit a home run that afternoon in the last game of our after-noon unofficial softball league. That made five for me on the year, only 12 behind Eddie, the league leader. Again, I was not a superstar, but at least I had contributed.

I raced home, opening the front door, searching for my mom. Ours was not one of those houses, like my friends', that smelled of a roast in the oven and the air permeated with the distinctive aroma of onions and garlic. That was probably because Mom never knew when my dad would be home, and who wants an overdone piece of meat?

"Hey, Mom. I hit a home run and we won!"

"That's great. Now go on upstairs and wash up and change so you can finish your paper."

An hour later I was back in her office with my rough draft.

"Bogota is spelled with two 'o's. And you have a run-on sentence here. Otherwise, it's really good, Austin. Write it up carefully and we'll show it to Dad."

Of course, by the time Dad got home, we kids had already eaten our two pieces of fried chicken and mashed potatoes, along with a small apple cobbler. After all, it had only taken 45 minutes to heat it up in the oven, only 42 minutes longer than a microwave dinner today, and 15 minutes longer than if my mom had actually cooked it from scratch. I was upstairs with Marty playing baseball with our stuffed dogs, deftly moving them around the floor as if they were multi-positional fielders and batters. No weekday television for us. That was for the family on the weekends.

"Dad, do you want to read my paper?"

"Just a minute, I've been working all day. Let me go to the bathroom first."

When he arrived at the dinner table, Mom was reheating their dried out dinners.

"Here, Dad. Read it, please."

After several minutes he said, with a laugh in his voice, "I think there's real potential here. You can follow in my footsteps as an Associate Editor." I beamed. And then he turned to Mom. "Helene, I know you're tired, especially from editing Austin's paper (he winked at me), but we're going to have to work on the last papers tonight."

"Can't I do it first thing in the morning?"

"Now you're sounding like Austin."

By the time they had finished eating, and my dad had recounted his day to my mom, we were sent upstairs to take our baths. And then it was time for bed. But I hadn't finished reading my book. And that book report was due in two days. So after giving my parents their goodnight kisses, I curled up outside their bedroom with my comforter and stuffed dogs and read until I fell asleep. I wanted to "stay awake just to hear their breathing," wishing, as Aerosmith would sing 25 years later, "I could spend my life in this moment forever."

THE MARCH FOR FREEDOM

August 28, 1963

Martin Luther King stood before a crowd of 250,000 civil rights support-
ers in front of the Lincoln Memorial. He spoke of a new nation where
blacks and whites would live together as equals.

"I have a dream that one day this nation will rise up and live out the
true meaning of its creed. 'We hold these truths to be self-evident, that
all men are created equal."

And then he concluded:

"Free at last! Free at last!

Thank God Almighty, we are free at last!"

THE END OF CAMELOT

November 22, 1963

The school year started like a new dawn for me: seventh-grade, junior
high school, with students from four different sending districts. Seventy-
five percent of the kids had no idea who I was, and that meant a fresh
start. That's not to say that there still wasn't an elite clique of "athletes"
who knew each other from the Majors Division of Little League, while I
was stuck in the Intermediate Division. But at least as far as the girls
went, it was virgin territory. Unfortunately, with my slicked back hair,
mildly buckteeth, and dowdy clothes, I wasn't going to be the target of
their affection.

The highlight of my fall had not been school, but a day in early October when my mom's first cousin, Bruce (for those of you who are confused, my first cousin "once-removed"), took me—and only me—to the
second game of the 1963 World Series at Yankee Stadium. Bruce was 30
years old, which put him somewhere between an uncle and a big brother.
To me, he was somebody every boy would want as his protector. He was

young and athletic, joked all the time, had a glamorous wife, Gail (who looked like a model in *Life* magazine), and had three young sons. My dad had his limp, walked slow, and had little sense of adventure. He was a far cry from Bruce, who smoked, gambled on baseball and football games, but was still considered "mainstream." His black hair was combed back, matching his black "Buddy Holly" eyeglasses, and his thick neck made it imperative that he keep the collar of his white shirt open at the top, with his thin, black tie loosened.

Older people may have looked at JFK as their token of youthful America, but for me, it was Cousin Bruce—not the "Cousin Brucie" on WMCA who played the Beatles and Herman's Hermits, but the man with the perpetual smile next to me. When one travels with one's parents, there is always some embarrassment about how they dress, how they talk, what they look like. This is one of the certainties of civilization, passed on from generation to generation, from me right to my daughter, usually accompanied by "Daaad." But to me, Bruce had none of the flaws that my parents had (although I am sure his kids found some), and I was proud to be in his tow that day.

This game wasn't like those I had been to at the Polo Grounds. It was between two teams who knew how to play the game. And our seats weren't in the upper deck. No, somehow Bruce had secured two front row box seats in right field. During batting practice, a line drive had bounced right past us, grazing my arm. That was my first "contact" with a ball at a major league game. And between innings, we could wave to Roger Maris as he trotted out to his position. I can't say I cared much who won, as my family hated both the Yankees and the Dodgers. But I have to assume that Bruce went home with his wallet a little thinner that day, as his team lost the second of the four consecutive games during their sweep by the Dodgers. Bruce took it all in stride, offered me a sip of his "cold beer," which I refused (it smelled awful), and he probably would have offered me a drag on his cigarette if he wasn't so sure that his cousin would make his life miserable the next time we all had dinner at his mother's apartment. But for one day, I was cool, and the next day, I made sure all of the boys at school saw my ticket stub and the bruise on my arm.

School life, unfortunately, quickly returned to its daily lessons and embarrassments. Although I excelled, of course, in academics, and was frustrated by being just not quite good enough to be among the best athletes, it was in shop class where I was most exposed. The shop room was set off from the rest of the school. Looking out the window, we could watch the teachers come in from the parking lot, taking the last drags on their cigarettes. The room itself was filled with sawdust and smelled of stain and finish. The ventilation system was inadequate, as we were as yet unprotected by the Environmental Protection Agency.

The room never appeared to have been cleaned regularly by the janitorial staff. After all, when was the last time in recorded history that men cleaned up after themselves? And we were boys learning to be men! Today, shop may be co-ed, and boys may be taking home environmental studies, aka "home EC", but in those days, the girls didn't drive in nails and we didn't learn to bake a cake or sew a dress. (Although when I did attempt sewing trying to mend my stuffed dogs, it was clear that I would not be a plastic surgeon in later life.) Our system didn't engender gender confusion, exemplified by Boy George or Michael Jackson, although the Charles Mansions of the world did come out of the '60s. Only one girl, Samantha Stewart, tried to enroll in our class. But that was because she wanted to learn her mother's primary skill—to "shop until she dropped."

Mr. Birch, my teacher, was a bit older than my dad, probably about the age of our president. His hair was somewhat unkempt, slightly thinned around the temples, and his voice was deep and gravelly. He always dressed in the same black pants, white shirt, and blue apron, and was the only teacher in the school allowed to go without a tie (it would have been a lethal weapon had it gotten caught in the lathe). The projects he helped us with were certainly not prime examples of American ingenuity or achievement. They were not going to make us carpenters, let alone future scientists or mechanics who would build the lunar modules that our president had pledged to support. No, I was constructing a tie rack for my dad, an interesting project, considering that even when it was completed, no one in my house would have the vaguest idea of how to attach it to the closet! But every day, as the project neared completion, as I drilled a hole, hoping it would be in the proper position, I dreaded having Mr. Birch arrive at my station, inspecting my project through his safety goggles, and uttering those fateful words, "You've wrecked your job!" Nothing, not even Miss Kimberly's scowl during English class, could match that phrase, heard by the entire class (girls, of course, excluded). There was no solace in hearing those same words said to Ralph or George or Ed. It just meant for me that the last 4 weeks of work, of planning and drilling and sanding, were wasted, with no hope of salvaging Dad's Christmas present.

The only project I had actually completed was my imitation of the game "Skittles." It took a certain amount of skill to wind the top tightly and then release it into the "playing field," a walled off square in which miniature bowling pins were standing, ready to be knocked over by the spinning top, producing havoc as it twisted across the board. I already had my gyroscope from second-grade, so all I had to do was build the sides, attach them to a floor with some Elmer's Glue, and cut ½-inch dowels into the mini-pins. The night I brought it home, everyone in the family played with it before Dad got home from work. Marty was first, but his weak effort was reminiscent of "Kaputnik," with no damage occurring. Mom was next, and with her pull the gyroscope spun fast and stood straight, at a precise 90- degree angle, so pure in its orbit that it caused no pieces to fall, no disruption of the dowel family. My spin was controlled, but at least it knocked over several pins. But Harlan, the hormonal teen, got the gyroscope to spin fast, but off its axis, causing the pins to splay. Only the 10-pin remained.

"I'm the champion!" And to my dismay, I couldn't dispute him. It was my game—why hadn't I won? I would need to practice, I told myself.

And thus it was in shop class where I first heard the announcement, over the loudspeaker, of the event that would so overwhelm our country's spirit. If you ask anyone who was born before 1954, they can tell you where they were, what they were doing, when they first heard the news. It was a little after 1:30 when we heard the loudspeaker activated. No one paid much attention to afternoon announcements, even unexpected ones. But this time, there was something about how Mr. Rice spoke.

"This is Principal Rice." Ralph didn't hear him at first, the motor of the lathe drowning him out. So we had trouble hearing, "Boys and girls, I am sorry to tell you that the President has been shot. I don't have any more information at this time, about how serious he is, but the reports do say he is being taken to the hospital."

Only the whirling of the lathe machine over in the corner broke the silence. No one knew how serious this was, and we looked to Mr. Birch for guidance. "Boys, I am sure the President's gonna be okay. Probably just a superficial wound. Otherwise, we would've been told more. Let's keep going with our projects or you won't finish them for Christmas."

We went back to work for the last ten minutes of our class, a bit frightened, but reassured by Mr. Birch's strength. This was in the days before audiovisual sprawl in our classrooms. There was no television in the room, and transistor radios were only "allowed" when they were smuggled in during the World Series. None of us, including students, teachers, or parents, for that matter, had ever been faced with an assassination of our president in this century. FDR had died of a stroke, but news had filtered to everyone through their radio consoles. This was the first political tragedy that our generation and the generations before us would see on a minute-by-minute visual level—our worries and despair to be shared publicly as well as privately.

As I rushed off to my math class at 1:45, President Kennedy was being rushed off to Parkland Hospital in downtown Dallas, his head and neck bloodied from the multiple, instantaneously fatal head wounds. His wife Jackie was caressing him, trying miraculously to sustain his life. Her pink dress was stained with blood, his blood, and maybe the blood of others. Who knew who else had been wounded at that time? What we hoped for, as we crowded into Mrs. Green's class, was that the report was wrong. Obviously everyone wasn't as concerned as I was, as I overheard several girls gossiping about who was being invited to Sally's party next Saturday. But any thought that this was a hoax, or a false report, was crushed by the site of Mrs. Green at her desk, head in her hands, praying out loud for our fallen hero.

"Hi, Mrs. Green, have you heard anything more? How is the President?"

"We still don't know. There haven't been any other announcements. I'm just waiting to hear from the principal."

As the minutes passed and we didn't hear anything, any attempt to conduct the class was abandoned. Although Mrs. Green said we were free to do our homework, multiplying fractions somehow seemed inconsequential. Aware of her distraction, Billy Rhodes and Johnny Singer sat in the back row, preparing spitballs as their weapons of mass destruction for a later assault on Sue Carter and Jennie Stack, who were passing notes under their desks. All of this taking took place under the usual reliable radar of Mrs. Green.

After 15 minutes, Ralph raised his hand, calling out "Why haven't we heard anything?"

It was a call back to reality for Mrs. Green. "Okay class, it was probably a flesh wound. Let's get back to our class work. Chapter 23— try the first four problems and we'll go over them later."

3/4 X 2/5 = 6/20 = 3/10

1/5 X 2/3 = 2/15

1 1/3 X 4/5 = 4/3 X 4/5 = 16/15

Math came easy to me, and even with this distraction, I proceeded with the problems. It would mean that much less homework that night— and more time to play with my baseball cards or with my stuffed dogs. I could see Betty, struggling as she usually did, conscientiously doing her problems, frustrated by her lack of understanding. She sat with her pencil in her mouth, twisting her curly blonde hair, about to totally lose focus. She leaned over to ask me a question and Mrs. Green got up and started to come over to the rescue.

We heard "static" over the loudspeaker, and then, "Boys and girls, teachers, this is Mr. Rice again. We have just received word over CBS radio that President Kennedy died at 2:00 p.m." . . . Static . . . "I can't believe it. I just hope they are wrong." And with that the loudspeaker went silent and so did our class.

I looked up and saw Mrs. Green's eyes filled with tears. She wasn't any older than my mother, and she had her own kids. I wasn't with my mother or father when we heard the news, and she wasn't with her kids. So our emotions, shared at this moment, would have to do for now for family mourning, for the immediate grief of our and their generations. Unbeknownst to us, as we all faced our own mortality and mourned together, that the death of this president and our sojourn in Camelot would soon be replaced by the turbulent events of the rest of the 60s. The race riots and the escalating Vietnam War would soon illuminate the immorality of racial inequality and the political and social divisiveness of the Vietnam War.

I turned around. Betty kept looking at her paper, playing with the #2 yellow pencil, the pink eraser used down to the end, the answers no more apparent. John and Billy were respectfully silent, although they were still hitting each other below their desks.

I stopped my homework. It somehow seemed trivial at that point. "I can do it later." I was oblivious to the fact that life would not go on with any semblance of normalcy for some time.

We couldn't leave school at that moment, as there were no buses or early dismissal. And parents weren't necessarily at home. I suppose I could have left, as my mom was usually home, but in the era before cell phones, I couldn't be sure she wasn't at the A&P. Instead, we sat in class and talked about what this meant. Here was the most memorable moment in all of our lives up to that point, and we were sharing it not with our parents or families but with our teachers, our principals, our classmates. And, much like during the Alan Shepard flight and the John Glenn orbits, it was not with Mom and Dad that I cried, cheered, and prayed, but with authority figures who now became one of us. They were our family surrogates, much as we were their children, sharing our closest secrets—the traditional family expanding out of my control.

None of us understood the politics surrounding President Kennedy, only that he was vibrant, alive, a man we admired as much, if not more, than our parents, a great father to John-John and Caroline. Who could have wanted more? But none of us kids had experienced the death of a loved one—except maybe an elderly grandparent or a family pet; and truly, none of us had ever met JFK. When we got home that night, our parents would still be there, our dogs would still be there, and even my brothers would still be there.

America would mourn this man for what he represented: youth and hope dying too soon. If only we could have felt the same depth of pain for our minorities in the cities and for the soldiers who were casualties of the war in Vietnam—for the youth and hope that they represented.

Mr. Rice came back on the loudspeaker. "There will be no school Monday." Way in the back of the room, a brief "Yeeeaa" was squelched by a collective look from our class, shattering that student's immaturity. "School will get out today at the regular time, but after this period, we will all come to the auditorium for a special assembly."

Mrs. Green was solemn when she spoke. "Children, let's observe a minute of silence to honor our president."

We all sat at our desks, faces buried in our hands, feet shuffling, noses running, eyes tearing, until our fidgeting made it clear it was time to start facing reality. A minute felt like an hour, until we had all looked up again.

"Mrs. Green, what will happen to Mrs. Kennedy and the children? Will they have to move?"

I thought back to my first move, when I was their age. I was in kindergarten. It wasn't so bad and, I thought, not as bad as later in fifth grade. They'd be okay.

And they probably would. Mrs. Kennedy would have to explain that they had bought a new house and were moving. They would have a dog. They would bring their toys and dolls and secret servicemen along with their legacy of tragedy. But how could she explain that they couldn't bring their "Dad?"

"What'll happen to the government?"

"Who'll be president?'

"Will they bury President Kennedy?"

"Do they know who shot our president?"

The questions kept coming and Mrs. Green had few answers, except that Lyndon Johnson would be president. As we walked to assembly, a few of the more savvy kids were talking about whether the Russians had done this, whether we would be bombing them. But most of the questions to each other were:

"Do you think we'll have school the rest of next week?"

"What about the book report due next Monday?"

What we weren't asking, either out of ignorance or denial, were:

"Did your parents like President Kennedy?"

"What will happen to us?"

"Will we be okay?"

As we would come to learn, this wasn't about me, my family, my friends. This was so much bigger that its affect would go beyond us as individuals. It was only later that I would appreciate that the U.S. government was like a barge on the Mississippi, and that no matter who was the captain of the ship, any change in the course would be slow. And although no one man or pilot could radically change the course of the vessel over a short period of time, the water's current had to be there to allow the shift to occur. In this case, Lyndon Johnson would take over and, using the momentum of this tragedy, guide the government on the path envisioned by President Kennedy—through Congress's passage of the great social legislation of the New Frontier, to enact the War on Poverty, Medicare, and the Civil Rights Act. Then he would lead us, with the support of Congress, into the quagmire in Southeast Asia—a course charted by President Kennedy as he attempted to be the warrior who protected us during the Cold War.

When I got home, Mom was there, holding Marty near her, ready to comfort Harlan and me as we arrived. She had lost her mom to breast cancer when she was 14, so she had experienced real loss at an age similar to ours. Although she wasn't politically inclined, she joined the rest of the country in being visually upset that this had happened to our president. Beyond the political and conspiratorial feelings that would arise later in our country, she was able to communicate to us the feelings on a more personal level.

I came weeping into her arms, aching for her to hold me, to tell me we would be all right.

I relaxed in her hugs, and we all basked in the warmth and comfort of her body so close to ours. Then we went into her bedroom to watch the television, all lying on her bed, waiting for Dad to arrive.

At 5 p.m. Dad arrived home, somehow able to extricate himself early from his office, probably because everyone else had already left.

Unlike the Kennedys, we were all together for dinner. We sat transfixed in front of the tube, eating our chicken pot pies and Pillsbury biscuits. My dad had already checked in with my grandmother, and we talked about when the funeral would be, who Lee Harvey Oswald was, and how sad it was for the family of Officer Trippet, the policeman killed by Oswald.

And then Dad started talking about his work, about a patient he had seen, about a new formulation of an oral drug that he was working on. And Marty was in tears, crying, "I'm going to get cavities and my teeth will all fall out!" because my dad had forgotten to bring him home his new electric toothbrush, which was promised to him just that morning.

A lot had changed since that morning when Harlan and I had walked together to school, each talking to our own friends. Marty got to stay home with Mom for a few extra minutes until leaving for his third grade class. A morning that had started out so inauspiciously reminded us by mid-afternoon about the frailty of life; that even sitting next to your loved one could not insure protection from outside, or, as I was to learn later, from evil forces inside of man or nature. But that night, still, we had each other. After dinner, what was there to do? It was like the Jewish holidays, too sacred to have fun, no homework to do; and so, like the rest of our nation, we sat in front of our television, the nation sharing the same pictures and commentary from Walter and Chet and David. We heard from Dan Rather that Lyndon Johnson had taken the oath of office on Air Force One while a drawn Jackie stood by; we learned of the funeral arrangements for the following Monday; and we wondered what was to become of John-John and Caroline.

Walter and Chet and David and Dan didn't talk to us about divisive politics that night. The revisionist historians who would later deflate JFK's reputation had not yet even analyzed his "1,000 Days" in office. JFK was from the elite Democratic class, and so it is not surprising that he believed that we could provide for the poor, without taking from the rich, by simply expanding the economy. But what made him special to my family that night was that he was, in his own way, a man of the people who believed in equal opportunity, in equality among the races, in truly supporting the Declaration of Independence, and the credo that "All men are created equal."

These were his ideals that my parents shared. They were not the ideals of the Republican Party, the other 50% of voters, who had supported Richard Nixon, nor the Southern Democrats. But it was JFK's visions, not his actual achievements, that were to become his legacy.

In the end, it was Lyndon Baines Johnson, one of those same Southern Democrats, but now serving the entire country as president, who gave JFK a chance at posterity through the passage of "The Great Society" legislation. But unfortunately, it was LBJ who followed JFK's questionable support for the corrupt Diem coup in South Vietnam. It had begun as a seed planted as military advisors, which then germinated into a full blown war under LBJ and Richard Nixon. Their inability to see the futility of our efforts in a civil war halfway around the globe led our country into a war that would leave so many mourning parents and spouses and children and impoverish our country's morality.

I broke the silence with the question that was asked much too often during the Cold War: "Are we going to be okay?" But this wasn't just about bombs and nuclear warheads; this was about my family, my fear of being, as John-John and Caroline were, one parent short.

"Of course, Austin, we have each other."

To paraphrase Paul Simon, we were on our own island, seemingly "safe." But although my parents would try to shelter us, to make us into rocks and islands, we would still suffer in "pain," and we would still "cry." For as with JFK's family, there was no parent so mighty to be able to protect us from the cancer that was already growing inside my reassuring Mom.

Sunday, November 24, 1963

The rest of the weekend went by as a blur. The country was in a quandary. We collectively wondered how much to mourn and how fast to get on with our individual and collective lives.

In the two days following President Kennedy's assassination, the United States was a country involved in a mass viewing. On a personal level, Jackie and the children would have to start their private lives, out of public service, but still perversely being scrutinized in their every move, held to a level of morality that far exceeded that of their father.

In Tenafly, the rest of us still needed to go to work, school, clean the house, make love, laugh, cry, begin to enjoy again. And for the Kutscher family, Sundays meant my dad's home-cooked Chinese feast. He would spend three hours in the kitchen, slowly chopping water chestnuts and garlic to put into the ground pork that would be steamed for an hour to prevent trichinosis. He would carefully measure a teaspoon of dark soy sauce with a tablespoon of light soy sauce, along with the appropriate amount of cooking wine. After slicing the flank steak with his cleaver, deftly avoiding adding any of his fingertips to the mound of meat, he would sauté the beef in molten peanut oil, adding Chinese vegetables to the wok at the last minute. He would then add soup stock and cornstarch to make extra gravy, to "stretch" the dishes, all to be spooned over mounds of sticky white rice.

What took ten minutes from ordering time to table time in Chinatown took most of the afternoon, but it was a labor of love, performed without "prep" chefs. The rest of the family sat around the dining room table, looking through the pile of change supplied by our grandmother, searching for that rare 1955 "double stamped" penny. We occasionally found a "rare" coin with a mint run of "only" one million, and we slowly filled our blue coin folders with the more common nickels, dimes, and quarters.

While we searched, Mom played her electric organ, practicing show tunes, including "You'll Never Walk Alone" from the musical "Carousel."

She sang,
"When you walk through a storm
Hold your head up high,
And don't be afraid of the dark.
At the end of the storm
Is a golden sky

And the sweet silver song of a lark.
Walk on through the wind,
Walk on through the rain,
Though your dreams be tossed and blown.
Walk on, walk on with hope in your heart,
And you'll never walk alone!
You'll never walk alone."

It was her mantra, somehow connected to her losses as a teen and her love of her family. It was her telling us how to survive, and it has forever been encased in my heart and soul as such.

Eventually, as the hours passed, the food began to take on the aromas of the peanut oil and garlic. We were ready to eat. It was at least as good as the local Chinese restaurant. The dishes were all steaming inside of authentic Chinese ceramic bowls sitting on the "Lazy Susan" that Harlan had built in shop. We used chopsticks and loaded our plates with food as the serving dishes spun past us. Steamed pork, beef with tomatoes, chicken with soy sauce, all piled on top of white rice.

But then it was time to clean up. Now the roles were reversed, with my father relaxing, exhausted by his labors, while the four of us would repent and wearily clean up the multiple mixing bowls, pots, woks, plates—all used without regard for the time needed to clean up. What took two minutes to clear the table in the Chinese restaurant took us an hour to do, as life began to return to normalcy at 66 Windsor Road in Tenafly, New Jersey.

In Washington, D.C., however, thousands of people lined up to view JFK's body as it lay in state in the Capital Rotunda. And thousands of people lined up to enter the football stadiums that Sunday, as Commissioner Rozelle felt that what this country needed to come to terms with its bereavement was to cheer as 22 men tried to decapitate each other on the playing field.

And the public appeared to agree with the commissioner to some extent, complaining to the network stations that cancelled their traditional Sunday shows. We watched, immobilized in front of the television, mesmerized, probably even hypnotized by the redundancies. We learned of JFK's days on PT Boat 109, his rise through the Senate to become president, his romance and marriage to Jackie, his football games on the grounds of the Kennedy estate in Hyannis Port. Everywhere, it seemed, was the image of the young vibrant leader and family man, his darker side still unrevealed.

In stark contrast, the pictures of Officer Trippet and his grieving family brought the foot soldier, the infantryman, into our living rooms, much as the pictures of the body bags from Vietnam would infiltrate the complacency of our middle and upper classes over the ensuing decade.

Theories of conspiracy, whether Lee Harvey Oswald acted alone, whether this was a Communist plot, were rampant. While we were watching the television, our minds foggy, overwhelmed by the monotony, the television cameras showed Oswald being transferred through the halls of the police station. Suddenly, there was a commotion on the screen, as Jack Ruby appeared from the edge of the crowd and stuck a gun into Oswald's torso and shot him dead. The nation would spend the next decade debating how many bullets were fired at JFK, how many assassins there were, but with Oswald now dead, the truth would be lost forever.

I may have lost sleep over what happened to JFK, and I mourned for Officer Trippet's family, even though his wife and children seemed to have been lost in the grand picture. But now I had to go to sleep, having actually watched a man killed right in front of my eyes. We weren't used to the death we would see from Vietnam, or the live assassination of Bobby Kennedy five years later. All of these people, one minute alive, the next dead, soldiers in the universe, "going, going, gone." That night, I would again sleep outside my parents' room. But I was still separated from Mom's comforting arms by that closed door.

November 25, 1963

The entire nation watched as the Kennedy brothers walked with Jackie behind the coffin through the streets of Washington to St. Matthew's Cathedral. The horse-drawn caisson carried the flag-covered box, which in the end was no different than any other resting container. Thousands lined the streets, while my family joined the millions of men and women and children, home from work and school, who watched on television. We weren't dressed in our mourning clothes, just everyday garb: pants, shirts, shoes, and socks. Nothing special, no ties or jackets. We didn't dare ask to go out and play, so I stayed in my room that morning, playing with my baseball cards, my dogs, and reading about Babe Ruth.

We must have eaten that day, as our grief wasn't as deep as the Kennedys'. I am sure that Caroline must have eaten something for breakfast that morning. Jackie wouldn't have let her out without at least some cereal and milk. But what I remember most, what is forever ingrained in our nation's photo bank, is the image of a very young man, a boy, his hair parted on the side, almost over his eyes, well groomed in his pale dress coat, knee length pants, white anklets and dark tie shoes. He stands tall, hand to his forehead, saluting the fallen solider. It is John-John's third birthday celebration, a parade for his father.

And then, we all began to return to our self-centered reality. I still had a book report due from before this tragedy—and it was due tomorrow! I knew I would have to stay up later, or get up early. So I read until 2 a.m., figuring I could get up at six to finish writing the two-page paper. Again, that night, I would sleep outside my parents' room, the "drill" no different, the fears still overwhelming.

LIFE'S MOST EMBARRASSING MOMENTS

Looking back through the years, I now record the six most embarrassing moments of my childhood, in approximate reverse order.

6) June 2, 1961: It was Debbie Goldstein's 10th birthday party. The appetizers, entrée and dessert are pizza, washed down by three glasses of Coca Cola. My stomach was only used to splitting a slice with Harlan after we got our haircuts. Was I proving that I could eat the most, or was the pizza and coke such a rare treat in my house? Seven pieces later (I wonder who ate the last piece?) I was proudly touching the fire hydrant near Debbie's driveway that represented third base, having kicked the ball way down the street, emulating Eddie Mathews, when up it all came, lurching onto the street. Mrs. Steinberg made it worse by rushing over to my side to make sure I was okay.

5) It was the end of fourth grade, and my last summer of fun with my friends before we moved. George and I were hanging out at his house, reading our Landmark Books about Amelia Earhart and Wyatt Earp, when Theresa, our classmate and his next-door neighbor comes over. George's brother had put up a small pup tent in preparation for his Boy Scout Jamboree.

"Hey," Theresa yelled, "Can we go inside?"

"I don't know if Tony'd like it."

"Ah, he'll never know."

"Well, what could we do?"

"We could play house."

"Doesn't sound like much fun to me," I said.

"Please!" Theresa begged.

So we crawled through the opening flap, with just enough light coming through.

We were bored, getting ready to go back outside, until George said to Theresa, "Hey, I'll show you mine if you show me yours."

It was fourth grade, and we were still innocent, still pre-pubescent, just biologically interested. And no one knew I had a crush on Theresa; that I tried to stand next to her on line for assembly; that I maneuvered to sit next to her on the bus on class trips—although my illicit desire was unrequited, as far as I could tell. That I was hoping she would marry me was a fantasy I couldn't let anyone know. It was fourth grade and everyone knew girls had "cooties."

Theresa thought for a moment, and then she said, "You show me first."

She and I watched as George unzipped his shorts and showed his small penis. There was no pubic hair or engorgement from hormones.

"Oh," she said.

"Now your turn," George demanded.

Theresa pulled down her shorts and showed us—nothing! No pee-pee, just a small slit.

"Well," she said.

"Thanks."

And that was it, my first "sexual" experience. And I had been a voyeur, a non-combatant, as my true lover barely acknowledged me. I was just an innocent bystander, an irrelevant participant in her eyes. And on a more philosophical level, I had allowed George to be exposed, along with Theresa. As with the Vietnam War in later years, I had taken the easy way out. I had gotten all of the pleasure, all of the knowledge, without being in the line of fire. Someone else had taken the bullet.

4) I was the star student of my third grade class, the best speller around. Like "Tommy," I never missed a "replay." The prize for any row of us classmates who all got a 100% on the weekly spelling quiz was a five-cent piece of candy. Today, everyone, even Esther, who usually got 70s, shocked us all with a perfect score. Until I noticed that Esther, who has corrected my test, hadn't noticed an error I had made on my test. As Miss Phillips handed out the candy, I was faced with my first moral dilemma. If I spoke out, not only me, but also Esther and my row mates, would be deprived. My honesty would cost her more than it would me. But would it really?

3) April 17, 1961: "What could I have done to make her so mad?" I didn't swear, so that couldn't have been it. I certainly loved her. And in the past I must have been obnoxious enough for my parents to threaten to send me to military school if I didn't watch my tongue. But this morning,

whatever I said, however I talked back to her, whatever "filth" came out of my mouth, my mother "washed" my mouth out with soap. Not "Dove for dishes" nor Palmolive, but Ivory Soap—so cleansing, so utilitarian, with its blue and white wrapper's slogan "no additives." It may have been mild on the dishes, but it was so bitter and acrid to the tongue. I was crying as I left the house, begging for forgiveness, blowing bubbles of filmy clear soap as I got onto the school bus. To this day, a visceral feeling overwhelms me whenever I see or smell a bar of this malevolent piece of benign cleanser. Why couldn't I just have gone with Theresa's family to confession at her Catholic Church? How much scarier could a priest be?

2) March 1963: I got my report card for the third quarter, with a B+ in English. I was shattered, as I had always gotten A's before. And although it's about time that I join the world of mortals, I begged with Ms. B, crying "My mother is going to kill me!" for this grade! That was an overstatement, obviously, as she didn't believe in the death penalty. Was it my perception or would she be that harsh? Tears falling down my cheeks in front of my teacher and classmates for a grade that 80 percent of the class would have "died" for, I forgot my mother's statement of support for me before any test: "Do well. Do your best."

Jane Miller was staring at me, her hands scratched by her cats. And then she looked down at her report card.

1) April 3, 1964: Eighth grade. Spring Break. My last educational trip with my mom, and my first visit to a cemetery.

There are moments of embarrassment that are remembered not because of any major character flaw, but because of shame in front of classmates or friends. But for me, on this date, my place in Dante's inner circle was assured. Like the ultimate charitable gift that is anonymous, this act was also anonymous, with no one else knowing the identity of the perpetrator.

All five of us were in Washington for Spring Break, and we decided to go to Arlington National Cemetery to see President Kennedy's gravesite. It was a long walk up from the parking lot, and my father obviously couldn't keep up with us. But the rest of the family stayed together— except for me. I somehow chose this moment to accelerate my entry into the long and winding line of respectful Americans who were waiting their turns, patiently, to honor their fallen leader.

I was at least 60-70 people in front of my family, as the line wove through the unmarked gravesites of other American soldiers, equally dead, equally brave, equally leaving behind family, but ignored today, not only by me, but also by the rest of the American public.

As I approached the gravesite, my trusty Brownie camera recorded for posterity its eternal flame and white cross. And then, a moment that will live in my infamy, I started waving triumphantly to my parents and brothers. Had I climbed Mt. Everest? Had I performed some miraculous feat? No, I had walked a little faster than my father, with his bad hip.

I would have to wait silently as they finally caught up, my glory turned to shame for eternity, my darkness extinguishing the memorial light. No one was hurt, Mrs. Kennedy and her children would never know. But I still remember.

A BRIEF INTERLUDE OF FANTASY

June 21, 1964

1964: Only 20 more years until George Orwell's Big Brother would dominate the world. Identity theft, computer viruses, all things that could never have been imagined except in his book, were part of the darkness that was left in the shadows at the 1964 New York World's Fair. Harlan was especially excited to be going to celebrate six days after his 15th birthday. He was already planning on going to engineering school, with a career at AT&T or IBM. I, of course, was most interested in that new building right across the Long Island Railroad tracks from the World's Fair, the house that Casey built, Shea Stadium, new home of the New York Mets.

I had already been to Shea Stadium on Opening Day, April 17th, 1964. Again, my father and mother had conjured up, together, the fantasy of our family being the faithful fans who had seen the Mets through each of their baby steps (and baby steps they were indeed). Unlike the Polo Grounds, which had its hallowed history and old-fashioned bathrooms, Shea Stadium was the first of the modern stadiums, with all of the conveniences and advancements of the '60s. It was space age technology for a team going nowhere!

For my dad, it was a moment of ambivalence. There were lots of parking spaces, there were no seats with obstructed views from the loge, but the symmetry of the stadium, not having to be wedged into the grid of city streets, was quite disconcerting. And of course, in the new environs, hot dogs not only didn't taste as good, they cost more. At least the day was a little better than that two years previously; but, unamazingly, the Mets again were upstaged by the Pittsburgh Pirates, with Willie Stargell hitting the first home run in Shea Stadium history, and the Mets recreating their opening day loss in the Polo Grounds, 4-3.

I was lucky enough the rest of the summer to piggyback visits to the World's Fair with games at Shea. I even watched Rod Kanehl on first base from the lofty perch of the upper deck. But although June 21, 1964, was not actually Harlan's birthday, it was Father's Day; and as it wasn't MY birthday, it was World's Fair, and the Fair alone, that we went to that day. While we stood in line for the GM Pavilion, and watched the talking figures at the Coca Cola exhibit, trying to figure out what the future had in store for us, I had my transistor radio close at my ear, following my boys playing the men from Philadelphia. We finally got into the GM Futurama building and watched from our moving seats as the Moon's surface was developed, with lunar vehicles and spacecrafts transporting people. We watched as deserts were irrigated (not so much the future as reality in Israel), and the Amazon rain forests were tamed by cutting down the trees for building materials. Naturally, there was no consideration of the effect that these actions or the GM gas-guzzlers of the '60s would have on the ozone, or environment in general.

Harlan had figured out which exhibits had the longest lines and had strategically planned our itinerary. "I think it's time for us to go to IBM," he stated with such certainty that even my dad couldn't disagree. "It's 11 o'clock and everyone will be here by 1 o'clock and we'll have to wait forever. So no matter where we go after this, we'll be stuck in line."

"Good, then you won't mind if we go over to Shea Stadium and see some real action." I was on a roll, the kind that usually tumbled me right into the "dog house." "Harlan, all you ever want to do is your science and math."

"Well, at least I'm spending my time productively."

Harlan didn't waste time on sporting events. He was going to Stevens Institute of Technology in Newark on Saturdays taking prep courses in advanced geometry, figuring to get a head start on his college classmates four years hence. "I need to see what IBM's computers are going to be able to do when I get my engineering degree. I hear they'll be able to fit them into a room the size of a closet by then."

"I hope it doesn't smell as bad as yours does now."

"Austin, enough of that! Keep it up, and we'll fill out those applications for military school," my parents said in unison.

"He started it, Dad."

"And we'll finish it, right now!" Dad was emphatic.

And Mom laughed. "Bill, remember that scene in "Car 54, Where Are You?" when the boy came into the room with the pool ball in his mouth? He couldn't say a word. Maybe we should get one of those for Austin."

"Make it gift wrapped, Mom." Harlan couldn't help himself.

Harlan pretty much pranced ahead, leading the way, showing me clearly who had won this battle. Marty stayed at his side, expecting protection should the feud escalate.

What a perfect "Leave It to Beaver" family we made. My mom, wearing a sleeveless blue blouse and a black skirt, sunglasses shading her eyes from the June sun, was walking slowly with my dad. He was dressed in his usual light blue, baggy pants and button-down shirt, with a pen and pencil holder and little note pad inserted in the pocket, in case a brilliant idea pop into his head. For once he was without his tie clasp, which usually held any of the loose sheets of note paper.

Not that we "three musketeers" would make the girls' eyes turn. Marty had his jeans with turned-up cuffs. I was wearing Harlan's hand-me-down pants, with cuffs let down and white socks and black shoes; and Harlan was striding along with his short hair coiffed back, his shirt, red and blue plaid, halfway out of his pants.

As we walked by the Belgium Pavilion, Marty's eyes lit up when he saw the line at the "Belgian Waffles" pavilion, the culinary discovery of this World's Fair.

"Can I have one, Mom? Please?"

"We'll get you each one if you are real good. But we just ate, so we'll come back after IBM."

"I want mine with whipped cream!" Marty yelled.

"And I want strawberries on mine, too" I yelled. I looked at Harlan, with a glitter of revenge in my eyes. "Harlan, it's too bad you're allergic to strawberries. You'll just have to eat yours plain. But they look so good, don't they Mom?"

It's a good thing that she was between us at that point, or I think the fight would have easily escalated from sticking out tongues at each other to something more "dangerous."

It only took us 45 minutes to get through the line to the IBM exhibit. We were led into a "people's wall," with 500 of us sitting in a tiered structure that was lifted up into the ellipsoid structure 90 feet above the ground. We were bombarded from all angles with slides of how the human brain, the ultimate computer, worked. Harlan was overjoyed and spent at least 20 minutes after the show in the grove below, watching computers translate from foreign languages and read handwriting—precursors to the Palm Pilots so common now. Harlan was fascinated by the 1,000 white balls that fell predictably into 21 slots, proving the theory of probability on a practical basis. It was his birthday celebration, and my making faces at my mom, begging her to make Harlan move faster, was met with a stare saying, "It's his birthday. You'll have to wait." I jumped up and down, pretending that I had to go to the bathroom, so we could leave and I could get my waffle. I had forgotten about the baseball game now, my stomach now in charge.

Finally, Harlan had enough, and we ran out of the exhibit towards the waffles line. What this had to do with the Belgian culture I'll never know, but we started speaking in foreign tongues.

"Oui."

"Ronzoni, son o boni."

"Frère Jacques."

Luckily for foreign relations, our parents arrived. We then each carefully placed our orders, and as they made each waffle — two with just whipped cream for Marty and Harlan and two with strawberries and cream, one for me and one for my parents to share—I marveled at the crisp, brown symmetry of the waffles, of the perfectly white whipped cream piled on top, and then at the delicious red fruit delicately laid on top.

The waffles paid for and carefully packaged, we trod over to the picnic table to enjoy our feast. It was better than any Chinese food I could imagine.

"You see, Austin, this is better than anything you could get at Shea Stadium today.'"

I bit into mine, and it was special. I could envision eating one myself every day. But then, as Marty went to sit down, disaster struck. His waffle fell from the plate and landed on the seat. It could have been worse—it could have landed cream side down! He started crying. The line had gotten longer, and was now at least a 20-minute wait.

"Marty, how could you?" Mom was about to give him some of hers, when I, with great chivalry, offered mine.

"Here Marty, have half of mine." Bonus points for my trip to heaven!

His tears welled up further as he reached down to the seat and put the waffle back on his plate. "You have germs, Austin. I'd rather eat this one."

We were such a loving trio of brothers.

We never did get to Shea Stadium that day. After the IBM and the Belgian exhibits, we went through the Coca-Cola Plaza, and then headed for the souvenir stand. I picked out a World's Fair glass with images of the Unisphere, the Hall of Science, where we had a simulated space ride to the Moon, and of course, Shea Stadium. As we left, Marty wanted a Coke from the Coca-Cola Pavilion, but when I said "Stupid, they only serve Pepsi there!" I lost my allowance for the following week.

I guess I was glad to be heading home down only one week's income, and I was starving by the time we reached my dad's goal for Father's Day, the China House restaurant. It wasn't until we got home that night and turned on the television that we learned that Jim Bunning had pitched a perfect game that afternoon in Shea Stadium, retiring all 27 Mets that he faced in a row. No hits, no walks, no errors. Not even Rod Kanehl, my hero, could figure out the Phillies' pitcher as he struck out ten Mets, including John Stephenson, to end the game. For Mr. Bunning, future United States Senator from Kentucky, it was sort of like getting 800s on the math and English SATs and then winning a game of hearts by "Shooting the Moon." And all I could do was read about it in *The New York Times* the next morning. When I got to the Hall of Fame in Cooperstown several years later, I went to the exhibit of that perfect game, and there was Rod Kanehl's name in the box score. At least he made the Hall of Fame, even if it was only with zeros after his name.

September, 1964

Eighth grade began with new classes and new classmates with each bell —more girls to look at, to worship from afar, to stare at their stockings and girdles. Something was awakening inside of me beyond mere curiosity, beyond the joys of the marriage of Ozzie and Harriet, of Ward and June. All around me in the locker room armpits and pubic regions were sprouting with hair. Acne became a common theme. And the girls . . .

One day after school, my mom asked me to go up into their bedroom to get her a sweater. My dad's bureau drawer was open a smidgen, and I saw a colorful magazine cover sticking out a bit. Hoping for the latest *Sport* magazine, I opened the drawer and pulled out a copy of *Playboy*. Alice couldn't have followed the white rabbit any faster than I opened the tome. The pages were decorated with the most beautiful women I had ever seen. Shame mixed with excitement as I flipped through the pages: bare bosoms, long suntanned legs, and naked buttocks. I was aware of a stiffening in my jeans. What was happening?

"Austin, what's taking so long? The sweater's just lying on the bed."

I'd been found out. She knew what I was doing. How could I face her ever again? I closed the draw carefully and raced down the stairs with her sweater.

"Sorry, Mom. I just stopped to say hello to my dogs."

"Don't worry. I was getting cold, that's all. Fall's coming too soon this year. Aren't you going out to play?"

"With whom?" I wanted to ask. "You won't let me try out for the football team." But that was a fight long lost.

"Nah, I've got a book report due Thursday. I've got to start reading."

"You're such a good student. I love you."

I went back up to my dad's dresser. I had a lot of reading and research to do! If only she knew. There were lots of copies of *Playboy*, a collection from months past. I calculated that if I took one from way down in the pile, he would never know.

I went back into my room and closed the door, ever mindful that my tattletale little brother would be home at some point. I opened to a folded page in the middle of the magazine, and there, almost life size, was my Venus. Her face seemed so sensitive, like she wanted to embrace me and hold me. But her flesh was so pure, her breasts so perfect, her bare legs so long. My eyes were drawn to some magical Bermuda Triangle, still unseen in the days of airbrushing and "pubic hair denial." I was lying on my stomach, feeling a strange sensation in my pubic area like I had to pee real bad, wanting to squeeze her tighter and tighter towards me, rocking on the mattress to get her closer. And then my jeans were all wet. How could I explain to my mom that I had peed in my pants? But then I realized that this was something different, much different, much more pleasurable. My confusion turned to shame as I lay there in my bed, a sinner, my soul to be offered to Satan. No bells rang out to proclaim the sanctity of the event. But I had this strange urge to light up a cigarette.

I heard Marty coming up the stairs, and then, as I would repeat millions of times (more like thousands), I pushed the magazine under my bed and picked up my book.

It was 1964, only 20 years until George Orwell's "Big Brother," but I knew that night, as I came down to dinner, that everyone knew, that my little brother had found out. But there was no need for such paranoia. My guilt was enough.

Was this what my mom looked like? Up until then, I guess I was convinced, as most kids are, that I was the product of "immaculate ejaculation." I was ignorant of what went on behind their closed locked doors at night. But if I looked at these women, was I peeking at my mom? I vowed that this was the only time I would pick up the magazine. I would honor my mother.

My vows lasted 23 hours, until the next afternoon. Patty Clark was sitting next to me in English class that morning, and as she sat down, her dress rode up to her stocking line. I was in love. And I couldn't wait until I got home that afternoon. After all, I had my math homework to do: 36-24-36. And I had to memorize my playmate's favorite food.

Five minutes later I was finished, spent, guilt-ridden, filthy. My innocence was lost for eternity, never to be reclaimed. I had to wash up, take a shower. And if I had known what the words meant, I would have felt like a "degenerate"—at least for one hour. Ah, the wonders of youth, wasted on youth! I realized that I would have to practice every night to become perfect at my new purpose in life. Patty's image, as represented by "Betty Sue" or Sally Mae" or "Rosemary" in my new "textbook," invaded my mind, but it spoiled my purity, poisoned my reverence for my mom. I couldn't face her that night without feeling lower than a serpent.

I was the only one who was committing these sins. But wait, what was my dad doing with these magazines? That was a question I never let come to consciousness.

1 9 6 5: A YEAR OF HOPE AND
A YEAR OF DESPAIR

Lyndon Johnson's landslide victory over Barry Goldwater in 1964 sig-
naled that the people of the United States were willing to let the federal
government play a significant role in improving peoples' lives, even as it
was a mandate not to use nuclear weapons in Vietnam. Who can forget
the image of Johnson's television ad against Goldwater, of the little girl
picking flowers in a field while the nuclear mushroom blossoms in the
background?

LBJ's 1965 State of the Union Address suggested that the "Great
Society" was just around the corner, promising equal opportunity for all
throughout the United States. Using JFK's legacy and his legislative
acumen, he was able to fight his "War on Poverty," working his magic
with Congress to obtain such progressive laws as federal housing and
higher education guarantees, along with Medicare.

He was able to work through the segregationist politicians to
achieve two Civil Rights Acts. He was at his best and brightest when he
spoke to Congress on March 15th, defending the use of federal troops in
Selma, Alabama:

"I speak tonight for the dignity of man and the destiny of democ-
racy. . . I want to be the president who educated young children . . .
helped to feed the hungry . . . protected the right of every citizen to vote."

In Tenafly, where the only blacks were the maids who commuted by
bus over the George Washington Bridge from New York City, we could
revel in Martin Luther King's proclamation, "We shall overcome!" In
our civics class, Mr. Brown extolled the virtues of our progressive gov-
ernment and had us write an essay as another piece of legislation was
passed.

In Norfolk, Mary's grandparents were much more ecumenical than
the rest of the city. They allowed Mary to have a black girlfriend—as
long as she was Catholic.

My dad, ever the health professional, was thrilled when the FTC
(Federal Trade Commission) ruled that cigarette cartons were required

to carry medical warnings, however small and inconspicuous they may have been.

And in Connecticut, the law banning birth control was declared unconstitutional. This gave Mary's friends hope that they would have some choice when they turned 18—as if the nuns hadn't already told them that sex itself was a mortal sin!

But all was not well in the United States.

As the Gemini missions continued, the Soviet Union once again beat us to the milestone—when Cosmonaut Leonov was the first man to walk in space.

It was the beginning of the escalation of the Vietnam War, as 3,500 Marines were landed at Da Nang, and LBJ ordered bombings in the north as reprisals for attacks on U.S. ground forces. The Domino Theory along with the fear of being perceived as soft on Communism had belied LBJ's statement during that same speech in March:

"I do not want to be the president who built empires, or sought grandeur, or extended dominion."

Back in the good old USA, antiwar demonstrations escalated in unison with the increase of monthly draftees to 35,000. LBJ took offense at Morley Safer's broadcast on Walter Cronkite's Evening News of a tape of U.S. Marines using Zippo lighters to set thatched roofs on fire in a Vietnamese village. The protestors were asking LBJ to truly understand the nature of the civil war in Vietnam, the lack of desire for the Americanization of Southeast Asia.

In the cities and in the South, despite the Civil Rights Acts, racial unrest showed that the "Great Society" had still not reached the blacks. Riots in the Watts section of Los Angeles after a minor police arrest (the usual catalyst, as the future would see) led to 24 deaths and almost 900 injuries. It was a rude awakening for us "liberals" in the North, who felt that we treated our "Negroes" so well. As Martin Luther King led the Freedom March in Alabama, it should have been clear that we should neither be complacent nor proud of our geographically and economically imposed segregation in Harlem and Newark.

But on a more personal and, therefore, more terrifying note, on February 21 Malcolm X was giving a speech at the Audubon Ballroom, *located only three blocks from my dad's office. A former member of the Nation of Islam, he was now interested in disavowing his previous conviction that all white men should be condemned and in promoting the idea of non-violence and brotherhood and human rights (although he still believed in violence against those who preached violence against the blacks). As he stood in front of a crowd of 400 followers, he was shot multiple times by supporters of the Nation of Islam. The entire area swarmed with police, but a lot too late. Even my dad's ID was checked when he went out to his parking lot around the corner from the ballroom. Malcolm X was pronounced dead on arrival at Columbia-Presbyterian Medical Center—a place to die that was to become too familiar to me over the ensuing months.*

THE DAY OF MY LIFE

It started out as just a lump. "Nothing much to worry about," according to my father. Only a year before, he had promised us that Mom would be okay. All she needed was a little radiation and the tumor cells would be killed. Forget the fact, unbeknownst to us, that her mom had died at age 41 of breast cancer.

Was my mom fooled? At 16 she had graduated from Julia Richmond High School; at 19 she had received her college degree from Hunter College; at 20 she was teaching typing skills to high school seniors only a year her junior; and at 22 she had married her high school sweetheart, my dad. She had grown up as a Jewish girl in a Christian Scientist home. In those days, there was no genetic evidence leading to the hereditary dominance of breast cancer in the Ashkenazi Jewish population. So I don't know if she equated the risk of her getting breast cancer with that of her own mother. But I find it hard to believe that my father was able to deceive her.

She dutifully went through three months of radiation therapy, which caused her axillary region to be reddened from the toxic rays we hoped would only affect the cancer cells. What irony that I had grown up worrying about the threat of nuclear radiation on our family, that we had considered building bomb shelters to avoid radiation, and now this "poison" was supposed to be her savior. For years, I had feared that my dad would be annihilated along with the rest of New York while we sat protected in New Jersey. And now she had her shield to protect the rest of her body while the X-rays did their damage.

How we believed, how we wanted to believe my dad's assurances that first and spring, as they celebrated their 20th anniversary at a Chinese restaurant with their friends, especially the Changs (a Chinese family who had become their best friends). Mom continued typing for Dad during the day but was at home for her kids when they returned from school.

We went away on our summer vacation, and throughout the summer she seemed to be doing well. She didn't swim, but she enjoyed herself. Maybe she didn't know. Hopefully she was able to enjoy her last summer with her boys. We certainly had a good time—more so than if we had known it would be our last with our mom. Our ignorance remained our bliss, as long as she was still "Mom." When school began—ninth grade for me, still in the junior high school building, but the beginning of high school, with grades that would count towards college—she was there for me when I came home. She still made our lunches, helped me with my reports, edited and proofread my papers, discussing with me the meaning of goodness in Atticus Finch, the protagonist in *To Kill A Mockingbird.* She reveled in my successes in school and in my being chairman of the Election Committee.

By early November, she and my dad were about to embark on a cross-country trip by train to a dental conference in San Francisco. November 3rd, the morning she was to leave, I had to get to school early to distribute ballots to each homeroom teacher's box for our mock election. I finished by 7:30 and, as school didn't begin for another hour, I walked the ¾-mile home to say goodbye one more time before she left us in the hands of our baby sitter, who would surely be more lenient, if not less supportive. We stood in the foyer and I hugged her one more time, told her I loved her and would miss her, and tried to remember what her touch and smell would feel like when she was gone. I had learned from my parents that you never knew what might happen when you left the house, that you always said goodbye, and that you never left home angry at each other.

I went back to school and she went to the West Coast. When she returned two weeks later, she couldn't keep any food down. She went directly into the Harkness Pavilion at the Columbia-Presbyterian Medical Center, November 19, 1965. Her breast cancer had spread throughout her warm, tender, loving body—with only her three boys and herself still in the dark, her diagnosis buried within her externally normal body, scarred only by the radiation treatment of the past year.

I had one last look at her in our house that early morning, which would never be "our" home again. The next time I saw her, she was in her hospital bed. All of us were assured by my dad that she would be home soon, that the doctors would be curing her, that this was a temporary setback. Because she was at Columbia, he could see her every day, most of the day, except when he was teaching or seeing patients. But he could do his writing and his editing in her room. He would break away while she was sleeping. He had more time to work, but got less and less done each day, as she got sicker and sicker. She needed more and more morphine to relieve the pain of her intestinal obstruction from the metastatic breast and ovarian cancer. We didn't know that the doctors had given up, no chemotherapy yet developed, and no need for further futile radiation or surgery.

Every night Dad would arrive home late, with nothing left to give, having left it all in the hospital room. We had a longed-for, but unwanted, freedom at home. Our neighbors baked us tuna casseroles and cakes. There was no one to supervise our homework, our daily chores, or our weekly hygiene. Instead of milk, we'd have the forbidden beverage, Coca Cola. Instead of studying, we played basketball and listened to WABC and WMCA, to Cousin Brucie, the Rolling Stones, and Paul Revere and the Raiders. Julie Andrews and the "Sound of Music" were out; the Beatles were now revolving on our stereo turntables.

On weekends, Dad drove us into the city across the George Washington Bridge. We would sit in the waiting room . . . waiting . . . waiting for her to come out of her morphine haze. He delayed our visits to protect us from seeing her so drugged or in such pain. We talked with her as if she were just visiting here, soon to be coming home. We told her about school, our stuffed dogs, and Christmas, which would was soon to be upon us. Then, after 30 minutes, we'd go back out to the waiting room, hoping to get one more chance, but wondering what to do with ourselves in this solitary room—a solarium without television, books, and radios.

If we were patient, my dad would send us down to the Chock Full o' Nuts restaurant in the lobby of the hospital, where we could buy crisply fried donuts with powdered sugar for five cents each, along with a date nut sandwich with cream cheese. How these foods brought back pleasant memories, of treats Mom would buy us after we had gone to the dentist, as we sat at the counter watching the waitress deftly pick up four crisp donuts and four sandwiches, along with a cup of coffee and three orange drinks, all with her only her. But when we returned to the solarium, our homework could occupy us only so long. And how long can boys 16, 14, and 10 remain on their best behavior? In this case, for as long as we could, although after a while we itched to get back home. We did not realize that the minutes we could be with Mom were slowly dwindling, like the particles of sand in an hourglass. In our case, however, we would have no ability to turn the hourglass back over and restart the sand.

When we would arrive home, there was no Mom to kiss goodnight before I went to bed with my stuffed dogs; no Mom to kiss goodbye in the morning. I would walk to school promising myself that, as long as I didn't step on the crack of the sidewalks, whoever controlled her destiny "up there" would spare her. I wanted to tempt fate, to step on the crack to break her back. But in this case, the consequences would be worse than an orthopedic problem. I wondered what it would be like to lose my mother. Would all of the kids in school be kinder to me, let me play on their basketball team or invite me to their parties? Or would they feel a momentary pang of pity for me and go their own merry ways?

Sundays were no longer devoted to my father's "Chinese Feast," his hours of preparation as we sat together as a family. For all of the rock 'n roll on my radio—for the "I Can't Get No Satisfaction" that blared throughout the house—what I still remember most, what still can bring tears to my eyes in an instant, is any rendition of "You'll Never Walk Alone." It makes me think of my mother singing while playing the organ, with my father cooking in the next room, and her soft voice emoting her love for her husband and her boys.

"When you walk through a storm
Hold you head up high
And don't be afraid of the dark.
At the end of the storm
Is a golden sky
And the sweet silver song of a lark.
Walk on through the wind,
Walk on through the rain,
Though your dreams be tossed and blown.
Walk on, walk on with hope in your heart,
And you'll never walk alone!
You'll never walk alone."

That song was my parents' anthem to live by. It expressed their love towards each other and their children, to be preserved for an eternity.

On New Year's Day 1966 there was no celebration. It was hardly cause for glee that she had survived to see the ball drop the night before, especially since she was fast asleep at that time. And there was not enough snow to make forts for a neighborhood snowball battle. Instead, we went back into New York City and the hospital on New Year's Day, for only a quick visit with Mom, who was groggy from her pain medicine. Then we just sat in the car while Dad remained upstairs in her room. We listened to the countdown of the year's "Top 100" songs on WABC: "You've Lost that Loving Feeling," "Like a Rolling Stone," "Satisfaction," "Turn, Turn, Turn," "Do You Believe in Magic," and then, "The Sounds of Silence." There was no discussion between my father and his boys about the certainty of her death; and as far as my dad would later tell me, there was no discussion with his beloved. How lonely it must have been for these two people who were always honest with each other. Now they had the biggest lie between them and no time to make amends or ask forgiveness afterwards. And there was no opportunity for them to say goodbye.

My Aunt Julie arrived from Chicago on January 2, 1966. If my mom didn't know how sick she was before that, the final clues were there now. We went with Aunt Julie to see Richard Burton and Claire Booth in "The Spy Who Came in from the Cold." A more sobering, depressing movie I cannot imagine for that dreary January winter day. It was nothing like the weird humor and sarcasm of "Spy vs. Spy" in *Mad* magazine.

January 8, 1966

It was a Saturday like any other Saturday in wintry New Jersey, only minus Mom's good night hug. We all drove in to visit, and then up the elevator we rode, with Marty and I each holding the last stuffed dogs that Mom and Dad would get us. We sat once again in the waiting room, until

Dad said, "You can come in now, but only for a few minutes. Mommy's very tired." I wondered why we came in just to see her for a few minutes. Her words of encouragement and interest got shorter with every visit.

I can look back at those days and hours and minutes and seconds with guilt, overwhelming guilt. How could I have been so carefree, so selfish, to be enjoying myself, listening to music, playing sports, laughing, enjoying food, lying in bed without pain, living as if time didn't matter?

How could my father not have told us the truth?

How could he have told us the truth?

We had the freedom from set bedtimes, from taking baths—at the expense of losing our mom. We had finished reading "Our Town" in English I, the same play I had seen in sixth grade. No wonder Emily was so distraught when she looked down from heaven and realized how inconsequentially we viewed each mundane day of our lives, instead of appreciating and sanctifying and cherishing every moment of our existence.

Except that really couldn't apply to my mom.

The last time I saw her, she was lying in her hospital bed, the curtains in her private room half-drawn, with a tube through her nose that no longer functioned as a feeding tube but, rather, just decompressed her bloated belly. Her jaundiced eyes and gaunt skin gave her the only color in what otherwise would have been her pale white cheeks. Thank heavens she had been spared the indignity of losing her hair to chemotherapy. Her IV provided fluids, but no nutrition. She was barely able to stay awake as the narcotics did their job, dulling the pain as it dulled her sensation.

She was in a dreamlike state while Marty and I sat with her, our new stuffed dogs each giving her a kiss. I do not remember, no matter how I try, what we spoke about that day. I do not remember saying goodbye, saying "I love you," but I know that I did. I cannot remember what she said to me that night as I left. There were no "final words" spoken that night for me to live by, no deathbed requests, no "take care of your father, and be good to your brothers." There was nothing said for me to play back in my head to pacify me, to console me in the years to come.

Because no one told us that she was dying, that we would never see her again. And even if she knew, was she unable to tell us because it was too painful for us or for her?

To this day, I can't tell you why I left her room that day.

What was so important that couldn't wait, that I had to start the rest of my life without her?

I should have just lain down on the bed with her, crawled under the covers, fallen asleep with her, dreaming, as the sun set. Together forever, morning never coming to awaken us, just her and me together. Everything is all right—we'll have lunch together, eat our cucumbers and diet dressing and Metracal diet crackers, study together, laugh together, be there with each other, forever, as all parents and their children are supposed to be.

I should have stayed and guarded her, guided her through the tunnel!

Only I left the room. And I must have known. I still remember my last look, Mom lying in bed with that tube in her nose, under the covers, thin, hanging on to life for who knows what reasons. I took that last look as if I would never see her again. I have that one last vision to last my lifetime. I had that vision to sustain me until I myself reached her final age of 41 years, 8 months and 25 days, feeling guilty that I had outlived her. I do not know whether she took one last look at us, to sustain her not only for a lifetime, but also for an eternity. But I'll always have that night, that goodbye. That last look was as precious to me as the photograph I have in my mind of the glance I give Jannie every time I leave her, and of the memory I have when I leave Mary in the morning.

January 10, 1966

It could have been any school night in my life. I was in my bedroom, reading John Griffith's *Black Like Me*, dozing off, waiting for Dad to get home for dinner. He called, "Wait up for me, boys. I'll be home around 7." He did not tell us that she had died sometime after 5 p.m. Still, I went back to my nap until I heard the car pull in the driveway, the door close, and Dad come into the house. He couldn't keep his secret from us anymore.

"Boys, come sit down. I have something to tell you."

We went into the living room, on the couch where we never sat, and heard:

"Mommy died tonight."

"Noooooo!" "Please Dad, don't." "Where's Mommy?" "I want my Mommy."

"Harlan, Austin, Marty, she's not coming home."

"What happened? You told us she was going to be okay. You promised that the doctors would take care of her. Why did this happen?"

"She had cancer, she never had a chance."

"Why, why did this happen, why didn't you tell us? I want to say goodbye, I want to hear her voice, to see her, to touch her."

"You can't Austin, she's gone. The cancer had spread through her body. It blocked off her intestines. I didn't tell you because I thought you wouldn't enjoy your last days with her."

"Why couldn't they fix her, Dad? They could've put tubes inside to keep everything open."

"It doesn't work that way, Austin."

"We can fly to the Moon, but why couldn't we save Mommy?"

"Dad, where is she now?" Harlan asked. "Is she comfortable?"

"Yes, Harlan, she's at peace. At least she's not in pain now."

The gyroscope my rabbi had given me when I was in second grade to comfort me on the morning my parents had dropped me off for Sunday school stopped rotating. Its center of gravity was gone; the spiral was interrupted. It lay on its side, inert. At some point, we would have to rewind the string, start it back in motion to regain our life, our energy. But not tonight or for many nights after that one.

For tonight we cried, all together, one family, minus one. Tears streamed down our cheeks on to the couch, on to the pillows, flooding the floor. We would be silent for a moment, only to start up again. Finally, there were no more tears left for that night, and we all followed Dad up to their room, now his room, now our room, and we all crawled into bed, one family, minus one.

Maybe if I hadn't fallen asleep that afternoon she'd still be alive? Or maybe I should have just stayed asleep, never to have awakened, suspended in life, traveling back in time with my mom—for the good times, and, hey, I'd even cherish the bad times.

Then a thought came into my consciousness, one that I couldn't prevent from taking control. I tried to block it out, but the images from my father's *Playboys* kept infiltrating every synapse, every visual fiber. BREASTS. I had become addicted to my centerfolds' breasts—all shapes, some larger than others, some with smaller nipples, some with larger. Now my obsession had killed my mother! The sins of the son inflicted on the parent! If only she didn't have breasts—she would be alive!! If only I had controlled my animal urges, she would be alive!! Finally, I could self-flagellate myself only so long, and the darkness that had fallen over her hospital bed earlier that afternoon took me into its arms and cradled me to sleep.

But then "mourning" came and I awakened. And then we went down to breakfast, to cardboard boxes filled with Frosted Flakes and Cocoa Puffs—and an unopened box of her Special K.

OFFSETTING LIFE'S MOST EMBARRASSING MOMENTS—OR "MAYBE I CAN STILL GET TO 'HEAVEN'"

January 12, 1966: My mother's funeral in midtown Manhattan. I would hear a lot about God that day—but it didn't make sense. What all-powerful God would do such bad things to good people? Salvation, heaven, soul, afterlife—they didn't make much sense, weren't much solace. Hitler lived while six million Jews died, each a mother, father, son or daughter, brother or sister. Each death was significant, none more or less, each mourning was no more or less painful. My faith was pretty much shattered—until much later, when I began to view God not as an omnipotent being, all-powerful, but as a spiritual force, a guiding light, helping me to understand myself, my strengths, my weaknesses, and helping me to love my fellow creatures.

At 11 a.m. everyone was present except for my grandfather, my mother's dad. It was 12 days into Republican Mayor John Lindsay's first term, and Transit Union president Michael Quill had called a strike that paralyzed the city. My dislike for the disruptive power of some labor unions began that day, reaffirming an upbringing based on economic conservatism with a social conscience. We had to hire a private bus to bring down the faculty from Columbia Dental School to be at the funeral. But not everyone could make it who wanted to be there. Not everyone could get transportation there. Not everyone could be there to say goodbye.

And now, Grandpa was stuck somewhere in traffic. Everyone was waiting, the rabbi was there, my dad's colleagues were there, my aunts and uncles were there, and they were about to start without Grandpa. "Pop, we can't start without grandpa," I pleaded. And he listened, and we waited. Finally Grandpa Leon arrived to hear the eulogies, to help bury his daughter, just as he buried his wife, at the same age, 41.

FUCK YOU, MICHAEL QUILL. MAY YOU ROT IN HELL.

EXODUS

A DAY OF THANKSGIVING
(OR)
TALES OF TWO CITIES

November 25, 1966 (Norfolk, Virginia, to Titusville, Florida)

"Mary, dinner'll be ready in 30 minutes."

"Thanks, Mother, I'll be down soon"

Life was different now that Mary was back in Florida with her mother, Ellen, and step-father, Bill. Three months earlier, in time for her junior year in high school, Mary had been unceremoniously placed on an airplane in Norfolk to fly down to Titusville, the home of the astronauts, to join her new step-family, who were already living in their own other world. After seven years with Gramps and Grammie, the decision had been made that Mary had to go back home.

"It's time for Ellen to live up to her responsibility to her daughter. You and Mom are getting too old to take care of her." Mary overheard her Aunt Susan and Uncle Mike talking after dinner one night toward the end of the summer. "And Mary isn't exactly the most sociable child. Maybe Florida will do her good."

"The times, they are a-changing," Mary thought. "Some 'Sweet 16' birthday party. I'm being thrown out of my home back to that bitch and whoever she's remarried. And now I have to deal with sister Kate and their new baby, William, Jr. A real un-Brady Bunch."

She went up to her room, slammed the door, and turned on the radio. The Stones' "Satisfaction" blared. She opened the window and pulled out the last cigarette which her Aunt Kitty had given her last week. She stood near the window and slowly twirled the Salem between her fingers, checked the filter, patted the tobacco carefully in place, and lit up. The smoke filled her lungs, even as she coughed. It felt soothing, relaxing, death-defying.

"I'll be leaving soon, Spider. They'd better let me take you with me. But you'll have to remain an indoor cat. You'd never survive without your claws down in Florida."

Before leaving her room, Mary pulled out a stick of Doublemint gum. She had once figured that 50% of its ingredients was for teenagers to mask the odor of cigarette smoke on their breath. Juicy Fruit just wouldn't make it. As she shoved the spearmint-flavored gum into her mouth, she thought, "I don't know what I'm so worried about. The whole house reeks of Grandpa's pipe smoke. God, how I'll be happy to get out of this town. Sailors everywhere, all day—and all they want is me."

And then she broke down and sobbed, overwhelmed by life. But when she ran out of tears five minutes later, there was no resolution.

At dinner that night, with the August moon appearing in the dusky sky, the family secret was the only ingredient of the silent conversation. By breakfast, it was over.

"Mary," her grandmother began, "we've all decided that it'll be best for you to go back to living with your mother in Florida. You'll have a better time there, with kids your age. And Grandpa and I just are getting too old."

"Please, please, I don't want to leave. I'll do anything. I'll get a job, I'll fix dinner, I'll do the dishes, I'll sweep the kitchen floor. I love you."

"Mary, don't make this any harder for us than it already is. We talked this over with Uncle Mike and Aunt Susan, and the decision is final."

"Yeah, but what'd my mother say."

"She's happy to have you," Grandma said.

"I'm sure." Mary's voice reeked of sarcasm. "And I'm sure that her husband, whatever his name is, must be delighted."

"Mary, please give your mom and 'Bill' a chance. For us, at least," Grandpa begged. And so, on Labor Day weekend, Mary got onto Eastern Airlines flight 273.

What Mary carried:

1. Her Calico cat, Spider, in his small cage.

2. Two suitcases, filled with two Sunday dresses, three Catholic school uniform skirts, five white blouses, three pairs of shorts, two T-shirts, eight pairs of white bobby socks, a pair of black patent leather shoes, a pair of red Keds sneakers, ten pairs of white underwear, and five white "cross my heart" Playtex bras.

3. A small case with her toothbrush and toothpaste and one lipstick.

4. Pictures of her grandparents.

5. Dolly, carried tightly beneath her arms, all dressed up in her summer best.

What she left behind:

1. Whatever existed from her childhood.

Her new house was a "ranch," with four bedrooms, two bathrooms, and a sunroom. It had typical Florida plaster, painted yellow, chipping at the corners, with a corrugated roof. It was old the day it was first inhabited.

Her first day at her new school was traumatic. Bill decided that they couldn't afford a private Catholic school, so Mary was introduced to co-ed public education. The building was painted white and blue, on a single level. The major focus was the finely manicured football field, which was the prime source of activity on Friday nights in the fall. The rest of the property was for the 98% of the students who were not on the football or cheerleading squad. Its lack of maintenance clearly showed where the school's priorities lay.

The good news was that there were no nuns telling her what to do, and thank heavens, the teachers weren't always praying to God. And there were boys—hormones on the rampage, sex exuding from every pore, acne in full bloom. Mary had never felt such excitement. She only wished that she wasn't so sexually repressed from her years in the Catholic Church. It hurt every day when boys ignored her, even though she wouldn't have known what to do. Maybe her long, plaid skirts with bobby socks and white blouse buttoned to the top—remnants of her old school—had something to do with it. Her "undergarments," white girdles and Sears' bras one size too large, added to the vacuum of sexuality. And Katrina (formerly Kate) didn't help. All of the boys flocked around her, drawn in part by her garter belt, easily seen by all. She was two years younger than Mary, but freely accepted all the boys' advances.

Mary sulked through her classes, answering questions only when asked. The rooms were not air-conditioned, and the cafeteria food was stale, starchy, and deep-fried, even the salad. During lunch, she sat by herself, unless there was no room; and then she would be shoved over by the cheerleader's squad, which ignored Mary's existence. She did her homework, got B's on exams, and felt herself sinking deeper into her hole of isolation and depression. Only Spider offered some solace when she would get home, settling down next to her, and purring as he was stroked for hours on end.

This Thursday afternoon, in late November, during the holiday dinner with her family, was her reality.

"Kate, could you pass the potatoes to William," her mother said. Only after everyone had been served did the platter of turkey arrive in front of Mary. The gravy dish was empty by the time it had made the rounds, and all of the marshmallows were unceremoniously spooned off the top of the sweet potatoes.

"Bill, would you like some more turkey? And please pass it to Kate when you are finished," Ellen said. "No seconds for me, I guess," Mary thought. "I'm just a second-rate kid around here. Only a year-and-a-half until graduation, and then I'm outta here."

It was the worst of times.

Late on Thanksgiving afternoon, Mary was in her room by herself as usual. Bill had made it clear that she was an outsider, not welcome in his house. She was Cinderella, the "ugly" step-daughter. She went to see "Dr. Zhivago" four times, falling desperately in love with her Prince Charming, Omar Sharif. She dreamed of sailing away in a "Yellow Submarine," far away from the geeky sailors of Norfolk. She learned to entertain herself, escaping with her 45s—"California Dreaming" and "Feeling Groovy"—that let her travel to another place. As she watched the black plastic discs spin around and around, she was transported out of this pathetic spiral that was keeping her here, and thrust far away from Florida. She could fly to the Moon to escape this boredom, this hell. But for now, she was still Earth-based, and she imagined herself over at the Cape with the astronauts, partying into the night, even though she was only with herself and her magic fingers.

November 25, 1966 (Tenafly, New Jersey, to Scarsdale, New York)

"Austin, get out of the bathroom. I've got to comb my hair."

"Shut up, Harlan. Who do you have to look good for today?"

"Just let me in, or I'll throw Waffles into the toilet."

I knew he wouldn't throw my stuffed dog into the toilet, because Dad would punish him. But could I take a chance? Dad was pretty distracted, since this was Thanksgiving and his wedding day.

"Don't you dare, I'll be out in a minute." What I would have added a year later was, "You ugly faggot." What I said instead was, "I hope you have an ugly zit on your nose today."

Instead of "Fuck you," he respected our mother and said, "Just you wait!"

After I got out of the bathroom, I surveyed my bedroom. All of the baseball posters of my favorite Mets and Orioles were off the wall, and only tape marks were left as a reminder of my heroes. All of the furniture had been labeled, all of my possessions were in several boxes, and my stuffed dogs were sitting next to my baseball mitt and my picture of my mom. Everything was ready to be taken to my new house. The "old house" was still full of our furniture, but it was devoid of life, as my mother's spirit had already exited. I trembled as I picked up my dogs.

"Nothing will be the same!" I cried as I held them tight.

We were moving to Scarsdale, where our new step-mom, Lil, and her four children had their home and friends and dogs; in short, their lives. The only thing missing was her husband and their father, who had passed on five years ago, also from cancer. Luckily the house had a finished third-floor attic, room enough for us three Kutscher kids, and room enough for my dad's work files in the master bedroom. The house also had a whole extra room over the garage and a basement, ready to be filled with Dad's work and journals—all about dentistry, Chinese cooking, and his soon-to-be purpose in life, thanatology, the study of death and dying and bereavement.

Tim O'Brien wrote in later years about *The Things They Carried*, a book about the foot soldiers in Vietnam. This is what we carried with us to our new home.

My things:

1. A colorized picture of my mom, smiling, her hair pulled back, her youthful beauty and love forever captured by a Sears' photographer.

2. My step-grandfather's desk and bureau for my bedroom, with labels "Scarsdale 3" (3rd floor)—labels that were so adherent that they remained for 20 years, ever a reminder of the "move."

3. Mom and Dad's bedside bureaus for our bedroom.

4. Two dining room chairs, Chippendale antiques, the rest of the dining room set left behind, as Lil had her own complete German Baroque set.

5. My stuffed dogs, "Senior," "Junior," and "Waffles," all woefully misshapen and resewn by me—replacement parts such as felt tongues and noses and new buttons for eyes. Yours truly did all of their reconstructive surgery, without the benefit of a home EC class, and it clearly showed. Only my newest friend, "Poppy," was still a puppy, having escaped injury and therefore, the knife.

6. My baseball mitt and bats, and baseball cards and Mets' yearbooks.

7. My Willie Mays Hartland's baseball statue.

8. My record player and records.

9. My *Playboy* magazines, stolen from my father, showing women with beautiful legs and perfect breasts, making my imagination overflow. "Bad girls," every one—to be fondled, groped—impersonal, unachievable. No need to worry about satisfying their needs.

10. My mom's letter. As we were packing up my dad's office, I found a box of Mom's Chinese language tapes, along with a four-page,

handwritten letter in her small, neat script, still somewhat difficult to read:

"Dear Harlan, Austin, and Martin,

If you are reading this, it means something terrible has happened to your Dad and me. It must have been God's will. We were lucky in finding each other at such a young age, and if God has allowed this to happen, it must be because he realizes we could not live without each other. Please remember to be nice to your grandmother; it will not be easy for her to bring you up. But most importantly, please be good to each other and love each other.

Love,

Mommy and Daddy"

Harlan's things:

1. Not much, as he wanted to stay in Tenafly.
2. His asthma medication.
3. His mathematics books.
4. His records.
5. His *Playboy* magazines.

Marty's things:

1. As far as he can tell me now, he did not have much of a memory of our mom. At age ten, his life was in front of him.

2. His stuffed dogs, "Cutey," "Happy," and "Popsy."

3. His comics (no, he didn't "read" *Playboy*!).

Dad's things:

1. An antique William and Mary Hutch from his Aunt Lily.
2. A Chinese sepulcher.
3. Three partial sets of china.
4. Two wine goblets he had received as gifts, even though neither my mom nor Dad drank.
5. Four reels of tapes of my mother practicing Chinese with Wonona and Irving Chang, our Chinese "family."
6. His work, his manuscripts—three rooms full.

7. His *Playboy* magazines, with young women with perfect breasts and airbrushed blemishes, were left behind, to be re-accumulated at a later time.

The family's things:
1. Two pinball machines, which the new family really loved.
2. Our new dog, Hope.

Hope's things:
1. Her four "boys" whom she had comforted.

It was the middle of the fall, I was in 10th grade in senior high school, and here I was moving again, driving with my dad, just the two of us. Except this time it was not us driving in the '57 Chevy, it was it was *Harlan,* with Marty alongside him, just the two of them. The station wagon was filled with our possessions, our clothes, and several boxes for my dad. My dogs, my mitt and Hope were with us, as we led the way to Scarsdale this Thanksgiving morning. There was no baseball game to listen to, and it was not the time to ask a lot of questions. The silence was deafening, as any reassurance from my dad could not overcome our grief.

Here's what I left behind:
1. Five years of unhappiness at a school in which I never felt comfortable.
2. One good friend, David, with whom I shared my summer and weekends, playing one-on-one stickball, basketball, and football. I didn't have the heart to tell him I was moving until three days before Thanksgiving.
3. A few girls I liked who barely reciprocated.
4. One student/athlete, who later became a movie star, and actually consoled me after I got cut from the high school basketball team tryout after one hour (which was probably 59 minutes longer than it took the coach to make his decision).

5. Two condolence notes from classmates after my mother died, along with one expression of sympathy from a teacher.

6. Ten months of life without Mom, freedom juxtaposed with grieving as my dad buried himself in his work.

7. Bars of Ivory soap, never to be used as discipline again, and never to be used by me to wash up again.

8. The name Austin, which I never liked because I felt it was too unique. I chose the name Ken—a name common enough to avoid ridicule but not as everyday as Michael or Paul or Richard.

9. The days of the winter, spring, and summer of 1966.

The void left in our family those first months after my mom died gave us the freedom we had so longed for only a couple of years ago, but which was now so unwanted. It was the worst of times.

Actually, the post-Mom era had started with "Hope." We had purchased (or she had adopted us) our black, mini-poodle puppy one week after Mom had died, and she was burdened with trying to guide our recovery. "Hopeless," as she was called, was overwhelmed. She was left alone during the day, thereby ensuring that she would be incorrigible for the rest of her life, never house-broken, only paper-trained. But she was as motherless as we were, having only recently been weaned. And we, especially I, became uncontrollably attached to her. As Marty stayed with our dad in his bed for comfort, Hope and I spent our nights cuddled together in my bed—just the six of us, including my four stuffed dogs, who were from the with-Mom era as opposed to the after-Mom era. Thank heavens Hope wasn't a chewer, although I could feel the pangs of jealousy pouring out from my stuffed dogs' fiber stuffing through the cotton skin of this loyal quartet, as their plastic eyes and felt noses maintained constant vigilance. I could hear them begging, "Daddy, we've been there for you all of these years, through all of your tests, book reports, projects. Don't forget us, don't abandon us."

I listened to rock 'n' roll with Harlan. My first "45" was "The Ballad of the Green Berets," a song honoring our clandestine heroes in Vietnam at a time when America still felt we were preventing the "dominoes" from falling to the Red or Yellow Menace. I had supported Barry Goldwater and Nelson Rockefeller's Republican Party only 14 months earlier, when, having not as yet read *The Ugly American*, I still naively believed in the benevolence of our mission to preserve democracy in Southeast Asia.

Our first album was a little more radical, the Rolling Stones' "High Tide and Green Grass." There was no way my mom would have allowed us to listen to this music, as show tunes and Andy Williams were the staples in our house. Now, we would go around the house singing the Righteous Brothers' "Soul and Inspiration." Finally, when my classmates talked about bands and music, I had some idea what they were talking about. This one girl I liked, Cathy, talked about her new favorite song, the Rolling Stones' "Paint It Black." I listened to the radio for hours on end, waiting to hear her song, constantly changing from WMCA to WABC, and finally hearing Cousin Brucie screaming into the microphone that his station would be playing it. I knew I would never have a chance with her until I could at least relate to her song. And then, finally, there was the "red door" being painted—now I had heard it, now I could talk with her—if only I had an idea of what the song actually meant!

In March, out of tradition, my dad had ordered tickets for Opening Day at Shea Stadium. Except now it was April 15, and there he was, lying on his side, recuperating from a hemorrhoid operation he had put off for years, praying that the surgery would heal before he had to have a bowel movement. I guess he hoped to relive our days with the Mets, but today we would be going without either my mom or him.

Instead, our favorite cousin, Bruce, volunteered to take his three cousins, once-removed. It wasn't quite as special as when he took me to the World Series in 1963, but he was still cool, much cooler than my dad. And it was a typical opening day for the Mets in their early existence. They lost.

Going to a game with Bruce was still like going to a game with my imaginary father. He was fun-loving, laughing, worry-free, and out to have a great time with his kids—not the serious, "everything and every moment counts" kind of guy like my dad. Did that make Bruce a better father? Would I have been better off with him as a dad or as a role model? Who can tell, but it was a relief having him play Dad for a few hours. Every kid, I think, wonders what it would be like to have someone else as a parent. On that day, we could run ahead with abandon, eat peanuts, and drink soda without worrying about rotting our teeth. And we didn't have to worry if we were "a pain in the ass" to him when we complained or argued about who would sit up front on the way home.

It was a day when the reality of life could be suspended, when I could forget that Mom was no longer with us, that Dad was so serious and despondent. Only the final score, the Mets losing, and Bruce returning us to an empty house brought us back to April, 1966. But the next day, while watching the game in my dad's hospital room, the Mets did have their miracle. A bases-loaded walk in the bottom of the ninth won the game. Maybe there was hope and joy for us! I started to jump up and down on Dad's bed.

"We won! We did it!"

"Austin, stop it. Stop it!" My dad was in pain. "You're killing my hemorrhoids!"—a forerunner to the statement, "You're a pain in my ass!"

But after he recovered and went back to work, my dad was too involved with his work during the day and trying to find a new wife and mother during the evenings and weekends to be aware of our not-so-clandestine habits. Our diet now included Coca Cola, the forbidden nectar, with its narrow bottle neck covered by a real bottle cap, not some plastic screw top. And Clara, or "Aunt Clara," who stayed with us during the weekday evenings, cooked and did our laundry. She was a friend of our backdoor neighbor and was also recently widowed. She was probably only ten years older than my parents, but she had gray hair and a warm but sad smile. She loved us as she would her own grandchildren, had she had any. We were partners in grief.

I was lost. I didn't even know enough to shampoo my hair on a regular schedule, although the Vitalis look was still acceptable. I stopped brushing my teeth before I went to bed—some dentist's son! I didn't have any dates, except with the two-dimensional women in Dad's *Playboys* that I had purloined, and now were officially mine, hidden under my bed. I was in that hormonal stage of super ability and no prospects, so that even the sight of a girl's girdle or top of her stocking was enough for me to fantasize throughout the evening. Harlan was lost, but he still found time to go to the movies and make-out with a real girl, much as that amazed me. And Marty, he didn't really know enough to be lost.

I even got my first detention for gym, probably for having dirty shorts. It actually turned out to be a pleasant experience, since I was "punished" by being the designated catcher, as Coach Reston hit grounders during infield practice for the freshman baseball team.

"Austin, why don't you come out for our team?"

I couldn't believe my ears. I had stayed up late the year before, waiting for a call from a Babe Ruth League coach. My dejection and plummeting self-esteem turned to elation when he finally called at 9:30 p.m. I wasn't a starter, but I surprised my coach with my fielding and with several key hits. And now, here was a "pro" asking me to play. I had my new Brooks Robinson "Figure 8" third baseman's mitt, all ready to be broken in. I went home to tell my dad, barely containing my excitement.

"Austin, there's too much pressure this semester after Mommy's dying. You need to concentrate on your work. This is the first year that your grades count towards your college application."

"Dad, you never let me do anything."

"Austin, you know your mother wouldn't let you. She'd be afraid you'd get hurt."

"I don't know, Dad." But without his permission ticket, I got no uniform shirt.

Instead, every afternoon I went to the local school and played stickball with David. This was usually followed by a tetherball "tournament." We would each try to punch the volleyball attached by a strong cord around the pole, which spiraled tighter and tighter in one direction, until the winner banged the ball snug against the steel totem. As the leaves began to change, we would often play one-on-one football.

After dinner, David had to be home, so I played basketball in our driveway with Harlan and Marty late into the night, under the lights. The only danger was a shot that could glance off the rim and carom through the garage window. It was usually Marty and me against Harlan. At age ten, Marty's jump shot, even if it wasn't rushed by the charging, scream-ing Harlan, even if it wasn't blocked by Harlan's outstretched hand, would chronically fall short of its mark. Harlan would triumphantly pro-claim, "I win, I win!" as if he were Bill Russell of the Boston Celtics proving his superiority over Wilt Chamberlain.

And Dad, he didn't know how to "date." He was an easy mark for other widows or divorcees, at least until they met us. Unless of course, they had their own monsters!

Words that I might have said to my dad were left unsaid, as he dealt with his grief by himself. Dad was trying hard to find something, some-one, to help him understand his grief, to overcome his loneliness. He be-came less involved in dentistry and became immersed in starting his "Foundation of Thanatology," to study the dying and grieving process, to honor my mom, his wife, and to find a reason to go on living. He also had to deal with the guilt of finding another wife, another mother for his boys, of remarrying, of loving another.

As his life changed, so did ours. He met Lil Steinberg over Labor Day weekend, and as he became aware that she might be the "one" for him, he reformed. He actually was able to leave his work and get up to Scarsdale on time—an amazing achievement considering how incapable he was of doing it for my mom. For several months, he was a changed man. He was relaxed, although I am sure he was also fearful of a new relationship.

He was ready for an adventure. Ready to break the mold.

That day would be October 5, 1966. The Baltimore Orioles were in the World Series for the first time. And as stockholders, we were given the opportunity to purchase two tickets to the third game of the series in Baltimore, to see the Orioles against the Los Angeles Dodgers. I clutched the tickets as we picked up my friend Peter Wallace from his house at 6:30 a.m. We needed to catch the 7 o'clock bus to New York City's Port Authority to make the 8 a.m. Greyhound bus to Baltimore. That would give us at least an hour to make our way over to Memorial Stadium. How, at age 15, we were being allowed to do this, when I know there is no way I would let my Jannie alone like this, is beyond me. But there we were, approaching Dumont Road, where we were stopped at a red light.

We watched with utter horror as our bus, with "Port Authority" above its windshield, went by us perpendicularly, sped by the empty bus stop off to our right, and continued on its way down the road.

"Dad, there goes the bus. What are we going to do? We'll never make the game."

He hesitated. "Don't worry, Austin. I'll catch up to it." My dad, who was the most law-abiding citizen I knew, made the choice. He knew that I couldn't take much more disappointment. Either we would take the 8 a.m. bus into the city and miss the beginning of the game, or he would have to run a red light to get in front of the bus.

Looking both ways, seeing no cars with red lights on the top, he took a chance, inching out onto the empty road, ignoring the red traffic light, speeding at 45 miles per hour, overtaking the black and tan bus. He pulled over into the next bus stop, and with the driver kindly acknowledged our desperate need to ride in his vehicle.

"Thanks, Dad! You are the greatest!"

"Thanks, Dr. Kutscher."

My dad was a hero to us, as much as the players on the field. I could tell that Paul was impressed that he was a law-breaker.

"Your dad is great. Mine would never have done that. You're lucky!" Peter shouted.

No one had ever said that about Dad. I was proud of him that day—he who was willing to take a risk, willing to take a risk for me. And my stock would go up in school, although only a little bit, as Peter wasn't too high up on the social ladder either.

We made it to Baltimore, but as we had no idea where to go, we just followed the crowds to Memorial Stadium. I was more excited for this game than I was with my Cousin Bruce, because the Orioles were my team. Later, I thought that maybe I should have reciprocated by asking Bruce. But for now, I wanted a friend, someone who would remember this next week in school. Pete and I celebrated together as my Orioles won their third game in a row, on their way to a sweep of the Dodgers.

On the way back, I reflected on my father. Little did I know that he was in love, that Lil had instilled a sense of adventure in him, and that instead of spending the whole weekend working, he would be on his way up to Scarsdale later that afternoon. Peter and I returned late that night, met at the bus stop by his parents.

It was the best of days in the worst of times.

On Halloween, we got the trick (or treat) of our lifetime. Marty and I were watching the television in my still-single parent's room, as Charlie Brown and Linus waited for the arrival of "The Great Pumpkin."

"Hope," I whispered as she lay on her back getting her belly rubbed, "Just watch how Snoopy gets whatever he wants."

We heard Dad's car arrive at around 9:30, and a few minutes later he came up to his room. We all jumped onto his bed to give him a kiss goodnight. My new-found hero sat us down.

"How was your date?" Harlan asked, strange words for a son to ask a father.

"Boys, I'd like you to meet Lil and her children on Saturday." He had asked us several weeks before, his words less fraught with fear than you might expect, as this was the third set of women and their children we had met over the past three months.

But tonight he asked, "Boys, do you like Lil?"

"Yes, Dad, she's nice."

"How about her kids?"

Cathy was my age. I'd never had a sister, so I didn't know what to expect. I wasn't exactly Cary Grant incarnate, but Harlan seemed a bit intrigued.

Paul, a year older, was a jock, if not a scholar. But he had friends, he played soccer and tennis, and he had everything he wanted (except for his C's in school). He didn't seem to pay much attention to us.

Michael, a freshman in college, was more threatened by my dad for his role as the man of the house, since his father had died five years earlier. Richard was a fifth-grader. His Beatle's haircut and wondrous laugh made him the life of any party, the ultimate clown who was used to attention and getting away with his antics.

"They're okay, Dad," I answered. "A bit stuck up, but maybe Paul will teach me tennis."

"I don't think they really liked us, Dad," Harlan added. "It's hard to talk with them. They all have so many friends."

"I like her, Dad, and Richie's funny," Marty chimed in.

"Well, I hope you'll all get along, because Lil and I are going to get married."

"No, Dad, No!"

"Where are they going to live in our house, Dad? There's no room for them here."

Dad hesitated, "We are going to move to Scarsdale. They have a big house and Lil doesn't want to move them."

"I'm not going. It's my senior year in high school, Dad. I'm staying here." Harlan was emphatic.

"Don't worry, Harlan," I rejoined, "You won't miss all of your imaginary girlfriends here. You'll be graduating in seven months. There's still plenty of time."

"Boys, we're getting married next month, on Thanksgiving."

Hope jumped into my lap, excited by all of the noise. I felt my pants grow wet, as she couldn't help herself. But I was too numb to scream at her. Then there was silence, broken only by the sound of her soft, pink tongue licking my face, the salt in my tears nectar to her palate. Harlan ran out of the room, and Marty climbed onto my dad's lap and held him tight.

Three weeks later, we were standing in the living room of our new house in Scarsdale, as we watched my dad and Lil join the families. Dad wore a dark suit, white shirt, and blue tie. For once, his tie tack did not hold pieces of paper with notes written on them. His shirt pocket was bereft of the pen and pencil protector. Absent from his pants were his pocket notebooks filled with the transcribed, cryptic notes. Lil, on the other hand, was a magnificent bride, dressed in a lavender dress with a white corsage.

We were all duded up, in our new suits, looking like an ad for Sears. Richie was jumping up and down, his pants a bit too short, his white socks showing, his tie a-kilter, excited that he was going to have a father. He had little memory of his own dad. Michael, the elder statesman of the step-family, stood near Harlan, who was already surveying Cathy's friends as potential prospects. Paul wasn't talking to anyone, his hair still short, jock length, with one inch sideburns, standing solemnly off to the side, wanting to be anywhere but here. Cathy, well-matured for her age, bursting out of her tight dress, was chatting incessantly with her pals, the gum cracking in their mouths, plotting on how they were going to get away for a smoke.

Marty and I just stood together. We didn't have much to say to Grandma Josephine Kutscher, her white hair freshly coiffed, her dark blue dress dignified but simple. And she said nothing about Mom, or about how difficult today must be for her three grandsons.

"Grandma," I asked politely, having been prompted in advance by Dad,

"Let me walk you to this chair. We saved it especially for you."

"Thank you, Austin," she said, in her Texas/New York accent.

As I helped her into the chair, she whispered, "Be sure to behave. Don't embarrass your father." If only Hope had listened—as she jumped right into grandma's lap, spilling her double scotch on her dress. I could imagine the lecture I'd get later in the day.

Unbeknownst to us, our weekly Sunday afternoon family visits with her would be forever changed. My mother seemingly had to apologize for her upbringing and the upbringing of her three children—our whole crew of four meant to serve my grandmother's honored son. My grandmother was proud that her son was remarrying so well, up to what she had always wanted for him, what with Lil being a Smith College graduate and a great friend of my grandmother's late husband's law partner. But best of all, she was a lover of Dewar's scotch, as opposed to my tee-totaling Mom and Dad. My poor Dad, torn between the woman he truly adored and his faithfulness and loyalty to his mother.

Grandpa Leon stood off to the side, his gray hair slicked back, drinking his third cup of coffee. He had already gone out for a walk around the block by himself. I doubt that he had talked to Josephine since the day their kids got married in 1945; and it didn't appear that today would be any different, especially as his stature in our family would now be dependent on my father's good graces toward him. (That, as the future played out, would be a loving relationship towards him, from both my dad *and* Lil, who treated him with kindness as a step-father.) He wore his typical vest-sweater, under a dark brown sports jacket, fresh with the smell of mothballs. Lord knows what he was thinking, having just buried his youngest daughter ten months previously.

Neither my Aunt Julie nor my dad's brother Bob was there. Gail and Bruce and their three sons were there. But none of my friends from Tenafly were there. And Hope and the Steinberg dogs were outside in their own respective cars, as yet not integrated.

I listened to the "I do's," realizing that there would be a lot of "don'ts" upcoming for me, and then spent the rest of the afternoon hanging around with Cathy and her friends, hoping that knowing them would help make my first day in school on Monday less devastating. I had the prospect for a new life, without the mistakes of my past or the prejudices of the jock clique in Tenafly.

We ate a beautifully catered spread of chopped liver, smoked salmon, turkey, roast beef, and a scrumptious wedding cake. There was a champagne toast, with cider for us young ones. The only thing missing for my dad from this party was Chinese food; the only thing missing for me from this party was my mom. I went to bed that night, and it was almost the same as before: Marty in the bed next to me, and Hope and the stuffed canines lying side by side under the comforter. But when I woke up the next morning, I knew it wasn't a dream.

We settled in as a family over the next weeks and months. Harlan kept his word and lived with friends and family and finished his senior year in Tenafly. Marty and I went to school with our new step-sibs. And my dad, after being on his best behavior for the first few months—getting home in time for dinner, leaving his work down in his basement office—soon reverted to his old habits.

My father has always been like a chameleon, able to fit into whatever household he came into, able to forget his past, his history, and to live for the future. But at the same time, he would shape his new environment with his work, with files full of manuscripts and correspondence which would metastasize from his office downstairs to the upstairs study.

Finally, he would make the bedroom his private office, his bed his private desk, and Lil his private editor. If he had started today, he could have been the ultimate space traveler, transported through space, unencumbered, with only his 512 megabytes of memory, all devoted to his work, taking up only the space of a laptop computer. But in those days, a computer wouldn't fit into any of the rooms of our house, and thus his work filled three times that amount of space. Only his Chinese sepulcher on the wall remained as a remembrance of his time with my mom. But he had nothing to remind him of his childhood—at least not until 25 years later, when we game him a signed Mel Ott baseball.

His dental research was rapidly replaced by his new obsession of "thanatology," the study of death and dying. Having found no help in resolving his own grief, he was determined to bury those feelings by soliciting papers and performing surveys that could be used as standard references for future generations who suffered from loss. He was honoring my mom and Lil's husband with his work. The rest of his academic life, and in many ways, his entire life, was dedicated to making thanatology a legitimate academic and health-related subject. (The only "competition" for his interest in thanatology was the Chinese cookbook he had started to write with my mom and the Changs.) And as his story has played out, including the frustrations of his journey, his efforts have been second to none, Don Quixote and Miguel Cervantes included. The windmills were never defeated, although they were, at times, controlled; his faithful sidekick, Lil "Sanchez," forever at his side. His son were his "donkeys," his supply team, at his beck and calling on weekends and evenings, loving their master, while at the same time feeling suffocated. This labor of love, in memory of my mom and in honor of my dad, had a chokehold over the entire Kutscher family.

As his obsession with the study of death became deeper and he drew me more tightly into his web, I grew resentful of the fact that I had learned to type two summers ago, that I had now replaced my mom as his emergency transcriber. I longed to escape, to lope like a man on the surface of the Moon at one-sixth the gravitational forces.

Or would I end up as we feared for our astronauts when they walked outside their capsule? They could soar off into space if their tows became disconnected, no longer held by any gravitational forces—just as members of my generation were getting high and free-floating through their existence on LSD and other drugs.

Wishful thinking was my immediate escape. I was more part of a traditional family, and I couldn't leave. And, therefore, the real question was whether the pressure exerted on me would leave me like the freeze-dried coffee which went up into space with the astronauts—able to be reconstituted to a state of culinary delight with the re-addition of water. - Or, scarier, would I be like the Hershey's chocolate-covered vanilla ice cream bar that I left out overnight in the kitchen sink—melted in its wrapper, with just some gummy chocolate syrup surrounding a little, white, thickened liquid, all of its "puffed-up with air" structure now lost in space, no way ever to be reconstituted into anything of any interest to the palate?

A ROSE BY ANY COLOR WOULD STILL SMELL THE *SAME*

Mike, Paul, Cathy, Richie: All-American names, nothing to make the Steinberg kids stand out in a crowd. Harlan, Austin, Martin: Distinguished names for professors or attorneys, but not for fitting in at high school. As I began my new life in Scarsdale, I wanted to leave behind my sense of difference that my parents had so tried to instill in us. In the '60s, the teen years were not about being unique, unless you were James Dean. What more radical move was there then to change my name? I have been told in my adult years what a distinguished name "Austin" is. I didn't want "distinguished;" I wanted to "popular." People have asked where I got the name Ken. Most have assumed it was my middle name. Well, there's not much to choose from when your name is Austin Harrison Kutscher, Jr. I could have chosen any name in *The Book of Names*, but there was no association with the name Ken that I can remember, no baseball star, movie star, or even friend in Tenafly. It just seemed like a name that no one would make fun of.

I was finally able to get a pair of penny loafers and to wear clothes that didn't look like they were hand-me-downs or belonged to the "Beaver." The "Beave"—can you imagine going through childhood with a cowlick and a name like that? Or worse, to have a brother with a friend like Eddie Haskel? Of course, I had Harlan, who was just as skinny and condescending to his "inferiors" as Eddie, although at least he could show some kindness.

In the beginning, I hung around with Cathy and her friends. If entering school in Tenafly in fifth grade was tough, it wasn't much easier in the middle of tenth grade in Scarsdale. The only saving grace was that the school was big enough, and the athletic program only average, so there was no one group that would be considered "in." As with everyone at Scarsdale High School, I was on the outside of most groups, although unfortunately, I wasn't on the inside of any group.

Having no friends, it was easy for my dad to expect me to do my homework and then help him with his thanatology foundation work. I was an excellent typist, having learned under the tutelage of my mom, and I quickly became his "go-to guy" for small typing jobs he needed in a hurry, which couldn't wait for his regular typist, who had a several day turnaround. My resentment started to build when it became obvious that the Steinberg kids could do as they pleased on Friday nights and weekends, but that I had to be available for my dad. Especially when his featured speaker at the next symposium was Elizabeth Kubler-Ross, who had described the five stages of death and dying. We were, after all, working in memory of my mom, and what shame I felt at any attempts to "shirk" my duty.

Only a date with a girl could potentially allow me to abrogate my responsibility. Intramural basketball or softball was a non-excuse. That did not give me much of a chance to build a social life among my peers, even with my new name. Cathy's friends were into either partying or dogs, and Paul's friends were into sports.

There I was again, in with the smarter, less physically adept kids, playing on second-rate intramural teams, when I was even allowed to play at all. I joined the math team, worked in the school store, and in my one attempt at sports, didn't make the JV baseball team. Two years of not playing organized ball, along with my borderline ability, did me in. I spent my afternoons with my homework and my *Playboys*. One afternoon, I was fantasizing about one of Cathy's friends, a delectable girl named Kris, who had slept over in her PJs the week before. I heard light steps coming up to the attic. I furtively started to get dressed and hide my contraband, fearing and hoping that Kris was coming to join me. As I closed my eyes, she hopped into bed with me, with no clothes on to come between us. Then I opened my eyes—as Hope licked me on the cheek, her black nose wet against mine. I laughed to myself, "Hey, at least it wasn't our maid, Willie, coming up with the clean laundry!"

April, 1967

Several weeks after Harlan was accepted by Columbia University, Reverend Martin Luther King spoke at the Riverside Church, only five blocks away from the austere educational institution. He told his audience that the Vietnam War was not only immoral but that it also drained U.S. resources from rebuilding our cities and funding domestic programs. He added that the percentage of black casualties far exceeded their percentage in the U.S. population, a statistic that would later prove to be as incorrect as it was inflammatory.

This speech was a keynote to the anti-war demonstration to be held in Central Park. Harlan asked my dad if he could go to the event. "Don't worry Dad. Remember, I'm going to college in New York in four months."

Later, my brother let me in on the secret. He hadn't gotten permission, but as he was still at high school in Tenafly, what our dad didn't know wouldn't hurt him. As our personal history would so often be repeated, Harlan was able to take a "detour" to New York City and be a part of the "Movement" several years before I was. He went as a passive participant among the 300,000 protestors—students, academicians, laborers, and radicals of all types. LBJ couldn't help but notice.

I was still 15 and living at home, too young to sneak out, too afraid to speak out, and too valuable to my dad's work at home. I was not yet emancipated. Instead, I read about the demonstration in the papers the next day.

June 1967

A week before, for my 16th birthday, we went to see the Mets play a doubleheader against the Chicago Cubs. It was probably our last family affair, with all of my brothers and step-brothers and Dad and Lil, but *sans* step-sis, who announced the day before, "I have a date with George. I'm not coming unless he can come also." To that Lil responded, "This is Ken's birthday celebration. There's no extra ticket. To that Cathy stormed out. "I'm not going. I have to study."

Of course, I heard her later on the phone with Kris. "You mean you went to 'third base' with Bruce?" Boy, here I was, "sweet 16" and I'd barely rounded "first base" with my dates. And Cathy told us she wasn't into baseball!

My dad, however, brought his work for the 25-minute intermission between games. Never one to waste time, he was known to do his work while sitting on the throne. So it was no surprise that he was prepared for a shutout against his team.

It wasn't a good day for the Mets. They brought in their long reliever in the fourth inning. But what a birthday present it was for me.

"Now pitching for the New York Mets, #33, Chuck Estrada, #33." He had on the Mets' pinstripe uniform with the New York skyline logo on the sleeve. His blue hat had an orange "NY" on it. It seemed strange that my hero—whom I followed since his rookie year as a Baltimore Oriole and had only seen on baseball cards in his Orioles uniform with the smiling bird on the sleeve, his boyish face darkened by his 5 o'clock shadow, just like my dad's—was now pitching. But now, he had fallen upon sore times. His rotator cuff was destroyed by the physiology of arm strain from throwing a ball at 90 miles per hour. As medical science had still not discovered the miracle of arthroscopic surgery, he had bounced around the major leagues. He was in the dusk of his short career, a has-been at age 28, sharing the clubhouse with a rookie at the dawn of his Hall of Fame career, Tom Seaver. But today, for one last time, Chuck pitched like the star he once was. And there I was in the Loge section, imagining what it was like to be a major league pitcher. I have the program, the newspaper printout, and the hope that Thomas Wolfe was wrong—that we "can go home again." I wanted to be ten years old again, to be back with my family, watching the young sensation, Chuck Estrada, pitch. But it was the wrong stadium, the wrong uniform, and someone was missing.

Now, a week later, the glow of that day had worn off. I was now 16—I had just gotten my learner's driving permit. Except there was no one at home willing to go out on the road with me to practice my u-turns and parallel parking.

Which was just as well as I really needed to concentrate on the upcoming New York State Regents exams. I wasn't worried about math, where I had a 99 average in the days when there wasn't extra credit to help pull our grades up. But French was a different story. I couldn't "think" in another language, and had to translate everything back into English before I could spit it out in French again. That's not to say that I didn't enjoy French class, what with Nancy Perkins, who sat across the room from me. She had discovered that perhaps the best way to get back at her parents was to wear the shortest mini-skirts that were manufactured. I guess you might wonder whether I would have done better in this class if I had paid more attention (to the teacher, I mean), but I can prove you wrong. Even at Columbia College, three years later, with an all-male class, I still couldn't think in French!

Marty was being particularly irritating this afternoon, working on his project for sixth grade science, a mock-up of the Apollo spacecraft. His friend Brian had come over to our house to work with him, and there was no peace to be had.

"Marty, couldn't you go downstairs and do this?"

"No, Ken. This is just as much my room as yours. And besides, all of the dogs are bothering us downstairs. Misty keeps coming over and knocking over the spacecraft. I'm afraid if we get up, he'll start chewing on it."

"Well, just make sure you don't go through my things. If I catch you, I'll tell Dad."

"Don't worry, we've got our comics to read if we get bored. Your *Sporting News* is so boring. The only thing it's good for is as paper for Hope to use."

"Come on, Hope. Let's leave these jerks alone. I'm sorry, Brian, I really only meant Marty. Just make sure you don't spill your milk."

As I left, I added, "Hope licked your milk while you guys weren't watching."

"I'm going to tell all of your friends your real name is Austin"

"Yeah, and your middle name is Lyle, for "Liar," I bet."

I didn't wait for a response as I went into Harlan's room with my books. Besides, it was a good excuse to use his new stereo, which was far superior to ours, to listen to the new Beatle's album, "Sergeant Pepper's Lonely Hearts Club Band." I certainly could relate, my heart being lonely at the time. As I listened to the album, through the upbeat songs to the inane "Lovely Rita," I found myself paying more attention to the music than my algebra. The interspersed drum beats were so compelling. The guitar music was unlike anything I had heard—synthesized, amplified, reconstructed; new techniques unknown to the music community. It was a true kaleidoscope of music.

I gave up studying the math and stared at the album cover. The Beatles were posed in military dress uniforms, mustached, looking somewhat sinister next to wax models of themselves in their classic black suits, with their clean shaven faces and haircuts looking like a bowl had been placed over their heads. A collage of peoples' faces formed a halo around them. I searched for familiar faces. W.C. Fields was the first to catch my attention. I had been watching his old movies on late night television, along with Mae West's "My Little Chickadee." What an evil man he was, his dislike for dogs only outweighed by his hatred for children. I waited up for Mae's line to Cary Grant, "Why don't you come up to see me sometime?" wondering if she had really ever said, "Is that a pickle in your pocket, or are you just glad to see me?" I knew W.C. probably drank himself to death and finally landed face side "up" for the first time when he was buried. His gravestone was satirical to the end, maligning his least favorite city: "All things considered, I'd rather be in Philadelphia." What was such a man doing on this album? And there was Sonny Liston, off to the side. Why not Cassius Clay, a much more colorful man, and a non-violent soldier at that? Laurel and Hardy, Tony Curtis, Karl Marx.

I stared around Harlan's room. Even though we had lived there as a step-family for eight months, Harlan had never become part of us. His room reflected emptiness, as he was staying in Tenafly with friends and family to finish high school with his class of '67. Life in this room was non-existent.

The Beatle's music gave it life. But, then again, as fantastic as their music was, their lyrics were somewhat mundane, talking about everyday life in Britain, with a frequent reference to getting high or leaving home. There didn't seem to be any real revolutionary ideas. It was more like James Dean's "A Rebel Without a Cause."

The last song came on, "A Day in the Life." The lyrics didn't seem to make sense to me, being in some way a non-sequitor.

"I read the news today oh boy
About a lucky man who made the grade
And though the news was rather sad
Well I just had to laugh
I saw the photograph
He blew his mind out in a car
He didn't notice that the lights have changed."

How sad this was, to have ended a life over such a stupid mistake — obviously a metaphor that I was missing.

The music was very uncomplicated, the guitar and drums playing a simple cadence against each other.

"The English Army had just won the war."

What a joke. We'd beaten them in the American Revolution and the War of 1812. And we were just studying about World War II. Boy, did the Allies need our help. It was only the American presence that had saved the day. (Although at least the Brits fought their hearts out—they weren't as pathetic as the French! Just look at what happened in the movie "Casablanca." And in Vietnam at Dien Bien Phu).

"But I just had to look
Having read the book
I'd love to turn you on."

On to what? Grass, marijuana, LSD, Lucy in the Sky with Diamonds?

Just as the music rose to a cacophonous roar, the orchestra playing almost atonal melodies, it was shattered by the alarm clock ringing.

"Woke up, fell out of bed,
Dragged a comb across my head
Found my way downstairs and drank a cup."

Sounds like a normal morning in my house. Although we were still an OJ family, Paul and Cathy couldn't wait to get out of the house for their early morning drag, *sans* their cup of coffee.

And then the inanity about how many holes there were in Albert Hall. What were they singing about? But the orchestral crescendo was overwhelming, culminating in that prolonged final chord that just drifted away into infinity. It wasn't clear when it ended and when all I was hearing was the underlying residual from the spinning plastic disc, noise in a vacuum of music. It was like a prolonged orgasm that just sputtered out at the end, leaving me drained.

But lest you forget, the album didn't end there. Ten seconds of gibberish by the foursome brought me back to the world of unreality.

The afternoon I listened to that record, lying on my brother's bed, with the blue bedspread tucked in so neatly by Willie after the last time Harlan had left to return to Tenafly. It was my freedom from my brothers and from my father, at least for an afternoon. This was music my dad would never understand—alien, almost sinister in nature to him.

And then from downstairs I heard, "Ken, what the hell are you playing upstairs? Turn that garbage off."

I guess he heard it after all.

"It's my new Beatles' album," I yelled, plaintively. "I'll turn it down."

"If you've got time to listen to that trash, get down here. I've got some work for you."

As I came down the stairs, I sauntered into his room. "Dad, I haven't finished studying for my finals. These are my first Regents exams. I don't know what to expect."

"Just a few letters, they are important. I need to contact the keynote speakers as soon as possible."

"If I fail, and I don't get into Columbia, it will be your entire fault," I countered.

"Don't you know that this work will help get you recommendations from the faculty I am working with at Columbia?

"I'm sure Columbia is looking for expert typists, Dad." And I muttered to myself, as I left with the letters, "For their secretarial pool."

And so, "It was just another day" . . . at the Kutscher mansion.

June 5, 1967

If December 7, 1941, will live as a day of infamy in United States history, then this date will live as the date that Israel showed that it wasn't going to be kicked around by the Arab nations and the Palestinians.

The Egyptians had closed the Straits of Tiran, which meant that ships could not leave Israel from Eilat. Israel's pre-emptive strike was led by Yitzhak Rabin, Moshe Dayan, and Ariel Sharon. With only 50,000 troops ready to do battle, they had inflicted casualties numbering 21,000 on Egypt, Syria, and Jordan, while losing only 679 soldiers. But most impressively, Israel captured the Gaza Strip and Sinai from Egypt, the West Bank and East Jerusalem from Jordan, and the Golan Heights from Syria—along with adopting a million Arabs and Palestinians who clearly had no interest in being under Israeli rule.

There was a "call to arms" at our temple, aka "monetary pledges," as the rabbi stood in front of the congregation and asked for support for Israel. Unlike for the war going on in Vietnam, which was beginning to be an albatross around our neck and for which many of my parents' friends had already developed a distaste, the contributions for the Israeli war flowed: a thousand dollars pledged here, a hundred dollars over in the next row, and ten dollars from my weekly secretarial earnings.

A tenuous ceasefire would remain until the 1973 Yom Kippur War, but at least the United Nations decreed with Resolution 242 the right of every state in the region to "live in peace within secure and recognized boundaries free from threats or acts of force." It also called for Israel to withdraw from the occupied regions in return for an end to belligerency.

Forty years later, Egypt and Jordan have made "peace" with Israel and have much of their land back. The Palestinian issue, however, just doesn't seem to go away. And our dependence on Arab oil, due to our inability to curb fossil fuel consumption (and the resultant global warming,) along with the emancipation of Iraq from Saddam Hussein's tyranny and "non-weapons of mass destruction" have replaced Southeast Asia as the breeding ground for world nuclear or chemical conflagration and as the bleeding ground for our U.S. soldiers.

June 17, 1967

It wasn't a rooster—it was Mary's clock radio awakening her from her reverie.

"*Good morning, good morning.*"

The Beatles again; that's all they were playing now.

"It's the last day of school. Thank the lord. I can't wait to get out of that stinking hell hole," Mary thought to herself. "Please, please let Bill be off to work this morning. I know I can't face 'His Ugliness' today."

Mary knew all of the kids were going to dress "groovy" today, on the last day of school. There was no way they could be expelled on the final day. She just had to figure out a way to sneak past her mom. She went to her closet and pulled out her tightest jeans, the old ones that fit last year, but that now showed off her figure to its fullest. They were already worn at the hem, and had a beautifully faded look, with a PEACE patch over a hole in left back pocket.

"Where is that pink top I like so much?" she asked Spider. "I've got to look cool today in case I bump into Mike before school ends."

Mary stepped into her pink bikini underpants, hooked her new white bra, and danced into her jeans. Her long, brown hair fell lazily down below her shoulders, and she spent the next five minutes carefully combing it out. Her paisley belt completed her outfit, all except for her leather thong sandals that she had left at the bottom of the stairs.

Bill growled as she wandered down into the kitchen. "You're not going anywhere like that. You look like one of those girls who frequent the bars up in Norfolk. Is that what you learned from your grandfather?"

"If you mean I'm dressed like a hooker, why don't you just come out and say it?" Mary retorted. "I'm so tired of having to hear your complaints every morning."

"Please, do we have to go through this every morning?" Mary's mom spoke resignedly. "It's like a broken record!"

"Ellen, if you'd brought up your daughter the way you should've, she'd have more respect for us," Bill lectured.

"Please, just let me be." Mary was already out the door, getting into her blue Corvair. She turned the engine on, flipped on the radio, pressed the button for reverse, and backed out of the driveway in America's most dangerous car.

"*Wednesday morning at five o'clock as the day begins.*"

"Don't they play anything on the radio except the Beatles anymore?" Mary thought, and then she listened.

"*Quietly turning the back door key*
Stepping outside she is free.
She's leaving home."

"It'll be my time soon," Mary thought. "One more year of high school, and then I'm out of here."

"*Father snores as his wife gets into her dressing gown*
Picks up the letter that's lying there."
"*Daddy our baby's gone.*"
"*How could she do this to me?*"
"*We never thought of ourselves*"
"*We struggled hard all our lives to get by.*"

Mary snorted, "No way this is real. Who wrote this crap? Do you think my mother and Bill would really care if I left? Yeah, they struggled, struggled to get rid of me."

As she pulled into the high school parking lot, she spied Martha Jane talking to Mike. She pulled into the nearest space, and pulled a Salem out of her pocketbook. She lifted herself out of the car, appearing to carelessly bend over to pick up her notebook that had fallen out of the Corvair, hoping Mike would glance over. She thought she saw him peek and then quickly glance away. Making the most of the situation, she walked over to Martha and Mike and asked, "Anyone got a light? I gotta get a smoke before I get my final grades."

"Only if you share."

"Sorry, it's my last one," she lied. Martha Jane was always grubbing cigarettes off of her, and at 20 cents a pack, that was expensive. "But I'll let you have a puff."

"Mary, Mary, quite contrary, I'd like to see your garden grow."

"Stop it, Mike. You're being gross. Do you have a light?"

"Sure." And as he flicked his Bic lighter up towards Mary's cigarette, he "inadvertently" brushed her right breast.

"Thanks, Mike." Mary ignored his gesture, but didn't move away. His hands appeared rough, like the other boys who worked on their families' farms during the spring. But she knew he lived in the trailer complex outside of town with his mother and step-father, who ran a junkyard. She imagined at least that his tongue would be smooth and sensuous.

"See you girls after class? A bunch of us are going out to my place after school to get wasted."

"I don't know," Martha Jane snorted. "We've gotten much better offers."

"Yeah, we were planning to cruise the Cape," Mary added.

"B.S. A pack of Lucky's says you're with us."

It was a short day, with 15 minute classes, report cards being handed out, books turned in, yearbooks signed. "Let it all hang out." "Peace, not war." "Baby, let's do it this summer." Mary couldn't bring herself to writing anything other than, "It's been fun, Mary M." Nothing memorable, nothing lost.

As she and Martha Jane sauntered over to her car at 11 a.m., now full-fledged seniors, she had just about forgotten about Mike. There he went, with Jimmy D. and two girls she barely knew, climbing into his '56 blue and cream- colored Chevy convertible. The door on the passenger side was so badly dented and rusted that it wouldn't open, which forced them to spill over into the rear seats head first, with their butts unceremoniously popping up.

Mike spied Mary staring over at them. "You're still invited. Mickey and Davey will be there soon. Just follow us."

"Will Peter be there?" Martha Jane winked.

"Yeah, then you can really act like the Monkees you four apes are." Mary laughed.

"Mary, they're just daydream believers if they think they're gonna get anything from me."

"Fuck you both," Mike screamed.

"MJ, it's going to be a long, hot summer. I'm already bored. It's time to act like seniors."

"What the hell, Mike. We don't have anything better to do. Mary, let's just stop by and tell my parents, and then we can stop by your house."

"No need, Ellen and Bill don't give a damn where I am. Let's just go."

"Suit yourself, it's your life."

By 8 p.m. the party was smoking. Mike had been hanging out with "Susie," the blonde with the butt. But now he came over to Mary, who was listening to the music near the stereo, smoking her last cigarette, drinking her third "Buzzweiser." Her head was already spinning, when she heard:

"Let's get out of here. It's much quieter in back of the trailer."

"Mike, I'm out of smokes."

"Don't bother, Mary. I've got my own, rolled right here in the Cape. You don't know what you've been missing."

The next album fell onto the turntable.

"Light my fire" started as they walked out the door.

Man, that's all I've been hearing all day on the radio."

"Would you rather hear the Rolling 'Stoned'?" Mike laughed as he grabbed Mary, pulling her by the arm outside, as the radio from inside the trailer blared out "Satisfaction," followed by Paul and George singing "A Little Help from My Friends."

THE SUMMER OF 1967

It was my first summer in Scarsdale, and Paul, Cathy, Marty and Richie are at sleep-away camp. No friends of mine are around. Harlan and Mike Steinberg are in New York City with my dad every day, working on research projects to help them get into medical school. I was stuck at home every day, tabulating a survey he had sent out regarding grief and bereavement.

The high point of my summer was Hope giving birth to four beautiful puppies. She was a natural mother, doing all of the work herself, with only a minimum of help from all of the "pre-meds" in the house. I set up a cot so I could stay down in the basement with Hope and her puppies, watching as breastfed them, making sure that each puppy got its equal share. And at night, when they were tired, and she was tired, she would climb back up on the cot with me to help us regenerate our strength. She cried when the breeder came to take a puppy, and she cried when Cousin Bruce and his family came to pick up another puppy. Hope was unaware that at least this one would stay in our extended family. And she started showing the ropes to the one puppy we kept—a pretty, black male my father named Ping Pong, Chinese for "united."

Harlan had also volunteered to teach me how to drive. As any 16-year-old male, I was both overly confident and scared shitless as I began to "solo," attempting to maneuver through traffic. It had always looked so easy ten years earlier, when my mom and dad got me a plastic steering wheel and console to hook over the back of their front seat in the '57 Chevrolet station wagon. It had a red horn in the middle, which I was forbidden to beep after I had scared my dad half to death one balmy Sunday morning on the way to the diner. The console even had directional signals. How I loved to mimic my dad, patiently waiting for the day when I could assume the captain's seat. Oh, would I be able to rule the roads—a regular Parnelli Jones.

As a sophomore, I had advanced to the simulators in "driver's ed," a step up from Mattel. We weren't on the road, but we had real steering wheels, brakes, gas pedals, and speedometers, along with a moving image of the road ahead. I felt like I was watching Cary Grant talking to one of his heroines in the back seat of a car in the old black-and-white films of the 1940s, with the car bumping along, in one place, and the backdrop showing the change of scenery.

"Boys and Girls, do not let me see that speedometer go over 40 miles per hour!" Mr. Buckminster was emphatic in his role as driving instructor.

"So this is what happens to shop teachers who want to move up in the educational system," I thought to myself. "They get reincarnated to teach us the skills of navigation." Only instead of "You've wrecked your job," as Mr. Birch would say, now we heard, "You've wrecked your car."

"If I catch anyone speeding, they'll be excused from class today and get detention," he bellowed.

That sounded bad—after school for speeding. How would I explain that to Lil? I didn't even have my driver's permit yet.

"But we're not going anywhere, Mr. B." Billy Clawson cried. "How can we get a ticket for speeding?"

"You're right, young man. And after school today, you're not going anywhere either!"

Whoa, the next thing would be suspension. That would be a first. But I wanted my license and it didn't seem worth it to challenge his authority.

After all, it was the spring of 1967 and we still respected our superiors.

Over that summer, Harlan actually spent hours teaching me to drive. He didn't spend much time that summer at our house, but somehow he got pleasure out of instructing me.

"Ken, be careful of that car on your right," he screamed. "Be careful! Beee careful!" as I heard the car doorknob scrape against our car, still the '57 Chevy, now with 100,000 miles on it.

I pulled over, got out, and sighed. It was only a small longitudinal scratch.

"I'm sorry, Harlan. I was afraid of hitting that oncoming car."

"Just don't be so frightened. You can't always drive so far to the right. You need to learn to drive with defensive confidence; being too defensive can be just as dangerous as driving overly aggressively."

He proved that to me that summer, when we took a road trip to Cooperstown, New York, my first visit to the Baseball Hall of Fame. We left at dawn in what was now "his" '57 Chevy, the windows wide open, forsaking the primitive air conditioning. As we headed north, we pulled over into the first service area of the New York Thruway for a quick "pit stop" and a sack full o' donuts and two cartons of milk for energy—a "Breakfast of Champions?"

"Ken, you drive."

My God. The sweat pored out beneath my underarms. No amount of Right Guard deodorant was going to protect me this morning.

"Harlan."

"Just do it!"

And so, first with trepidation, I went 50 miles per hour in the right hand lane, and was passed by an elderly couple in a Rambler sedan. Then I accelerated into the middle lane at 65 miles per hour. I was coached by my older brother on how to watch for unmarked police cars, how to find the perfect flow of traffic, and how to drag race with a pair of pretty co-eds (just kidding).

We spent four hours in the Hall, my Mecca, though hardly Harlan's. Whatever was the reason he went with me, I cannot remember, but it was an unselfish day on his part. We saw Babe Ruth's bat and locker, Joe DiMaggio's bat, and Lou Gehrig's uniform. Chuck Estrada and Rod Kanehl were there, if only as footnotes of history, in the box-scores of games such as Jim Bunning's perfect game.

As we left, I realized it had been a perfect day for me.

"Thanks, Harlan. Thank you so much." My day was complete.

We stopped at the ESSO gas station on the way out of town. A pimple- faced boy came over to the car, with ears wide apart, bright red hair, and a smile like Alfred E. Newman's that said "What, me worry?" He started filling our tank.

"Harlan, do you think we have enough money? It's 35 cents per gallon. We've got to go 180 miles at 15 miles per gallon with our station wagon. That's over four dollars!" I was beginning to sound like I was at a Math Team competition.

But he wasn't listening. Next to us were two girls in a pickup truck, probably straight off of the farms of Kansas.

Harlan, who was hardly a man of the world, smiled at them.

"You girls need some company?" is what he wanted to say.

"Do you know the way to the highway?" is what he said.

"Three blocks down, turn left and you'll be on Route 28."

"Thanks," Harlan grinned.

"Chicken," I muttered to him under my breath, as they drove away.

"So big shot, do you want to drive home? It's time to really earn your wings." I could hardly imagine what he had been sipping on. Or what fumes he had inhaled.

"Can I? The whole way?"

"At least until you scare me to death."

And off we went; back down Route 28 from Cooperstown towards Route 81, the superhighway. I was having fun, gaining confidence, ready to do 60. Until . . .

"Harlan, what do I do now?"

In front of us was an 18-wheeler going 40 miles per hour in a 55 zone. We were on a two-lane road, with traffic steadily coming up north towards Cooperstown. And we still had 16 miles to go before we reached Route 81.

"Just pass him." Harlan barely looked up, as if he were telling me to pass the butter at the dinner table. His computer magazine was much more interesting to him.

"When?"

"Stupid, when there's no traffic coming towards you." And he went back to his magazine. I could have understood his disinterest if it was a new *Playboy* he had sequestered. But computers . . . I needed his help now.

I tentatively pulled out towards the yellow-dotted line.

"Now?"

"Just make sure we're safe."

I checked and rechecked.

"Here I go!" and I put on my directional signal like the driving manual said, pulled out, took one more quick peek, and then put the "pedal to the metal." I sped up to 60 and passed the truck, then pulled smoothly back into our lane.

I felt like the rookie in the major leagues who hits his first home run. Harlan never looked up, never acknowledged my triumph—much like the "non-reception" reserved for the same rookie when he gets back to the dugout.

July 1967

No sooner did I get my driver's license than my dad began to use me as a courier to drive manuscripts and letters back to his old stable of typists in Tenafly, New Jersey. Whenever I wanted to become nostalgic or sad, I could drive by our old house. But, as Thomas Wolfe said, "You can't go home again." As I no longer went to the high school there, and I hadn't had a lot of friends to begin with, I never actually visited my old classmates.

But on July 12th riots broke out in Newark, as a black cab driver was arrested and beaten by the police—a familiar catalyst. The riots were fueled by segregation, both racial and economic, as the migration of middle class Jews and Italians to the suburbs exacerbated the eroding infrastructure and inequalities. I'd never been to Newark, and only had heard of it because Harlan had gone to the Stevens Institute of Technology for a weekly Saturday course in advanced mathematics. The riots were as remote to me as those in Watts and Detroit.

On the following weekend, a night after a fight broke out at a local diner in Plainfield, New Jersey, blacks began rioting and looting, throwing Molotov cocktails, until they were finally dispersed by the local police. The next day, rioting resumed, and a white police officer was killed after shooting a black youth. To make matters worse, an arms factory in a nearby town was broken into, with 46 military style carbines stolen and distributed to the black youth. As Governor Hughes proclaimed a state of emergency, the police searched homes without warrants, but were unsuccessful in their attempts to locate the weapons.

As opposed to my semi-interest in the Newark riots, what was happening in Plainfield had much more than a passing interest to me. This was a city that I knew. This was the city where I went to synagogue ten years earlier and where the rabbi had given me my gyroscope and miniature Torah one morning, when I was in tears, lonely without my parents, feeling abandoned—although they had of course come back for me. My gyroscope and Torah, which were to travel in my cigar box with me as we moved from home to home, had been there to assure me of my parents' love. They were my "Rosebud."

This was my youth being desecrated—the five books of the Bible in shreds. This was my innocence being fractured, my gyroscope beginning to quiver and shake, ready, as in my Skittle game, to cause some real damage.

DAYS OF MY JUNIOR YEAR 1967-1968

September

Grades, SATs, Achievement tests, colleges, letters of recommendation—all paramount for any student intent on going to an Ivy League University. The junior year, I'd been told, was the most important one—the grades the colleges looked at. I was determined to work hard, study regularly, be focused on my goals. And I succeeded in getting A's in math, English, history and chemistry, with French still a mystery as opposed to a romance language for me. Minute by minute, classes went by, teachers droned on, except for Mr. Rothschild in American History, who energized the students. No wonder he won "Teacher of the Year" for our class. But I was also part of a social structure, the academic part easier to deal with than the personal relationships I was attempting to establish with my peers. I struggled to become more than a scholar, to define myself as a mature teenager—an oxymoron if I ever heard one.

As Harlan went off to Columbia that fall, I inherited the '57 Chevy. Although I had to drive Cathy to school each day, by the afternoon I was on my own and could hang with any friends I might have had. I had a girl friend, one of Cathy's pals, and we went to the football games at Scarsdale High School. "Frankie" was, I guess, the unfortunately not a boy that her parents had hoped for—although she was ten pounds overweight with smallish breasts and a full waist. But we had fun dating and necking at parties, until I became enamored with Robin, one of the girls in my math class.

I was developing my own circle of friends, and in an ungentlemanly fashion, I gave up Frankie for Robin. I was on my own now, and drove by Robin's house every morning. I hoped to time it just right so that she would just be leaving to walk the one block to school, which would put me in a position to offer her a ride. This created the paradoxical situation, however, of the parking lot being farther away from the school entrance than where I had picked her up!

"Hi, Robin," as I passed her house. "Want a ride?"

"Sure."

We were sounding like an old married couple.

"Did you finish your English paper yet?"

Nothing like an original conversation to move this relationship along!

"No, I'll finish it this weekend."

Just when was I going to get the nerve to ask her out? Maybe today when we got out of the car.

"I know. I still have some research to do on mine. Are you busy Saturday afternoon? Maybe we can go to the library together?"

"That would be great. What time?"

My heart was palpitating. In a split second, I was imagining the Junior Prom, summer days at the beach, going to college together.

"How about 12 o'clock?" Should I be adventurous? Should I ask her if she wanted to go to lunch first?

Thankfully, I didn't have time to add the rest.

"Let's make it at 2. Alice and I have to go to Korvette's in the morning, and we'll be going to Friendly's for lunch. So we'll meet you at the library."

I guess I had gotten a little ahead of myself. But for now, I'd settle for a group study date. At least she didn't ask me to bring one of my friends.

We entered the hallowed halls of Scarsdale High School together.

"See you later, Ken."

"Okay, I hope we survive math today."

And then I was on my own for the rest of the morning, waiting for math class that afternoon, when I would see her again, sitting one seat up and one seat over, close enough to talk if things got boring.

It was difficult as I sat in the hallway after lunch, watching two seniors making-out in public across the hall. The girl's short, black dress rode up her thigh and her white panties gleamed at me, if I sat at a certain angle. Her boyfriend's body was pressed close to hers. His blue shirt was open at the collar and his package of Winston's was sticking out of his side pant's pocket. She wasn't particularly pretty, and her long, dark hair had split ends, but I'm sure he didn't care. I could only imagine what pleasures they were having over their weekend. They were probably "doing it." I remembered the "sex test" that we all took from Ann Lander's column, giving 1 point for first base (kissing), 2 points for second base (breast fondling), 3 points for third base (hand jobs) — and I forget how many points for a "home run." I don't think it even listed oral sex, or "sodomy" as some of the Southern states would define it, which was illegal even between married couples. I was sure those two seniors were way off the chart. And here I was, having barely gotten a "single" and rarely a "double" in the past—and now, with Robin, just a few practice swings in the on-deck circle.

But that afternoon, Robin was actually paying attention to Mr. Winters, who was reviewing the material from the last test. Math genius that I was, co-captain of the Math Team (aka "geek club"), I had gotten a 100 on the test, and was pretty bored. So I started playing with myself. I would roll my 6-inch cylindrical object, which functioned as a substitute bat. Only it was my yellow #2 pencil, with its six sides, each marked with a number that served as a self-made baseball game. Odd numbers were outs, "2" was a single, "4 "a double, "6" a triple, with a roll again, and another "6" making a home run. I had box scores, lineups; I could play a whole nine innings during a boring class. And the Mets became equals to the Orioles, because this was a statistically balanced game. Frank Robinson was no more powerful than Ed Kranepool. And the game could be delayed for rain (i.e., questions from the teacher) whenever necessary. I had my own baseball game that was much more simplistic than my dad's invention from his college days, which he had saved all these years in a box in the attic. And even more primitive than the "joy sticks" used in today's Xbox360 baseball game.

But I was distracted from my game. What I really wanted was to talk with Robin.

"Can I drive you home after school?"

"No thanks, I've got to talk with Miss Wilson. But I'll see you at the library on Saturday."

That was the best I was going to get today. It was enough to hold out hope for the future. Now, all I had to do was figure out how I could get out of the house on Saturday. My dad had another symposium coming up the following week. And he was expecting big things out of me this weekend. I could just imagine the last minute typing that he would need.

I remembered the day I had pleaded, "Dad, I've got an intramural basketball game on Saturday."

"I need you here. There is too much—we'll never get ready for the symposium."

"Another 'Festival of Death." I muttered to myself, my anger mixed with guilt.

"I have eight letters that need to be typed today. And you know Raymond Moody is speaking." He wrote about the "bright light at the end of the tunnel" that patients with near death experiences had described. Only, of course, he didn't describe what I wanted to hear—my mother's voice, back among the living, singing to us "Walk on, walk on, with hope in your heart, and you'll never walk alone, you'll never walk alone."

"Dad, I told you about the game last week. Paul has a game, and you're letting him go."

"Paul is different. He is a real athlete. It's his team, and he needs to be there."

"Yeah, Paul's different," I muttered to myself. "He's a Steinberg. You'd never tell him what to do."

I guess I was lucky Dad has a bad ear, because all he heard was "Steinberg." "What was that, Ken? You know all of this work will get you letters of recommendations."

That was his mantra. But, somehow or other, I didn't think typing letters was the attribute that made me an Ivy League candidate. I remembered back to eighth grade summer school, when my mom insisted that I learn to type (along with hormonal, sophomore girls who had failed the course during the school year). She helped me practice when I got home each day, with my mind more in fantasy about the older "women" in my class. After all, she had taught typing in the local New York City high schools while engaged to my dad. So I guess I practiced with the best. And for those born in the computer age, we didn't have word processors, we didn't have spell-check, we didn't even have electric typewriters in those days (we did, however, have running water.) Any error would have to be corrected individually, by hand, with an eraser or "correct-tape." A whole document could be ruined by a mistake and need to be retyped in its entirety, especially if you left out a letter and couldn't fit it in.

The stress level of "maeking" a "misteak" was "tremeendous," "expesially" if it was a final draft.

In the end, I had semi-replaced Mom in my dad's work life, although I was nowhere as good. In the new millennium, if I can type this manuscript at 60 words per minute, without worry regarding making any mistakes, I wonder what speed her magic fingers could have achieved.

But that weekend, I didn't want to be in Mom's typing chair. I needed to go to the library. Should I try, "I have to work on my English project"? That might work, but then Dad might say, "You can go later in the afternoon after I finish my work."

Knowing the inherent dangers of that tactic, I went back to the only one that ever worked.

"Dad, I need to go to the library on Saturday at noon!"

"I need you to type for me until 4."

"Dad, I'm meeting a girl there."

There, that was it. My dad—at least for the beginning of a relationship, either for himself or for his three sons—would allow that to take some precedence over work. As the relationship became more settled, he would expect the woman (his wife or my girlfriend) to understand the importance of his work, and become, at least for his wife, more like an old dog at his side while he worked. For now, my tactic would have to suffice.

"Why didn't you tell me? What's her name?"

That was the problem. He now had to know my business. And if Cathy overheard, the whole school would know.

"Robin."

"Do I know her?" Lil asked. Lil had lived with her kids in Scarsdale all of their childhood and she knew everyone.

"Robin Taylor."

"Of course, I played bridge with her mother last year. They're a very nice family. Bill, you need to let Ken go."

Lil was, if anything, overly fair to us. She treated us as equals to her kids, and we treated her with increasing love as the years went on. In later years, I routinely referred to her in conversation as "my mother," not needing to suggest that she treated us in any way like step-children. The only time I made a distinction was when someone would say at a party, "Gee, you don't look anything like Paul. Are you sure you are related?"

Thankfully, on this day, my dad listened to his new bride. They had been married less than a year, and he still wanted to please her whenever he could. "Ken, it should be okay for a few hours. But Lil, can you please type this one letter so we can get it out in today's mail?" He had a one-track mind when work was involved!

Over the next months, to say that Robin and I had a "thing" would be an overstatement. I was madly enthralled and she was lukewarm in her affections. We saw an occasional movie, and on her birthday I took her to see "Guess Who's Coming to Dinner," in which a white girl brings her black fiancé home to meet her parents. Liberal white Americans could watch the film and proclaim the end of their society's intolerance towards blacks. That the black man happened to be played by Sidney Poitier, the most trusted name in "Negro" film history, made it easy for the movie to be praised. (And it was a great reprise for Mr. Poitier, coming on the heels of his performance in "To Sir, with Love," where as a black teacher in a white London high school, he again broke the social and educational color barrier.)

It shouldn't surprise the reader that my dates with Robin were irregular, that even my "birthday" kiss ended up only being an "infield single," although we still continued to be the best of friends in school. Each night I watched my television, (I was especially enamored by "Gadget," with Sally Fields—now that was a girl to have a crush on!), I would promise myself that, after it was over, I would call up Robin. Eight-thirty would come, and I'd turn on the "Smothers Brothers Comedy Hour" and give myself whatever excuse it was to wait another half hour. And then, it would be 10:00, clearly too late to call her. So it would have to wait until tomorrow night, when "Laugh In," followed by "I Spy," repeated the procession. Again, I was saved from the potential embarrassment of rejection for another day, but remained in my celibacy, curling up at night with Hope and Johnny Carson, praying that my sheets would remain dry through the night.

What's a lonely teen age boy to do on those long Saturday nights? I turned to Jay Reisberg to be my regular weekend companion. Jay lived differently than the other kids in Scarsdale. His mother was an industry nurse, his dad an assistant manager and tailor at the local dry cleaners. They lived in an apartment over one of the stores in downtown Scarsdale. The Reisbergs had sacrificed for their two sons by living in a railroad flat, but their Scarsdale address provided their kids with a Class-An education. Our favorite Saturday night entertainment was *RISK* tournaments. *RISK* was the greatest war game ever developed, with dice as ammunition and plastic pieces as armies. No real soldier ever got killed as acts of bravery or cowardliness were enacted. Treaties were made between players, only to be broken as easily as our government did with our Native Americans.

It was a strange game for Jay, who was to become a Conscientious Objector. But he saw no contradiction—it wasn't "soldiers" being wounded and killed. It wasn't "bullets" being fired. Instead of a war game, he considered it the ultimate in military strategy.

We made a comfortable pair. I was 5' 11" with a lanky build, blond hair short and wavy, and a Jewish nose. I wore heavy, black-frame glasses, which were fashionable for those times. I had little need to shave, and now when my daughter looks back at my yearbook pictures, she howls "What a geek, Dad." Jay was 5' 9", of a heavier build, with a darker complexion and curly, black hair, cropped close. He already had a "5 o'clock shadow." Neither of us was particularly athletic looking, and we certainly were not the objects of the lascivious stares of the cheerleaders.

Bart and Seth were our third and fourth players. Although Jay and I were able to find occasional dates, they were always available. Bart was too shy to ask anyone out, despite the fact that he wasn't bad looking except for his acne. Seth, however, looked like a "dork"—one step above a "geek." He wore old-style, tortoise-rimmed, round glasses, button-down white shirts, and khaki pants with cuffs. He was three decades too early for the "me" generation, who bought from LL Bean's or The Gap. However, his greased, combed-back, blond hair, along with his white socks and black shoes with laces, made him a decade too late for the James Dean look. He was truly a man in fashion's twilight zone.

Between games, the losers would walk down the street to pick up the pizza—browned crust with tomato sauce and oily cheese, melted to perfection. When we added a couple of quarts of Coca-Cola in green-tinted bottles, we had a feast in the making. And don't forget the Cleara-sil ointment for the extra zits that would sprout up in the morning.

October 22, 1967

We watched television while we played RISK that night, as 70,000 pro-testors peacefully rallied at the Lincoln Monument. Jay had wanted to go down, and although I'd just gotten my driver's license, we had no place to sleep and no car in which to travel. We were still young enough not to feel guilty for not going—or at least I was. However, as Jay watched the mass draft card burning, it must have planted the seed for his subsequent Conscientious Objector application.

As the march went on to the Pentagon, Seth unfolded the board and, as usual, we all strategized internally—about the color and continent we would try to control first. I had a fondness for North America, "Team USA." The whole continent was worth five extra armies, with complete control of the U.S., Canada, and Mexico (our "allies" in the real world). But it was vulnerable from South America through the rest of Central America and vulnerable from the Soviet Union as the Russians could see across the Bering Strait into the Governor's Mansion in Alaska. At least North America was easier to defend than Central Europe. However, Europe was also more difficult to conquer, with its multiple potential attack points and fronts. No wonder Germany was unable to win either world war.

South America was not only an attack zone to the U.S., but in RISK it was also in military competition with Africa, (the continent, not the country!). So there was not only the specter of the slave raids of the previous centuries, but also the potential of armies attacking from the "Dark Continent," where the names of the countries were changing daily, as British colonization was coming to a close.

As our plastic armies advanced or were defeated, it was time to consider who would be potential allies. Jay seemed to be bent on dominating Africa and Bart went after Europe.

"Jay, if you don't attack me, I'll leave you alone in Africa, and we can mount a dual offense against Bart in Europe. We'll annihilate him."

But three moves later, Jay announced, "Ken, babe, I'm going after you"

"What about our treaty?"

"Bart's a now a non-entity. He's got no power anymore. And besides, he's only a threat to you now."

"Yeah, but what about Seth?" He was sitting pretty, almost ignored by us, as he built up his armies in Australia and the lower Asian corridor.

"Hey Seth," I entreated. "How about a treaty?"

"I don't know. I just want peace."

"Is that why you always start with Australia?" Bart asked Seth, "So you can be a woozy non-confrontationalist? That's not the name of the game. Remember, RISK."

"Because I can at least control that area. It gives me some sense of security that your armies can't wipe me out at the beginning of the game without spreading yourself too thin."

Australia was isolated, of limited strategic value, but a good stronghold, easily defended—only vulnerable from Southeast Asia.

"So that's why you think holding Southeast Asia is so strategic?" Jay had that quizzical facial expression that really suggested this was more than a rhetorical question.

Southeast Asia, with the small countries of Laos, Vietnam, and Cambodia, were all unidentified and unified as one strategic entity on the RISK board. They were dwarfed by China, India, and the Soviet Union.

"It is the only way into Australia." Seth was adamant in his opinion.

"So we build up more troops in Vietnam and Cambodia, to protect Australia? I don't think that's what General Westmoreland is telling LBJ." Jay was on a roll. "It's the Yellow Menace, the Domino Theory, that's the lie. Do you think we care about Australia, the Philippines, Indonesia? Why are we afraid of 'Communism' all the way over there. What have those people in Vietnam done to us? The French colonized them until they bravely threw them out at Dien Bien Phu. And then what do they get, the 'Ugly American,' who feels that it's 'Our way or no way at all.' We're just imperialists. We want to control the entire world."

"Jay, do you think that the Russian people under Stalin were treated so well? Is that what you want?" Seth added. "Remember the Hungarian Revolution—Communist imperialism and dictatorship at its worst! Is that your type of government?"

"But the Vietnamese aren't Stalin or Mao. This is just a civil war!" Jay started yelling.

"No politics for Ho Chi Minh, eh?" I mocked.

"You think the Diem regime was any better, Ken? The corruption in the South makes me sick. And Kennedy supported it."

"Jay, you're beginning to sound like you're against the war."

"Fuck, yes. LBJ's telling us we can win it, but he must be smoking some good shit. It's time we woke up! Look at what's happening at Berkeley. Those students have it right. I'm not gonna fight in this war!"

Down in Washington, in real time and real life, soldiers were now confronting the protestors at the Pentagon. The more radical contingent was ready for the first acts of civil disobedience.

"Don't worry, Jay, we'll all have student deferments until '73. It'll be over by then." I was sure of that. Big talk from a bunch of non-jocks, none of who wanted to go to war! I certainly didn't want to join the army. I certainly didn't want to die. "Better dead than Red." Or did I have it wrong? Was it "Better Red than Dead?" No, that was Jane Fonda's line—let the Commies take over Vietnam.

"And, meanwhile, it's all the poor, ignorant blacks who get to fight our war. It's such hypocrisy. We're so insulated from the inner cities—

the prejudice, the economic disparity, the lack of jobs, the lack of education. No wonder there's all of the rioting in the cities. Black Power!" Jay screamed.

"All of the rioting, but all of the looting, the robbing, even of the black- owned stores. All of the killing." Seth said. "They're murdering their own people. They're addicting their own kids with drugs."

"Seth, stop blaming them for everything. It's the white establishment that is addicting the black population. They feel it keeps them in their place." I was trying to see both sides of the story. "Maybe they shouldn't be rioting, but what does the government do for them? They've got to get their frustration out somehow. Maybe not with killing; maybe with more protest."

"Ken, civil disobedience doesn't work for the blacks. Civil unrest, maybe. When they gather at peace marches, just look at all of the police brutality." Jay answered. "How many of the 'pigs' are black? All of us 'whities' here in Scarsdale, insulated, protected by our rich parents, or at least your rich parents. How many black students do we have here? One, maybe two? And look at how many are being sacrificed in Vietnam, being killed or getting addicted to dope. It's no worse for our black brothers there than here."

In Washington, the soldiers were now in control of the protest at the Pentagon. Gradually, even famous activists like Normal Mailer would begin to leave the scene.

"Well, if you feel that way, then why don't you enlist after high school?" Bart asked.

In fact, despite Scarsdale's liberalism, only one male student from our high school class would decided not to go to college and forgo his 2S classification and join the Marines. For the other 99% of our class went on to college, the 2S deferment may have been worth more than the college degree. It was worth its weight of the college tuition payment if it kept you from getting drafted and killed.

"Because I don't believe in war." He was chomping at the bit to burn his draft card.

"Yeah, that may be so, Jay," I was exasperated. "But right here, it's your turn. Who are you going to attack?"

"Yeah, Jay, let's see what kind of general you are. Sending those plastic men into battle, to be destroyed by a roll of the dice."

"Not as bad as the military commander who said, 'We had to destroy the village to save it!'" Jay blurted out, barely able to contain himself.

All of this was a harbinger of things to come—of the peace movement becoming non-peaceful; of SDS and the Black Panthers changing the focus from non-violent protests of racism and an immoral war to clashes with authorities; of riots on the streets; and of the campus protests beginning to make headlines. The non-violent movement led by Martin Luther King and Eugene McCarthy was to be challenged by Eldridge Cleaver, Bobby Seale, Tom Hayden and the rest of the Chicago Seven.

February 1968

Another night of RISK, another night of celibacy, another night of debate about the war. As we watched Walter Cronkite on the news, as we saw body bags being airlifted back to the U.S., it was clear that it was truly the roll of the dice as to which soldier stepped on the landmine or was ripped apart by shrapnel.

We were seeing the effects of the Tet Offensive. The Communist Viet Cong ("PLAF," or the National Liberation Front's Peoples Liberation Armed Forces) and the North Vietnam's "PAVN" attempted to prove to both themselves and the South Vietnamese and American troops that the North would be victorious, that they could infiltrate and win over the rural towns and then move on to control the southern cities.

Although we later found out that the Communist casualties outnumbered the American and South Vietnamese by 10:1, the fact that the Communists were able to mount such an attack was a blow to the American hope for a quick victory.

"Jay, didn't you read what happened? We beat back the attacks. No way did we lose," Bart stated.

"Shit, Bart, read between the lines. U.S. propaganda. We never expected them to beat up on us so much."

"And, if we're so close to winning, Bart, then why did Westmorland ask for 200,000 more troops to win the war," I asked sarcastically.

Jay couldn't control himself. "Westmorland is such an ass. Why doesn't he fight himself? Let him slop through the mud!"

"Jay, you're much too angry to be a pacifist!" Seth had had enough.

"Fuck you." Jay's face was contorted with anger.

"No, Bart, Jay's right." I hated to admit that Jay had me thinking. "You know, Westmorland and his talk of troops and sacrifices; LBJ and he act like only 4,000 men killed against their 45,000 is a victory. What the assholes neglect to mention is that in this human experiment, in this war, where lives are counted in the thousands, for each soldier, the n=1. Each soldier is a single life, not to be fractionated, multiplied, percentagized—either he lives or dies."

"A regular philosophizer—but, unfortunately for you, I just rolled three 6's, and your armies are wiped out of North America!" Bart gloated.

"Shut up and stuff your face with some more Fritos!" I yelled, realizing my Maginot line had just fallen and I was about to be swept under the surge of Bart's attack. At least I could get home earlier tonight.

And I was right. Within five minutes my armies had been razed. "See you next Saturday—unless, of course, we get real dates." I knew they'd be there, but I still had hopes that Robin would be available. And the next week, I was lucky. The movie "The Graduate" had just come out, and she was anxious to see Dustin Hoffman and Katherine Ross. As it turns out, the movie represented one spectrum of our generation that didn't have a clue what it wanted to do, but that rebelled at the suggestion to go into "plastics." But it was pretty depressing, and although we enjoyed the music for the rest of the spring, we were bummed out at the end of the movie. I barely got a kiss goodnight. How could I blame her, after watching what Dustin's character did to Anne Bancroft (aka "Mrs. Robinson")—his girlfriend's mother?

February 27, 1968

Lil and I were watching the news as she wondered about the proposed income tax surcharge and its effect on the economy and the stock market. We were waiting for my dad to call from the city to let her know that she should put the steaks in the broiler. Early on in the marriage she learned that only when he actually phoned and said he was on his way out the door could she believe he was leaving; and even then she tacked on another ten minutes for the forgotten phone call to a patient.

Walter Cronkite, probably the most respected man in the United States, ended his CBS Nightly News broadcast with an unprecedented "personal" editorial. He had gone to Vietnam to see the action first-hand, to file video reports of what was going on. He had been on the frontline with the troops and flown in a helicopter with body bags filled with Marines. He had met with leaders who assured him the Communists had been dealt a terrible blow—that we could win the war with another infusion of troops.

We listened as Cronkite said, "Tonight, back in more familiar surroundings in New York, we'd like to sum up our findings in Vietnam — an analysis that must be speculative, personal, subjective. Who won and who lost in the great Tet offensive against the cities? I'm not sure. The Vietcong did not win by a knockout, but neither did we. The referees of history may make it a draw.

"For it seems now more certain than ever that the bloody experience of Vietnam is to end in a stalemate.

To say that we are closer to victory today is to believe, in the face of the evidence, the optimists who have been wrong in the past. To suggest we are on the edge of defeat is to yield to unreasonable pessimism. To say that we are mired in stalemate seems the only realistic, yet unsatisfactory, conclusion. . . . But it is increasingly clear to this reporter that the only rational way out then will be to negotiate, not as victors, but as an honorable people who lived up to their pledge to defend democracy, and did the best they could.

This is Walter Cronkite. Good night."

For our generation, and those who cared about their sons at risk, he was Moses, carrying down the Ten Commandments, exposing LBJ's Golden Calf for the pagan sacrifices it represented.

"Wow, Lil. What do you think?"

"Maybe Johnson will listen to him."

And even though LBJ was reported to have said to his aides, "If we've lost Cronkite, we've lost Middle America," it was General Westmorland who won out. Additional troops were sent to Southeast Asia. How many tens of thousands of American and Vietnamese lives were lost, while LBJ and Nixon fought a lost cause, their military strategy ending like a poorly played game of RISK? Down the tubes went LBJ's "Great Society," as the economy began to shows signs of inflation and was in no shape to finance the domestic programs at home along with the drain of an obvious (to me and my generation, at least) futile war effort halfway around the globe.

March 16, 1968

What we didn't see, what was too real for our games, be they "RISK" or the Guerrilla Warfare class exercise during our high school's summer school, was what was happening in Vietnam that morning, 14 time zones away, where Lt. William Calley had led members of Charlie Company into the village of My Lai. They had apparently recently lost a beloved sergeant to a Viet Cong boob-trap. Upon entering the town, they had anticipated insurgents, an elusive enemy that always seemed to be one step ahead, behind, or to the side of them. It was a perfect "petri dish" for disaster. They had been prepared for a major attack, but had come upon only women, children and old men.

As we would only find out 18 months later, this was a day that would live in infamy. Psychologically, the soldiers had been "broken;" they were as good as brain-washed, deluded—a reverse mirage of an oasis in a desert. Their leaders were not the "best and the brightest" Ivy Leaguers who were avoiding the draft. Rather, they were junior officers, unable to avoid the draft or unwilling to suffer the shame of fleeing to

Canada, men who never received the appropriate training to prevent this kind of revengeful massacre of over 500 Vietnamese civilians.

We suffered no angst as our dice and plastic armies were our battle-field. The strategic maps and troop movements and briefings were the real generals' battlefield, but this, the actual killings, the bodies, was the soldiers' battlefield.

As winter melted into spring, and the warm weather started to lift our spirits, I still spent most of my evenings studying and watching television, with Hope curled up next to me on my bed, lying next to me. I wondered why Robin wasn't reciprocating my advances. It wouldn't be until our high school reunion 25 years later that I found out the secret. It wasn't my acne, my breath, my glasses, or even my lack of experience at kissing. I had a wonderful time talking with her after the reunion—about her career and her life-partner.

So, other than studying, there wasn't much to my life. The Columbia Lions basketball team advanced to the NCAA Eastern Regional semi-finals against Davidson. Hard as it might be to believe, back in 1968, the Lions had a 7' 1" white center named Dave Newmark, a volatile black 6' 4" guard, Heywood Dotson, and a future NBA all-star, 6'5" Jim McMillan. I listened to the game on WKCR, while Harlan was down in North Carolina at the game. With the score tied, Columbia's Bruce Metz went to the free-throw line with six seconds left in regulation time. He missed his shot, and the Lions lost in overtime. I actually watched the game on delayed tape later that night, staying up until the bitter end, still believing that this time Bruce's shot would actually go in!

The rest of the television news wasn't so great either. All we heard about was the aftermath of the Tet Offensive, and the official version of how victorious we were. But the nightly broadcasts of the body bags being shipped home only reinforced Cronkite's editorial opinion and eroded any enthusiasm for a war that seemed to have no end in sight. Jay's lectures and emotional assaults were beginning to take their toll on us, and we were all distraught at the possibility that we might at some time have to fight what seemed to us to be a futile and immoral war being fought half way around the world. And as liberals, we were increasingly willing to go on record in support of Martin Luther King's statement that the blacks in the South and the cities shouldn't be forced to go either.

I signed up to work on Eugene McCarthy's campaign. "Jay, I really think he's got a chance," I naively stated on the way home one night.

"You're an ass, Ken. LBJ's the establishment, and he controls everything. We're stuck with him and his fucking bombs for four more years. Either that, or that creep Nixon."

"Not if we all work together. We've got to get organized for the primaries. Gene needs our help. You should shave your sideburns and 'Go Clean for Gene.' Let's get out into the community. Maybe we can convince our parents that the war must end." I was beginning to rebel myself, letting my hair grow that extra inch and come across my forehead rather than being greased back with Vitalis.

"Don't waste your time. This is America." Jay depressed me, but I wasn't quite ready to believe he was right. Especially when, in mid-March, Senator McCarthy, from the "Great State of Minnesota," won a stunning 42% of the vote versus LBJ's 49% in the New Hampshire Democratic Primary, and actually gained 20 of the 24 delegates.

"Jay, you see what I mean! We can do it. Here's the razor blade."

But it wasn't only me who believed that LBJ could be defeated.

March 31, 1968

"Good evening, my fellow Americans."

Lyndon Johnson was addressing the nation in prime time.

"Tonight I want to speak to you of peace in Vietnam and Southeast Asia."

I'd heard this speech before. What could he say that was new?

"Tonight, I renew the offer I made last August—to stop the bombardment of North Vietnam. We ask that talks begin promptly."

Wonderful, I thought, but that offer had already been turned down.

"Tonight, I have ordered our aircraft and our naval vessels to make no attacks on North Vietnam, except in the area north of the demilitarized zone where the continuing enemy buildup directly threatens the allied forward position. Even this very limited bombing of the north could come to an early end—if our restraint is matched by restraint in Hanoi."

They haven't gone for it yet, I thought. What makes him think Ho Chi Minh will agree now?

And of course, it followed with, "But if peace does not come now through negotiations, it will come when Hanoi understands that our common resolve is unshakable, and our common strength is invincible."

John Wayne to the rescue!

"Yet, I believe that now, no less than when the decade began, this generation of Americans is willing to pay any price, bear any burden, meet any hardship, support any friend, oppose any foe to assure the survival and success of liberty." Words . . . spoken by John F. Kennedy.

Where was he going with this speech? I wondered. He seemed to be repeating himself over and over, like an old man.

"There is division in the American house now. So I would ask all Americans, whatever their personal interests or concern, to guard against divisiveness and all its ugly consequences.

I have concluded that I should not permit the Presidency to become involved in the partisan divisions that are developing in this political year.

Accordingly, I shall not seek, and I will not accept, the nomination of my party for another term as your president."

"Hope, did he really say that?" She looked up from me with sleepy eyes and droopy ears, and came over and licked my face. But her tail was wagging with enthusiasm. And as I screamed for joy, she started barking, at first small yips, than escalating into her own imitation of a wolf's howl. "That means McCarthy will win the nomination," I thought. "We'll be out of Vietnam before I have to go." I thought I could hear the cheers throughout the neighborhood.

The next morning, Jay and I couldn't stop yapping. We were both beside ourselves, getting ready to volunteer for Gene.

"Far fuckin' out! Finally, something worthwhile to do this summer." Jay's usual ennui was overcome by the potential for change in this land that he so despised. "I'll follow him wherever he needs me, to whatever primaries he is involved in." Jay couldn't stop rattling on. "Gene's too good for this country, but he'll show them how."

"Jay, don't get an erection." I was a little more pragmatic than he was, less idealistic. "He still has to win the primaries, get the nomination, and then face Nixon or whoever else runs against him."

And we were both right. "Clean Gene" had made quite a presence, and he had knocked over the champion. But, despite the adoration of the college generation, those ready for emancipation from the political process, he had not built the support he needed to carry him forward. He was like the pacesetter at the horse track, tiring out the favorite, only to find that he had served his purpose and that it was his barn-mate who would take over the lead in the end. Bobby Kennedy, who had previously declined to make a run against LBJ, now announced his candidacy. McCarthy had softened his foe, taken the blows, and walked the minefield to make sure it was safe. All of a sudden, Bobby Kennedy decided that he could be president, as LBJ no longer stood in his way. He acted like he was the adorned "white knight in shining armor," a "Kennedy" risking all to rescue the "damsel in distress."

But as Gene and Bobby were joined by Hubert Humphrey in the fight to get the nomination to succeed LBJ, I was distracted by the upcoming SAT's, getting ready for my assault on college applications the following year. I had listened to Harlan's experiences as a freshman at Columbia College, only 30 minutes away from Scarsdale. For all of his time spent at home, he might as well have been in Boston or Baltimore. On his mind were only two things—his new girl friend, whom he had met at a New York Philharmonic concert, and his upcoming finals and papers. His seven page paper for his Contemporary Civilization course dealing with Henri Thoreau and "Civil Disobedience," as it was being practiced at University of California at Berkeley, was almost completed. But he had yet to begin his paper on racism in Shakespeare's "Othello."

April 4, 1968

Mary was upstairs in her bedroom reading Shakespeare's "King Lear." It was difficult enough to understand the 16th century English without having her mind distracted by worrying what kind of a mood her mother and Bill would be in tonight. They didn't think much of LBJ, but Bill, in particular, thought that Eugene McCarthy, unlike Joe McCarthy, was a Communist.

"What's this country coming to if those Commie students and politicians can get LBJ to resign? We should've elected Barry Goldwater and just nuked Ho Chi Minh," he pontificated the night after LBJ's speech.

"Bill," Ellen spoke softly, "Don't worry, there's no way McCarthy will ever get the nomination. He'll never get the support of the Southern states."

"Ellen, the Northern liberals control the press, they'll make sure he wins."

Mary just sat and ate her fried okra and catfish, not daring to say a word. How many times had she thought that it would be easier to be taken to a nunnery and a vow of silence. At least then she wouldn't have to take orders from Bill. She'd take her orders from a higher power.

She was listening to the radio, playing the great songs from the past year: "To Sir, with Love," "Daydream Believer," "All You Need is Love," and "Ode to Billie Joe." She didn't know whether to be hopeful or mournful. She thought of Hamlet:

"To be or not to be.
That is the question."

Then the news flash: "Martin Luther King has been shot in Memphis Tennessee." That's all they said for now. "A minute ago he 'is,' and now he 'was,'" she thought. "What's this country coming to?"

She ran downstairs where her mom and Bill were having their gin and tonics.

"Mom, Reverend King has been shot."

"Is he dead?" Bill asked, sounding hopeful.

"You're the kind that killed him, Bill!" Mary screamed.

"Mary!" her mom stood up to defend her from Bill's glaring approach. "Take that back. Bill didn't pull the trigger."

"Mom, you know how he talks. He always talks about keeping the niggers in their place."

"Mary, I may hate the niggers, but I don't want them dead. I just don't want them in my house or marrying Kate."

Mary ran out of the house and was in tears as she drove away towards town to find MJ. Titusville was a poor town, but it was mainly a poor white town. And the blacks were mainly illiterate farmers. So, unlike the rest of the country, there were no riots in the streets. The small black Baptist Church had its bells ringing, and there would be a memorial service there the next day. Mary and MJ sat in the car and smoked a pack of cigarettes, crying.

"They only shoot the good people," Mary whispered. "First John and then Martin."

"Don't forget Abe Lincoln," MJ added.

"I hope they catch the killer soon," Mary wiped her eyes. "And give him the 'chair.'"

Within a few months, the first part of Mary's wish would come true, as James Earl Ray was caught in England. But, as with JFK's assassination, it wasn't clear (and still isn't to this day) if he was the killer, or if he had been framed, perhaps even by our own FBI who wanted their nemesis, the leader of the civil rights non-violent movement, permanently benched.

April 23, 1968

Life went on in Scarsdale, despite LBJ's announcement, MLK's assassination, and the massive American casualties in Vietnam. We still had school, our tests, our papers, and our social lives.

I had gotten home late from our intramural softball game. I wasn't good enough to make the JV baseball team, and none of the jock teams had wanted me, so I formed my own team among my friends and the scattered leftover kids who wanted to play. It was intra-mural, so we didn't have any uniforms or caps. And the "ballpark" had only a small backstop and two benches without bleachers. There were no outfield fences, and the outfields overlapped with the neighboring diamonds. We weren't very good, but at least I got to play shortstop, was captain of my team, and hit cleanup. I had my Brooks Robinson Figure 8 glove, which allowed me to emulate the Gold Glover, at least in my own mind. And that day was my most memorable, as I hit grand-slam home runs in consecutive innings. It was quite a feeling rounding third base the second time, listening to the roar of the "fan," then jumping up and stomping on home plate. And, of course, I could only thank my teammates, who had gotten on base before me. It was only too bad that our defense failed to hold in the seventh inning, and we lost a heartbreaker, 17-11.

I scoffed down a turkey sandwich and went upstairs. We were reading Josephson's book *The Robber Barons* in American History. It contained tales of 19th century capitalism gone wild and industrialists raping the land and the citizens of the country—all in the name of money and free enterprise. Anti-trust legislation had been necessitated by their actions, with the unions becoming the savior of the working class.

As I had no social life except for Jay and pals, I once again had "Gidget" on in the background. She was still beautiful, perky, my dream girl. And she dated nice boys, nice boys like me. The upstairs phone awoke me from my reverie. I ran to pick it up, then stopped for a second, not wanting to appear too anxious if it was Robin.

"Hey, Ken, let me speak to Pop. You can't fuckin' believe what is going on here at Columbia. Turn on the fuckin' news."

"Harlan, you better not let Pop hear you. Anyway, the news isn't on for another 90 minutes."

"Wrong, baby bro! SDS and SAS just took over several buildings at Columbia. All of the news stations are here!"

"What happened?"

"I'll let you know later, but you know Columbia was trying to build a gym on Morningside Heights down into Harlem?"

"So? Didn't you say it would be open to the community?"

"Well, they were going to let the kids from Harlem come in through a back door entrance. Anyway, some students went down to the site, protested, and were arrested. Then there was a rally on campus last night and they went into Hamilton Hall, one of the classroom and office buildings."

"So where are you? Are you okay? Is anyone hurt?"

"Not so far, but all of the press is here."

"But what about you?"

"We're all out on South Field."

"Let me get Pop. Are you sure you're okay? I've got to call Jay as soon as you hang up. I'm going to turn on the television."

"Just make sure you watch Channel 7. I'm in the background while they're interviewing one of my friends. I'm a celebrity!"

I yelled down, "Pop, pick up the phone! It's Harlan!"

I ran into my room to check out the news. Nothing. Still "Gidget," with Sally Field looking so innocent. And then, across the bottom of the screen, I saw a news flash regarding Columbia.

I went back to the phone to call Jay, but Harlan was still on. "We didn't pay all of this money so you could be on strike. What kind of grades will you get?"

"They're talking pass-fail if the strike takes hold, Pop."

"You'll never get into medical school if your first-year grades are pass-fail."

"Pop, I gotta go. Talk to you tomorrow. Luv ya."

"Keep me posted. If there are no classes, you need to come home tomorrow. I don't want you anywhere near the police."

"Dad, I'm staying."

"God help us if this ends up at the Dental School," I heard my dad say to Lil as he hung up the phone.

Finally, the phone was mine. "Jay, did you hear what is going on at Columbia? Harlan just called. SDS is occupying the president's office. They're destroying Columbia."

"I don't think so, schmuck. Think of it as an invasion. It's about time we got the East Coast liberals doing what they did at Berkeley. Is your brother in there? What's he up to? Is he as straight as you?"

I answered, with my usual sarcastic tone, "You've got to be kidding. He's on the outside, looking in." A familiar sensation shuttered through my body, as I recalled a time back in sixth grade, when I stayed in class after school one day with all of the boys in my class. We were about to be punished with detention because they had tormented one of the new students. I wanted so much to be a part of the "club," even in infamy, that I was devastated when Tom Stone yelled out to the teacher, "Austin can't stay! He wasn't there with us!" And I was sent home, devastated by my innocence, no criminal, indeed. I couldn't even try out for a career in civil disobedience.

"Maybe we should go down there this weekend?" Jay had wanted to protest in Berkeley, but he couldn't quite scrape together the money to go.

"I'll keep in touch with Harlan. Maybe it'll be all over by then. Do you really think the sit-in will last that long?"

"I doubt they're going to move by themselves. Anyway, let's find out what they want first." Jay was beginning to even sound rational.

"I'm going back to watch the TV, Jay. I'll see you tomorrow." I watched pictures of the university, with longhaired students yelling into bullhorns, screaming to anyone who would listen. Off to the side were several ROTC officers. With their stern faces, crew cuts, pressed khaki shirts, and black thin ties they were a striking contrast to the protestors. And then, as the reporter showed up on the screen, there in the background, was Harlan, with his disheveled blond hair and mustache. He was trying to look so serious, but had that silly shit-eating grin that says, "I'm on television."

April 24, 1968

By the next night, it was clearer. The black students of SAS (Student Afro-American Society) had held a meeting and informed Mark Rudd and his SDS contingent that they wanted Hamilton Hall all to themselves, that their issues were different. The black revolutionaries were overturning "Brown v. Board of Education." The whites had to leave and find their own building to occupy—"separate but equal?"—as segregation re-appeared on the campus. Of course, from the dingy basement of

Hamilton Hall, Rudd led his students first into Low Library and then into President Kirk's office—the lap of luxury, with carpeting, beautiful leather chairs, and elegant cigars. Other SDS members occupied the Math Building, while Avery Hall was taken over by the graduate students and Fayerweather Hall by more students the following morning.

Harlan called to let us know that the protest outside the buildings was a little more organized. The jocks and the rest of the "Majority Coalition" were protecting the buildings from the outside and attempting to restore order, liberate the campus from the rebels, and prevent the liberal faction of students trying to get nourishment to the protesters. The faculty was divided as it met, with some willing to compromise and others holding fast with President Kirk, but all were trying to keep the peace. As of yet, there was minimal police presence, which kept the protests from escalating.

The demonstrators made their demands, which revolved around the University's "racist" relationship with Harlem and the gym, and the University's role in both the Vietnam War and the Institute for Defense Analysis.

"And Ken, best of all, we have no classes. At least I can work on my paper."

April 25, 1968

Every night, conversation at the dinner table in Scarsdale focused on the strike.

"I won't let these punks ruin my University!" the "Professor" would scream.

"Pop, you know that some of what they say is true."

"They're just spoiled college kids. They have no respect for the institution that's protecting them."

"Bill," Paul said, testing the waters, slowly entering the fray, "They're not just fighting Columbia. They're against the war."

"Paul, just . . ." My dad never got to finish his words, which I can only imagine would they have been something like, "It's none of your business!" because Richie yelled,

"Bill, where are they taking their showers? They must smell worse than Cathy."

Cathy glared at Richie, yelling, "I'd better not catch you in my room, or I'll give you a wedgie."

Lil finally diffused the conversation, "Enough is enough. Cathy, let the dogs out."

April 26, 1968

My dad disagreed with the strike against his institution, but above all was worried about Harlan's welfare and safety. He prevailed upon Harlan to come home for a few days, which he did under protest. Of course, Harlan made it seem like it was all about being where it was happening, neglecting to tell us about his new girlfriend with whom he was making such sweet music now that his roommate had gone back to Brooklyn!

Happily for my dad, the Dental School—hardly a hot bed of political action or defense research—was three miles to the north and appeared isolated from the storm downtown. I guess the students had worked too hard to give up a year of their lives if they didn't graduate, including a year of lost earnings; or they felt they were exempt from serving on the front line, except for the few who had deferred their military service in exchange for the government paying their tuition under the Berry Plan. Although some of them must have sympathized with the cause, classes and clinics continued, ensuring that the blacks and Puerto Ricans and poor Irish Catholics of Washington Heights would get some semblance of dental care.

Harlan arrived home after the rest of us had finished dinner.

"Pop, I heard the faculty was meeting today to try and negotiate some agreement." Harlan was talking with his mouth full of sirloin steak, ravenous, as if he hadn't eaten for days.

"Harlan, I only heard through the grapevine that they sat in an Ad Hoc Group and made some proposals."

"Such as? Did they say the gym construction should be stopped?"

"That's the easy one for now. The defense thing probably can also be resolved. I think Columbia can survive without defense research, even if it means losing a few of our faculty. But they also recommended a tripartite committee of students, faculty, and administration."

"Huh," Harlan laughed. "I can just imagine Kirk and Rudd sitting next to each other, sharing a cup of tea."

"I don't know, Harlan," I was hopeful. "It sounds like things will be okay."

"Not so fast, Ken," our dad and Harlan both spoke as one.

"The SDS wants amnesty," Harlan interjected.

"And the administration won't give it to them," Dad said emphatically.

"Can't they settle anyway? Aren't all of the students tired of all of this?"

"Ken, the campus is divided, faculty versus faculty, student versus student. Only the administration seems to be standing firm."

"On what?" I innocently asked.

"On the issue of amnesty for the protestors. It seems to be the deal-breaker."

April 27-28, 1968

More talk, more meetings. Things that universities and radical students seem to do well. Tom Hayden from the national SDS was in town, working with Mark Rudd. The stalemate continued.

And, according to Richie, "They must smell like dudu by now."

April 29, 1968

My dad couldn't keep Harlan away any longer. And of course, he wanted to play sweet music with his new "squeeze" he had met at the Philharmonic. Anyway, he packed up his backpack and took the 12:15 back to the city.

My dad and I were having another of our debates that night when Harlan called.

"Ken, rumor has it the police are being called in."

"You're shitting me."

"No, it looks fucking crazy here. There are all of the jocks and the rest of the Majority Coalition down here surrounding all of the occupied buildings, while the rest of us try to get food into the protestors."

"So?"

"I bought a salami for them and we're trying to throw it in through the window."

"Hey, where's Tom Seaver when you need him?" I laughed.

"Or Joe Namath. You know what really sucks—that there are Barnard girls sitting across the street watching Martha Peterson be inaugurated as the president of their college instead of supporting our efforts."

"I just hope there's still a school left for me to apply to," I bemoaned.

April 30, 1968

I guess it had to happen. When there is trespassing and no end in sight to occupation by "squatters," the owner has no choice but to force an evacuation of its property. And so, the occupation turned to a "riot" when the NYC Tactical Police Force "violated academic freedom" by following Columbia University President Grayson Kirk's decision to ask for outside help.

Amazingly, the 86 blacks in Hamilton Hall—having been unmoved by the appearances of H. Rap Brown and Stokely Carmichael earlier in the week—were removed peacefully, and subsequently arrested by Chief Police Inspector Sanford Garelick's forces which had entered through the tunnels below.

"Ken, it was awful. The police swarmed the other buildings; they were dressed with helmets and face protection, and pulled the demonstrators out by their legs. They had billy-clubs in hand. There was blood all over the place. Most of the students in Low Library, Fayerweather, and Avery were removed with minimal casualties and lots of arrests. The protestors just went limp. But it was really crazy at Mathematics Building; the protestors refused to be 'liberated' by the police and they fought back, throwing filing cabinets down the stairs. The police beat on them as they dragged them out."

"Where are they now?"

"Who the fuck knows? I just know that when the police started moving through the crowds of us who were on South Field, all hell broke loose. I mean, they were chasing us. I just managed to get away."

"Are you going to tell Pop?"

"No way, he'll drive down to get me. I'm staying. I'm sure there won't be any more classes. But I'm not leaving now. We're all on strike."

"God, I wish I was there."

"You don't belong—it's not your school! And besides, they won't let anyone in without an ID."

I was on the outside, looking in, once again. In the background I heard "On strike, shut it down!"

I went to bed and awoke the next morning to the news and images of police brutality intermixed with pictures of students bombarding policemen who just might have started out with civility on their minds. "Are there two sides to every riot?" I asked myself. "Was either side blameless?"

May 1, May Day, 1968

Harlan called in the morning to let us know he was okay. I picked up the phone while he was talking to our Dad.

"The police were everywhere. We were running, just trying to avoid being hurt."

"You must have done something to irritate them."

"No Dad, we were just watching."

"Harlan, get your ass back to Scarsdale. I don't want to see you on the evening news again. And I don't want you to be arrested."

"Dad!"

"Don't 'Dad' me, just take the subway uptown and we'll drive home together."

"Well, I'll come home tonight, but I'm going back when it calms down."

That night, Harlan and Dad couldn't stop arguing, Lil was the moderator.

"Dad, the faculty has to support us. We're calling for a strike."

"You kids are ingrates. Look what Columbia has done for you. Look at what it's doing for the community. They're even building a gym for them."

"Yeah, with a separate entrance, Dad. And what about the war research?"

"Hey, Harlan," I added, "just be careful when you go back down that you don't get hit with a billy-club—although a broken nose might not be too bad. They could fix it up nice and get rid of that Jewish nose, and insurance would even pay for it."

Harlan gave me the finger as he stormed out of the room.

"You know, we've got to do everything we can to stop this war, Pop. I'm sure most of the protestors only want peace. The cops didn't have to be so brutal."

"But, Ken, what about the punks who fought back? Who insulted the officers' wives and mothers?"

"Pop, the police are professionals. They should've known better. They should've remained controlled behind their shields. Remember what you taught us, 'Sticks and stones can break your bones, but names can never hurt you.'"

From Jay's point of view, it was clear which side to blame. From my dad's point of view, it was clear which side to blame. Unlike both of them, Harlan was actually in the midst of the debate; and he seemed to know where he stood. For me, the lines were a little blurrier.

That semester I was taking an English elective, "The Black Man in White America." Only in Scarsdale, with less than ten black students in the entire school, could we have the balls to have such a class. But this English course was taught by Roberta Wilson, a young, single, white woman whose short, straight, black hair, white sleeveless blouse, and non-descript breasts gave her an asexual honky aura.

We were assigned a project to become involved in a "Black Experience." I chose an interview with Willie Mae, our black maid (or "domestic engineer"). It began the afternoon I overhead her talking on the telephone to a friend, saying that Sam was going to be in jail for the next 20 years for killing his girlfriend. I was distraught. Who was Willie hanging out with?

"Hey, woman," I asked—my attempt at "black" dialect far inferior to my little step-brother Richie's soulful conversations with Willie Mae. "Which of your friends gonna do time?"

Willie Mae came over, towering over me. Her 6' 1" frame was hardened by the scar across her left cheek. She boomed with laughter, "Booy, that ain't my friend. That's Sam from my show "As the World Turns" (or as Richie would say, "As the Turd Whirls!"). "He messed up his woman pretty bad."

"Willie, you watch too many soaps!"

"What else is a black woman got to do while she washes your clothes? I love to watch all those pretty, white boys making it with those tramps on "Days of our Lives."

And though we fought, we were almost like brother and sister at times. When I got my license, I was glad to drive Willie home to her apartment in White Plains. But even as I wept for Martin Luther King, I understood why Lil and my dad were afraid that Willie Mae might take her anger out on us. Luckily, she loved her little Richard so much and considered him family (and still does to this day) that we had nothing to fear.

This was all quite different than the book we were reading for the course, *Native Son*, by Richard Wright. In this novel, Bigger is a black chauffeur who inadvertently suffocates the white teenage girl in his charge as he tries to silently carry her back to her bedroom to keep her parents from discovering how drunk she had become on a night out with her friends. Clearly, the Chicago community would have his life if he were caught in an accidental crime caused only by the fear of the racist society. White man's justice would be a black man's injustice—until Bigger escaped into the tenements and, during his escape, brutally murdered his own black girlfriend.

My essay on the novel described my sympathy for him regarding his certain execution for the white girl's accidental death, but I refused to exonerate him for the subsequent murder of his girlfriend. Ms. Williams, knowing that I was planning on applying to Columbia the next year, wrote on my paper, "I hope Columbia makes you more of a radical!" I didn't believe in Karl Marx, "that the ends justified the means," and I felt that some semblance of humanity and justice must still prevail. I was still 16, had never been laid and never had a drink or a smoke, but I yearned to be an independent thinker.

Two days later, Harlan announced, "I'm going back down. They've organized the strike, but they're holding ad hoc classes on South Field. I'm not gonna miss this."

"On strike. Shut it down," became their mantra, and they lit bonfires in the evening. Pictures on the front page of *The Columbia Spectator* were captioned, "SDS burning South Field to the ground."

I called Harlan one night, to see if he was coming home over the weekend and would need the car.

"Hell, no, Ken. Let Dad know I'm sticking it out."

"Harlan, what are they striking about now?"

"Mainly about the issue of amnesty for the protestors."

"But, isn't this a form of civil disobedience?"

"Fuck, yes."

"Then doesn't civil disobedience require some degree of responsibility?"

"You've got a point. But I think that some of the faculty might work with them. Not that it matters. President Kirk won't budge."

The next week the stalemate was still at hand. Protestors again took over Hamilton Hall, this time demanding amnesty for the protestors. And predictably, again the police were called in to clear the Hall. When they came, they wreaked havoc as they swept through South Field. The students and faculty were united in their stand against the police brutality, which was clearly unwarranted against the students and faculty outside of the buildings.

Finally, as the students and faculty were united, a more moderate faction took control of the conflict and the Students for a Restructured University negotiated reforms, such as an end to the gym construction and defense contracts, the end of ROTC on campus, and a tri-partite senate made up of faculty, administration and students to dish out punishment. As for the students involved, suspension as opposed to expulsion became the fate of the multitudes of the occupation forces.

The gyroscope that I had counted on to steady my course began to vibrate and started migrating across the floor, leaving me without a center of gravity. I was no longer capable of locating my position in the universe. My tightly spun spiral ascension was now in disarray.

The world that had made so much sense had become chaotic. I didn't condone violence on either side. But, after listening to Harlan, it was obvious that, while the police were physically threatened and provoked in the Math Building, the rest of the "protectors of the laws'" lawlessness outside the academic buildings against bystanders and my brother's classmates demonstrated that they were the enemy to the students, just as they were to the blacks in the inner cities. They lived up to their description as "pigs" and deserved the command, "Up against the wall, motherfucker!"

Social injustice, civil disobedience, immoral war, police brutality, carnage of private university property, flying filing cabinets, and racism—this wasn't the "South," this was New York City. The "Robber Barons," the military establishment, and the revolutionaries were all a threat to the great majority of our country who were trying to earn a decent living and have a decent home for their families. And the blacks—whose second-class status was still apparent in the South, and who had a separate-but unequal-status in the North—were striving for the American Dream, with the civil rights movement in its infancy and black power emerging as a national force.

June 4, 1968

"Not a whole lot happening tonight," Mary thought to herself. "Fuck, it's the summer, one week after my graduation, and I'm stuck here at home watching television."

"Mary, don't bother applying to college. Get a job, work, pay us some rent, and we'll let you stay here." Her mom was so encouraging after graduation.

"What am I supposed to do around this God-forsaken town? Titus-ville sucks."

"Mary, there's plenty of work over at Cape Kennedy. I don't want to hear any of your crap about this town," her step-dad lectured.

Mary applied to the local bank, to the McDonald's, and to the Kennedy Space Center. With the Apollo missions in full development, she was able to talk her way into a job in the accounting office, although her short skirt and sun-tanned legs didn't seem to hurt her interview with the tired junior-assistant-vice-president in charge of finances. He wanted her to begin work this week, but, as Mary told him, "I'm still exhausted from my finals! [aka graduation parties]. Can I start next week?"

But this week wasn't worth being off. Martha Jane had already started her job at the bank, and Mike had been called up by the Navy two days after his graduation. So she was home by herself with Spider, not much to do except sneak a few cans of Budweiser up to her room and turn on the "boob tube." By 11:30 at night, there wasn't much else except for the preliminary results of the California Democratic presidential primary, so she turned on Johnny Carson and the "Tonight Show."

Tiny Tim was the special guest—a grown man, ugly as sin, with a long face, a nose the size of Pinocchio and long, straggly hair which gave him an aura of freakiness that far surpassed any of the radical hippies or rednecks Mary was used to avoiding.

"Tip toe through the tulips" he sang (?) in his high-pitched nasal tone, while Johnny sat next to him in hysterics.

After he finished, he sat down to a round of applause and jeers, as Johnny could just not stop his laughing. The dialogue only became more inane as the interview went on, and Mary nodded off during the run of inane commercials which paid for Johnny's insane salary.

What awakens someone in the middle of sleep when the television is droning on in the background is unclear. But clearly the mournful screams of Bobby Kennedy's supporters—as they watched Sirhan Sirhan gun down their hero—could have awakened a hibernating bear. Mary awoke with a chill, and was mesmerized by what she was seeing on the screen. Over and over they replayed Bobby's exit from his victory speech, out through the hallway to the kitchen, and each time he fell to the ground, unable to be saved. The bullet wound was so reminiscent of what had smote his older brother.

"Oh my God, Oh my God," Mary wailed, "what have they done?" She ran downstairs to wake up her mother, with much trepidation, as her step-father was known to have friends who walked around like ghosts on Halloween, lighting bonfires the likes of which would have made the football fans proud on Homecoming Weekend. Nonetheless, Bobby, just like JFK, was also a Catholic, and her Mom had spoken kindly of him, forgiving him for his friendliness towards the Negroes (although never in front of her husband).

Mary knocked quietly, hoping Bill would continue to snore in his drunken stupor.

"What is it, Mary?" her mother whispered. "Why are you here in the middle of the night? You know I have an early day tomorrow."

"They shot Bobby Kennedy, Mom, they shot him!" Mary wailed.

Her mom got out of bed quietly, put on her robe, and came outside the room, softly closing the door behind her.

"Is he hurt badly?"

"He's dead, Mom, he's dead."

"I'm so sorry, but I guess it serves him right, with all he's been saying for the Negroes. He's too far ahead of this country."

"Mom, he wasn't killed by a white man; he was killed by a man from the Middle East."

"Do they know why?"

"No, Mom, no."

"Come on downstairs, don't wake up Bill," Ellen pleaded. "We'll turn on the television and watch together."

After watching the scene over again, and hearing the commentators discuss how this assassination left the nomination open for Hubert Humphrey to wrest it away from the Eugene and Bobby anti-Vietnamese faction, Mary could only think about Mike, who now surely would have to serve halfway across the world in a guerilla war, in a country in which we were not welcome.

"Abraham, Martin, and John." And now Bobby.

Morning came much too soon, as the alarm went off for Bill to get up at 6 a.m. for his morning shower. Mary, sleepy eyed, crawled back up to her bed for ten more minutes of sleep, before she got up to go to work at the Space Agency. It didn't seem to matter much what she wore today or whether she put on any makeup. She wandered back down to the kitchen and poured herself a cup of coffee left over from last night, reheating it in the percolator, not really caring about straining the grinds. Her mother's emptied glass still smelled of cheap scotch, and the remnants of her Kent cigarettes were crushed out in the bottom. The milk container was almost empty, so there wasn't much to do for breakfast except to put a raspberry Pop Tart in the toaster. It was going to be a typical Florida summer day, so she put on a tank-top, skirt, and sandals and walked out to her VW beetle. She started it up, flipped on the radio, and set off to help man reach for the stars, as if there wasn't enough to fix here on Earth.

The Summer of '68

The Space Center was a beehive of activity. It existed now to put a man on the Moon, fulfilling the promise spoken by Bobby's brother: "We will land a man on the Moon by the end of the decade." Mary's part was to help keep everyone happy (i.e., to keep their paychecks coming on time). It wasn't much fun through the early summer, through the hot days of June, with insects swarming around her every morning and every evening whenever she went outside. Only the pungent smell of tobacco and marijuana seemed to keep them away. She remained lost, wondering what the next day would bring, often hanging out at the local bar with Martha Jane and Sally, watching the boy/men come over, trying to cop a feel, never intent on any serious relationship. It was as if the summer would never end, although it wasn't clear what the fall would bring, what with the tedium of work and the added pressure of her "Introduction to Psychology" course at Brevard Community College. As she listened to Richard Harris singing "MacArthur's Park," she fantasized about the recipe for his cake, about being in his kitchen, cooking up some love. She thought of Billie Jo McAllister contemplating suicide from the Tallahatchie Bridge, and wondered what she would be feeling during the seconds after jumping, when you were still alive but knew the end would soon be here. Would it seem interminable? Or just timeless? But most of all, she spent evenings alone, "On the Dock of the Bay," listening to Otis Redding, as the tide rolled in.

Then, at a 4th of July picnic, Mary met Ronnie, a Native American who was one of the mechanics at Grumman. They went out on a couple of dates, going to the movies to see "Alice's Restaurant." Then they headed over to the River's Edge on the Banana River. It was a little too sophisticated for Ronnie, who was more into the Satellite Restaurant, with its ethnic Mexican food.

The following weekend, they went down to the Westland Marina and Ronnie took her out for a day of fishing. They came on shore with several nice groupers and even a sea bass, which he deftly filleted for her on the boat and packed in ice. They went home to the trailer park where he lived with his parents and he grilled up the fillets, while Mary tried her hand at frying up some green tomatoes and okra. They sat and watched as the stars came out, drinking slowly from their bottles of Bud. As Ronnie started to kiss Mary, she felt, for the first time, some sense of love and acceptance, something different than she had felt when she was with Mike or the other jerks from high school. But she wasn't quite ready to commit; she'd only seen crazy relationships in her past, except for her grandparents, who seemed beyond sexuality.

The work-week crawled by as Ronnie and Mary waited for their next date. Mary was surprised when Ronnie showed up in a bright, blue sports coat two sizes too large, a blue shirt with a bright, red tie, and his best bluejeans. His black hair was shoulder length, and he was trying to make himself look older, with his fuzzy, black mustache and attempt at a beard.

"I'm taking you out to something nice tonight, Mary."

"Ronnie, I need to change. I can't go like I am with jeans and a T-shirt. Where're we going?"

"Mary, you look great. We're going over to the Captain's Table. I have some deep shit to talk to you about."

Mary felt adored for the first time in her life as Ronnie wined and dined her, buying a full bottle of California cabernet, not just a carafe of Gallo red table wine. They each had surf and turf, and Mary was beginning to get a bit giddy.

"What's the occasion?" Mary's eyes were twinkling.

"Besides that I've fallen in love with you?"

Mary's eyes started to tear.

"I got my draft notice today."

"No, it can't be."

"I need to report next week to the induction center for processing."

"This war, why does it have to keep on? Why can't Nixon just end it?"

"Mary, I'm sorry."

"What about us, Ronnie?"

"There's the telephone and the good old U.S. mail. And there's at least two to four weeks before I have to report to boot camp. And maybe they'll give me a furlough over Christmas before I ship out."

"Then we don't have any time to wait." Mary had already made up her mind that Ronnie was special, and that if there was any man who was worth her losing her virginity to, it would be him. Maybe he would come back in December and they could get engaged.

That night they went back to Ronnie's room in the trailer, tiptoeing past his Mom's door, and when he started caressing her, she didn't move his hand away. She was in love and Ronnie was worthy of her, despite whatever the nuns would say. This wasn't like her sister's friend, Susan, who'd gotten knocked up in the back of some football player's car. No, Ronnie was gentle, he didn't leave her side after they made love, and he made her coffee in the morning after they had again consummated their relationship. But by 11 a.m., it being Sunday, she had to leave to meet Martha Jane at church.

"You look exhausted, Mary, but there's a certain glow to your face," MJ chortled.

"What do you expect, after how I just spent the last 18 hours?"

"Did you and Ronnie have a good time?"

"The best! It's finally happened for me. There's someone who cares, that I can trust." Mary started crying.

"Then why are you crying? He was a typical man, wasn't he? Came in 45 seconds and then went to watch TV with his beer?"

"No, Martha Jane. It wasn't like that at all. He made me feel special. It's just that he's been drafted and he'll be leaving soon."

"Then you better make up for lost time, honey."

"I know."

"Well, after he leaves, I've got plans for us."

"What do you mean?"

"We're going to fight to get him back home soon. We're going to Chicago for the Democratic Convention."

"Damn it, MJ. They just had the Republican Convention down in Miami. Wouldn't that have been easier to go to?"

"What, are you a Republican now? No way, Nixon's the biggest jerk I ever saw. And besides, didn't you see those riots in the darkie section? I think there were four people who got killed along with lots of arrests.

"I still can't go to Chicago. What about Ronnie?"

"It'll take your mind off of Ronnie's leaving. And you'll be doing your service to our service men, bringing them back home out of harms way."

"But I just started working. They'll have my ass soon enough."

"Don't worry, my friend Jeannie works for old Dr. Grant and she'll forge a note for you, stating that you had contagious strep throat."

Mary and Ronnie spent every evening together, knowing that, at least for now, he was only going to basic training—not yet to 'Nam—and that they would have more time together. But when he packed his two duffle bags and was off on the Greyhound Bus, Mary was alone again.

And just as simple as that, in mid-August, Mary and MJ set out for their road trip. Mary's VW convertible was packed with their two duffle bags full of underwear, jeans, and blouses. Mary refused to bring a bra, and MJ was too flat to need one, so they were going to truly be in the spirit of free expression. Toothbrush, toothpaste, and underarm deodorant made up the rest of the packed goods, with gum and cigarettes to be bought along the way as needed. They got an early start on Saturday morning, drove straight up I-95, and were halfway through Georgia by the time they found a roadside camp to spend the night.

Dinner was a bag of pork rinds washed down with a couple of beers they bought at the camp store. Too tired to even pitch their small army surplus pup tent, they slept in their sleeping bags under the stars, smoking their last cigarettes.

At dawn, Mary awakened to a beautiful sunrise. MJ was still asleep. Mary slowly got out of her bag, trying not to disturb her.

"Where are you going, Mary? What time is it?"

"It's 6 a.m."

"Fuck! We need to get going now if we're going to make it to Chicago by nightfall."

"First I need my shower."

"We don't have time."

"Don't worry, MJ. I'll make it up on the road. They don't call me leadfoot for nothing. I'm not going anywhere 'til I take my shower and wash my hair. We don't have any idea of where we're staying in Chicago and whether there'll even be running water!"

"Just make it quick, then."

Fifteen minutes later, Mary was back, her hair dripping wet, with a pint of Jack Daniels and a package of powdered donuts from the camp store.

"Breakfast!"

"Of Champions!" MJ retorted.

They packed up their sleeping bags and were on the road again.

As they headed northwest, through Tennessee and up through Illinois, they kept the top down, their hair "blowing in the wind." They were singing, smoking, honking their horn at any one traveling in their direction who looked like a hippie. Any car with the bumper sticker "Make Love, Not War" was an ally.

But when they stopped for gas outside of Springfield, Illinois, they realized they "weren't in Kansas anymore." The pimple-faced teen who came out to pump their gas had a crew cut and torn jeans, with his Winstons protected in the fold of his dirty white T-shirt. His buddy was in his army fatigues.

"You girls need some company?" he asked as he topped off the tank. "We've going out this evening 'fore George here goes off to boot camp to be trained to get shot up by the enemy."

"Hey, Andy, not so fast. Those Cong won't have a chance against me. I won't trust anyone, not even the little yellow women or children. Bang! Bang! I'll shoot them down."

"Just be careful, or they'll be bringing you home in a body bag," Andy warned.

"So how about it, young ladies? Where you off to? All we've seen today are long-haired hippies off to Chicago to protest against our boys."

"Yeah, but they haven't gotten very far. I just leave the gas cap off and they plum run out of fuel on the interstate."

"We're off to see our aunt in Wisconsin," Mary said, figuring a little white lie would go a long way here. "It's her 60th birthday and we're due there tonight."

"Well, you girls better get going. Only watch 'bout ten miles north of here. That's where "Old Elmer" sits in his cruiser, waiting to give tickets for out-of-state libs."

"Thanks a lot," MJ said, prodding Mary to go. "Mary here tends to go a bit fast."

"Good luck in 'Nam."

"I'll think about you in my dreams. You two sure are pretty."

At the end of the parking lot, Mary turned around towards the guys at the pumps and pulled her blouse up, showing her small dark nipples, which stood out in contrast to her pale white breasts.

"Pleasant dreams!" she yelled. "Don't wear out your right hand!"

With that, Mary spun her wheels and screeched out into the highway.

"Damn, I thought they only had rednecks down in the South."

"I guess not, MJ. I can't wait to get to Chicago."

By 8 p.m. on Friday night, they were just south of Chicago. Instead of riding into town at 9 p.m., they found a cheap motel off the exit of the interstate. By 10 p.m., they were asleep. And at 5 a.m., they heard the goats outside their window, letting them know it was time to go.

August 24, Saturday

The streets of Chicago were filled with police, National Guardsman, and the protestors. None of them were yet in their "respective corners." Mary checked the fliers on the telephone pole.

"Hey, MJ. There's a Women's Strike for Peace picketing at the Hilton Hotel. I say we go over there. I'm ready to join the sisterhood!"

But she wasn't quite ready for all of the Women's Lib movement, (although going bra-less meant freedom at last, especially if men were around). She was turned off by women not shaving under their armpits (a little gross to see them looking like men!) or forsaking deodorant (why not just live in a stable!) And when a woman started to come on to her, she yelled "Get the fuck away from me!"

MJ insisted that it was much better to spend the night in Grant Park, where heterosexuality was rampant and they could watch the guys walk around, especially those who were "well hung."

"MJ, we're not here to get laid. Get focused. I want to hear what Abbie Hoffman is saying."

"Sure, take all of the fun out of this. Let's get over there."

The only problem with getting over there and with sleeping there was that Chicago Mayor Richard Daley had declared war on the protesters, denying them permits to spend the night in the park. With almost 12,000 police, 7,500 Army troops, and an equal number of National Guardsmen to enforce the Mayor's "point of view," violence was unavoidable.

As Mary and MJ ran over to hear Tom Hayden, the police were swarming through the park, and then officially closed it.

"Keep moving, Mary."

"MJ, I hear screaming up ahead."

Two black men, with Afros and full beards, were walking past them.

"Don't worry, whitey, the "pigs" won't hurt you."

"Or if they do, Leroy and me, we're ready to do battle to protect your lily white asses," his comrade added. "Bitch, you'd better find yourself a large stick to defend yourself."

"MJ, do we really want to go up there?"

"Mary, we didn't come here just to leave."

As they moved forward, the police were coming towards them, carrying their billy-clubs on their horses' saddles, ready to do battle. Leroy ran towards them, his own tree trunk swinging wildly, only to have the wood broken in half as the billy-club came down, landing on his shoulder. As his friend George went to protect him, he was knocked off his feet by another cop, and both men were dragged out of the crowd to be arrested.

"We better get out of here, MJ." Mary was choking, her eyes unable to tolerate the tear gas that was surrounding them.

"Pour the water out of your canteen onto your bandana, Mary. Put it over your face."

"I am, MJ. Let's get the fuck out of here."

As the crowd scattered, Mary felt the breath of a mare at her side. She looked up to see a "pig" up close. He did not look like Andy Griffith in Mayberry, but more like one of the football players from Titusville, who was avoiding serving his country in Vietnam by serving in the National Guard. As a photographer ran over to take a picture of the scene, one of "Chicago's Finest" rode up and, in one motion, knocked him off his feet and pinned him to the turf, handcuffing his wrists together.

"MJ, where are you?"

"Mary, fuck this. We're outa here."

They started to run, got winded easily, and then started to walk the three miles to where they had left their car, which thankfully still had four intact tires and an unbroken windshield. They reached Springfield by nightfall, the birthplace of Abraham Lincoln's political career, and were back in Florida two nights later.

August 27, 1968

Mary and MJ decided to turn on the television to see what was happening. They were just in time to watch the police slashing through the crowds of protestors. They felt like they were still part of the event when Senator Abraham Ribicoff nominated the "peace" candidate, George McGovern, inflaming the crowd when he said, "With George McGovern as president of the United States we wouldn't have Gestapo tactics in the streets of Chicago."

"Pop, are you watching what's happening in Chicago?" I was hoping he would see the brutality being inflicted on the peace protestors. I ran into his bedroom, where he and Lil were editing a manuscript. "We have to turn on the television. Senator Ribicoff just made a great speech, attacking Mayor Daley."

"Ken, I have to finish this paper."

"Bill, watch. I'll work on the paper later. This may affect Paul." Lil was adamant.

We stared at the television: images of the police swarming through the protestors; pieces of earth and sticks and bottles being thrown from the crowd; and the National Guard and Mayor Daley's Police, the "Red Army of Chicago," responding with tear gas and clubs, as they chased the proletariat through Grant Park, capturing and dragging them off in police vehicles.

"Dad, they can't do that. Those people were trying to get away."

"Then what the hell were they doing there in the first place?"

"Dad, they have the right to demonstrate. Isn't that what you always said? That's what makes America so great."

"Not when they start throwing sticks and bottles. It's no different than what happened at Columbia. Just ask Harlan. They're just out to destroy the very society their parents gave them on a silver platter."

"I know, Dad, but it's not so simple. The police don't have to be so brutal. That's what turns peaceful protestors into violent SDS recruits."

"Ingrates! Why don't those kids at least cut their hair? They look disgusting."

"Bill, just wait. You're condemning Paul. His hair is long." Lil was the protecting mother bear.

"Dammit, Lil, he's the one I'm most worried about. What if he decides not to go to Temple University? Then he'll be drafted."

"That's why we're out there, Dad. Didn't you read the Democratic Platform? Even with all of the support for McCarthy and McGovern, the Democrats still refused to propose unilaterally suspending the bombing. They're waiting for Hanoi. And you know that won't happen."

As our "discussion" went on (and on), the convention delegates nominated Hubert Humphrey by a substantial margin.

"At least he's not LBJ," Lil interjected.

"No, Lil, he doesn't look like LBJ, but his speeches sure sound like him." I emphatically added: "What a choice, Nixon versus Humphrey."

"I still love you, Pop." And I reached into my back pocket. "Happy 45th Birthday!" as I handed him a card from Hope and me with a big PEACE sign on the front!

September 1968

The disappointment of the Democratic Convention was a fitting ending for my summer of either working for my dad or hanging out with Jay and our buddies. Robin had been away at summer camp as a counselor—not that it really mattered! With September would come the excitement (and entitlement) of my senior year. We were the Kings and Queens of the Hills of Scarsdale High School. Although Cathy and I had learned to co-exist, by this time I had developed my own set of friends, and we had fairly separate lives—except, of course, at dinner time, when she was still the hormonally challenged teenage girl and I the acne-faced horny boy. Thus, our main interface occurred nightly, when I would be in charge of carving up the chicken or steak, and Cathy would come down, pick off pieces of the freshly carved meat as her dinner, and then, much to Lil's "dismay," would proclaim at the dinner table, "I'm not hungry." She would then get up with a grunt and go off to the telephone closet. If I had the urge to carve off one of her fingers every time she went for the roast, I can only imagine Lil's anger at her "pride and joy."

I prepped for my SATs and achievement tests once again, prepared my applications for Columbia University, Brown University, Johns Hopkins, Union College, and University of Wisconsin—all, as it turned out, except for Johns Hopkins—hot beds of student and radical political activity. I went with Jay to visit his brother at Union College, and took the bus myself to Baltimore to the Johns Hopkins campus. My dad and Lil took a weekend off to drive me to Brown University and Cathy to the University of Bridgeport, but we got our traditional late start. Not wanting to miss an afternoon working on his files, he "allowed" Lil to drive—much to our relief, as she was a much better navigator. By the time we got to Providence, it was late Saturday afternoon—not much chance to look around the campus or interact with the college kids.

October 1968

The Olympic Games, held in mile high Mexico City. The United States' reputation on the line, the Free World against the Communist World, the amateur Americans against the professionals from behind the Iron Curtain and Asia. This was the closest thing to warfare without loss of life — at least, unfortunately, until the 1972 Olympic Games in Munich.

And white America relied on black America to prove our superiority against the Reds, much as white America relied on black America to fight our battle in Vietnam against the Reds.

On October 18, two black Americans, Tommie Smith and John Carlos, won gold and bronze medals in the 200-meter dash. On the winners' platform, Smith raised his right arm while wearing a black glove on one hand and Carlos raised his left arm. They wore no socks. More importantly, during the National Anthem, they kept their heads bowed. All of these actions were a form of silent, non-violent protest against black discrimination and poverty in the United States. Their reward for expressing their feelings, their First Amendment rights, was to be sent home by their team under threat by the International Olympics Committee. They were barred from all further Olympic Games, and subsequently viewed as outcasts in their own country, their lives threatened by countrymen who disagreed with their expressing their rights of expression.

The Red Communist Bloc must have been savoring the moment of Western hypocrisy towards the blacks. As Jay and I watched, we felt their pain, and awaited more of the violence that had erupted. White America had shown its true color.

November 1968

All of the enthusiasm we baby-boomers had for a new approach to ending the war in Vietnam, for a society free from our parents' generation's prejudices and economic priorities, was dissipated by Gene McCarthy's poor showing and spirited away by Bobby Kennedy's assassination. The Democratic Convention had left us without someone we felt we could trust. We were totally unaware of the liberal causes that Hubert Humphrey had fought for as a young man in Minnesota, and pigeon-holed him only as an "Establishment candidate" of the pro-war contingent of the Democratic Party. It was hard for us to become excited, or even, more importantly, emotionally involved with his campaign, even though we were fighting for the same social liberal causes. The result, as often happens, is that our lack of involvement helped "Tricky Dick" Nixon get elected, only six years after he had pretty much resigned from the political arena. At that time—after he lost the California gubernatorial election —he told reporters, "You won't have Nixon to kick around anymore, because, gentleman, this is my last press conference."

Now instead of Hubert Humphrey and Edmund Muskie, honorable senators from Northern states, we not only had Nixon, but also Maryland Governor Spiro Agnew as vice-president. When I had interviewed earlier that fall at John Hopkins University in Baltimore, I had innocently asked people whether they were going to vote for Spiro for VP. They responded with, "Of course, anything to get him out of Maryland." For now, we would have to wake up in the morning to their pictures on the front page of *The New York Times,* and go to bed with these future felons' images on the CBS News with Walter Cronkite, right before seeing Dan Rather reporting on the carnage taking place half-way across the globe. In only five years, Agnew would resign under charges of tax evasion and Nixon would leave office under the threat of impeachment for the Watergate cover-up. But in 1969, it was only OUR enlightened generation that realized they were crooks; they were still considered "honorable" men by mainstream Americans.

November 11, 1968

Veteran's Day, Titusville, Florida. Mary called Ronnie's camp, but was unable to get through to him. She had hoped that now that he was a "veteran" that the country would be honoring him. But then again, she thought, if they gave all of the veterans the day off, who would be protecting us? And Ronnie was still just basic training. Whatever, she was so proud of him, whether or not he got the chance to call her.

Veteran's Day, Scarsdale, New York. If Memorial Day was just viewed as another holiday, then image how unimportant this day felt to everyone except those families were related to a veteran. At home, my dad continued working on his symposium—it was just another day.

November 18

I needed some relief from my parents' world and the mess they were leaving us. In October, the Westchester County Center had advertised that Janis Joplin be giving a concert. She was not yet a national star, but after I'd heard her on Paul's stereo, I bought my own copy of Big Brother and the Holding Company's album "Cheap Thrills." Not that I could play it on my stereo at the appropriate wall-throbbing level, since my dad would inevitably yell, "Turn that garbage down."

I got two great seats for the show: fourth row, center. And best of all, Robin agreed to come with me. I know I anticipated her company more than listening to the "Big Brother and the Holding Company!"

The County Center was hardly what could be called a "symphony hall." Our seats would have been ON mid-court at a Harlem Globetrotters game that Harlan and I had attended the past spring. We had laughed as the black athletes who made up the Globetrotters had their way with their slower white counterparts of the "Nationals," a team that was destined to lose every time. That spectacle was so unlike real life in White Plains, where racism was an unofficial fact of life. It was more similar to "Amos and Andy," with the races reversed. My fellow white Americans applauded—just as long as the victories remained on the basketball court.

And only two months ago, our fourth row center seats had been occupied by suddenly pious members of our synagogue—the number of congregants swelling to five times the capacity of our own sacred temple building. Prayers for Atonement for our sins filled the air as we sang religious hymns during the High Holy Day services.

On this night, however, there were no flowers, no hoops, no choir music. And there was certainly no piety. We waited the traditional 30 minutes past show time before Big Brother came out to tune their instruments. Janis finally came out, shuffling, assuredly stoned or drunk by that time, 20 pounds overweight, her shoulder-length hair uncombed. She began to talk to us with in hoarse, gravelly voice. The band started to play, with the rhythmic guitars and drums setting the tone, until she was ready to sing. The spotlight moved from band member to band member, and then finally illuminated Janis.

Her sultry voice quieted the crowd—a white singer's rendition of a black song written by a white composer in the 1930s: "Summertime."

I'm not sure all of the audience actually knew what to expect, as it took several minutes for the teens around me to get the beat, to feel the white soul, to internalize the sadness of her love.

I'm not sure that Robin was ever moved by the music, and there was no way that I could get her to be a part of the moment. I should have known when I picked her up from her house and she was dressed in the early "Natalie Wood" fashion, wearing a blue skirt and stockings, with a white button-front blouse, that this wasn't her scene. (Not that I was exactly a poster child for the '60s. My only attempt to break away from the "Buddy Holly" look of the '50s was to have a wave of my blond hair over my forehead, as opposed to having my hair slicked up with Vitalis. But I still had my thick, black-rimmed glasses, my hair cut short in the back, and my yellow Arrow shirt tucked "stylishly" into my beige chino slacks.) There was no holding hands, no hugging, no dancing in the aisle between us. I could smell the pungent scent was that drifted over from the surreptitiously lit "cigarette" four seats down from us, but I didn't dare inhale for fear of being arrested. But if I was a "square," then Robin was a "square" squared!

Finally, I decided that I would just enjoy the music, and be less concerned with how the date was going, and less worried if Robin still liked me. As if I really could be that detached. I kept looking at her, hoping she would be turned on to the music, be thankful I had brought her here to be with me.

Then the song that I wanted Robin to hear, "A Piece of My Heart," filled the auditorium

Oh, how much the words reverberated inside me as Robin sat like a stone (but clearly not "stoned") next to me. If only she had one-tenth of the emotion for me; if only Janis would be singing about me, through her Southern Comfort and drugged-out state, I could heal her pain.

The next 90 minutes were a schizophrenic experience for me. I wished I was with Janice backstage, high on something, while at the same time sitting next to Robin, who I know couldn't wait to get out. Her level of discomfort rose with every song. And I experienced Janis' pain, knowing Robin would never "Hold me in her arms."

And as we walked out into the parking lot after the concert, Robin reached into her pocketbook and pulled out a cigarette, quietly lighting it, taking a deep puff. She had heard me pontificate on the evils of cigarette smoking, how much I was disappointed when I found my fourth-grade teacher smoking one afternoon. Even a hammer and nails couldn't have sealed the coffin on our "relationship" more profoundly.

But, uncharacteristically, I was able to rebound from this disappointment, flowering like a cherry blossom tree in April in Washington, D.C., when I qualified to be one of my high school's three contestants on the television show, "It's Academic." We were to be pitted against two other teams of the "best and the brightest" students from high schools in the New York City metropolitan area.

And so, the next week, there we were on the front page of the school newspaper, Josh and Don and myself, pictured as the three monkeys: "Hear no evil, See no evil, Speak no evil." And the following weekend, we arrived at the Channel 4 studio for the taping of our first show, ready to make our loyal supporters from the high school proud. Even several of the cheerleaders were there, eager to start with "Give me an S, Give me a C," until they realized there were no basketball players running around in shorts. Several of our teachers, along with the student government, were there, much as the ladies went to watch their heroes prepare for mortal combat in medieval days of yore. Our brains were our swords—something that, at last, I would be respected for in my class. We were dressed in our best suits, our faces covered with makeup to hide the acne. My stark white shirt, purple tie, and navy blue blazer appeared much like funeral garb; my glasses freshly cleaned to prevent any glare from the cameras; and my hair was combed just right across my forehead. So everything was counterproductive to my attempts to be declassified as a "geek!"

After our introductions, the audience's attention turned to the moderator, Art James. He was dressed "middle-aged cool," wearing a pale green suit with wide lapels and a red and yellow polka dot tie six inches wide. His hair was groomed and his sideburns came halfway down his cheeks.

He tried to calm us all down with small talk about what each of us liked, and then, he warned, mimicking Jack Webb from "Dragnet," the popular crime show:

"Don't forget, 'Just the facts, ma'am.' "

He launched into the initial first round, a series of "toss up" questions, worth ten points each, and then allowed that team to proceed to another question.

"The first American president to die in office . . . "

I buzzed, waiting to be acknowledged. "William Henry Harrison!"

"Correct, ten points for Scarsdale High School."

Cheers emanated from the "peanut gallery." I couldn't have been more ecstatic; it felt like hitting my first home run for the varsity baseball team. We were on the board!

"If a barber cuts a customer's hair every 15 minutes for $8 dollars a haircut, how much will he earn in 90 minutes?"

I went for the bell, about to blurt out $48, when I realized that Wantagh High School had beaten me to it. I went sick inside, hearing the right answer come from a different team.

Back and forth we went, but gradually we built up a lead. I found myself watching the clock, like a soccer coach whose team has a one goal lead, not exactly knowing how much time was left, but waiting hopefully for . . . the final whistle.

"And Scarsdale High School is the winner!"

With a sigh of relief, Josh, Don and I smiled at each other, ready to bask in the glory of our triumphant return to the high school. Luckily for us, this was the night of our senior party at the American Legion. As I entered, for once I was recognized by the rest of my classmates, who came over to congratulate me, to say they couldn't wait for the show to be on television. I was the student athlete, my math genius propelling me to the adulation of my classmates. If I couldn't do it on the football field, at least I could be a TV hero.

Only Robin was missing from my life—I wasn't that dense not to have gotten the picture. Jay didn't bother to come either. He was ready to blow this town, and high school parties had little left for him. And like the one-dimensional jock, I was soon sitting alone, my glory days almost behind me. I went over to the "bar" for a Coke, still smiling, but wondering how much longer I would be staying.

"Hi, weren't you on 'It's Academic' today?"

I looked up and there was this pretty girl from my French class talking to me. I thought her name was Lynn, but she was so quiet in class I couldn't be sure. She had on a black, mid-thigh-length skirt, and her long legs looked beautiful in her beige stockings. Her white blouse had the two top buttons undone, and her chest revealed as yet unblossomed breasts.

"Sure, we won."

"I'm so happy for you. I'd love to try out for the team, but I'm just not that good in math."

"Maybe I could help you?" What a great pickup line!

"That would be nice." Lynn was friendly to me. I had never been "picked up" before, so I didn't have the vaguest idea where to begin.

"Can I buy you a Coke?"

"Sure."

And so, over a couple of Cokes we started with the small talk about our families and how our class was so big that it was impossible to know everyone.

Finally, I got up the nerve to ask, "Would you like to come with us to next week's taping of our quarter-final show?"

"I'd love to."

"I can pick you up from your house and we can ride to the high school together to take the bus into the city."

"That'd be great! What time?"

"I'll call you during the week and let you know. What's your number?"

"555-2589" (Did you ever wonder why every number in the movies begins with "555"?)

And so it was the beginning of a nice, although not wonderful, six weeks of dating, including several movies and one dance. I learned that Lynn was interested in modeling, in going to the Fashion Institute of Technology, and had little interest in science, math or history. She was beautiful, tall, thin, and had a striking face and breathtaking smile. She was of some comfort to me after we lost the second round of "It's Academic," and still went out with me after that. But if our relationship started with the optimism of James Stewart and Donna Reed in the movie "It's a Wonderful Life"—which I had just seen for what would be the first of 30 annual viewings—it ended more like a scene from an Elliot Gould movie about relationships gone flat in the '60s. As was the case with Art Garfunkel and Candice Bergen in "Carnal Knowledge," we just didn't have enough in common to really sustain a longterm relationship.

Our last date was New Year's Eve, 1968, ushering in 1969. We went to the city to see "Funny Girl" and took the train home to Scarsdale, where my dad went the extra mile to pick us up at the train station at 12:30 a.m.

Lynn and I sat in the back seat, with Dad playing the roles of dutiful chauffeur/facilitator, following Lynn's instructions on how to take the shortcut to her home, going up the hill to the fashionable section of town. We held hands in the back seat, and when we arrived at her "mansion," I escorted her to the front door. With my dad unobtrusively watching from the car, there was no, "Would you like to come in for a drink?" And obviously, there was no "good night fuck." What there was, in full view of my father, was a good night kiss, not on the cheek, but also without any lingering on the lips. Not much to hope for in the future!

The next morning, the first day of 1969, I awoke with a stiffness in my jaw, a temperomandibular spasm. I was unable to open my mouth more that two inches. For the next three months, I saw several specialists who prescribed exercises, heat, and muscle relaxants. It wasn't until I saw the last dentist that I was told that the disorder was often psychosomatic. I guessed that, in my case, it was because my father had seen me engaged in "sexual activity!" At least I wasn't caught masturbating.

January 1, 1969

"What time is it?" Mary whispered, her head throbbing. "Ronnie, do we really have to get up this morning?"

Ronnie was lying next to her in bed, his body taut from basic training, his previously long, black mane so proudly tied in a pony tail now shaved into a crew cut. He still had his baby face, barely able to grow whiskers, and his angular jaw and long, chiseled nose made him a poster child for an Army "grunt." He'd had some trouble assimilating into the redneck, Southern culture in Georgia, and as he'd not yet learned the knack of turning the other cheek, he'd spent several of his days doing KP duty. But when he stepped off the bus a week ago, Mary was elated; her "savior" was home. She embraced him and gave him a big kiss, but when she went to jump in his arms, she noticed his right arm was behind his back. He had this crazy smile as he presented her with his prize, a live turkey in a poultry case.

"For Christmas Dinner."

Christmas was joyful his year, because even though Ronnie's family was poor, they actually seemed to love each other. With all of the gifts that Mary's mother and step-father gave, there was no love. Bill gave Ellen a new washer and clothes dryer, and Ellen gave Bill a new charcoal grill and hair dryer. Even the clothes under their perfectly adorned Christmas tree were all Sears-Roebuck specials. But, at Ronnie's, there was a small doll for his baby sister, Dawn, some homemade jam for Mary, and woven mittens for Ronnie. They were all under a small, evergreen Christmas tree with ornaments that Ronnie and Dawn had made in elementary school. Mary brought the family a box of blue and gold Christmas tree balls, and she bought Ronnie a new transistor radio that played both FM and AM and had a small earphone, so he could listen to his music in private. And Ronnie gave her a beautiful pearl necklace that he purchased at the local pawnshop at the camp.

As she rolled out of bed, she realized the sun was halfway up in the sky. She took one look in the mirror, saw her disheveled hair, and wondered when they had gotten home. The she realized that they must have celebrated New Year's Eve well into New Year's Day.

"Ronnie, get your butt out of bed. I'm not going to waste our last day together."

"Mary, I need some java first, then one of those three-egg omelets with real eggs, not the powdered kind, along with some hot cakes and grits for breakfast with some genuine Vermont maple syrup."

"Right, Ronnie, but I'm not a waitress. Just get up and brush your teeth. And there's no way you're gonna find any other syrup than Aunt Jemima's at George's Coffee Shop. I just hope they're open."

"We both deserve better. It's not fair that Ronnie has to get shot at in Nam" Mary thought. She went into the shower, first turning on the cold water to awaken herself, and then the warm water, letting it soothe her muscles. After 20 minutes of the pulsating jet, she felt rejuvenated. Ronnie, however, was still asleep as she toweled off, zipped her jeans back on, and pulled her sweater over her braless torso. She brushed her teeth with her finger, using what was left of the Crest toothpaste, and poured some cold water over Ronnie's face.

"Up and at 'em." She laughed.

Fifteen minutes later, Ronnie was dressed in his khaki uniform. And they were out the door, into the brisk January morning. As they got into her VW bug, she decided to put the top down, to feel the cool air rushing through her hair, punishing her face as it invigorated her body.

"I need some coffee now. I can't wait 'til we get to George's. I'll get us a couple of cups," she said aloud, as they heard the radio announcer playing the top hits of 1968, down to #44, "Good Morning, Sunshine." At last she found a 7-Eleven that was open. She pulled up, parked her car, and went inside, joining a group of repentant revelers pouring themselves extra large cups of black coffee. She recognized one of them from Grumman Industries where she worked, an engineer on the lunar project. He grunted, "Hello," and Mary gave a half-smile, half grimace, simultaneously expressing her delight at seeing him and dismay at being up this early.

"I guess I'll see you tomorrow at work," she said.

"Yeah, bright and early, we're at least a week behind schedule." He was too serious for her. And she felt sure she was would be protected from any unwanted advances by that gold band on his left hand.

Back in the car, the radio was still on, the manic voice announcing #41, as the Beatles sang "Lady Madonna." "What a life," Mary said. "I can't believe I've gotta go to work. I can't believe you've gotta leave."

"Who was that guy you were talking to in there?" Ronnie asked.

"One of the guys at work."

"Doesn't he know you're taken?"

"Ronnie, he's just a guy at work. Don't worry, I'm all yours," she said, as she put her arms around his neck and gave him a big sloppy kiss.

"When'll I see you again?"

"Soon as you can."

"Depends on when I'm gonna ship out to the West Coast. Can you come up to see me?"

"I'll try to get time off, I promise."

They were quiet over breakfast.

"What's wrong, Ronnie?"

"Nothing. I'm just thinking."

As they parked the car at the Greyhound Station and walked up to the gate, Mary started to count down the minutes until he took off. They held hands, the bus pulled up, and Ronnie started to get on. She hugged him again, gave him another big sloppy kiss, and he started up the steps.

"That guy knows you're taken, doesn't he?"

"Yes, Ronnie, I love you."

"I love you too. I'll see you before I ship out?"

"Of course. I'll try to get out to the coast."

As the bus pulled out, her apprehension began to grow. Ronnie's behavior had become obsessive, overwhelming her with his unfounded jealousy. "I just don't know, this may be too much," she thought. "I wonder if I'm celibate for a month, do I qualify as a virgin again?" She would have to ask Father Joe that question, but then again, she would have to go to church again to get an answer.

She drove back to the Callahan's, where she was renting a room, although it was not clearly "renting" because they'd given her a place to live in return for nominal babysitting for their eight-year-old son, Philip. Marge Callahan was the senior teller at the Titusville National Bank where Mary had worked during high school, and she knew that Mary's step-dad had pretty much thrown Mary out after her graduation. For the first time since she left her grandparents back in Virginia four years ago, Mary felt part of a family. It was because of this love for Marge and her husband, Ryan, that Mary would have self-recrimination when she went overboard, get stoned out of her gourd, and had to be driven home. Marge had spoken with her last week, and now Mary resolved to turn over a new leaf. It would be easy today, for when she was babysitting for Philip, she took her responsibility seriously. If only she could keep it in moderation on weekends.

Marge and Ryan were sitting at the breakfast table, with Phil on the sun porch reading the newspaper, when Mary walked in.

Ryan looked up and spoke in his softest, almost pleading voice, "Mary, why don't you sit down and get something to eat with us?"

"Not this morning. Thanks, anyway."

"Ah, please, Mary?" Philip's voice reverberated through the passageway from the garage, as he entered the room. "I didn't get to watch the ball drop with you last night."

"Philip, I'm sorry, honey, I was out. But I'll have some Cheerios with you this morning."

"No, I want my Wheaties! I want to a champion!"

"And then you can become a big football player, just like one of the Titusville High School Astronauts." Ryan volunteered his enthusiasm for an athletic son.

"Ryan, I don't want him getting hurt. He's my son also. I want him to become an accountant. That's where the money is."

"Philip, what would *you* like to be?" Mary was behind him all the way.

"I want to be an actor. Just like Robin in "Batman.""

"That would be cool."

"Yeah, and then I could ride around in the 'Batmobile.' "

"Only if you give me a ride!" Mary laughed.

"Silly Mary. I don't have enough money saved up, yet. But you can take a ride with me on my new bike I got for Christmas."

"Hey, why don't we all go for a ride this afternoon?" Marge chimed in. "I know the old station wagon isn't a "Batmobile," but at least it holds four of us. We can drive up to the Breakers."

"I don't know, I need some rest," Mary answered.

"Please, Mary, you can rest later," Philip pleaded.

"Well, if you all insist. But just make sure we get back in time so I can get a good night's sleep before I go back to work tomorrow."

"We promise, Mary. The fresh air will do you good. You spend too much time cooped up in that building over at the Cape."

"Don't forget Max," Philip added. "He'll be lonely at home without us."

An hour later, they were all packed into the Ford wagon with wood side panels, Marge and Ryan up front and Mary sitting with Philip in the back seat. Max, their handsome golden retriever, had the back area all to himself. He reached over and grabbed Philip's Twinkie out of his hand, leading to a wail from the eight-year-old that could have been heard halfway to the Moon.

"Philip, that's okay, just calm down, son."

"No, Max, you doo-doo bird, you stole my Twinkie." Philip was half-crying, half-laughing now.

"Philip, I'll buy you another one when we get to a '7-Eleven,'" Mary comforted him.

"Make sure you buy two, Mary, so I can give him another. Did you see him eat it in one bite?" Philip had forgotten the trauma and was enjoying his dog's antics.

Mary reached over and hugged him, her loneliness evaporating. They both closed their eyes and slept for what seemed like a long time, with Max's muzzle resting between their two heads.

January 2, 1969

The first day back at work at the VAB—the Vehicle Assembly Building—and Mary was determined to start the new year right. She had dressed carefully that morning, in her pink sleeveless blouse, royal blue skirt, and a new pair of panty hose. Her make-up consisted of a minimum of lipstick along with her mascara.

As she rushed through the doors at 9 a.m., the rest of the Grumman employees were straggling in. The partying would now be over as there were only six months to get the final lunar landing module ready for man's walk on the Moon. The engineers all wore their starched white shirts, sleeves rolled up, with blue or dark red ties and black slacks. The supervisors usually kept their ties on, maybe a bit loosened at the collar. But those who were physically working on the projects were tieless, not wanting them to get strangled by the machinery.

"Hey, Mary, you don't look so bad!" MJ had spent most of New Year's Day in bed with a hangover.

"That's what love will do for you." Mary laughed as they gave each other a hug.

Mary went up to her office, lit a cigarette, and started working on the timesheets from the Christmas week. "What a mess! Do I give them each a holiday or a vacation day? Whatever, I'll just put down the holiday and let Grumman decide."

By lunchtime she was back in the groove, her radio blaring in the background, still recounting the greatest hits of 1968, by the Stones and the Beatles.

"Hey, MJ, you think if they ever send up another chimpanzee they'll play music from the Monkees? 'Day Dream Believer.' Or 'Take the Last Rocket to Clarksville.'"

"Mary, you look exhausted."

"No, MJ, just too much in love to know any better."

"Well, don't be too happy. I need someone to go with me to the Mousetrap tomorrow night. The first Friday night after New Year's is always a hoot."

Two nights later they were all at the Mousetrap, the local watering hole, with 25-cent drafts and 50-cent well drinks. Mary and MJ were sitting at the bar when Jack and Arnie walked over.

"You girls looking for someone to buy you a beer?"

MJ laughed. "Yeah, Arnie. Like you're looking for some action. I know you got your pretty wife and two little girls back home in Long Island. I saw their picture on your desk. And that ring on your finger doesn't lie."

"Where does it say that two men on assignment can't buy two pretty girls a drink without having anything but a friendly chat on their mind?" Jack was too serious. He still had his tie and jacket on. His hair was slicked back and he had a thin, black mustache on his upper lip—the Clark Gable look, a couple of decades out of style.

"That'd be a new one on me," Mary cackled.

"I don't know, Mary, you girls are cute, but this is a pretty small town, and believe me, all we want is some conversation. Maggie and the twins are at her mother's house tonight at a party. I told them where we were going."

"So, Arnie, tell me about yourself," MJ said, willing to give them a chance.

"Graduated from Lehigh University, married my high school sweet-heart, moved to Long Island when I got this engineering job, and then I took this opportunity to come down here to help build the lunar module. The pay is pretty good, and it's exciting to know that we're a part of history. But I do miss Maggie and the kids."

"MJ, they must be okay," Mary whispered in her ear. "No one would mention his wife and kids twice in two minutes if they weren't homesick and in love."

As they all talked, the music on the jukebox started playing "Un-chained Melody" by the Righteous Brothers. Tears started welling up in Arnie's eyes. "You'll have to excuse me. I'm going to go back to my apartment and hope that I can reach Maggie."

"Hey, we all have a long day tomorrow. I've got to get up early also," Mary added.

As they got into their cars, MJ whispered to Mary, "I think I'll hang out with the rest of the guys. They're fun, and they don't want anything from me, just my laugh and smile. And then she paused, "What a shame!"

"Well, I promised Ronnie I'd be true. He's just so jealous."

"Mary, you're not married to him. Take care of Number One!"

January 12, 1969

It was a harbinger of things to come in the new year for New York and Baltimore sports fans. The New York Jets, from the lowly American Football League, were underdogs to the Baltimore Colts in Super Bowl III.

The fledgling American Football League, whose champions had been blown away by the Green Bay Packers the previous two Super Bowls, had as its spokesperson Joe Willie Namath of the Jets, who brashly guaranteed that his team would beat the Colts. The odds makers disagreed with his assessment, making the Colts the 20-point favorite.

Final score from the Orange Bowl in Miami:

New York Jets 16

Baltimore Colts 7

Spring 1969

There was lots of time to wait for our letters of acceptance or rejection from colleges. The old adage was: thin letter, rejection; thick envelope, acceptance. It was exhilarating to come home from school every day to check the mail, as if Lil hadn't already perused it with the same knowledge base, since three of her kids had already gone through the process. In school every day the talk was about from which schools each of us had received a "yea" or a "nay."

"Ken, there's a letter from University of Wisconsin on the counter," Lil said with a smile, as I came in the back door. Her smile told it all—my first acceptance, even if it was my safety school. At least I knew I'd be going somewhere.

I heard from Johns Hopkins—another yes! That was actually the school I really wanted to go to. It had a great political science department and the students all seemed homogeneously pleasant and politically and socially liberal without being radical. And best of all, after my freshman year I'd be required to live off-campus in an apartment, and I had already made "plans" to bring Hope down to live with me. However, there were only two problems: I had a full faculty child's tuition exemption for Columbia, if I got in; and Lil and my dad made it clear I couldn't take Hope down with me.

Jay finally heard from UCLA—it was a thick envelope! He started packing his bags that night.

So I waited until April 15, the date Ivy League admission letters would come. It was also "senior cut day"—a time either to celebrate victories or drown oneself in defeat. Josh Goldman, who had appeared with me on "It's Academic," couldn't wait to find out whether he'd get into Harvard, Yale, or Stanford, the only three schools to which he had applied.

That day, I got one thick letter (from Columbia) and one thin letter (from Brown). Josh got three thin letters.

As we played our Scrabble or RISK games while eating pizza or take-out Chinese, little did we know, of course, that President Nixon had authorized the secret bombing of Cambodia by our B-52 planes. It was only seven weeks after the Paris peace talks opened, with the U.S., South Vietnam, North Vietnam, and the Vietcong all in attendance.

April 8, 1969

It was Opening Day for the New York Mets, and I was determined to restart the tradition of going to Opening Day at Shea. So far, however, if tradition held, I would be disappointed. The Mets had managed to lose all eight previous opening days in their short, non-illustrious history. But today could be different. After all, they had their new ace, Tom Seaver, on the mound. And to make it a sure thing, they were playing the Montreal Expos, an expansion team playing its first game.

I hadn't missed much school this year and it was the last semester of my senior year, so my dad was happy to write a note describing my awful sore throat on this Tuesday afternoon. No one else was willing to miss school to see my losers, so I was off to the ballpark by myself, arriving way early at 11:30—plenty of time to find my seat, buy my program, and start reading the 1969 official Mets' Yearbook. As always, it was filled with optimism, describing the young pitchers, Tom Seaver and Jerry Koosman, who would anchor our staff, along with rookie Gary Gentry and hard-throwing, albeit wild, Nolan Ryan, a rising star. We had a great young shortstop, Buddy Harrelson, who, although he would be missing some games over the summer while serving in the National Guard, would be there to solidify our infield.

The fans cheered when the Mets took the field, and we were instructed to remove our hats while we listened to the National Anthem.

"Oh Canada!
Our home and native land!
True patriot love in all thy sons command.
With glowing hearts we see thee rise,
The True North strong and free!
From far and wide,
Oh Canada, we stand on guard for thee."

I'd heard this anthem before, on the New York Rangers hockey games broadcast from Montreal on Saturday nights on Channel 9, but here I was in the good old U.S. of A., at the American National Pastime. I guess it shouldn't have surprised me—and the Canadians were our allies, after all. They even allowed those who didn't want to fight for their country to come live there in pursuit of pacificism or cowardice. Finally,

"Oh say can you see
By the dawn's early light."

Now I felt right at home—and even more at home as the Mets promptly surrendered the lead to the Expos in the first inning. It had taken the Mets nine games to win their first game in their first season, and here were the upstart Expos already flexing their muscle. But in the second inning we came back to score three runs, only to have the Montreal pitcher, Dan McGinn, hit the first Expos' home run. In the ninth inning, we were down by five runs, when those fans remaining in the stands started to chant "Let's go Mets." Again, I stayed to the final out, not wanting to miss the "rally." But in the end, we went home tired, angry, depressed, "the same old Mets." Wait until next year went through my mind, if not for the season, then certainly for an Opening Day victory.

At least my hoarse voice convinced my teachers the next day that I was really ill.

May 1969

The glory days of high school were really coming to a close. All of us seniors knew where we were going. I'd already received my housing application from Columbia, and Cathy had hers from the Centenary College for Women in Hackettstown, New Jersey. My 2S draft "evasion" was locked in for four years, even as our troops in Vietnam peaked at over 540,000 men and women. I figured, no way are we going to still be in 'Nam by the time I graduate.

But then I picked up *The New York Times* and read about the secret bombing of Cambodia. As Jay would say, "No way this fuckin' war is gonna end soon." The month before, students at Harvard had taken over the administration building, only to be thrown out forcibly. But, amazingly, the college campuses weren't in an uproar over Nixon's secret bombing of a neighboring country. Maybe we were all shocked by the assault on "Hamburger Hill," where over 40 men soldiers were sacrificed and 400 wounded in a battle in which the commander of the 101st Airborne ordered the "Hill" abandoned after our "victory," returning it to the Vietcong. Should it surprise anyone that American soldiers' morale was dropping and drug use was escalating—anything to get through the days and weeks and months in the mud and rain? Even "Gomer Pyle, USMC," who was stationed stateside during the entire five-year television series, would have lost his goofy innocent smile had he been part of this fiasco.

Jay couldn't be appeased. "Cannon fodder, that's all they were. And to prove what, that we could take the hill?"

"I guess we showed them," I mocked. "Like the bully who takes a toy from a little kid and then just throws it away."

"And you wonder why I'm going to be a Conscientious Objector."

"Hey, Jay. What I really object to is the lack of conscience of our president. He told us he was running on a platform of peace with honor. I don't see the peace or the honor."

Of course, that week, on May 14, Nixon did go on television for damage control. But his peace plan to have America and North Vietnam pull out of South Vietnam over the next 12 months was obviously rejected by Hanoi. Why should they leave? They knew our country was losing its appetite for war. Their military intelligence must have been watching Walter Cronkite, translated into Vietnamese. And the Communists must have been encouraged when, in June, Nixon told South Vietnam's President Thieu that we were going to start withdrawing our troops and nationalizing the South Vietnamese fighting forces.

May 29, 1969

It was my 18th birthday, and I was old enough to drink, to order a beer. I was old enough to drive in New York City. But in the back (or front) of my mind, I realized "Now I'm old enough to be drafted in the Army or the Navy. I'm even old enough to enlist in the Marines. But I'm not old enough to vote for our president or congressmen who will decide whether we end the war in Vietnam, or whether to send our soldiers, my fellow Americans, into battle. Or whether we end 2S deferments."

Memorial Day Weekend—an extra day off from school to ensure that I wouldn't have to be in class on my birthday. My family never went to the parades or services I am embarrassed to say. No one we knew had died in the line of duty. My father and grandfathers had not served, so I just considered the holiday as part of my birthday weekend. Maybe I had a double-header baseball experience, if the Mets were home at Shea Stadium. But I certainly had no reverence, except for the moment of silence at the beginning of the game.

But as Memorial Day was a holiday, we had to visit my grandmother in her fancy Madison Avenue apartment that Friday—a weekly Sunday ordeal that came a few days early. We three Kutscher boys (the

Steinbergs were exempt, unless they had nothing better to do) would be forced to sit in the den with my dad and Lil and Grandmama. We would sit and listen, as we understood Grandma's mantras, "Children should be seen, not heard," and "You're here to take care of your father." These were operative words for all children save her own, whom she enshrined.

This visit was in stark contrast to our semi-monthly visit to my other grandparent, my mom's dad, which took place earlier in the day. Grandpa Leon was now destitute except for his social security checks and the money that Lil and my dad gave him. He lived in a "pretense" of independent, assisted-living in Yonkers. Supervision was provided by his roommate, Frank, whom we paid $2 per week—although Frank was often absent, as he used the money for his daily 15 cents draft beer at the local bar.

Visits with Grandpa Leon were much shorter, more of a show-and-tell of what we'd been doing. His life had become so miserably mundane and excruciatingly protracted after his youngest daughter had died. My dad, with the help of Lil, remained loyal to his beloved first wife's father until Leon's depression became so overwhelming that he was relocated to Chicago to live in a nursing home near my Aunt Julie, his one remaining daughter. He became a shell of the grandfather I had once known, and now communicated by way of brief, government post cards. His handwriting became more disorganized with the years of progressive depression and dementia. Julie visited every week, until one day we received a call that he had finally put an end to his misery, strangling himself with his telephone cord.

June 15, 1969

Yearbook Day. Prom Night. My picture made me look like a real "dufus" (not even spell check can tell me how to spell this word). Looking back, I could have passed as a twin of Chip on "My Three Sons," my black eyeglasses complementing my puffy cheeks. At least I didn't have a crew cut—or even worse, have my hair combed up in the front. Still, I didn't look that different from most of the guys in my class. Everyone had their hair a bit longer than five years earlier, and all combed across their fore-heads—the look of mini-rebellion, the calm before the storm. And we all had on a white shirt, dark tie, and darker jacket.

Not that the girls broke with their fashion mode. All present and ac-counted for had shoulder-length hair, straight, parted on the side, and, again, combed across the forehead—the longer version of their sexual counterparts. It portended the unisex fashion statements of the '70s, when, as my dad would say, you couldn't tell the boys from the girls. Even more importantly, the airbrushed pictures of the women's breasts made them all equal in the eyes of their beholders.

Each of us had our senior quotes, which usually were hopeful, ideal-istic, or funny.

True to my idealistic hopes of making the world better, beneath my picture was:

"Some men see things as they are and say why.
I dream things that never were and say, why not."
　　Robert Kennedy

Everyone was going around asking friends to sign their yearbook. It wasn't like kids didn't want to sign my book; it only seemed that I'd have to ask them first to sign mine, and only then would they offer up theirs.

Even my sister didn't bother to ask me to sign, and Jay was boycott-ing the whole bourgeois idea, so the space next to his picture remains blank to this day. Only his "thought" remains:

"My grandfather told me there are two kinds of people: those who do the work and those who take the credit. He told me to try to be in the first group; there was much less competition there."

Seth signed next to his picture. He was the only boy with his hair still combed back over his forehead. Under his photo it read:

"Well, if I called the wrong number why did you answer the phone?" He added, *"I expect to see you playing basketball with Jim McMillan at Columbia next year."*

Robin and I were still friends, and I loved her picture. She wanted to be remembered by:

"There's only one corner of the universe you can be certain of improving, and that's your own self."

And her special message to me was:

"We've had a lot of fun in these olde hallowed crumbling halls. Oh well, anyway, BEST OF LUCK at Columbia next year—and don't be too rambunctious. Luv, Robin. P.S. No I'm not gonna be stupid—I'm gonna cook pills" (as in pharmacy school).

Ginny, who was on the math team with me, was certainly not a brilliant mathematician; but she was a great counterpoint to the rest of us "geeks"—a distracting presence to our opponents. She wrote next to my picture, with her smiling face expressing her inner beauty:

"Dear Kenneth Harrison Kutscher, Jr, the math genius and the Columbia star-to-be, knowing you these past 2 years has made my years happier! I'll miss your smiling hello in the hall."

LeeAnn, one of the beautiful cheerleaders, made my day when she wrote,

"Have a fantastic summer and I'll probably see you at the pool this summer."

We were an integrated school, and Chauncey, one of the two black students in my class, scribed:

"No angels singing-up above today," above his note to *"Be what you will be for I know you will be great."* Chauncey, with his short-cropped hair, black glasses, and suit and tie, was hardly a candidate for the Black Panthers. But he was one of the founding members of our Civil Rights Committee, with all of eight members.

We were all so uniform in appearance, so optimistic regarding what we could do for the good of society—except for my colleague, Barry Flowers, the founder of the Conservative Club. I unfortunately was a member in my sophomore year, before I understood what he wanted it to represent. Barry's hair was actually longer than the rest of ours, but he had such a menacing look as he wrote, "Liberalism reconciles western civilization to dissolution." I think he was the only member of our class who failed to stand and applaud Georgia's black representative, Julian Bond, when he came to the high school that spring to speak to us of the hopes for the black people in America. Looking back at Barry's picture, and remembering him now, he was pretty angry.

The last person to sign was Lisa White. She had a slightly crooked smile, angular Scottish features, and long hair that obscured her flat chest in the picture.

"*Don't grunt, said Alice. That's not at all a proper way of expressing yourself.*" But her inscription wasn't true to her statement. She wrote, instead of grunting, "*I hope your dog gets cavities! And you better develop some intellectual honesty before you go to college, you crossword cheat. And when my all-star baseball team becomes famous, then you'll be sorry. All seriousness aside, I didn't enjoy fighting with you all year. Remember Pawling and the corn. Lisa*" (but, no Love, Lisa).

I remembered our senior outing in February, in upstate New York, in Pawling, where Lisa and I hid all of the cans of corn in various parts of the complex, including the car glove compartments. Minor senior pranks—jokes just between us. I even got to ride home with her in one of the teacher's cars, a British Rover, as Lisa had a broken ankle and needed special services. But I didn't have the nerve to ask her out then —or now to our senior prom.

I'm not sure why I didn't ask her. She was funny, we had a lot of laughs together on the senior outing in February. I think maybe she was too wholesome, more like a best friend than a girl I would date. Sort of like the girl you'd want to marry and have sex with in the dark: in short, the girl next door, but not someone about whom you could have lascivious thoughts or who would be the subject of a wet dream.

I did ask Ginny, who was more of a friend, but she already had a date. Romantically, my senior year was puttering out—the fizzle all gone from the Coca Cola.

Even Jay had a date, a junior girl named Judy, kind of pretty, whom he had met on the School Store Committee. I had met her a few times, just in passing. What she saw in Jay I couldn't tell. She was nice looking, although not gorgeous, but with a developing body and a quick smile. And she knew how to talk with us seniors. I guess Jay liked her enough—and at least she wasn't a "giggler."

My step-cousin, Jane, also a junior, took some interest in my dilemma. Although she was one of the prettiest girls in her class and one of the most popular, she didn't offer herself as my date. We (meaning she) would have made a spectacular entrance! Instead, she arranged for a couple of double dates with her and her boyfriend and my prospective date, Randy Weinstein. Randy was also a junior, and well aware of the prestige of going to the Senior Prom. Our dates were stiff, but the die was cast, and she was in no way going to pass up this opportunity.

However, despite her thin, freckled, drawn face, shoulder-length, dirty-blond hair, small breasts, and body devoid of any adipose tissue (she was almost anorexic from her one pack-per-day cigarette addiction), she made an acceptable presentation with me, as she was pretty in her own Jewish Princess way. Her tasteful lavender full-length dress contrasted with my blue tuxedo jacket—something I realize now would have been worn by some cheap lounge singer. I had stopped eating pizza for several days before the prom and had prayed to the "Acne God" that morning. Luckily, there was only the old zit from several days ago that had dried up nicely with Clearasil. The band was The Left Bank, a group of musicians who had one mega-hit, "Don't Walk Away, Renee." The fact that they played for our prom was significant both for the fact that we had the money to pay them and they needed a high school gig to eat.

As the night proceeded, I realized that I really wanted to spend more time with my friends than with Randy. I looked over at the couples really having fun, really "in love." Robin was with her boyfriend, Peter, from a private school in White Plains. And Jay looked out of place in his dark burgundy tux. His body and face were still composed of baby fat, which contrasted with his progressively longer and wider sideburns that came two-thirds down his cheeks and almost to the side of his lips—in mockery of the school policy regarding appropriate facial hair. He and Judy were dancing, too close for my comfort, to the slow songs. Randy and I sat out the very romantic songs, and by the time the dance ended, we were both ready for the end of my senior experience. As Randy went to the "little girl's room" to freshen up, I noticed Jay off in the corner making out with Judy. His right hand was inching closer to her breasts, as she discreetly tried to preserve her modesty by shifting around to the side.

Fascinated, I watched as he started to move his hand up her lower thigh, under her semi-formal, light blue, satin dress. I looked away, having had enough—she was, after all, only 17. But still, I began to sense the beginning of an erection. Maybe he was going to get "some action" tonight—something I wasn't going to get from my Jewish Princess Barbie Doll date.

When Randy returned, we started to walk outside. I overheard that most of the class was going to spend their first all-nighter at the local pool club, which had offered its services, probably as the first attempt to keep drunken promsters off the road. Each year, the local paper listed the number of students killed by drunken drivers on prom night in New York. No one wanted to be a number, a statistic, and most of the class was planning on going.

I mused briefly about taking Randy, but I really didn't want to spend the rest of the night with her. I excused myself as being too tired and drove her home. She was even more bored than I was as the evening approached 1 a.m.

It was close to 1:30 a.m. when I arrived at the pool. Finally, I was free to have some fun. Lisa was there, along with others who hadn't gone to the prom. This became our true senior outing. I spent most of the night talking to Lisa, all hyped about the Mets, who were finally playing decent baseball. As the morning progressed, I was even more aware of my foolishness in not asking her to the prom. After breakfast, as we left each other, we promised to keep in touch during the college year, and to root for the Mets. We parted as great friends, but there was an ache in my heart. We had our funny, sardonic repartee. But I knew we would never be more than friends. I had missed my opportunity for physical intimacy.

I drove home, my heart devoid of the sustenance of love and companionship. "We could be so happy," had changed to "I could've been a contender." Not to mention the ache in my groin that only Betty Sue, in her two-dimensional image, would be able to satisfy that night. I groaned with internal longing as I fantasized about which of my classmates and their dates would be "hitting a home run" tonight.

As for me . . . I arrived home to an adoring Hope. Crawling into my bed on this Sunday morning, I fell asleep, with only my dog to keep me company under my covers. As the Bee Gees sang, "One Is the Loneliest Number," Lisa was on my mind.

What was I scared of? Why didn't I ask Lisa out? I wasn't certain. My ambivalence had resulted in solitude and teenage despair. Maybe I thought she was too pure for me, or maybe she reminded me of my mother—so smart and so witty. And who could have sex with his mother?

NUMBERS

June 17, 1969

I'd slept most of the previous day, but now I was ready for some fun. It was Harlan's 20th birthday, and he was still old enough to drink, to order a beer. He was still old enough to drive in New York City. He was still old enough to be drafted in the Army or the Navy if he flunked out of Columbia and lost his 2S deferment. He was still even old enough to enlist in the Marines. But still he was not old enough to vote for our president or congressmen, who would decide whether we would end the war in Vietnam or whether we would send more soldiers, our fellow Americans, into battle.

Everyone was still asleep when I woke up. As I stumbled down the stairs, I almost kicked Hope for a 40-yard field goal. I let her outside, watching her from the corner of my eye. I opened the fridge, poured a glass of milk and stirred in a package of Carnation Instant Chocolate Breakfast as I sat down at the dinette.

I was bored, so I started looking through my yearbook. I scanned the pictures, looking at the different club and committee group shots. I thumbed through all of the senior pictures, all 350 of us, in our suits and ties or white blouses, depending on our sex—no cross-dressing allowed. I sat wondering if there was anyone I needed to ask to sign my yearbook before graduation next week. Where would all of us be as autumn arrive? Last week the school paper published the college list for our class—only one male student wasn't going to college, wasn't going to be 2S, and therefore would be susceptible to the military draft. All of us would be alive for the next four years, unless we became a motor vehicle statistic (drug overdose was still something that didn't happen in Scarsdale, only in the ghettos).

I finished my drink and, still hungry, popped a Pop Tart into the toaster. It seemed to take forever to heat up, so I started to glance through that week's copy of *Life* magazine, with a grim soldier's face on the cover. It was filled with yearbook pictures, all guys. Some military school graduation pictures, I surmised. But then I flipped back to the first page of the layout:

VIETNAM: ONE WEEK'S DEAD.

There they were—there we could be but for the grace of our good parent's wealth and social setting and our 2S draft status—pictures of the 242 U.S. Servicemen killed in Vietnam whose names had been released by the Pentagon during the previous week. It was as if the entire male class from my school had been terminated, along with half of our female students. They didn't look any younger or older than we did, because they weren't. We were all the same age. Half were dressed in their military garb, but the other half were dressed up for their high school senior pictures, taken during a previous summer of innocence. Some were smiling, some were serious, some wore glasses. Most of them had shorter hair than we did, probably because the pictures were taken a year or two earlier. And for some, there were no pictures, just their names—no one to remember what they looked like.

Their ages and hometowns were listed. Most of them were in their early 20s, many from the Midwest, Florida, Texas, or California. But here was a soldier from Middlesex, New Jersey. He probably went to the same stores in New Brunswick that I went to, ate in the same restaurants, even went to the same drive-in movie theater my family went to—although he probably went with his girl and didn't even watch the movie. Was he there the night we saw "The Music Man," with the loudspeaker attached to our car door window? He was 26 when he died—would I reach that age? He was a PFC in the Army, not even an officer. Did he want to be there? Had he enlisted in support of the war? Or was he just doing his patriotic duty? Or was he drafted after college, his 2S deferment no longer a safety bubble around him in his attempts to avoid death?

I wondered how he had died. By now, we were seeing enough clips from Vietnam on Walter Cronkite's CBS Nightly News, with Dan Rather on the scene. Had he died from shrapnel? Was he booby-trapped while walking through the jungle at night? Did he even come home in one piece? How were his parents now? How was his girlfriend? How were his friends?

Families in Scarsdale wouldn't have to endure this grief. While we worried about our grades, our parents worried about their stock portfolios. Is this what our servicemen were needlessly dying for in a foreign land?

Was this a moral war? Would our soldiers get to heaven? These questions had no definitive answer. If the United States left now, then the soldiers would have died in vain, our defeat a shameful reminder of the first war our country had lost. But if we continued to send our men (and women), then more would die; more lives would be lost just to justify those who had fallen before them.

As I left my formative school years behind me and became a college student, with my own values paramount in my mind—these were the issues that would percolate inside me as protesting students took center stage. We would anger our parents and citizens who believed in America's "holy cause," the sanctity of the United States' moral prerogative (or imperialist design) throughout the entire Earth, the entire solar system.

My meditation into the meaning of our lives was interrupted as Paul wandered down, his long hair disheveled, his beard now full grown. He was wearing his torn jeans and a Grateful Dead T-shirt, with leather sandals on his dirty feet.

"Hey, Paul, want some of my Pop Tart?"

"Fuck, no. My head's splitting. I guess I partied too much last night."

He hadn't spoken much to any of us since he got back from Temple University the week before. All I knew was that he and Lil had a major fight three days ago when he got home at 3 a.m. He was still waiting for his final spring semester grades, as he had an incomplete in his American History I class, his paper long overdue. The unspoken fear was that if he was suspended or flunked out of school, he would lose his 2S deferment. He'd have his drugs and his army gear.

I looked at the cover of *Life* again. Then I looked up at Paul. I imagined him in a crew cut, clean shaven, muscles taut from basic training—a grunt.

I went upstairs and looked at my registration and housing package for Columbia, but the number 242 men lost in a week in Vietnam stuck in my head. Multiply that by 52 weeks and we would have lost 12,584 men this year—the equivalent of the entire population of Columbia University being wiped out. Were we college kids the best? Were we the brightest? I doubt it. We certainly weren't the bravest. Were we like Paul, struggling to stay out of Vietnam? Were we like Jay, ready to become a Conscientious Objector on his 18th birthday? I didn't know who I was. Would I serve when my 2S ended, or would I run in protest, in fear, in cowardice? I could only hope that we would, by our protest, bring all the soldiers home safely — as if they were "sliding under the catcher's tag"—one by one. What a grand slam, what a perfect game that would be!

LEVITATE US

July 9, 1969

It was a beautiful July day. I was working in New York City at the Columbia University library on my summer project for my dad. I had graduated from typing to compiling a bibliography on all of the books published on thanatology. It was tedious, but he wanted to get me "published" for my graduate school application four years hence. I spent most of my time on the Columbia campus, commuting with him in the morning, taking the subway down to 116th Street, and copying information by hand from file cards. No wonder I looked forward to lunchtime, when I could lounge on South Field, pretending that I was already enrolled at Columbia. Today, it was littered by hordes of summer students, a few studying, and several with their dogs, who were playing "Frisbee" with their owners. My summer reading list included Plato, which was opened to the same page it was yesterday, a little greasy from my meatball hero. My mind was unable to concentrate as my eyes wandered over to the female student, about 20 feet away, immersed in conversation with her girlfriend. She had short, red hair, an average body, and her nose was turned up a bit, giving her a slightly "waspy" appearance. She was lying on her back, and her short skirt was inching its way up her thighs. I was hoping that she would get up, or move her legs, so I could get a glimpse of her panties — which hopefully would be "virginal white," for my fantasy, my viewing pleasure. Sensing no movement on her part, and my being too shy to actually make eye contact or get up and try to talk to her with anything but lust in my heart, my telescopic eyes shifted to the blond to my left. I was salivating as she bent over, which allowed me a wonderful view of her breasts beneath her lowcut top. Oh, how I loved the new braless era!

I didn't have a girlfriend at that time. Oh, these young girls, these women—were they aware of what they were doing to me? Did it make it more exciting for them if they were enticing me? Or were they just unaware of what they were doing? But why else were they wearing tight skirts or blouses? Unless they were pre-med—and just using a ploy to distract the males in the class, to enable them to get better grades. Soon enough, I fantasized, I'll be here at Columbia fulltime, and I won't be alone by myself with only their images at night.

I went back to my Plato, which was even more difficult to comprehend with my erection caught bent in my tight jeans. And then a girl approached, barely 18 or 19, in shorts and a Rolling Stones T-shirt, with no makeup, hair cut short, and sandals worn at the heels.

"Hi. I came down to see my boyfriend, but when I went up to his room, I heard the bed rattling and some girl's voice." She started to cry. "I spent my money for a train ticket into town, and then he was supposed to give me a ride back to New Jersey. I have no idea where I'm going to get the $4 fare. Could you help?"

I fought off my desire to help her in more than one way. "I'm sorry, all I have is a $10 bill and I don't have any change. I need to read this chapter; I've been working on it for a week." I lied. I really didn't want to move because I sensed the red-haired fantasy girl was about to get up to go to class.

"I could go to the store, buy you a Coke, and bring back the change," she said softly.

I was thinking that she looked sad, and in addition to the red-haired girl, there were several other prospects sitting down near me. "Sure, I'm sorry what he did to you. He must be stupid to lose someone like you."

I gave her my ten-spot, and went back to studying—Plato, the co-eds, and my fantasies. After ten minutes, I was still thirsty and she hadn't returned. After 15 minutes, I worried about her. After 20 minutes, I realized the long-legged girl with a sad face and shorts had scored a $10 bill off of a rube—me! And I thought I was New York street-smart. Who was I going to tell? I was pretty embarrassed. Even the Hare Krishnas chanting at the entrance to Columbia wouldn't have fallen for that line.

But, as so often happened that summer, the Mets came to my rescue. My depression was lifted by the lunacy of the events at Shea Stadium. My "Mutts" had become pedigrees, despite the absence of AKC papers. They were actually playing baseball the way Abner Doubleday had suggested—with pitching, good defense, and timely hitting.

On July 8, the Chicago Cubs came to Shea, only 4-½ games in front of the second place Mets. It was the first important series the Mets had ever played in their existence. There was no joy in Mudville that day until the ninth inning, when the Mets rallied from two runs behind to win 4-3, scoring on a hit that the Cubs' center field lost in the sun.

Now we were only 3-½ games out of first. I knew I had to go to Shea the next night. But Jay hated baseball, and there was no way he wanted to see the Mets. So I asked around, but even my Mets pal, Steve Krauss, couldn't make it. Harlan had a date, Paul was busy, but Mike — the least sports-minded of my step-family—said, "Why not?" A true "closet" Mets' fan.

I had gone to several games already this year, and had a five-game personal winning streak going. So I was pretty excited when the Mets took a three run lead in the first two innings, knocking Ken Holtzman, the Cub's starter (and one of the two Jewish players in the major leagues, along with Art Shamsky of the Mets) out of the game in the second inning. By the seventh inning, we were up by 4-0, behind Cleon Jones' 10th home run and a double and triple by Tommie Agee, his Mobile, Alabama hometown neighbor.

But it wasn't just the 4-0 lead that was becoming exciting, leading to the tension. Tom Seaver was pitching a perfect game; he had faced 21 Cubs and retired all of them through the first seven innings. No Met had ever thrown a no-hitter, no less a perfect game. And now, Tom Terrific was only six outs away from immortality, on a night we would show the Cubs we were a force to be reckoned with for the rest of the year. The fans were roaring with each out, and Mike and I were high-fiving each other as each Cub, one by one, went back to the dugout.

In the later innings, Gil Hodges has inserted his best defensive players, including Rod Gaspar in right field to replace Ron Swoboda, who was known to make every play that came his way into an adventure.

"Where is Buddy Harrelson? Why is Al Weis still in at shortstop?" Mike complained. "What the hell is wrong with Hodges? He knows Buddy is better than Al." When did Mike become a baseball freak, I wondered?

"He's away for two weeks at National Guard summer training," I suddenly realized, and wondered, "Why of all times does he have to be serving his country?"

"Well, we all have to make sacrifices," Mike moaned. "The Mets will just have to do with a backup player for these two weeks. I just hope he doesn't get hurt during basic training."

Had Jay been here, the conversation would have gone like this:

"Who are these major league baseball players that they can get out of fighting in Vietnam just by serving in the National Guard? They play baseball all summer, miss a few weeks for training, and then they're back on the field." Jay would have moralized.

Jay was right. The players were given a bye by the fans. Even the military establishment allowed this perfunctory service to count as patriotism. In the good old days, our players had gone to war. Ted Williams had his career interrupted twice, by World War II and the Korean War. Even Willie Mays had served his two years in the military. And now, while poor black kids and white kids—from the South, the ghettos of the North, and the farms of the Midwest and Texas—were being blown away by Vietcong bombs, baseball players were being blown away by an 0-2 inside fastball. While Bill Clinton was not inhaling in England and George Bush was not pulling back on the throttle above Alabama, our ball players were spending their two weeks of basic training at military camps throughout the country. But with the rare exception of units called up to quell the riots of Chicago in 1968 at the Democratic Convention (and later at Kent State in Ohio in 1970), they escaped any threat of bodily or psychological harm. The National Guard was the haven for those who wanted to get credit for serving their country with only minimal risk of loss of life or limb. They were not labeled cowards; they were not conscientious objectors; they were not protestors; and they were not maimed or dead.

This was the year that Curt Flood challenged the reserve clause in Major League Baseball, ending the system whereby a player was a "serf." Every player remained the property of the team that originally signed him, until he was released or traded. But the true "reserve clause" during the Vietnam War was the two week National Guard training every summer which could provide for any given player the moral protection from the condemnation of the patriotic Americans who backed our presence in Vietnam.

But Jay wasn't with us this night, so there was no such soul searching. As the Mets came up in the eighth inning, the tension was becoming unbearable. We actually were happy as the Mets failed to score, wanting to get to the climax of this game.

We started cheering even before Tom Terrific made his first pitch of the ninth inning. And when Randy Huntley bunted unsuccessfully, "we" were almost there. Not only would "we" have pitched our first perfect game, but "we" would now be only 2-½ games behind the first-place Cubs—a lofty perch for our lowly Mets so late into the season. Only two more batters were between "us" and immortality. "Light-hitting" Jimmy Qualls came up to the plate. After Tom would retire him, all that would be left was a pinch-hitter. The roar was deafening. And then there was silence . . . and then a loud groan from the crowd as he went with Tom's next pitch and lined a single to left-center field, a clean hit. And from the silence, from the groan, came cheers, cheers for our hero, who had taken us so far. It's ridiculous to say we were disappointed in only winning 4-0 after Tom dispensed with the next two Cubs. We all gave a standing "O" for our hero.

The stands gradually emptied, with everyone exhausted and exhilarated at the same time. There was no need to rush out to the parking lot—we'd be stuck for an hour anyway. We realized first place was in sight, and as we made our way down the ramps, "brothers-in-arms," we were young at heart. But not young enough to still be there with our respective Dad or Mom—holding our hands, watching us run down the ramps, yelling at us to wait for them so we would not get lost in the crowd.

July 16, 1969

The preparations had been on-going for months, ever since the successful Apollo 10 mission in May. Mary's "Merry Men" at Grumman's Lunar Assembly Building were hard at work assembling the module that would take Neil Armstrong and Buzz Aldrin to the lunar surface and then return them to the mother ship. The highlight, of course, was the day that Armstrong, an ex-Naval officer, with blond hair slicked down to the side, and Aldrin, an ex-Army man, with his "buzz' cut making his ears his prominent facial feature, came to encourage the workers. On most days, Mary would happily walk among the engineers, taking messages, lending a hand—anything in addition to the drudgery of her primary role as payroll manager. Of course, the engineers weren't working for nothing, and they always received their paychecks, insurance claims, or vacation requests with a smile—along with asking Mary to help them spend it at the Mousetrap Lounge.

"Sure, Steve—I'll go with the bunch of you. But don't forget to wear that gold ring on your finger."

"Mary, you're breaking my heart. Who else can I daydream about?"

"As long as it's just a fantasy."

There wasn't much else to do nights in Titusville, after the streets were rolled up for the evening. The engineers, and even the astronauts who were not prepping for the next upcoming flight, would hang out—drinking, dancing, flirting. Mary didn't know about the other girls who went with them, but for her, the guys were off-limits after they left the bar. No way she was going to break up a marriage.

On the nights leading up to the launch, the talk became a little more serious, much more philosophical. What would Armstrong and Aldrin find on the Moon? What would they say? What would be the first words from the lunar surface? On a more practical level, would the television transmitters work? Were there any bacteria on the Moon that could contaminate all of mankind?

All this was discussed, but there was no talk of what was really on their minds. Would the lunar module that they had helped design and build land safely? And more importantly, would all the rivets hold, all the computers work? Would the module take off from the Moon with the two astronauts and their payload—the lunar rocks?

Today was launch day for Apollo 11. Mary wasn't in Firing Room I, where the 400 men and women who were the heart and soul of the launch were situated. Nor was she in the viewing stand with ex-president Lyndon Johnson. At least she was closer than President Nixon, who was watching the launch from the White House. She stood with Martha Jane on the sand at Cocoa Beach, not far from where she had stood with her parents 12 years previously watching the first successful rocket launch. She looked around for the bushes where Kate had peed those many years ago, wondering whether there was some bush that had grown extra tall after being fertilized. At 9:32 a.m., everyone cheered as the Saturn 5 rocket took off flawlessly, propelling Apollo 11 towards the Moon. But unlike that morning 12 years ago, the launch was only a preliminary step, not an achievement in itself. That would have to wait several more days, as the astronauts made their way towards "Moon dirt."

That night, with their job done—like students who have studied as hard as they can and now only have to take the test—most of the Cape workers relaxed, ate a burger, had a few beers, danced and listened to the juke box for a while. They went home "early," however, knowing that there was no real reason to celebrate yet.

I had persuaded my dad that we should stay home to watch the launch together. Although Lil interrupted her editing for the actual takeoff, he barely looked up from the letter he was formulating for his latest symposium. He was too self-absorbed in this "humanitarian" project about whether a terminally ill patient should be told the truth about his condition to actually be involved in this historic event. But, as interested as I was, by 10 a.m. the rocket became merely a speck seen through the camera's lens, and I went back to my work.

The Mets had played the Cubs in Chicago that afternoon, in the era before there were lights at Wrigley Field. I made sure to have the game on in the background as I typed another repetitive letter, using Correct-Type to eradicate my errors. I found it ironic that even as I strove go make my letters perfect, my dad would often add something in his own handwriting to show the recipient that the letter was truly personalized. In the 60s, there was a clear-cut distinction between a form letter and a "personal" letter. Nowadays, what with word processors and address mail-merge, even personal letters are often regarded as junk-mail.

I had watched as the Mets took an early six-run lead in the first two innings against future Hall of Famer Ferguson Jenkins and gone on to victory. So, as the day ended, as the Apollo 11 sped towards the Moon, the evening news recapped both the launch and the Mets' heroic victory.

I imagine Mary was already in bed by the time I went up to my bed-room. I had broken open a Miller High Life, but as I still had not ac-quired a taste for beer, the can sat half empty. (I obviously was a pessi-mist, as opposed to an optimist, who would have said the can was half full—although the engineers down in the Cape would have said that the problem was that the can had been made twice as large as it needed to be!)

I was lying there in bed with Hope, for whom I had brought up a glass with water—iced cubes included, for my somewhat spoiled dog—listening to Johnny Carson on the Tonight Show. I usually made it through his monologue, but often, unless he had some beautiful actress as a guest, I would be asleep after the first commercial. Johnny sat with Ed McMahon, kibitzing about how terrible Ed's tie was that night, watching Ed pick up his coffee mug, which most likely contained coffee and not the alcohol suggested by his mannerisms. Johnny was excited about the lunar mission, but knew his New York audience was enjoying their team's emergence as a "powerhouse," as they approached the divi-sion-leading Cubs.

"You know, Ed," he quipped, his smile demonstrating the lunacy of the moment, "I always said the Mets would be in first place the day we walked on the Moon!"

Sunday, July 20, 1969

The weekend was passing as our astronauts were hurtling towards the Moon. Yesterday they had entered into its orbit. Their compatriots had done this previously on Apollo 8 and Apollo 10, so it was more like watching batting practice before the actual game began.

The Mets had won again on Saturday, a victory now only a footnote as my worldly—or should I should "solar system" interest remained the focus of my imagination. On television, Walter Cronkite listened with all of us to the Apollo radio broadcast, explaining how the lunar module— known as the LEM, but named the Eagle—would separate from the command module, Columbia, that afternoon. I spent Saturday evening, bored, playing RISK with Jay, Bart, and Seth, but not until I had finished typing Dad's manuscripts at 7:30 p.m. I finally got a break when Lil angrily reminded him that he had to get ready for a dinner engagement at a friend's house. Oblivious as usual to social amenities or obligations, his work was the center of his universe on Earth, the gravitational pull that could suffocate all those around him.

We were distracted by the reports from Chappaquiddick, Massachusetts that Teddy Kennedy had been involved in a fatal car accident on Friday night on another Cape 1,000 miles from the Cape named for his brother. Little did we know, at that point, that although the youngest of the three Kennedy political sons would use Massachusetts justice to escape significant punishment for the death of Mary Jo Kopechne, this accident would signal the end of his presidential aspirations. It was ironic that on the day the United States achieved the promise his brother had made eight years earlier of our astronauts navigating 250,000 miles and landing safely in the Sea of Tranquility, Teddy had attempted to navigate only miles from home and landed in anything but a sea of tranquility. It was more like the Bay of Pigs.

But, for all of us in the United States and the free world, today was to be THE NIGHT. It was quiet when I went downstairs at 8 a.m. and walked outside in my PJs to pick up *The New York Times*. I read the headlines quickly about the lunar landing, and then turned just as quickly to my "Bible" — the sports section, Section 5.

"METS 'EXPOSED!' Lose in Canada 5-4."

"CUBS IN FIRST"

"YANKEES . . ." Who cared?

Other than Hope, who came down with me to the kitchen to see what I would give her for breakfast, not a soul was stirring. Richie was still at sleep-away camp, and Marty was sleeping over at a friend's. Harlan had been out the night before. And who knows what the Steinberg kids had done?

There was not much to do this early in the morning. My dad wouldn't be up until 10 a.m., when Lil would bring him his morning orange juice and English muffin, and she would have her cup of tea and rye toast with orange marmalade—the same breakfast every morning, without fail. Thank heavens she never bought Tang instead of OJ, or my dad would have had a fit. He wouldn't be starting his work until around 10:30, so Lil actually had 30 minutes to work on her one remaining hobby that my dad allowed her to keep once she had become the official editor of The Foundation of Thanatology—finishing *The New York Times* Sunday crossword puzzle—in pen, no less. She knew all of the three-letter Greek words, or the early English spelling of "ornery." Anything she didn't know right off the bat she'd have to work on clandestinely later that evening, while he was in the bathroom.

Predictably, by 10:31 my fingers were quickly at work, dexterity my middle name. "Dear Dr. Jones:" I typed. "On behalf of the Foundation of Thanatology, I would like you to write a paper on . . ."

"Too bad," I thought, "I don't have any important plans to escape his routine this morning, or any plans for that matter." Hey, even no plans at all seemed to get the Steinbergs out of helping.

"Ken, I just found these doctors' addresses and I need these letters out by tomorrow or else the symposium will fail." I would need to type the same letter five times. With only the name and the subject changed—oh, was I born a decade too soon before word processors!

"I doubt it, Dad." I whispered as I walked away, knowing he was deaf in his left ear and wasn't looking up to "read my lips."

I was planning on watching the Mets later, but for now, I was watching and listening to the lunar goings on. The lunar module was about to separate from the command module.

On the television, as I watched the lunar module undock, Neil Armstrong told Houston control, "Unlocked."

When Houston control answered, "How does it look?" Armstrong replied, "The Eagle has wings."

The astronauts even had a sense of humor. Michael Collins, left behind in his command module (and in the history books as an asterisk), commented, "You've got a fine looking flying machine there, Eagle, despite the fact you're upside down."

The Eagle replied, "Somebody's upside down." As Einstein said, "It's all relative."

"I hope they watch out for that 'cow' jumping over the Moon!" I laughed.

Walter Cronkite stayed on the television, letting us know what was happening as the lunar module was coming into orbit around the Moon —how it would land, how important the landing angle was to ensure a proper takeoff so the astronauts could leave the lunar surface when their job was completed. I flipped back and forth between Channel 2, watching Walter, and Channel 9, watching the Mets, with Lindsey Nelson, Ralph Kiner, and Bob Murphy my anchormen.

Around 3:30, the Mets, who were losing the first game of a doubleheader up in Montreal, Canada, took second place to the Moon men.

"Dad, I'm taking a break. They're about to land on the Moon. Can we all watch together?"

"Sure, Ken. Bill, put down your paper and let's watch together. Ken, see if any of the other kids are around."

"Lil, I haven't finished this letter . . . "

"Bill, no harm will be done if we get them done tomorrow."

"Yes there will," he said, as he began to raise his voice.

"Bill." Lil's voice was quiet, but it was the first time I'd heard her use that tone. Luckily, that was all that was necessary—just a stare, but not "Give it a break" or "Go fuck yourself," in today's vernacular. Just "Bill."

"Well, let me at least finish the letter."

"Lil, that channel?" I asked gingerly.

"Channel 2—CBS. Let's watch Walter Cronkite."

Marty was upstairs, reading Charles Dickens' *Great Expectations,* which was required reading for incoming freshman at the high school.

Cathy was around, but she was on the phone with Karen. Harlan arrived about ten minutes later and Mike came up at 4.

We listened to the static filled radio transmissions as we watched the simulations of our engineering prowess. Cronkite needed to use all of his years of reporting experience to fill the time while the astronauts were in orbit above the far side of the Moon—the dark side—where they were out of radio contact with Mission Control in Houston. It was the 1960's version of dead areas for cell phones, the "no bars" equivalent. Magnify today's communicators' frustrations by 250,000 miles to understand why the boys in Mission Control needed their extra strength deodorant that day. But as the lunar module emerged back into radio contact, we heard Armstrong's steady voice say, "The burn was on time." The Eagle was now ready to make its approach to the lunar surface.

Walter was trying his best to scientifically explain to his lay audience what was happening. He described, from his notes and briefings, what was occurring as the Eagle approached the Moon, its "landing gear" in place, the three legs ready to keep the module upright.

Once we heard from Houston, "Forty-two hundred feet. Go for landing," the anticipation grew. We knew from Walter that the module was just about ready to land and how the angle had to be just right. We watched as the lunar module proceeded over the lunar surface, and listened to the astronauts as their ship was guided closer to the surface: ". . . 100 feet . . . 60 seconds . . . 30 seconds." The surface was getting closer, and it appeared somewhat rough and treacherous, as the module got closer. Buzz Aldrin calmly said, "Down two-and-a-half. Forward, forward 40 feet. Down two-and-a-half. Picking up some dust. Thirty feet. Two-and-one-half down. Shadow. Four Forward. Four forward. Drifting to the right a little."

We all held our breaths. I don't think that even Richie, our resident jokester, had he been there, could have made us laugh. The shadow of the module was on the television feed, as the Eagle prepared to land.

Neil Armstrong said, the radio crackling. "Stop." Then, "Okay, engine stop. Engine arm off."

Houston responded. "We copy. You're down, Eagle."

Then we heard the words we were waiting for. "Houston, Tranquility Base here. The Eagle has landed."

Cronkite's voice combined excitement, relief, celebration, elation, and exhaustion, all in one. "We have a man on the Moon."

Wally Schirra, another astronaut who would have loved to be there instead of sitting next to Walter, simply said, "Oh, Jeez."

As we exhaled, Houston answered, "You've got a bunch of guys here about to turn blue. We're breathing again. Thanks a lot." The picture from Houston told it all, as the engineers in their white shirts and black ties—with a rare renegade in a yellow or blue shirt, early 70s in style—all began to shake hands, pat shoulders, and inhale on their cigarettes or cigars.

We saw Cronkite remove his glasses and wipe his eyes, while Schirra was in tears.

Of course, as we later would find out—what was possibly known in Houston and on the Cape but was unknown to us viewers in New York or in New Jersey or California or, if they were watching, in the Soviet Union—was that Neil Armstrong had actually flown the module the last 90 seconds searching for a spot to land, because the original computer calculations would have put the Eagle down in a football-sized crater with boulders and rocks. In guiding the module to a safe landing area, Armstrong had less than ten seconds of fuel remaining before he would have had to abort the mission!

It was ironic that the jeering the original Mercury Project received from the early test pilots like Chuck Yeager, the fearless navigator who broke the sound barrier and whose Southern Appalachian drawl has been imitated by commercial pilots for the past 50 years—was based on the belief that astronauts would me merely passengers (or was it chimpanzees) in space, not real commanders. I can't imagine Yeager's feelings when he realized that Armstrong had "the Right Stuff," that he had flown the Eagle to safe harbor!

"Lil, wasn't that great?" Mike yelled. No "Mom" used by the Steinbergs — just "Lil," an old joke from Richie's kindergarten days that had become habit.

"When do you think they'll do the Moon walk?" Marty's enquiring mind wanted to know.

"At least we landed safely." I was the down-to-Earth kind of guy.

"Yeah, but they still have to get back to Earth," Paul said, unable to just enjoy it.

"Paul," Mike added, "if they got stuck, it would be like a Robert Heinlein story. You know, they'd have to survive while we sent another lunar landing party up there."

Cathy stood up and yawned.

"Anyway," Cathy said. "Lil, I'm going out with Jim."

"Where are you going?"

"Out."

"To do what?"

"We're going for a drive."

"Funny how Jim's car only shifts into 'Park,'" Marty quipped.

"Will you be home for dinner? We're going out for Chinese. "

"Doubt it."

"Just make sure you are home by 10." Lil wasn't smiling.

"Why?"

"Because."

Cathy turned and walked out of the bedroom. Her pants were one size too small and her sleeveless, pink blouse was two sizes too small, but her attitude more than made up for any deficiencies.

At 6:30, we arrived at General Tso's Restaurant. My father had long ago given up on cooking his Sunday feasts, as there was no longer any family to sit around and be a family while he cooked—or to stick around afterward as the clean-up crew. Instead, we had our weekly dinners at his favorite Chinese restaurant in White Plains, where he could order his specially prepared dishes, such as braised octopus or 100-day-old eggs that were buried in the ground for three months, only to emerge with a foul-smelling, sulphur odor. Of the Steinbergs, only Mike was adventurous— he ate everything. Paul ate only a good-old American grilled steak. And Cathy, who usually tried to order tuna fish, was good tonight, probably because she had stopped by and brought Jim with her—no permission asked.

"What do you think they'll find on the Moon?" I asked Mike.

"Probably cheese," Paul answered.

"What time will they be walking on the Moon?" Cathy blurted between bites of her pork-fried rice.

"They said they were supposed to take a nap, and go out around 3 a.m."

"Hell," said my dad, "You'd think they'd be excited enough to do it before they took their nap."

"I bet they'll have a snack, and then they'll go out." I was pretty sure of myself.

"I wonder what they'll have for dinner?"

"Maybe they brought Russian caviar?"

"Or Chinese dumplings?"

"Or French fries?" Jim added.

"I think," Mike said seriously, "probably dehydrated hamburgers and apple pie with vanilla ice cream."

"And real American cheese from the surface of the Moon!"

A genuine "country barbecue!" We joked as we stuffed our faces with wonton soup, pork lo mein, chicken egg foo young, and "toe food," (or tofu) as Richie liked to call it, with smelly cheese.

And for dessert we had canned pineapple and lichees—and that flavor ice cream found only in Chinese restaurants: green pistachio.

Finally, out came the fortune cookies, inedible wafers, a Chinese sacrament.

Mike opened his first. "A serious relationship will be in your future."

"Whoa, Mike, Diane better watch out."

Paul's said, "Beware the dragon's breath."

"Hey, Paul, I guess something got lost in translation."

Mine said, "The unexpected is to be expected." I hoped it meant the Mets.

And Cathy's read, "Only a fool believes in fortune cookies."

I couldn't believe my dad's: "To each according to his needs."

"Hey, Pop, that must have been smuggled in from Red China."

But Lil's said it all: "Be happy for today. For tomorrow is another day."

We got home a bit early because it was unclear exactly when Neil Armstrong would be setting foot on the lunar surface. By 9:45, I was sitting at the foot of the bed in my parents' room, wearing my pajama bottoms and a Mets T-shirt. We were listening as Walter Cronkite and Eric Severeid waxed eloquently about the humanist implications of today's events.

Harlan and Mike came in around 10 o'clock, discussing how the computers would fire the lunar module back into space. Paul had gone over to his friend's home for a while, although Lil had made him promise to be back by 10:30. Cathy was, as usual, showering and doing her hair.

At 10:15 the kitchen door slammed closed, and downstairs Cathy's gray poodle, Misty, ran to greet Paul, while Hope just looked up from her comfortable position next to my dad. If it wasn't food, she wasn't interested.

Paul arrived upstairs as Cathy sauntered into the bedroom, her hair in rollers, her face smeared with Clearasil and cold cream.

"Cathy!" Mike screamed. "You'll scare the astronauts."

"Mike, they're a quarter-million miles away—they can't see her." Harlan was coming to her rescue.

"Yeah," Paul regaled as he looked up. "But they have telescopes. They'll see her and they'll be afraid to return home."

"Screw you all!" yelled Cathy, as she ran out of the room crying.

"Cathy, grow up." Lil yelled. "They're just joking."

"Yeah, you always take their side."

"Cathy."

"Yes, Lil."

"Come in here and watch with us."

"Not until they apologize."

"I'm sorry, Cathy," Mike said, unable to keep from smirking. "They won't be afraid of you."

Paul added, "They're too busy with other things."

"Shh," I said, "watch the TV."

It was now 10:18 p.m., EDT. There we were—my dad and Lil under the covers, with Lil in her nightgown and my father in his blue pajamas. For once, his pile of work was on the floor next to him, which allowed space for them to hold hands, while Hope snored away at their feet.

I wondered what they were thinking, as both had lost their spouses at a young age—the husband and wife and father and mother weren't there to watch what JFK had promised in May, 1961: that we would land a man on the Moon by the end of the decade. For them, the 60s had started as a decade of such promise—of love, family, and growth. It had seemed so hopeful, as they and their families watched the first Mercury and Gemini missions. But that hope soon transformed into the disillusionment and pain of the Cold War, the Kennedy and King assassinations, the racial and urban unrest, the mess in Vietnam, and ultimately, loss and grief and teenage angst. Tonight, however, was a triumph, which promised to bring back the spirit of America to all citizens.

Despite this, in so many ways it seemed awkward for me to be sharing tonight with this new family—without my mom and with my dad holding someone else's hand, a wonderful new wife and a great stepmother. But, it just wasn't the way it should have been. Maybe we should have put out our pictures of my mom and Mike's dad so they could have watched with us.

We continued to watch and wait, until finally the pot of water boiled, the Eagle's hatch door opened, and a shadow of the lunar module appeared on our television screen as Neil Armstrong released a TV camera that would show man's first step on the Moon.

None of us moved our eyes from the TV, as Walter Cronkite and Wally Schirra watched with us and described Armstrong's descent. We saw him emerge from the module, a grainy picture, but clear enough, in stark black and white and gray. Across the screen, in simple white block letters, it said, "LIVE FROM THE SURFACE OF THE MOON."

As Armstrong put his left boot down on the lunar surface, the words "ARMSTRONG ON THE MOON" flashed across the screen in archaic, white letters, along with 10:56 p.m. EDT. It was unadorned, as if describing the arrival of the UPS truck. Although some skeptics would later say that this was just a fabricated picture, that none of this really happened, I—along with 600 million other Earthlings—believed in the truth of what we saw, and understood there was a time delay of 1.3 seconds as the radio waves reached Earth. So what if we were several seconds behind in viewing history? I mean, how long did it take before Columbus was able to tell Queen Isabella that he had discovered America? (Although Columbus did get his own city, right near where Armstrong grew up in Ohio, along with his own national holiday and fraternal organization. Armstrong only got a call from our president, a hero's welcome, and a ticker-tape parade.)

"That's one small step for a man;
One giant leap for mankind."

The first words spoken from the Moon, and Cronkite didn't understand.

"What did he say? I didn't catch it."

Schirra hesitated, then misquoted Armstrong, saying "That's one small step for man; One giant leap for mankind."

I couldn't believe it. Neil Armstrong had two years to come up with the line that everyone would remember forever, which would go down into history. At least he didn't stutter or miss his cue. But I'd heard baseball announcers with more excitement, more everlasting statements. "The Giants win the pennant. The Giants win the pennant." Give me Russ Hodges any day.

With the "excitement" of the opening statement over, we watched as Cronkite intermittently commentated on the ensuing events, letting us listen to Armstrong and Buzz Aldrin's conversation and repartee.

Armstrong's first act upon walking on the Moon was supposed to be accumulating rocks according to a contingency plan. In case he had to rush back to the lunar module and abort the mission, NASA wanted some samples from the Moon. But as we watched, we saw the first disobedience of lunar life, as Armstrong ignored his orders and took pictures before getting his rock samples.

As Buzz Aldrin arrived on the surface, we were in a trance-like state as we saw them frolic like two playful kids, bounding around in an environment with one-sixth the gravity of Earth, their footsteps in the lunar dust making the surface a virgin no more. Aldrin described the "magnificent desolation of the lunar surface"—a view that would be forever spoiled by the remains of their scientific equipment.

They kept taking pictures—of each other, of their scientific experiments, of where Armstrong grew up, or suburban New Jersey, the home of Aldrin, could have had a better time. All of the "toys", the futuristic Buck Rogers' gear of our past, were in their hands in the present. Their huge backpack carried all of their atmospheric needs. Their sun visors reflected the Earth's oceans and continents. They were the home team, dressed in white, the good guys. The only thing missing was a bat and a ball. Rocks had to do instead, as Aldrin quipped to Armstrong, "I didn't know you could throw so far." Could you imagine how a how far Babe Ruth could hit a ball up there, I thought.

After about an hour, we became bored. Even porno films begin to get redundant after a while; even ice cream loses its excitement if eaten for every meal. My dad fell asleep, Cathy left to go into her room to finish setting her hair, and Paul listened to his stereo. Only Lil, Harlan, Mike and I remained, along with Hope who was lying on her back sound asleep . We had watched the tedium of rock collecting and heard President Nixon's uninspired conversation with the astronauts. His voice sounded "computerized" as he said,

"This certainly has to be the most historic telephone call ever made. Because of what you have done, the heavens have become a part of man's world. And as you talk to us from the Sea of Tranquility," Tricky Dick droned on, "it requires us to redouble our efforts to bring peace and tranquility to Earth."

Armstrong, as if on cue, replied in his Midwestern mode, "Thank you, Mr. President. It's a great honor and privilege for us to be here representing not only the United States but men of peace of all nations, men with interests and a curiosity and men with a vision for the future."

How out of sync this message was to the battles going on halfway around our Moon's Earth. Then the astronauts placed the plaque that symbolized victory in the "Race for Space," aka the Cold War: "We Came In Peace For All Mankind."

I fell asleep around 12:45 a.m., and Harlan had to wake me to watch the last moments of the walk on the Moon. One hundred and forty-one minutes after Neil Armstrong set foot on the surface, the two explorers were back in their nest. That was it—2 hours and 21 minutes—and I hadn't been able to stay up the entire time. "At least no one had died while I slept," I thought, remembering back to January 10, 1966.

Meanwhile, at the Mousetrap, the guys from Grumman were watching their "baby" do its job. Mary sat with the engineers at the large table in the middle, their tense "laughter" a distraction during the blackout period. They were all silently holding their breaths during the LEM approach when Arnie grabbed her hand as Armstrong maneuvered the spacecraft beyond what he knew was the landing site.

"What's he doing? He doesn't have that much fuel! Dammit, land, land! " He was hysterical.

No one had enough time to reassure him, but Mary's hand went numb from his grasp.

And then, they heard, "Okay, engine off. Stop."

And they knew everything was okay.

The rest of the afternoon, they went down to the beach and partied. The Mousetrap advertised the "prettiest waitresses in the area." But, they may have exaggerated just a bit. All the guys had eyes on Mary, who as usual was oblivious to their stares. MJ didn't mind the attention, though, as she flirted with several engineers off in the corner. However, this was a serious day, and no one took advantage of the fact that the bar was located in the Polaris Motel.

Not knowing when Armstrong and Aldrin were actually going to walk, the crowd thinned out a bit.

"MJ, I'm going back to my place to take a shower and change."

"Sounds like a plan, Mary. How 'bout we meet over at the River's Edge for dinner later?"

"Don't you feel guilty, dining on pompano or a casserole of shrimp and crabmeat while all they have up there in outer space is dehydrated chicken and Tang?"

"Hey, they'll get plenty of rubber chicken when they do the banquet circuit after they return. It's just getting them in training. Besides, I'm going to finish my dinner off with a nice glass of Chablis. Do ya think they have any of that up there?"

"What an idea. Powdered wine."

"Or a double Dewars scotch, on the "rocks.""

"So, I'll meet you at 7?"

"Sure."

"Do you mind if I invite Arnie and Jack?"

"MJ, does it have to be Jack?"

"You know he likes you. And besides, he'll probably pick up the check."

"MJ, what kind of women's libbers are we? You know I don't lead guys on."

"Don't worry; we'll come back here to watch the moonwalk. There'll be plenty of us to protect you from yourself."

Dinner was boring, but the party was rolling at the Mousetrap when they arrived back at 9:45. Mary wore her pink capris and white blouse tied below her breasts. MJ was more sedate, with blue jeans and a wrinkled blue shirt. The guys were in shorts and polo shirts, with black socks and white sneakers. There was a "buzz" in the air waiting for the first step. Everyone had his or her idea about what Armstrong should say as he stepped down.

"Fuck you, Ruskies, we're here first," Arnie joked.

"First come, first serve," said Jack, a bit more civilized.

"May the force be with you," quipped James Lucas.

"Tough luck, Yeager, keep flying those jets," chimed in Arnie.

Finally, Armstrong's leg appeared on the screen. He was talking to Houston at the same time as he was climbing down.

"You've got a good picture, huh?"

"There's a great deal of contrast in it and currently it's upside down on monitor. But we can make out a fair amount of detail . . ."

Armstrong continued to climb down. "I'm at the foot of the ladder. The LEM foot beds are only depressed in the surface about one or two inches, although the surface appears to be very, very fine-grained as you get close to it."

"Don't blame the LEM, Armstrong!" Jack cried out. "You're the one who piloted it."

"I'm going to step off the LEM now. That's one small step for a man, one giant leap for mankind."

"What the fuck did he say?" Jack couldn't make it out.

"Something about a small step for man, a leap for mankind," Arnie replied.

"Shit, that's the best he could do."

"No, I think Neil also added, 'And good luck, Mr. Gorski.'"

"What are you talking about?"

"Just a joke Steve told me earlier. I'll tell you later."

"Shh," Mary shouted. "I'm still trying to hear what they're saying. Look at the way Armstrong is bouncing around."

The jukebox started playing. "My love is taking you higher than you've ever been before . . ."

"Who put that on? That's so corny." MJ started choking on her drink in laughter.

"Who wants to dance?" Arnie grabbed MJ and they started whirling around the floor.

"Next round of drinks is on me," Jack bellowed. "We made it."

"Not until we take off and make it back to the Columbia," Steve reminded them.

"Don't you worry," Jack said emphatically. "That engine was the one I built. No way it's going to let us down tonight."

Mary glimpsed up at the screen from time to time, but it was much too happy a party to stay glued to the TV.

"Steve's right, MJ. They've got to get back before we celebrate. We've only completed half the mission."

"Don't worry, my little chickadee," Jack whispered in her ear. "We'll be celebrating soon enough, and you'll be my date." He slipped his hand under her blouse. Ronnie would've beaten the crap out of him if he saw this.

"Jack, off. Do that one more time, and you'll have to clap with one hand." Mary laid it on thick.

"Can't blame a guy for trying."

"Can't blame a girl for crying," Mary responded.

The partying continued well into the night, long after Armstrong and Aldrin had retired back into the Eagle. Everyone went home to their respective lairs. It was too important an event historically—the only one-night stand that night was up on the Moon.

The next day, everyone sort of stumbled in to watch the lunar takeoff. They were back in their work clothes—white shirts, dark ties, black pants. The smokes were not celebratory cigars but, rather, Camels, puffed down to the fingertips. This was business —the moment of truth for their baby! There was no laughter at the Cape this morning, as they listened to the LEM radio report at 1:55 p.m.: "9, 8, 7, 6, 5, first stage engine on ascent. Proceed. Beautiful, 26, 26 feet per second up. Little pitch over, very smooth, very quiet ride . . . " And four minutes after takeoff, "Eagle is back in orbit." When the LEM docked with the Columbia at 5:35 p.m. and the astronauts had returned to their command module, the mission of Grumman Aircraft Engineering—made possible by all of the engineers and professionals who had left their families back in Bethpage, New York—was finally completed, and successful in all respects.

Along with proving that the surface of the Moon was not made of cheese, the astronauts had left behind much more sophisticated equipment. Some of it was important for scientific testing, but other things they just no longer needed to carry, including boots, cameras, an aluminum pole, and equipment boxes—things that would only make their "backpacks" too heavy as they made their way out of alien territory. They were the first litterbugs in outer space. Millions of dollars of taxpayers' money was left for near eternity.

Now all that remained was for the rest of the project to be as successful in bringing the astronauts home. The uneventful return, the floating down into the Pacific Ocean, the arrival on the U.S.S. Hornet, was almost anti-climactic. President Nixon—there he was again—stealing the thunder with his speech. Praise from the rest of the world poured in. We watched interviews with our adoring public in London, in Paris, and even with the Pope. There were somber congratulations from the Russian cosmonauts. Janice Armstrong, Neil's wife, was interviewed over and over. "If anyone were to ask me how I could describe this flight, I can only say it was out of this world." She had as much imagination as her husband, exuding mid-Western American corn.

The New York Times on July 21st had the following headline:
"MEN WALK ON THE MOON
Astronauts Land on Plain, Collect Rocks, Plant Flag."

In China and North Vietnam the event was ignored. In the Soviet Union, *Pravda* downplayed the event.

Mary and all of the workers at Grumman got patches and certificates to thank them for their efforts. I had just been a passive participant and could only bask in the glory, as the historic venture was recounted. All of the interviews began to merge into one, with platitudes aplenty and discussions about the meaning of space exploration. But for me, the most insightful interview was with a foot-soldier in Vietnam still halfway around the world — a full day's air flight for the rest of us but just 45 minutes for the astronauts. He couldn't have been much older than 22 or 23, still with a youthful face partly hidden by his combat helmet. His lips stood out in the spotlight of the television camera. "This is the most fabulous event of my lifetime, and in the end I hear 25 billion dollars has been spent on the space project to reach the Moon. Man will have to decide if we believe he can afford more money, say, for the cities, the slums, urban renewal, or the war effort here."

Although for one week, for one night, all of this was forgotten, reality would again have to take hold. Our misguided priorities would again be revealed to the world. New Year's Eve only lasts for one night.

And what about Mr. Gorski's good luck? Arnie told Jack that Armstrong had recounted that when he was a youngster growing up in Columbus, Ohio, he had been playing baseball one Sunday afternoon in his backyard, when the ball got hit over the fence into the neighbor's yard.

He had been elected to climb over and retrieve the ball, but feared that Mrs. Gorski would come out with her broom handle. The ball had landed under their bedroom window. As he slowly and quietly went to pick up the ball, he heard Mrs. Gorski say to Mr. Gorski, "Oral sex? You want oral sex? I give you oral sex the day the boy next door walks on the Moon!"

July 25–August 4, 1969

Less than a week after our triumphant walk on the Moon and only a couple of days after our heroes had returned to Earth, Vietnam was again in the forefront, as President Nixon's "Doctrine" was made public. It promised economic and military assistance for those countries fighting against Communism but no further use of American ground troops. It was the ultimate admission that our involvement was a mistake, and would never be repeated again during his administration. Of course, he still had to get us out of this quagmire, and he sent Henry Kissinger to Paris for secret negotiations with the North Vietnamese government.

August, 1969

"Jay, one more month 'til college—I can't wait. I'm getting horny as hell around here. What do you want to do this weekend? Are you hanging out with Judy?"

Jay's new hairdo now included a full Jewish Afro and a beard and mustache. He was even more ready to leave Scarsdale than I was.

"Don't know, I haven't spoken to her."

"Hey, she's got a cute friend, Patty Franklin, you know, the math teacher's daughter. Maybe she can get me a date and we can double?"

"Shit, Ken, I'm getting ready to go off to college and you're gonna start up with some high school chick. You really think you'll get any action?"

"I don't know, Jay. You seem to get along pretty well with Judy."

"Yeah, but she ain't traveling with me out to UCLA."

"Still, call her for me. We could all go to the Mets game."

"Call for yourself, Ken. She's still pissed at me after last weekend."

"Wouldn't put out, huh?"

"Nah, that wasn't it. I told her she was richer than I was and that she'd have to pay for her own movie."

"You're a class act, Jay."

"Yeah, but you're right. I'm ready for some college pussy. I'm sick of being a virgin."

"I'll call her anyway, Jay."

As I picked up the phone, Jay just shrugged. The phone rang twice. "Hey Judy, it's Ken Kutscher."

"Hey, Ken."

"I was just wondering if Patty Franklin and you were still hanging out. I was hoping you could ask her if she wanted to double date with you and Jay and me, and go to the Mets game on Saturday."

"I don't know. I'm not sure she's even around. But I'll call her."

"Call us back, I'm at Jay's."

"Is Jay there?"

Jay overheard, shaking his head violently.

"No, he went out for some pizza."

"Sure, anyway, I'll get back to you in a flash."

"Ken," Jay said, coming to his senses. "I'm not sure I really want to do this. My brother's friends are going up to that Rock festival in upstate, and they may have room for me in their Beetle bus."

The phone rang.

I looked towards Jay.

"Answer it Ken, it's for you."

"Hey Judy, what did she say?"

"She's going camping with her family."

"That's okay. Hey, I still want to go to the game. You wanna come with Jay and me?"

"That'd be fine. Sounds like fun," came a voice through the telephone earpiece.

"No way, I can't stand baseball," came another disjointed voice, creating a stereo sound, from the other side of the kitchen.

"Jay doesn't want to go."

"Why don't we go anyway?" Judy responded, as Jay said, "Why don't you go without me?"

And so it was the moment when universes began to move away, as positive ends of magnets repel each other—the beginning of one "beautiful" and long (at times too long) friendship and the ending of another, now too-long, friendship.

Jay went up to Boston that weekend to visit his brother. They were supposed to go to Woodstock, but all of the guys in the apartment got so stoned that they never made it out of Cambridge. Judy and I went to see the Mets play. I wasn't sure if it was a date until I arrived at her house, and she came out dressed in tight-fitting red and blue striped bellbottom pants, along with a sleeveless blue blouse.

We had an exciting night, with the car overheating as we sat in traffic. That forced us to walk to the nearest gas station just to get some water for the radiator. Even that couldn't dampen the spirit of the night, however, as the Mets won—the eighth time in a row that they had been victorious while I was in attendance! I don't remember any details of the game, but I know we didn't get home until 1 a.m.

In the morning, my dad asked how the game was.

"We won. We'll be in first place by next week."

"Did Jay enjoy it or not?"

"Jay didn't go."

"It was just you and . . ."

"Judy."

"Oh."

The phone rang.

"Oh, hi. Who is this? Oh, hello Judy. It's for you, Ken."

"Sure, Judy, I'd like to go to the pool with you. Let me check with my father to see if he has any work I need to do."

My dad smiled. "I guess I can wait for you until later. Try to be home by 4."

I was excited about going to her family's club for the day. My excitement turned to disappointment, however, when I found out it was the town pool where we had our post-prom party and of which we were both members. But at the end of the day, after lying at the pool's edge, about 30 yards away from Jay's mother, even "dense I" got the message that maybe Judy had more on her mind than just a pool date.

By the time Jay got home from Boston midweek—four pounds lighter from lack of food and three atmospheres higher, already out of orbit—Judy and I had seen the Mets, had our second date at the movies, done the ice cream social, made out in the park, and had plans for the following weekend.

Of course, Jay didn't know this. I figured he pretty much didn't care about Judy anymore. And although I had probably broken the rule about dating your best friend's girl, Jay's mind was already on UCLA. Even more importantly, his 18th birthday was coming up on August 29th.

On August 28, at 11 p.m., I arrived with Bart and Seth at his apartment.

"Hey Jay, it's time to go out for your first legal drink. Let's get the RISK game set up for our final tournament of the summer." Bart was a geek, but he was trying to learn how to party.

"I want to be the blue armies." I added.

"Are you sure it's not too late?" Seth still ordered a Coke whenever he went out, even though he was two months past his 18th birthday.

"What about it, Jay? Are you ready to party? Are you ready to rip through Africa?"

"Or overrun the Vatican and put the Pope out to pasture?"

"That would be somewhat hypocritical, wouldn't it, my man?"

"What are you talking about?"

"Like, man, 'Make love, not war.'" Jay was maturing into a free radical. "Peace, brother."

"Jay, you're . . ."

"Stoned. Shit, yes. How else can I go down to the draft board to-morrow and register."

"Jay, you got your 2S," I answered. "Just show them your college acceptance letter."

"Ken, didn't you hear me? Make love, not war. I'm registering as a conscientious objector. I've already got my Bic lighter to burn my draft card if they don't give it to me."

"On what grounds? You're not even religious."

"Ken, do you believe in war?"

"Not this war."

"How about any war? Would you fight and kill your 'brother?'"

"Yes, if we're attacked, like at Pearl Harbor. Certainly, I would defend our country."

"Wouldn't you, Jay?" Bart asked.

"I don't believe in war!" Jay restated his position. "I'm a pacifist."

"Jay, you're full of shit." I was not going to let him off the hook so easily. "What about the Israeli Six Day War last year? You're Jewish, didn't you contribute any money? Weren't you proud? Did you think about enlisting?"

"Ken, when was the last time I went to temple? And I didn't see you hopping on a plane to go fight."

"Shit, Jay, I was just making an example. I mean, that was a necessary war."

"Not for me."

"Well, Jay, I'd hate to have a mugger come up to us and demand our money. You'd probably show him where you lived. Or what if someone was breaking into your house and stealing your stereo?"

"Let him have it; he probably needs it more than I do."

"And if he was threatening to kill your mother, and you had a gun, would you shoot him?"

"Ken, you and your fucking theoretical hypothesis. I would try to talk him out of it."

"And if he was running towards your mother with a knife . . .'"

"I'd try to grab the knife out of his hand."

". . . and you were 20 feet away from him and you had a loaded gun—would you let your mother die?"

"I don't know if I could pull the trigger."

"Jay, if you really wouldn't, you're a great pacifist and a lousy son." I couldn't believe my ears.

"Why, Ken, could you really do it?"

"I wouldn't like it, but, yeah, I would."

"Ken, you sound so tough, but you're being a pussy. You applied for a 2S, you're still avoiding this war, and you're letting the blacks and poor people fight if for you."

"That's because, first, I'm a chicken—I'll admit that—second, it's an immoral war, and, third I'm going to college. But don't think I won't be protesting the war."

"Ken, that's chicken shit. Columbia would defer your admission."

"Listen, Jay, I'm willing to admit that I'm scared. I don't want to get blown away over there, especially for no good reason."

"But you'll let some poor black or white man get the bullet in the head instead of you?"

"Jay, don't think that doesn't eat away at me everyday. I mean, I'll go to all the protests, sign the petitions, march wherever."

"And you'll yell—'Hell no, we won't go!'"

"Sure."

"Knowing your 2S protects your lily white ass."

"Hey, I didn't make the laws. Why don't you write to Congressmen Reid or Senator Javits? You're always yelling 'Power to the people.'"

"Fuck it, Ken. You know, if they did away with student deferments, this war would be over real quick. You think the middle and upper class would put up with this war? Writing to government officials is a waste of my fucking time."

"You know, Jay, they didn't have this problem in World War II. You know why? Because we were attacked—everyone enlisted. Even the baseball players. You'd have brought shame to your family if you'd have stayed home."

"Not everyone was in favor of the war."

"Yeah, like Charles Lindbergh—that fascist. He was an isolationist who loved Germany."

"You mean the guy who flew across the Atlantic?" Seth asked.

"No kidding," Bart said. He couldn't believe it.

"So what's different, Jay?" I asked. "Would you've fought in WWII?"

"Probably not. But I would've found a job in a non-combat area in the military."

"Jay, making bombs at home still would kill people. What would you have done, swept floors in the factories?"

"Anything not to have pulled the trigger."

"Hey Jay," Bart asked, "why don't you become a medic? That way you only save lives."

"Yeah, Jay," I said. I was on a roll. "They get to shoot at you instead of your shooting at them."

"No way, I hate blood. I'd rather run off to Canada. Hopefully, it won't come to that and I'll get my C.O. and do community service."

"Jay, I don't know if I could run away. Somehow I think the shame of desertion would be worse than the fear of being killed."

"But is the shame worse than being killed?" Seth asked.

"Ken, I only have one last thing to say—there is no honor in an immoral war." And that was the last we spoke that night of the war.

"Let's get some pizza and beer," Bart interjected. "I'm thirsty and I'm hungry."

We had two pepperoni pies that night, along with a six-pack and a bottle of Canadian Club with ginger ale. By 2 a.m., we had all had enough, although Seth was still nursing his second beer. Jay was bored, so he started "flicking his Bic." Seth pulled out his own "Bic."

"Seth, what the fuck do you need a cigarette lighter for?" Jay asked. You don't smoke cigarettes, and you certainly don't smoke dope."

"Hey, I just want to be ready in case I go out on a date and the girl wants to burn her bra."

"Your friend's a fuckin idiot." Jay's brother Andy had arrived. After listening to Seth's bullshit, he poured himself a couple of shots of the C.C.

"Hey, boys, want to listen to some real music? Led Zeppelin."

We didn't have a boom box or surround sound, just a small record player with two small speakers. As we listened to "Whole Lotta Love," we started strumming our phantom acoustical guitars and using our fingers as drumsticks. Little did I know I was hearing the group that would release "Stairway to Heaven" that winter—the rock anthem for our generation—and that the "Led" was ours to keep, not to be usurped by the generations of the 80s, and 90s, as much as they tried.

I didn't make it home that night because I passed out on the couch. Bart and Seth left sometime around 3 a.m., and Jay spent half the night in the bathroom.

I unfortunately awoke the next morning . . . wondering whether this was what college life would be all about, with my head pounding as Andy started up with "Whole Lotta Love."

It was Monday morning, so Jay's parents were already up, showering for work. As there was only one bathroom, I squirmed while waiting my turn. Jay's dad was "old," about 55, shorter than any of his kids, about 15 pounds overweight. He was dressed in his work clothes, loose pants and a T-shirt, ready to walk to his tailor's shop down the street. His mom walked out of the bathroom with her hair up in curlers, bathrobe tattered at the sleeves, and pink slippers worn to the point that her big toe came through.

"Hey, Mr. R."

"You boys had quite a night."

"Not many more before we go off to college, Mr. R."

"I certainly hope not."

"Jay . . ."

"Yeah, mom; I'm still asleep."

"Make sure you clean up this mess before you and Ken leave."

"Sure, Mom, whatever you say."

"Don't sass your mother."

"I'm not, Dad. I'm just tired of living in this apartment, filled with all of your crap, while you get on my case."

"Then I guess we'll have more room once you go off to college," his dad shot back.

"Ernie, don't say that; we'll need to keep his room ready for when he comes back for vacation."

"Don't count on that too soon, Mom."

"Why, are you planning on running off to Canada—no guts, can't fight for your country?" His dad wasn't about to back down. I could tell this was not going to be a good morning.

"I'm sorry, Dad. I can't be like you. I wasn't there at Normandy with you on D-day. I'm not going to kill some other man, just because he lives in another country and the politicians sent him and me to do their dirty work."

"Jay, don't talk to your father that way."

"Why not, Mom? He thinks because he got some medal for killing three Germans in a fox hole that he deserves sainthood?"

"Come on, Jay." I was trying to be the peacemaker, the Secretary General of the United Nations. "Let's just clean up. Your father's only concerned that you do the right thing."

"Shut up, Ken. What do you think this is, one of those Arthur Miller plays we read last year—father and son fighting it out, moral degradation?"

"Jay, all I did for this country so that you could get a good education, be free from Communism, go to UCLA. Irma, why did we do it? Why do you go off to be a nurse at the factory every day? For this?"

"Dad, let me be myself. I know you never read James Joyce in school, but read *A Portrait of the Artist as a Young Man.* I'll even leave you my underlined copy—page 256. 'I will not serve that in which I no longer believe whether it call itself my home, my fatherland or my church.' Then maybe you can understand that I want to be free to express whatever feelings I have."

"Don't think you can talk to me like that and still come back to this house!"

"Ernie, just let him go."

"Jay, please let's go."

"Sure. Let's blow this joint. Mom, I'll clean up later."

And we left, walking down the stairs.

"Jay, let's go get some breakfast at the diner."

"Sure, sure."

Jay was silent as we rode over to Central Avenue. We walked into the diner filled with mechanics in their grimy T-shirts under denim shirts with "Tony" or "Billy" embroidered on the pockets, their hands covered with grease as they sat smoking their cigarettes, laughing. And there were the regulars, the old guys, sitting at the counter, nursing their cups of coffee.

We sat in the booth farthest from the door. Jay ogled the waitress behind the counter working on the coffee pots. Some of the anger melted as she turned her taut, young body towards us, with a smile on her weary face. Her hair was pulled back in a ponytail and her lips were red with a fresh coat of lipstick.

Five minutes later, we still were having a love affair with our menus.

"What'll it be, boys?"

We turned to see another waitress come over to our table. In her white blouse, stained with eggs and coffee, a cigarette pack in her vest pocket that covered her once voluptuous but now sagging breasts, she could've passed for Jay's aunt.

"We may have been boys when we came in, but we've been waiting here so long I think we've become men!" Jay retorted sarcastically.

"Hey—why do you think we're called 'waitresses!'" she cackled.

"How long have you been waiting to use that line?" I laughed. "I'll have a "Number 2"—eggs over easy, rye toast, with coffee," I continued, with all the officiousness of a trucker.

"Give me a coffee, black."

"Is that all you want, honey?"

"It's all I can afford at these prices—99 cents for a breakfast?"

"Jay."

"I need to save my money for UCLA. You don't think my parents are going to send me any?"

"Jay, let me buy you breakfast."

"What, with your Daddy's money?"

"Fuck you, Jay. You know I worked all summer."

"Yeah, typing and working in the library for your dad. You call that real work?"

"Probably harder than yours. At least you weren't on a seven-day-a-week call schedule. Whenever he needed something typed, it was always: 'You can't go out until you've finished typing this letter for the Foundation.' We fought all of the time. You know how I was always late getting to your house."

"You make it sound like packing groceries was easy."

"And you think working for your father every day is easy? Being told that it was my obligation to help out with his symposium in memory of my mother. You can't even be in the same room as your father for more than five minutes."

"Well, at least I didn't get any help getting into college. My old man knows no one."

"You're right Jay. But I still had to get 1,522 on my SATs." Jay glared at me.

"Miss." Our waitress walked back over. "Give him what I'm having." Then I said to Jay, "Just call it a loan."

When the food came, we pretty much ate in silence. I paid the bill, and Jay left a quarter as a tip, for the proletariat.

Driving back to his apartment, there were no tears in his eyes, no attempt at a grand summation of life. As he got out of the car, I pleaded, "Jay, please make up with your mom and dad. Life's too short to be so angry. There are too many beautiful California girls waiting for you."

"That's the first fucking truth you've said all morning. I can't wait to graduate to college chicks. And one last word of advice, Ken."

"What, is this the Pope pontificating?"

"Don't trust anyone over 25."

"Jay, aren't you afraid of leaving?" And I paraphrased what appeared today to be Jay's favorite Irish author. "You'll be alone, all alone. Without any friends. Are you sure you're not afraid?"

"I'll take the risk," he answered, in communion with Joyce. "There will be others."

This was really our last night together as compatriots, Jay and me. I was going to go to Columbia College, 40 minutes from home, and 20 minutes from where my dad worked. I was still a New Yorker, and still part of my family. Harlan had offered to share a two-room suite with me, and I was going out with Judy, a high school senior-to-be. But Jay was now firmly entrenched in LA mode—grass, rebellion, hatred of his parents and authority.

Jay was angry, jealous, and superior. He was comparatively poor yet guilty because he also was comparatively rich. He knew what his friends had and what he didn't. He knew what he had and what the inner city blacks didn't. His bags were physically packed three days before his flight to UCLA, although mentally he was packed months before.

Jay's hearing before the draft board was successful. He was granted 1-O, alternative, non-military status. He didn't have much trouble since all but one of the male students in my class enrolled in college and were 2S, which left plenty of spots for conscientious objectors. The poor black students in Yonkers and White Plains gave the board plenty of the cannon fodder it needed to choose from. And I guess he never told them about how he ransacked the Vatican as his RISK armies swept though Europe.

In the end, Jay wouldn't be going to the jungle; he wouldn't be stuck in the rice paddies without a paddle; he wouldn't be shooting at the Vietcong; and he wouldn't be used as a human mine sweeper. Instead, he would spend his obligation doing community service in Watts. If he felt any self-recrimination or guilt, he didn't show it. For Jay, the United States was founded on resistance to intolerable government; it was established through acts of defiance. He was being a patriot, resisting the unjust.

As for me, I was complacent with my 2S. I wasn't worried, as Jay was, that the selective service would change the rules. There were too many congressmen who would have to answer to their "valuable" constituents if, all of a sudden, upper and middle class white students were sent to Vietnam.

Jay certainly didn't want to hear my argument that he wasn't actually saving another grunt's life, as he would have had he been 1-A, or even served as non-combat military. His arguments weren't so pure, but I didn't even try. Others would still die while he lived.

During the end of that summer, I often wondered whether Jay really knew or cared that I was dating Judy. But as Percy Sledge sang,

"When a man loves a woman…"

But as much as I had turned my back on Jay, he had turned his entire back away from me and from Scarsdale. Physical laws dictate that for each action, there is an equal and opposite reaction. So it didn't surprise me that Jay and I didn't talk much those last few days (or for that matter, after we went away to our colleges.) We separated no longer best friends, having gone our individual ways, with separate cultures, separate priorities, and separate peaces as we flew to opposite sides of the solar system.

As Jay was moving on, higher and higher, away from Scarsdale and me, Judy and I were steadily getting closer, talking about continuing to date while I was at Columbia. Would I come home on weekends and have to deal with my father's requests for me to work for him, typing letters and organizing files, as if I had never left? Would he have control over my free time and would Judy put up with it? Would I escape the home base to spread my eagle's wings, to soar away from Scarsdale and my family's gravitational pull?

In the end, however, it would be ironic that Jay, the conscientious objector, who would never fly in a B-52, who would never drop bombs or spray napalm, and who would never be subject to anti-aircraft fire, would die as a result of the gravitational forces dropping a plane out of the air. But it wasn't over an unnamed jungle in Vietnam or Cambodia; rather, it was in a commercial airline crash the following year over San Diego. By then, it was an event that was only a footnote in my personal history—the first person to die from my class. His name was listed in Scarsdale's weekly paper's obituary section—along with the names of people who had already lived their fulfilled lives—all in the absence of the names of "this week's dead in Vietnam" which were too often in local papers around the country.

Jay was lucky regarding his own words: he would never be "untrusted" by the youth of America because he never reached the age of 25. In that way, he was like 50,000 Americans who died in Vietnam before they were 25—men and women whose role in the world he so hated.

August 18, 1969 (Woodstock)

My brother Paul walked through the kitchen. His sleeping bag was rolled up, his canvas knapsack was on his back, his bellbottom jeans and tie-dyed shirt were wrinkled, and his leather sandal's clip was clopping on the floor.

"Which car are you planning on taking?" Mike demanded, his older brother's superiority seeping through.

"My Pontiac."

"Your Pontiac?" Mike's upper lip, now covered with a thin mustache, was quivering. "It's my last weekend home before I'm going back to U of Mass and I need it."

"There are plenty of cars here, Mike."

"Paul, just sit down for a minute with Mike and we'll discuss this."

"Lil, I need to go!" Paul turned quickly towards his mom and then went back out towards the door.

"Lil, I need the car also," Cathy chimed in, as she arrived downstairs wearing cut-offs with a hole in the backside of her tight jeans covered by a rainbow sew-on. Now three of my step-siblings had become rivals. "Darcy and I are supposed to go to the movies tonight."

"Can't she drive you?"

"Her parents took away her keys."

"My God," Lil exploded. "We have four cars, my insurance is over $1,000 a year, and spoiled brats can't come to an accommodation."

"Lil, I need the car." It was like the Kingston Trio, all in harmony, all as one, only with a Steinberg whine.

"Let me check with Bill to see if he needs Ken or Harlan to drive somewhere."

I overheard the last part. I ran upstairs before Lil could leave the breakfast nook and pleaded my case with my dad.

"Please, Dad, I think I might have a date with Judy tomorrow afternoon. It's important that I don't have to work after 10 or 11 a.m."

"Ken, I know you like this girl, and it's important that you spend some time with her, but this symposium starts in three weeks and I don't even have the draft of the program done. I need you and Lil to work on it."

"Dad, I'm about to go to Columbia. I won't be around every day or weekend to do this. I'm going away to school."

"Don't be so ungrateful. You're part of this family. This Foundation is in memory of Mommy and Harvey Steinberg. We work for a team."

"I doubt it, Dad, more like for a taskmaster. I'm gonna go out, no matter what. Judy and I were invited to a picnic at her friend's house."

"Well, buster, you better have a ride, because you're not using our car, not with that attitude."

"Then I guess we'll just walk. And since it's two miles away, I guess we'll just have to leave at 10 a.m." I turned to walk away.

"Do not leave this room, Ken. You'll do as I tell you."

"I'm not 14 anymore."

"Then pay for your own college expenses."

Luckily for us, Lil walked in. She caught only the aura of the conversation, but she was not in a good mood herself.

"Bill, everyone wants a car this weekend. Paul wants to go away with some friends camping, Mike needs it for his last weekend in Scarsdale, and Cathy wants to go to the movies."

"And Ken wants it for a date with Judy," I added.

"Bill, they're all ungrateful. Why don't we let them all get rides with someone? I'm tired of us being the rental fleet."

"You'll have to figure it out, Lil. You know they won't listen to me."

"We'll come to a compromise, then. Bill. Maybe we should just get rid of all of the cars."

Paul had stormed up the stairs. "Lil, I gotta go or I'll be late."

"Where are you going that's so important, Paul?" Mike was close behind.

"To upstate New York."

"Lil, ask him if he's going to that rock concert. We'll probably never see the car again."

"Shut up, Mike."

"Paul?"

"I promise I'll be careful."

"Yeah," I thought, "like the time I drove Paul's car last year and found this funny looking cigarette in the glove compartment." I had been confused at first, in my innocence, as to what it was, and then I was shocked to realize that Paul was actually smoking grass. Maybe it wasn't his. Maybe it was a friend's stashed away. No matter what, I was shaken. What if I got into an accident on the way to school? I felt the paranoia grow, having watched "Reefer Madness," a 1930s movie in health class. And I hadn't even inhaled!

"Lil," Mike pleaded, "If you let him go, they'll probably paint the car with psychedelic flowers."

"Hey, that would be cool. I'm getting the car for school this year. My friends would really groove on that." Cathy was excited all of a sudden.

"Look, boys, it's your last weekend." My dad was becoming Solomon. Would he split the car in half? "Let Paul take the car for the weekend. You other ingrates can share. Lil, I'll drive Cathy to the movies if Darcy's parents pick her up. That'll leave two other cars for Mike and Ken and Harlan—more than enough for the rest of the weekend."

"Thanks, Pop. I'm out of here."

"Wait a minute, Paul, where are you staying? How can we reach you?"

"Lil, it's gonna be cool. I'll call you from the campsite at the concert."

"Paul?"

"What, Cathy?"

"I hear they're expecting 50,000 people. Do you have your tickets?"

"We'll buy them there."

"Paul, please drive safely."

"Lil, I won't go over 90. Just kidding."

"Especially with an ounce of dope in the car," I almost heard myself utter.

Ten minutes later, Paul was at Ben's house.

"What took so long?"

"Mike wanted the car. I had to negotiate."

"Huh?"

"My step-dad let me have the car."

"Well, we got to roll."

"You got the grass?"

"All rolled up inside the sleeping bag—there's a special compartment."

As they drove out onto the Bronx River Parkway, Ben rolled his first joint. "Man, did my parents buy my story about going to a college retreat for religious self-knowledge up in New Paltz."

"Well, rock 'a' roll is a religion, and we'll definitely be getting some self-knowledge," Paul laughed, as he took his first toke.

"Lil, do you know where Paul's going?" Mike asked a few minutes later, munching on his chocolate-covered Ring Ding.

"To a concert in upstate New York. It sounded okay."

"I just hope your car comes back in one piece."

"Don't worry about Paul, just because his hair is long. Anyway, Ben's a good kid; he'll be alright." Lil's voice became softer, as if filled with some concern.

There hadn't been much in the news about Woodstock that week that Lil had seen or read—certainly not in her bible, *The Wall Street Journal*. And the nightly news was mainly filled with negative reports about our progress in Vietnam and with coverage of the student protests around the U.S.

But the next night, as I waited for Mike to return from his activities so that I could use the remaining car to pick up Judy, Woodstock was the lead story—the mud, the trashed farms, the drugs, the naked bodies, and the music. I knew that Lil and my dad would be watching the 11 o'clock news, so there was no need to worry them yet. And as I came home that night, sometime after midnight, I saw their light was still on, and Lil was talking to my dad. In the morning, Lil stayed by the phone. She called Ben's mom to see if she had heard from him. And by the evening news, all she saw was the destruction, the chaos, the litter, and the drugs being passed around. She looked for her son and swore what she'd do to him when he got home. As I kissed my dad and her goodnight, I was amazed at how her face had aged that weekend. Was it a figment of my imagination, or were there a few strands of gray hair?

It must have been 3 a.m. when the car lights came into the driveway and Hope rolled over in my bed.

In the morning, we saw the mud-coated car with the rear hubcap missing, the dirt on the kitchen floor, and the muddy jeans and shirts at the bottom of the basement stairs.

It wasn't until noon that Paul came downstairs—to stares from his mother, stares of relief that did not at all mask her distrust and anger.

"Lil, I wasn't even there. We got stuck in traffic five miles away and parked in a field. We tried to get in; we camped in a field nearby where we could hear the music. But there was no water, the stench was awful, and not a porta-potty in sight."

"Why didn't you come home?"

"Lil, it took us eight hours just to find the car where we thought we had left it. It was 10 o'clock when we left and I figured you'd be asleep."

Lil didn't ask any more questions, and Paul didn't trust any of us to tell the truth, if there was more to this than he let on. But no police came knocking at the door, there were no traffic tickets in the mail, and what I learned of "Woodstuck" was muddied by the press and the drug-tempered stories of those who were there. I would have to vicariously live the "social" event of the '60s. It wouldn't be until the following year when "Woodstock: The Movie" came out that I would actually see what had happened. For others, who had been there stoned, it would also be their first appreciation of what had really happened. And from all accounts by my step-brother, watching that movie would also give him his first glimpse of Jimi Hendricks live.

August 1969 (Florida)

"Anyway, it looks like a quiet weekend down here. Did you read about that rock concert in New York State this weekend? Thirty bands and they expect 50,000 people."

"Yeah, Mary—what of it? It's over 1,000 miles away!"

"If we leave right after work Thursday and watch out for those Georgia troopers who love you so, we could be there by midnight Friday."

"Can you miss work, MJ?"

"Sure, I'll call in from the road."

"Well, I can't leave until Friday afternoon—there's too much going on at the Space Center."

"Miss Responsibility!"

"Damn it, MJ, I forgot. It's my mother's birthday Saturday."

"So?"

"She'll be 40!"

"And married three times, with a jerk for a husband."

"MJ, I need to be there for the party."

"Earth to space, Mary. What universe are you living in? Like she's ever been there for you—your fifth birthday, your sixth birthday, your seventh birthday. Get the picture? You know, it's like last summer, you didn't worry about her birthday when we blew this town and traveled to Chicago. Somehow you were able to escape Mother Earth's gravitational pull then—but I guess she's got hold of you again."

"She's still my mother."

"Yea, and the only effort she ever put forth on your behalf was when she pushed you out of her womb on the day you were born."

"I know, God do I know. I guess it's my Catholic guilt."

"I'll remind you of that the next time you get stoned."

"Are you going to New York, anyway?"

"Not without my sister-in-crime. Anyway, I'm not sure either of our cars is really ready for that long journey. 'Mission control, this is Cape Kennedy. We have a no go.' Mission aborted."

Predicably, the birthday party was a disaster. It was like a scene out of *Who's Afraid of Virginia Wolf?* expanded to include family and "friends." The liquor was free-flowing, as were the threats, and Mary was insulted one too many times by her step-father.

"Mary," he bellowed, "Go upstairs and change that blouse!" The countdown began for the retrorockets on the second-stage to fire, to propel Mary once and forever out of Titusville, far from this abuse.

Later that night she sat crying, "MJ, I'm out of here."

"What about your job?"

"Hey, I'm not exactly a rocket scientist—they'll be able to replace me."

"Where'll ya go?"

"Does it really fuckin' matter? Shit, maybe I'll call up dear old Dad out in San Diego. Haven't seen him for years."

"That's a good start—at least you haven't been fighting with him."

"Yeah, time to pack up the old VW bug and head on out. Surprise the bastard!"

One week later, Mary was packed and had given notice to the Space Center. That was followed by a small going away party at the Mousetrap, perfunctory kisses from Mom, and false expressions of "We'll miss you" from her step-father. Only MJ would really be missed—and Spider, whom she willed to Philip.

The trip to the West Coast gave Mary plenty of time to think, to ruminate, to hope. Should she call her father or just show up? If she called, he might tell her not to come. But maybe he was away on assignment from the paper and wouldn't even be there.

She hadn't made it to Woodstock, but as the radio blared—as she switched from station to station, as each one would fade away—she could imagine the bands playing. She sang along on the radio to Credence Clearwater Revival's "Bad Moon Arising," The Incredible String Band's "Maybe Someday One will Come Along," Janis Joplin wailing "Take Another Little Piece of My Heart" . . . to Sly and the Family "Stoned," the Grateful Dead . . . . It was her own rock 'n' roll marathon.

She stopped the first night in Biloxi, Mississippi, and went into Sam's Café, a dive on Route 66. There were enough cars parked with Mississippi plates, including the Sheriff's black and white, to suggest that at least the locals ate there. Her duffle bag was in the back seat, along with her case of 45s and LPs tucked under a blanket, to keep them from the sunlight.

The burger she ordered was overcooked, the roll was stale, and the fries were greasy, but she was hungry and she washed it down with a chocolate milk shake.

"Excuse me, Miss," she said to the waitress, a 30-something bleached blond with black roots coming out and a lapel label emblazoned with "MAUDE." "Where's the nearest hotel that I could afford?"

"You by yourself, or are you all 'specting company?" She glanced around at the guys shooting pool in the dark corner.

"Me? There's not a guy here I'd be seen with."

"Smart lady. I've been with 'em all!" Maude cackled. "And ain't one that's worth a roll. About a mile down the road—the Satellite Motel. Nothin' special, but at least the roaches stay outside!"

"Thanks for the tip. Even if they did steal the name from Cocoa Beach!"

Mary got up to go, leaving a dollar extra for Maude's advice.

"Thanks for the tip," she heard as she walked out the screen door into the poorly lit parking lot.

"Shit!! Fuck!!" Someone had broken the back window of her bug and stolen her bag and records! The seven-year-old "Pollymaryanna" would have said, "I guess someone needed the stuff more than I did." Instead, Mary chose not to hold back her tears as she screamed, "Fuckin' rednecks! Dirtbag misfits!"

Two guys dressed in uniform (jeans and cowboy boots) sauntered out and glanced down at Mary as she sat at the side of her Beetle.

"Somebody broke into your car, little lady."

"You're a fuckin' genius."

"Need a place to stay. My mama's out of town!"

"Yeah, but where's your old lady. Or are they the same?" Mary squealed.

"You probably shouldn't have left that stuff in the car," Maude interjected as she wandered out for a smoke. "This is Mississippi—spelled with four i's and four s's."

"I thought it was still Alabama," Mary retorted, "spelled with four a's, as in assholes! Should I call the police?"

"You mean the sheriff inside? He's out back with the cook. I doubt he'd care about some hippie with Florida plates."

"Thanks for the free advice!! Shit, I'll just get in my car and try to forget this place even exists on this earth."

It was a long night as Mary drove through to Louisiana. She crossed the Mississippi River at four a.m. and pulled over on the side of the road for a few hours to sleep. In the morning, she was back behind the wheel, after having a large cup of coffee and a couple of greasy donuts for breakfast. There were lots of highway, lots of concrete, lots of asphalt, lots of roadside dives—all distracted by rock which rolled into turned to Country-Western music—as she littered the back of her car with empty bottles of Coke and Twinkies wrappers.

The sign read "San Diego 60 Miles." It was 6 p.m. and she'd be there in a couple of hours. She wanted to make sure her father was home, so she pulled over at the Sinclair gas station with the big green dinosaur out front and looked up his number in the phone book. After she dropped her last two dimes, she heard, "Hello."

"Dad?"

Silence. Bob didn't have a daughter—just his two sons from his second marriage, Billy Bob and Bobby Bill.

"Dad?"

"Mary?"

"Yeah. I'm glad you remembered my name."

"What are you doing? Where are you? Is your mother okay?"

"I'm somewhere about 60 miles outside San Diego."

"What are you doing there?"

"I'm on my way to see you."

Another "voice" interjected, "You have ten seconds remaining on your phone call," in a monotone.

"When?"

"Tonight."

"Well, we just finished dinner."

"Dad, I'll find a . . ."

"I'm sorry, your time is expired," the monotonic voice said. Then a dial tone.

Mary banged her head against the telephone booth, too tired to cry.

She got back in the car and started towards San Diego on the free-way. Florida was flat, with lots of 90-degree right-hand and left-hand turns. But here, in California, there were jug handles, circular exit ramps that intertwined with each other like a pretzel. She got lost several times, driving off one cloverleaf exit, then back around to another, circling almost randomly as she tried to make her way towards the northeast suburbs near the mountains.

The house was modern Western—ranch style with a two-car garage and cacti growing in the front yard. The lights were on as she rang the bell.

"You look exhausted."

"Haven't slept in a bed for six days, Dad."

"Well, there's not much room here."

"We can make up the couch, Bob," Mary's "step-mother," Carol, interjected.

"Anything. I'm fagged out."

"Are you hungry?"

"Of course she is, Bob. How about some mac and cheese? That's what we had for dinner?"

"Thank you, Mrs. McAuliffe." It was the name Mary used to have, before . . .

"Mary, call me Carol."

Billy Bob and Bobby Bill came bounding down the stairs in their PJs—Roy Rogers and Hopalong Cassidy in tandem, with their holsters at their sides and guns drawn to protect the homestead.

Carol looked at her husband.

"Boys, this is Mary. She's your aunt from Florida."

"I didn't know I had an aunt in Florida."

Mary looked at their dad. They didn't know.

He shrugged, as if to say, "I'm sorry. I'll tell them later. What did you expect?"

"I didn't know I had little nephews in California," Mary said with a subtle tone of sarcasm in her voice that easily passed over their pre-teen heads.

Over Coke and mac and cheese Mary told them about her trip through the "Wild West." The boys went off to bed while Carol—a bit frumpy looking in her house dress, as middle age had not been kind to her figure—fussed with the dishes, refusing Mary's help to clean up. She and her Dad went into the living room. Mary had a Coke in her hand.

"Want a real drink, Mary?"

"Sure, what're you having?"

"Irish Whiskey. Jameson's."

"Never heard of it."

"I don't doubt it, down in Titusville. Try it, you'll like it."

"How'll it go with my Coke?

"A new taste sensation, I'm sure."

After Bob poured their drinks, he asked quietly, "What are you really doing here?"

"I left Florida. I've decided to move to California."

"Why?"

"Many reasons. Change, mostly."

"How's your mother?"

"Bitchy as ever. What a farce. Her 40th birthday party and she kicked me out, she was so drunk."

"Now maybe you'll understand why I left. What'll you do here?"

"Hey, I did payroll at the Cape. I've worked in a bank. I'll find something."

"Where'll you stay? I mean, it's fine for you to stay here for a few days, but we don't have the room."

"I know, Dad. Just give me a few weeks, I'll get my job, my first paycheck, and then I'll get my own place."

Carol walked in. "I'll get the sheets. Where are you staying tomorrow?"

"Carol, Mary needs a place until she gets settled here."

"Bob, you know my Mother's coming next week."

"Don't worry, Carol. I'll be long gone by then."

And during the night, as Mary went to the bathroom, she could hear her Dad and step-mom talking about who had first dibs on the couch next weekend.

In the morning, Mary listened for the *San Diego Courier* to be thrown up onto the porch. She went outside in her T-shirt and panties, carefully bending down to pick it up. On the editorial page was "Bob McAuliffe, Associate Editor, Local News."

She walked into the kitchen and put some water on to boil. Then she spooned in the Folgers's coffee and stirred some milk and sugar into the cup.

She turned to the Help Wanted section.

"BANKING"

"First National Bank of California. Teller wanted. Experience Required."

She circled the ad, along with a few others.

"How'd you sleep?" Carol inquired as she came down the stairs.

"First soft bed in a week," she said, as the java began to percolate to her brain.

"I see you got the paper already. Anything?"

"Yeah, looks like First National needs a teller. I'll go by there first."

"Dad," Mary said, as he lumbered down the stairs in his bathrobe — his middle-aged gut adding about 25 pounds to his previously taut military body. "Can I borrow $20 to get new clothes for my interview?"

"Sure." He reached for his wallet on the kitchen table and handed her an Andrew Jackson. "Consider it a gift."

A dollar for each year, Mary thought.

The next morning she was in training as an assistant teller. She arrived wearing a short (but not mini) navy blue skirt, stockings, and a white blouse tastefully unbuttoned one or two notches. Her long hair was carefully entwined in a ponytail.

"Hi, I'm Tammy," said a tall brunette with cute bangs, and a winsome smile, wearing an even shorter skirt. She had tight buttocks and long legs, and was wearing high-heeled, leather boots and a sweater that exaggerated her A-cup breasts.

"Oh, hi, I'm Mary."

"Glad to meet ya. You're gonna love it here. This is a great place to work."

"I hope so. I just got in from Florida a couple of days ago. I'm crashing with my dad and step-mom and their two brats. I really need a break."

"Hey, we have an extra room in our pad. You can crash there, and if we're all cool, we can split the rent."

"Groovy," Mary said in "California speak."

Over lunch, Tammy introduced Mary around, and after work they went for a drink.

"Friday night," Tammy announced, "we got an invite to a really great party at a friend of my boyfriend's house out near La Jolla."

"Really? Can I come?"

"Of course."

"He's not military, is he? All they ever think about on their leave is getting drunk and getting laid."

"Maybe it's because they're about to get their heads shot off in 'Nam and they don't want to think about it," answered Rosa, one of the other tellers. She was a third-generation Mexican immigrant who had changed into her bellbottom jeans with red paisley strips for hems. Her dark, black hair was long and braided in the back.

"I don't know," Mary responded. "My dad wanted to go to war."

"Not this one, he wouldn't," Tammy answered.

"You're wrong, Tammy. He's country first, family second. God old U.S. of A."

"Don't generalize, Mary," Rosa added. "You'll get to meet my boyfriend, Frank, a seaman. And he got drafted. He doesn't want to go. He's not straight-laced or hardened by his commanders. He's just a softy at heart."

"That's not what you told me the morning, Rosa," Tammy laughed. "You told me last night how you hardened him, got him straight."

"Is the party gonna be all military?" Mary was beginning to get exasperated.

"You kidding. My boyfriend is one of the San Diego Padres. He's a reserve infielder for the team. And he backs up Cito Gaston in the outfield."

"Who are the Padres? Some minor league team?" Mary wasn't ready for second stringers.

"No, Mary. They're Major League. New expansion team."

"Can't be any good, can they?"

"I don't know, Mary. He seems pretty good with his bat."

"Very funny. Does he have any friends?"

"*Si, si, señorita.* He told me to invite a few of my pals to the party. The Padres just brought up a few of their minor leaguers for a look-see at the end of the season. They're just sitting on the bench, so I'm sure they'll be ready for some action."

"Shit," Mary thought out loud, as she scratched behind her ear. "I don't know nothing about baseball."

"Neither did I," Tammy laughed, "but now I've learned all about their bats and their balls." She cackled as her cigarette ash was about to fall into the ashtray."

"Tammy," Rosa quipped, "no wonder the guys all love you. They never strike out with you."

"You got that straight. My Stan's kinda quiet, but he sure carries a big stick."

"A real Teddy Roosevelt."

"Well, I don't know. I'm still pretty tired."

"You'll be there, Mary, if we have to drag you."

"What should I wear? I've got nothing. Everything was stolen on my way out."

"Come with me. You can borrow my skirt and Rosa's blouse."

They arrived at the house around 8:30. The stereo was booming "Don't You Need Somebody to Love," with the bass rocking the neighborhood. Mary's makeshift outfit showed off her sunburned legs, since Tammy's mini-skirt only came down to her mid-thigh. And Rosa's blouse, which she had borrowed, was one size too small, allowing (or forcing) Mary to go braless.

They wound their way through the crowd until Tammy found Stan, who was standing off to the side with a Bud in his hand, wildly replaying an error that the Cincinnati Reds' second baseman had made that night.

Several of his younger teammates were watching the "pro," getting tips on how to be cool.

"Hey, Stan."

"Hi, Tammy. Come on over. I'd like you to meet some of the rookies."

"Sure, Stan. This is Mary; she's the new teller I told you about who's going to be living with us. And this is Rosa, you remember, from the bank."

"Hey, Rosa. Hey, Mary." Stan's eyes glanced briefly at Mary's smiling face, and then focused on her breasts—an action that was not lost on Mary or Tammy. "How's it going out in sunny Californiaay?"

"I don't know. I just got here."

"Stan, where's your manners? Introduce us to your friends. And why doesn't someone get us a brew?"

"Mary, this is Reggie Weaver. And Sammy Green, one of our new pitchers."

"Hi, Mary."

"Hey."

"Hey, guys."

"Stan, I need to talk to you for a while," Tammy said, winking her eye.

The night was fun for Mary. She danced with the guys, drank beer with the guys, got stoned with the guys. Before she knew it, it was 2 a.m., and Reggie offered to drive her home.

"Sorry, Reggie. I got my own wheels. And besides, it's not even our first date."

"Babe, this is California. Free love, you know. Love beads."

"I guess I'm still on Florida Standard Time."

"Well, how about a second date. We're all meeting up after the game tomorrow with some of the Reds who are staying at the Coronado Hotel downtown. I'll leave you tickets for the game."

"No promises."

"Just a party."

"I'll pick them up at the box office. Make sure Stan leaves a couple for Tammy and Rosa."

"*No problema.*"

When Mary got home that night, she quietly opened the front door, hoping everyone was already asleep. But her Dad was still downstairs, watching TV in his overstuffed avocado tweed chair—a remnant of the 50's, a piece of furniture that easily could have been used as a prop in "All in the Family."

"Watch'ya watchin?"

"An old rerun of 'Citizen Kane.' Now there was a newspaper man."

"Dad, have you seen Orson Wells recently? He looks like a pig, a stuffed pig at that."

"I know—I guess that's what middle age and money will do to you."

"And bad TV commercials." Mary's voice got deep, "Julio Gallo: We will sell no wine before its time. Like what month it was blended?"

Mary walked over towards her dad. The gray light from the television illuminated her figure. He glanced up at his daughter, recalling long-past memories of her toddler years. His eyes moved from her face, which was without makeup, her natural beauty shining through, to her breasts, with their natural beauty, to her long legs, with their natural beauty.

"You went out like that?"

"Dad, I'm not five years old."

"Don't expect to come in here at all hours without wearing any clothes."

"Don't worry Dad. I've already made arrangements with the girls at work to try out their apartment. I'm gonna move in tomorrow."

"So fast? You just got here."

"Dad, I heard you and Carol talking . . . her mother, etc. I know you really didn't need me to upset the center of your universe. I mean, everything seems to be so perfectly in sync here. Each little knickknack in its place."

"It's not so simple, Mary. You think everything is okay. But, the boys are always arguing, Carol's bored at home. Half the time I come home from work she's already had a couple of martinis, two sheets to the wind.

"But you're still here."

"Yeah, where'm I gonna go. I'd be a two-time loser."

"Dad, you're still young. Why didn't you ever try to reach me?"

"I figured you hated me. I figured that you'd forgotten me."

"Dad, I cried every night after you left. I prayed to God. I prayed that you'd call me, that you'd rescue me."

"You think it was easy?"

"Dad, no phone calls, no cards, no 'Happy Birthday.' You stopped existing. You went inside my black box. I protected myself from you and Mom."

"Are you going to stay?"

"Dad, I'm not the little girl you never knew. We'll have to try as adults. Love ya." Mary walked up the stairs.

"See you in the morning." His eyes followed her natural beauty.

September 4, 1969

Hope stared at me as I packed my suitcase and boxes. I had 14 pairs of socks and jockey shorts, allowing two weeks between laundry runs. I had washed my two new pairs of jeans at least ten times, going through an entire box of ALL detergent, hoping to give them that worn, washed-out look.

Hope yawned. After all, she didn't have any possessions. But this is what I carried downstairs to the car for my trip to Columbia:

1) My record albums, filed in alphabetical order: Beatles, Chicago, Cream, Janis Joplin, Jefferson Airplane, Moody Blues, Procol Harum, the Rolling Stones, and Simon and Garfunkel—along with Beethoven's Fifth Symphony. Brahms' Fourth Symphony, and the Strauss waltzes from "2001—A Space Odyssey."

2) My new state-of-the-art turntable/FM stereo and floor-model speakers, each weighing 20 pounds—all purchased with my summer's earnings.

3) My full size IBM electric typewriter, ready for industrial-length term papers

4) My 13-inch portable color television with rabbit-ear antennae.

5) My portable refrigerator—just the right size for a couple of six-packs.

6) A toaster-oven and hot plate with a sauce pan and frying pan that Lil had donated to the cause.

7) My small travel bag, packed with my toothbrush and Colgate toothpaste, my Old Spice deodorant, and my Remington electric razor.

8) My sterling silver Parker 75 Fountain pen that my family had given me for my graduation, so I could take my copious notes.

All of this barely fit into the trunk and backseat of my dad's Ford Galaxy. And just for comparison sake, flash forward to Jannie's trek to college circa 2006, with her IPod and CD player and CDs, her laptop compute, and a microwave, all fitting on the front seat of her Honda Civic—a car that was barely a glimmer in the eyes of the motorcycle company of the 60s.

As I clumped down the stairs, Lil asked,

"Ken, I have an electric frying pan. Why don't you take that with you?

"Thanks, Lil. That'd be great. Are you sure?"

"Don't worry, I won't use it. Especially with just your father and Marty and Ritchie here at home."

"Won't Cathy need it?"

"No, she can barely boil water. And besides, she's on the meal plan out there. And there's always tuna fish—all she'll need is a can-opener."

"Thanks, again."

"And pick out some cans of soup and some spaghetti and sauce."

"You act like I'm never coming home again."

"If only it was so simple. And go downstairs to get some laundry detergent."

"Now I know you really think he won't be coming home." My dad was coming into the kitchen. "You know they always come home to do their laundry. He'll be home on weekends before we know it. Laundry, home cooking—I just hope you have some time to help with the symposium next month."

"Dad, more like coming back to see Judy."

"We'll worry about that when the time comes," Lil said, deflecting the potential disaster.

I ran back up the stairs to get what I really needed to carry me through the night!

9) My two-foot by three-foot picture of Hope mounted onto a blue poster board—my wall decoration that would surely freak out my roommate and any girl I would hope to bring up to my bed.

10) My stuffed dogs, Senior, Junior and Waffles, looking up at me, waiting for their last hug. As I held them, I made a spur of the moment decision. They needed a college degree also—although I figured they'd have to stay in a drawer in my dorm room, lest I face ridicule from my dorm mates.

"Ken, let's go. I have a 9 o'clock meeting," I heard my dad yelling from downstairs.

"Be right there!"

Here's what I left behind:

1) My Monkees and Tommy James and Shondells albums for Marty. And my Andy Williams and Broadway show original cast recordings—along with so many memories of listening to them with my mom and dad.

2) My picture of Mom—a bit too much for a college "stud."

3) Hope. But as she rolled over on her back, I promised, "I'll be home soon. I love you. I'll miss you." And I let her lick my nose, my ears, and my cheek. I knew the salt tasted good to her tongue, as I got one last moment to savor this intimacy with her. As I left, I turned around and took one last look back at Hope, in case I didn't see her again.

I ran down the stairs and out the backdoor.

"Bye, Lil."

"Good luck."

A peck on the cheek and I was out the back door.

"I'll drive, Dad."

"Sure, that'll help me; I can get ready for the meeting."

"Will you be home for dinner?"

"No, Lil, it's my first night."

"Ken, I wasn't talking to you. I was talking to your dad."

"Sorry."

"I'll be home late. Can you wait for me?"

"Sure, I'll just feed Marty and Ritchie earlier."

"What'll you do with the car, Ken?" my dad asked, as we backed out of the driveway.

"I'll just bring it up to you and take the subway back."

We drove down the Bronx River Parkway, my dad immersed in his work, my mind immersed in the first day of the rest of my life.

"Dad, did you watch the end of the game last night?"

"No, we fell asleep. Who won?"

"We did—we're only two games out of first place."

"Who'd of thought?"

"Aren't you excited?"

"I will be when they win the pennant."

"Dad, you need hope. Remember Bobby Thomson and the '51 Giants."

We talked for a few more minutes about Seaver and Koosman and the rest of our boys.

"Ken, I have to finish reading this paper."

"Sure, Dad." And I concentrated on the driving.

Twenty minutes later we were at his office at the Columbia Presbyterian Medical Center campus of Columbia University at 168th Street and Broadway.

As I dropped him off at his office, he said, "Thanks, Ken. Are you coming home tonight?"

"No, Dad, didn't you hear what I told Lil? It's my first night."

"You could always drive me in tomorrow."

"For what," I thought, "so you can work on your papers?"

"Dad!" I said.

"Okay, just get the car back to me by four p.m."

"Sure, love ya."

"Love you too." After a cheek-to-cheek goodbye, I drove off down Broadway towards 116th Street.

That was it, no fatherly advice, no "Be careful!" no "Study Hard." Just have the car back by 4. Like, "Just be home by midnight."

I turned onto Riverside Drive and towards the downtown campus. It was only three miles away physically but miles away psychologically—and geographically, too, through Spanish Harlem, with reality check on all sides. Was I really going away to school? Jay had flown away to Los Angeles; he was gone, maybe to return on Thanksgiving. I'd be back in a few days.

I flipped on the radio and heard the Beatles' "Hey Jude." After a few commercials, Richard Harris sang his interminable song, "MacArthur Park," about leaving a cake out in the rain—some ridiculous lyrics. I drove by 125th Street, home 20 years ago of Ruby Foo's, now no place I would want to even park my car. Two minutes later I was at Columbia, 114th Street and Broadway. Carman Hall, the undergraduate dorm, my dorm, loomed before me. It was constructed out of utilitarian cinder blocks during the last decade, lacking all of the charm of the ivy-covered buildings on the rest of the campus.

It was 9:30. I had only 90 minutes until I had to move my car for the alternate side of the street parking regulations, which allowed the streets to be cleaned—an oxymoron in New York City, if I ever heard it. Having no friends, I'd obviously have to unload the car myself. All the carts were in use, so it was one trip up after the other. Luckily I was on the second floor, in a two-bedroom suite with two double rooms and a bath-room.

Harlan had magnanimously invited me to share his four-student, two-bedroom-suite—in different bedrooms, obviously. It would either make my transition a bit easier or delay my maturation. After 45 minutes I had taken up eight loads and worked up a sweat. I stretched out on the bed, with the room all to myself. Only two more boxes to go!

The lobby was congested with freshmen moving in for orientation, most with parents helping them. From their appearance—their crew cuts and T-shirts—many were from the Midwest. A few had longer hair, bell-bottoms, and tie-dyed T-shirts. There were guys who had already unpacked and were hanging out in their own groups. The blacks, too, were together—"brothers," street-talking, laughing, hanging high-fives; and the Asian engineering students were quietly talking to each other, side-kicks already, their slide rules in holsters on the belts, ready to do battle.

After I unloaded the last of my clothes, I wandered out into the hall. Two doors down I heard activity. I poked my head inside. A couple of dorm-mates were hanging pictures.

"Hi, I'm Ken."

"Hey yo'all. I'm Tex. This here is Rick. I'm down in 207."

Tex wasn't tall, or mean looking, but, rather, a teen with short, straight, black hair, combed off to the side. His face was boyish, still disfigured with acne. At 5' 7", 140 pounds, he would hardly be called formidable. Rick was more scholarly looking, an engineering type, with short, curly, close-cropped hair, a white, button-down shirt, and brown chinos. All that was missing was the pen protector in his shirt pocket.

"Yeah, so I'm in 201. I got to run, I'll be back later. I got to move my dad's car and return it to him."

"Hey, check it out. We're setting up my stereo now."

"Cool. Later."

I went down to the car at 10:50 and made it ten minutes from getting a parking ticket. I drove the car back uptown, parked it in its space, and went upstairs to my dad's office at the Psychiatric Institute Dental Clinic.

"Is my dad around?"

"No," said Nancy, his dental hygienist. "He's teaching over at the school."

Nancy was the best thing about his office. She was "mature," at least 23, and had a model's figure, although her face was not that pretty. She wore her blouse open at the neck and her skirts provocatively short, which always made me wonder how her male patients could follow her orders to let their lips remain relaxed and go limp while she was cleaning their teeth.

"Okay." I wanted to hang around for a while, as Nancy was comfortable female companionship and I had some small hope I could get lucky. "Please give him the keys. Let him know I'll call him later once I get my phone number."

"No problem."

"Bye. Hey, do you want to get a bite to eat?"

"Thanks for the offer. No, I've got a patient due in ten minutes. I'll take you up on the offer some other time."

As I walked to the subway, I thought, "Ten minutes, that's all I would have needed with her!" But walking down the stairs to the #1 IRT line, I was now officially without ties to my family.

As I got off the subway at 116th Street, I checked out the graffiti — "187" in green, blue, and red, a rainbow of spray paint; "Lindsay sucks;" and on the stairs going up, in black spray paint,

"God is Dead."
Nietzsche

"Nietzsche is Dead"
God

Ah, Ivy League graffiti.

I climbed the stairs into the sunlight as the campus spread out before me. I stood at the gates, security guards scanning me over as I entered. Over the summer, I had been a visitor, an imposter, a "wanna be." Now I was a Columbia Lion. And without any class work for a couple of days, I was not yet behind in my courses. I walked by Sam Steinberg, "artist-in-residence," a disheveled, elderly man who painted Picasso-esque pictures, and pledged to myself to buy one later, to adorn the cinder block wall of my dorm. I watched as the students were playing football on South Field or flinging their Frisbees. I headed back to Carman Hall and walked up the stairs, hearing the music blaring from 207 already. And wafting from 206 was the sweet smell of marijuana. I wasn't ready to get expelled on the first day, so I went back to my suite to finish unpacking.

The door was open. "Hey." There was my new roommate—tall, angular Aryan face, with a broad smile and longish, blond hair fashionably cut and combed, like a model out of *Vogue*.

"I'm Ned. Ned Darrow."

"Hi, I'm Ken, Ken Kutscher."

"I hope you don't mind. I was setting up your stereo. I'm glad you brought yours—mine sucks."

"I'm glad—I'm no good with wiring. You must be studying electrical engineering."

"Fuck no. I'm a Greek theatre major."

"That's a relief. I'm pre-law. I was afraid I'd get someone without any culture."

We got to know each other as we read the instructions and figured out where to place each wire, putting our soon-to-be Ivy League education to use.

"What albums do you have?"

"Take a look."

As he thumbed through them he said, with each new flip of a cover, "Cool. Great. I've never heard that one. I have that too. Do you have any Laura Nyro?"

"Who?"

"The greatest female singer today."

"Better than Joplin?"

"Only if you like soft singing."

"Well, did you bring it with you?"

"Of course."

And we were serenaded by her sweet voice as she sang, "Up on the Roof."

After that side, Ned pulled out something a bit harder. Out came Jefferson Airplane, Cream—heavy metal, but hey, college was a mind-expanding experience.

"Ken, we're gonna be great together."

Of course, I had the hot plate, the refrigerator, the typewriter, and the stereo. And Ned had the good looks, the easy manners, and the sexuality that attracted men and women alike. His Regis High School Catholic education was about to evaporate.

By 3 o'clock we were starving. "Let's get some lunch."

"Have you been to Mama Joy's."

"No, why?"

"Best subs in town."

We walked down to 112th Street and Broadway, just four doors up from where Jerry Seinfeld was to hang out for so many years on Channel 4. We stood in line behind several students and three police officers who took their overstuffed sandwiches and sodas out to the car, *gratis*. I ordered a meatball hero and Ned ordered a cream cheese and ham hero. He offered me a bite, which I couldn't refuse. It was the best, and it was the start of my "Freshman 20"—the 20 pounds I expected to put on, like most first-year college students, from eating junk food.

We were walking back to the dorm when I said, "We've got to get our girlfriends down and cook dinner for them. Spaghetti and salad."

"With Ripple and sausages," he laughed.

"Judy already begged me to let her come down. Can you get Corinne over?"

"Give me a week or two. I want to see who else is around. I don't want to be viewed as 'taken' too soon."

Such independence, such sexual self-assurance, and such freedom of expression I wouldn't have. Nor would I have any sexually transmitted diseases that might be lurking around.

I spent the rest of the afternoon trying to get a head start by concentrating on the first chapter of Aristotle for my Contemporary Civilization class on Monday. Ned had already read the Greek plays we were studying in Humanities, so he was preparing for his night out.

"Aren't you going to hang around for the dorm party?"

"Ken, look out the window. There is New York City. Look in the hall. There is the Midwest. A bunch of horny guys with nothing more to do than watch some porn flicks and stack their Budweiser cans along the wall. I'm meeting some friends in the Village, and we're going to a party to get stoned. I'd invite you, but it's a pretty close group of people from my theater group."

I wasn't ready for Ned's scene, even if he had invited me. And the porn films didn't sound that bad. As for the beer, I still hadn't developed a taste for the suds, but I knew any college student worth his salt would have to finish a 6-pack that night.

I called home and spoke quickly to Marty, then to Lil and my dad, letting them know I was okay and giving them my phone number. By 9 p.m. we were all heading down to the lobby where the flicks were about to begin. They were a lot more exciting than the sex education movies we'd seen in high school that warned us about the dangers of sex or pregnancy. The sex was degrading and the women were haggard and sexually used, if not abused. The first fucking scene, the first penetration, the first blowjob, the first ejaculation were arousing. But by the third or fourth time, the sex had "becum" mechanical, much as my masturbation would be later that night in my room, after having called Judy and spending 20 minutes on the phone telling her about Ned and our dinner plans for a few weeks from now.

Orientation was scheduled for 9 a.m. the next morning, followed by classes the next day: Humanities and Contemporary Civilization, the Core Curriculum for Columbia, along with French II, English Composition, and Political Science I. Papers, readings, exams, all were to follow.

As I listened to the news before I went to bed, setting the radio alarm clock, I learned that Ho Chi Minh had died of a heart attack 48 hours ago, the North Vietnamese keeping his death a secret so as not to disrupt their Independence Day celebration. But I knew that any thoughts that the Communists would go away were clearly only fantasies. They were fighting a war that meant more than one man. It was about a nation that didn't want any foreign occupation, even if it did take military assistance from the Soviet Union and the Red Chinese.

If we thought the Communists were nefarious in their censorship of the news, we were eons ahead regarding hiding the details of the 1968 My Lai massacre. Those soldiers who finally arrived to stop the genocide had been ostracized. The conspiracy of complicity overwhelmed all sense of goodness. And thus it wasn't until this day, 18 months after the attack, that Lt. Calley was secretly charged by the military for premeditated murder. It would take two more months, not two more days, before the story broke in the national news, becoming a focal point for those who hated the military, hated our leaders, and proclaimed the devil within us.

September 6, 1969

Mary had already said goodbye to her "family" and taken her toothbrush and hairbrush, along with her small suitcase of clothes, as she moved into Tammy and Rosa's pad.

"We figured we hadn't cleaned in two weeks," Tammy laughed as Mary walked in as they were spending their Saturday morning scrubbing the bathroom tiles. "We wanted to make a good impression."

Mary cringed. The fixtures were 40 years old, and two scrubbings wouldn't even begin to touch the scum in the bathtub. "Here, let me help."

They spent the rest of the afternoon cleaning the kitchen, while getting to know each other over Ajax and Mr. Clean.

Tammy was one of seven kids from a good Catholic family in San Luis Obispo. Her father was a longshoreman and her mom took in sewing to make ends meet. She was the oldest and when she moved out after high school there was much Papal angst about her waywardness, about the immorality of being a bank teller in a city and living with a female roommate. Her parents called every evening at around 10 p.m. to make sure she was home, and they called every Sunday at 8 a.m. to make sure she was ready for Mass.

Rosa's mom worked as a maid at one of the hotels downtown, and lived in a two-room shanty at the outskirts of town. Her father was rarely around. He was a second-generation, migrant farmer who had been selected by Cesar Chavez to help organize their union.

Mary figured she didn't quite fit in with these two girls, who were part of the mainstream lower class of the United Sates. Just as she was trying to escape her segment of the dysfunctional middle class, they were attempting to gain access to it. They loved the parties and the consumerism.

They'd made plans to go out for a spin in Tammy's '62 Chevy convertible before getting ready for the night. Mary went back into the bathroom, which still looked like it belonged in a cheap motel. She couldn't take a bath, no way, no how. Thank heavens she'd brought a pair of rubber flip-flops from her beach days. She could wear them so her feet would never touch the shower floor.

"Mary, come with us to the Sub Shop. We're getting a couple of meatball heroes for dinner to hold us over until the party after the game."

"Shouldn't we at least go out to the game to watch your boy-friend?"

"No way. He's not playing tonight. They're letting some rookies get a shot. I don't need to watch him sitting on the bench."

Rosa pleaded, "I don't want to be doin' nothin' til then. How about a movie?"

"Mary, you brought the paper. What's playing?"

"'Easy Rider,' 'Bob and Carol and Ted and Alice,' 'Butch Cassidy and the Sundance Kid'."

"They all sound groovy."

"I just drove cross-county through the South. I'd be interested to see how those hippies were treated. Couldn't have been any worse than me."

"Well, let's get the subs and then get ready to go. There's an 8:30 showing of 'Easy Rider' downtown."

Four hours later they left the movie theater. "Fuck." Randy was pretty freaked out. "Can you believe they shot Peter Fonda like that?"

"Doesn't surprise me at all. I'm just glad I didn't get blown away in my VW bug outside of Biloxi."

"But those guys . . . those bikes were cool. They were so stoned. Do you think they even felt anything as they were shot?"

"No different than getting wasted in 'Nam." Mary interjected.

"But at least there it isn't our own Americans killing 'em off."

"It's amazing," Rosa said, dreaming to herself. "My grandfather snuck into California for the better life, my father fought for decent wages, and my brother's over in 'Nam fighting to save the world from Communism—and some big, ugly redneck from the South is blowing away guys just because they have long hair and wear an American Flag."

"Biggest joke is that those rednecks probably weren't even in the military. Back home in Florida, they all defend the U.S. of A. from the comfort of their local bars; their old knee injuries keeping them from serving."

They all climbed into the Chevy and drove in silence up to a mansion in the hills.

"Want a smoke?" Rosa asked.

"Sure." Mary took the Virginia Slim, lit it, and inhaled deeply. "This isn't bad, but I'd rather have a toke."

"Don't worry. I'm sure they'll be plenty there."

As they drove up the circular driveway, two valet attendants rushed to assist the "ladies." The first, hair cut short and face clean-shaven, looked much more military than 60s; the other was about 18 with a pudgy face, long, black sideburns, and tight, curly hair. They were both probably moonlighting from their sociology classes at the University of California, San Diego. And they all wanted to assist the women for a night.

Tammy gave the tallest one her keys. "Make sure you don't scratch the doors."

"I'll keep it here for you. Maybe we can go for a drive in it later?"

"I'm sure," she laughed as she pulled out her pack of Lucky Strikes, "That the only luck you'll get tonight is from one of these." And she slowly inserted one between her lips, carefully wetting the end with her tongue, then lit up and blew smoke in his direction, as she turned away and pranced with her friends into the house.

Tammy was dressed up for Saturday night. Her pink, green, and purple striped bellbottoms were brand new, as was the white linen blouse covered with a leather vest and some multi-colored beads. Rosa had gone more for the "screw me" look—a short, denim skirt that barely concealed her white panties and a pink T-shirt that said "Make Love, Not War" on the front. Her firm brown nipples unfettered by a bra accentuated the look.

Mary dressed more in her "Who would even notice me?" outfit—a black mini-skirt offset by her ironed, white blouse and a paisley, blue scarf that pulled her hair back.

As they passed through the lobby, Tammy looked at the trio. "Girls, we're no angels." And she laughed as Rosa added, "Girls, we better get laid tonight."

"What about Frank?" Mary was a little puzzled.

"Fuck Frank. I saw him with another chick at the bar last night."

"Well, just don't count me in on any of your plans." Mary was already turned off.

They wandered into the kitchen, the party obviously well under way. The Reds' players had mingled with the Padres', as the festivities flowed from one room to the next. Jimi Hendrix's electric energy filled the entire house.

"It's lucky that a couple of Stan's teammates are friends with the 'enemy.' This is guaranteed to be a great party!" Tammy was already dancing up a storm.

"Hey, Tammy. It's about time." Mary turned expecting to see the dashing duo, Stan and Reggie. Instead, she saw this gorgeous, black man standing there. As he winked at her, the bigotry of her parents and Southern roots reared its ugly head. But she grinned back.

"And what would Dad say?" she thought, as Stan said, "Tony, this is Tammy. I've been telling you about her. And I forget her girlfriend's name."

"Mary, Mary McAuliffe." Fuck, Mary thought, I haven't used my dad's last name since I was five. She was distracted as, off in the distance, she saw Reggie flirting with several girls wearing more makeup and less clothes than the prostitutes who "hung out" outside the Naval base. Then Mary smiled her politest smile, just like her grandmother had taught her. "Nice to meet you."

Reggie saw her and started to walk towards her. Mary's "I'm really not interested" look was evident from across the room, as she turned to Tony and said, "Maybe I'll talk with you later." And she walked down through the other rooms, where the music wasn't so loud, so she could close her eyes and imagine being back in Titusville as a teen, listening to Marvin Gaye singing "I Heard It Through the Grapevine."

This room was darker, and she realized she'd been drawn there by the sweet aroma. She saw the yellow-red light at the end of several joints being passed around—and finally passed to her. She took a deep drag. By the third go-round, she was mellowed. She stood up to dance to the music, really just to sway, as a handsome, broad-shouldered man put his arm around her.

"I think I'm taking you back to Alabama."

The gentleman seemed somewhat out of place, more mature, with his Afro graying a bit at his temple.

She laughed. "Wow. Is that sort of near Mississippi?"

"It's too noisy in here. Let's find some place to talk."

"Nah, I just became unavailable!"

As she reached out her hand to sort of push him away, Tammy came in with Paul and Tony.

"There you are, Mary. Tony and Paul were invited upstairs to a smaller party—less people. Wanna come?"

"What about Rosa?"

"Don't worry, she left long ago with Reggie."

"I knew I couldn't trust 'em. Sure, let's go." As they left, Mary turned back to her older friend. "See ya."

They walked away, with Stan whispering to Mary, "Don't you know who that was?"

"Some guy old enough to be my father."

"Oh Mary, if you don't know who one of the greatest ball players is, just give it up." Tammy said.

Upstairs, Stan and Tammy found a couch off in the corner, while several other couples were on the bed, co-mingling.

Mary sat with Tony on the small loveseat. She told him about her trip to California from Florida, and he told her about his trip to California from the Caribbean.

"I'm sorry, Tony. I know you expected more," Mary blurted. "I think the champagne's gone to my head. I think I better go home."

She glanced over to Tammy and Stan. They were "engaged." Tony took her hand and said, "Let's go downstairs and I'll get you a cab."

As they left, still with a virginal relationship, Mary tried to save the evening. "Maybe I'll see you again. The season's still young, isn't it?"

"Not really, it's almost over. Can I see you when we get back from our road trip?"

It turned out that the season was much too short, as Tony and Mary's affair blossomed. Mary had finally found a man who knew how to satisfy her, who made her feel like a woman. But then she found out that Tony had long ago made arrangements to play winter baseball back in the Caribbean and would be leaving in October. There didn't seem to be much reason for her to stay around after that, as she was rapidly becoming bored with the bank and her roommates, as well as with her non-existent family.

"Do you have to leave?" Tony asked.

"What am I gonna do here? I don't want to fly down to Puerto Rico just to see you play. You know I don't speak Spanish. What would I do all day?"

"I'm sorry, Mary. I signed a contract. If I don't show, I'll be blacklisted in the future. I need the dough to help my mom with her rent back home."

"Don't you make enough here?"

"Are you kidding? The owners have us by the balls. Haven't you heard of the reserve clause. They own us until we die. Play with their team or don't play at all."

"It sounds like slavery."

"It is, but it's not like the slaves 100 years ago. We could always do something else, like sell cars." He laughed.

Just when Mary was beginning to feel hopeless, Tony asked, "Mary, I've got to go to New York on some business in a few weeks. Wanna join me?"

"Sure. Just make sure you stay in a quality hotel. Clean showers are important to me."

"Don't worry. The Roosevelt isn't the Waldorf, but it is where the Padres stay when we're in town. And, as a special bonus for the woman I love, I'll make sure they leave a couple of extra clean towels. You'd never have made it traveling with me in the minor league clubhouses."

"Tony, you should know me by now. I only travel Major League."

September 24, 1969

It was Thursday and I had English class tomorrow, but this night the Mets were to play at Shea against the St. Louis Cardinals, with a chance to clinch the Championship of the Eastern Division of the National League. Even though there would still be eight games to play, this could be the night that they'd make their history—and I could be there!

Ned and I spent the afternoon in Central Park with his girlfriend. Nixon had announced the week before that he'd ordered 35,000 troops to be withdrawn from 'Nam, and that there would be a reduction in the amount of men drafted. That was good news for Ned, who was already two papers behind in Freshman English.

We sat on the rocks in the park near 89th Street as Ned introduced me to the real vice of my freshman year. No, it wasn't a cigarette, it wasn't liquor, it wasn't even marijuana. It was Haagen Daz ice cream—smooth, creamy, no pretense at "low calorie, low cholesterol." He bought two pints, one chocolate and one rum raisin, and three plastic spoons. We let the ice cream melt a bit so we could easily remove it from the white and brown containers. Every minute or so we tried to dig in, but not push too hard for fear of breaking our spoons. It was truly sinful, smooth nectar to the tongue, and guaranteed to corrupt. And it didn't leave me much room for dinner. So I wouldn't even have to pack peanuts for the game.

But not so fast! Back at the dorm, Clark invited Ned and me to a party of his theater friends on East 83rd Street. Only two weeks into my college career, and I'm faced with my first major decision: Do I hang with my old buddies, who haven't let me down this year, or do I go out with Clark and Ned and explore New York and its gay theatrical life? The Mets' gravitational pull weakened as I pulled on my newly faded jeans, followed by my boots, which were still polished and new looking. My face remained clean-shaven, but now I had a pair of wire rimmed aviator glasses, and my hair was beginning to grow out, with its natural curls extending an inch down the back of my neck. It was New York City, the "entertainment capital of the world," and I was 18 years old and about to go to a party with the "beautiful people."

Clark was one-half of a set of identical twins, a gay black student who lived in the suite next to us. He was flamboyant, dressed in tight jeans with a paisley shirt unbuttoned one-third of the way down. His hair was cropped in a short "afro," but he remained clean-shaven. An Eldridge Cleaver he was not, as he was trying to assimilate into the theatrical world from his middle-class environment in Queens.

We were listening to Beatles albums, trying to find out if there was a secret message that Paul had died. One of the engineers had lent us his tape deck, which we used to play the albums backwards, as rumor had it that the sorrowful drone we were hearing actually said "Paul is dead."

"Hey, Clark, do you have any of that great shit left?" Ned was hopeful.

"Just enough for a couple of joints."

"Good, because the shit I got last week sucks and we need to get high before we go."

I was in the room with just the two of them, but I was still a "virgin. I watched intently as Clark carefully rolled the first joint, making sure that none of the "Acapulco Gold" got wasted. Ned licked the paper, lit the joint, and took a long draw, inhaling deeply and holding his breath. Clark took the joint, its telltale aroma filling the room, and sucked in deeply.

What was I going to do? I could refuse—or grow up and be a "man," a college student of the '60s, one of "our generation."

As the burning cylinder was passed on to me, it felt like a time bomb, or more like a homing device. I imagined the police were outside our dorm room, with the distinctive aroma penetrating their nostrils, and their axes ready to break down the door. I took a look outside the window to make sure there were no patrol cars in the street. Ned was watching me impatiently, waiting for his next hit, worried that the priceless grass would burn up in smoke. What the fuck!! I put the joint between my lips and inhaled deeply, emulating Ned as best I could.

And then I choked, with the smoke exhaling rapidly from my partially filled lungs and the room filling with secondhand hallucinogens.

"Ken," Ned laughed, as Clark gasped. "That's no way to treat a lady. You've never smoked before, have you?"

"Ken, it is, isn't it?" Clark added.

"No, it isn't"

"Yes it is."

"So . . ."

"Welcome to the club."

"Hey, hit me again," I demanded, after my friends had another round.

"Go easy, Ken. Don't inhale so much."

After three more rounds I was just getting the hang of it when Ned took the last toke. I wanted to feel high—to feel crazy—but all I worried about was being caught and that everyone in the street would know of my sin. I knew I'd be arrested, kicked out of school, sent to Vietnam.

We walked out of the room and down the stairs, with Ned and Clark laughing and singing. I wanted to feel stoned, but somehow I hadn't escaped the gravitational pull of my existence. Stoned I wasn't and stoned I wouldn't be, now or in the future. Paranoia, bad first experience, immunity to the chemical reaction—yes! Morality issue—no! My own "reefer madness."

As we sat in the Checker cab, Clark squinched up on the jump seat. I heard the Mets game on the radio. Ned and Clark were cackling, telling stories about parties they had been to, speculating about who'd be there tonight. As Bob Murphy announced the score, I whispered loudly, "Shh."

"Did you guys hear the score? The Mets are winning 3-0!"

I looked over at Clark who, although he grew up ten blocks from Shea Stadium, was oblivious to the conflict I felt. My thoughts, whispered silently, were "How can this party be more important than seeing my Mets clinch the pennant?"

I was already beginning to feel a twinge of regret for my decision to forgo my trip to Shea. After all, for the past eight years I had lived and died with the Mets. My day was made if they won, ruined if they lost—nless, of course, I had a great date the night before. In the past seasons, when the Mets were terrible, it really didn't matter; but this year, it did.

I wondered, "Does baseball become bigger than life or is it life itself—replacing relationships and substituting for what's not there? How could the citizens of a city develop such a cult-like attachment to any team in a league where the players could be traded at the whim of the owners? And this was in the days before player free agency, when the image of player or owner loyalty became an illusion.

We got out of the cab, me last, and thus in charge of paying the cabbie.

"We'll get the fare coming home, Ken," Clark chirped.

"Sure," I said, knowing that there was no way I would still be with him when he arrived back at the dorm at four a.m. in the morning.

I was excited with the anticipation of my first party in the city, on the 14th floor overlooking the East River, with all the important people of New York, celebrities who I would remember meeting for the rest of my life.

"Come on, Ken," Ned said, assailing my baseball senses. "You're not going to worry about the Mets tonight!"

Clark started his lecture on the way up the elevator. "Baseball is only a game played by men. It has no social or moral structure, no lasting benefit. Movies, acting, magazines—that is immortality; old movie reruns to be watched on TV late at night, starlets in the making."

"Or standing in line in the rain to see Fellini's '8 ½'," I mocked.

"Clark, you're full of it! Do you really stay at home at night watching movies?" Ned was jesting with him. "You must have a sucky social life. You should be out partying, drugging, getting laid."

"Yea, Ned, but while you're getting stoned, did you ever watch to see who is that actor, or was this his first role in a long career, while you're looking at the credits roll by at the end to see if there were any young actresses or actors in it?"

"Hey Clark. If you're so smart, I bet you don't know who played 'Boo' as his first role in the movie 'To Kill a Mockingbird'." It was my favorite book, made into a movie, and I loved watching Gregory Peck play Atticus, my attorney hero, the man I was expecting to fashion my life after—attorney, state legislator, great father, loved by his community. I could dream on and on.

"Who cares?" Clark groaned. "That's not a modern movie."

"You don't know, do you? It was Robert Duvall! See, you think you know everything."

"I know that was a 'simple' movie, a straight adaptation. I'll take you to see Fellini's 'La Dulce Vita.' Now that's directing."

I didn't let on that I'd seen another Fellini movie the previous week and hadn't understood anything—maybe because I wasn't stoned like the rest of the audience!

As we entered the party, I looked around for the "famous" people. I didn't recognize any famous faces, but I assumed that either they'd be arriving later or I was an inept people-gazer. I'd just have to wait for the "credits" to go by! Clark went off in a flash, selling himself (not his body, just his theatrical soul), while Ned went over to a "hot" couple, hoping to set up a threesome for later that night. I picked up a jug of Mondavi table wine, choosing the red (vintage June, 1969) over the white, and poured it into the plastic wine glass. What a high-class party —no Thunderbird or Ripple, no Boone's Farm in sight. I looked around. There were couples on the sofa, smoking, drinking, laughing. There were groups of guys talking frantically with their hands, as their mouths moved in unison. The uniform for the night appeared to be hip-hugger jeans, frayed at the bottom, with the girls in printed Indian madras shirts slit down to the bosom, and the guys with T-shirts that said "Make Love, Not War!" emblazoned with the peace sign. The only variations on the themes were whether the women were braless (I counted at least six, two of whom didn't need a bra and another one who looked like a swollen cow without one) or whether the men wore sandals or boots. Except of course the "professor" type off in the corner wearing his dark Nehru suit, pontificating to whoever would listen.

From the den I heard that familiar voice of comfort. It was Bob Murphy announcing the eighth inning of the Mets game. As I wandered into the room I saw a double image. There on the television was the Mets game while the view from the window showed, not the aurora borealis, but the lights from Shea Stadium six miles away. It was like a scene out of the "Twilight Zone"—not at the ballpark but in another, altered, parallel baseball universe.

The people who weren't concerned with being with the "beautiful people" were here. Some sat on the leather couch and others were in the Wasilla chairs around the room. Although people were talking to each other about John Lindsay's chances in the upcoming mayoral election, all eyes would intermittently return to the television screen. While everyone at this party may not have wanted to come and were dragged (or blackmailed or seduced—whatever the case may have been), the people in *this* room wanted to be at Shea, at least in spirit.

The ending was somewhat anti-climactic, as Joe Torre—later to be an unremarkable Mets' manager before he found success as the Yankees' skipper—grounded into a double play to end the game.

Bob Murphy started yelling, "The Mets Win! It's All Over! Ohhhh, the roar going up from this crowd! An unbelievable scene on the field."

First the Mets' players erupted from the dugout, running onto the field, joyous but aware they still had two more series to win before they could be declared World Champions of the United States. Then the fans poured out on the field, excited but somewhat respectful of the fact that they had to keep the field in playing condition for the rest of the championship season. The players, however, in the clubhouse, were anything but subdued—what with the champagne flowing and the players lathering each others' hair with a most expensive shampoo. Tom Seaver, Gil Hodges . . . they were all interviewed. The miracle was just beginning, but the fairy tale had not yet reached its happy ending.

You can only imagine my feelings at this time. My team had won! We were the champions of the Eastern Division of the National League! I was exuberant after eight years of suffering watching cellar dwellers. Finally, we were Number 1. I had gone to games, first, with my mom and dad and my family, then with my Cousin Bruce, then with friends from high school, and finally with my girlfriend as baseball merged with romance.

I felt alone in this room as I celebrated with all of New York. We were all cheering while the other partygoers were somewhat oblivious to our cadre. But I was not with my family or my old friends or my girlfriend. I was with strangers, pretending to be someone I wasn't. My "old acquaintances were forgot" as I'd forgone being with my "baseball buddies" at the ballpark where—although we were strangers—we still shared an implied intimacy as we would sit or stand, cheering on our team, keeping score, downing cold hotdogs and warm beer on a hot summer afternoon. Shea was six miles away, Scarsdale only 20 miles away, but I was in college, trying to redefine myself. At least for tonight, however, I wasn't where or with whom I should have been.

By 11 o'clock I'd had enough. I went out and looked for Ned, but after five minutes of searching the room, I assumed he had left with his latest playmates. Clark was stoned, holding court.

I left alone, wandered out of the building, unaware of the homeless man on the corner of 86th Street and Third Avenue. It wasn't raining or cold, but as I boarded the cross-town bus, I looked for a seat amongst the passengers. I wondered who were the "reactionaries" and who were the "visionaries" in my life. I had just left a party where it was supposed to be "happening," but here at Paul Simon's "zoo" I thought I saw the honest working-class people of New York. Simon and Garfunkel's lyrics— voices for our age, allegories for our generation.

As I stood to change buses at Broadway, a few of the passengers were talking, but mostly they were napping on their way to work. These were the "proletariat" we were fighting for!

I felt a twinge of . . . what? Guilt? Self-importance? Me, a college freshman, getting my "free ride" in life while these people worked. But then:

"Did you see the game?"

"Yeah, wasn't it great? My brother went out tonight with my nephew. I guess he'll be pretty tired for school tomorrow."

"Shit, why doesn't he just skip a day?"

"It's just the third week of school."

"But it's only fifth grade."

It was a cast that I hadn't reckoned on seeing. I was overcome with a sense of disloyalty, of having abandoned my team.

I had the munchies when I got home, but the vending machines were broken in the lobby and everyone was asleep on my floor. All that remained in my frig was some moldy cheese; so I contented myself with eating the sugar-coating of candy off of the multivitamins Lil had sent down in a care package. I lay awake in my bed with the streetlight from 114th Street shining through a crack in the curtains.

It was not until the next morning that I would recognize the full level of my despair; when I understood the regret that I had not been at Shea to experience this wonderful night; that I couldn't say that I had been there. I was inappropriately angry with Ned and Clark. After all, did I not have free will? I knew I should've been at the game, and that what comes with believing in one's maturity—the ability to make appropriate decisions—was the gut-wrenching feeling that I had only myself to blame.

October 1969

I had bought my first pair of bellbottom jeans the week I arrived at Columbia. They were low cut, hip-hugging—my trophy, the new signature of my "hippiedom." Now that I was away at college in the city, I no longer was under my father's power regarding my grooming habits. No more, "Ken, get that haircut or you're not coming out to dinner with us." Judy promised that she would cut it for me when it got too long, and begged me to forsake my local barber's antiquated style of combing the hair back up off my forehead with a curl. Not only that, but Judy persuaded me to grow a mustache, probably to impress her high school friends whose boyfriends were still seniors back in Scarsdale and weren't permitted to grow facial hair. My father didn't know what to say the first time he saw my upper lip covered with coarse, blond hair, but he managed, "Ken, shave that off if you want to come into this house."

"Dad, I don't hear you telling Paul that."

"This isn't about Paul. You're my son."

"What's fair for the Steinbergs is fair for us. I'm not shaving it off. "

"You'll do what I tell you if you want to come into this house."

"Judy likes it. And anyway, I'm living at Columbia now."

With that, I walked out of his room, went downstairs, and called Judy. I slammed the back door as I went down the driveway and started walking towards her house, waiting for her to pick me up in her parents' car so she could drive me to the train station.

"Judy, I'm not going back to my house for a while. Do you think your parents would let me stay in your spare bedroom?"

"Ken, what happened?"

"My dad demanded that I shave my mustache if I want to come back."

"Ken, he'll get used to it. Paul and Michael have them, don't they?"

"He seemed pretty mad."

"Just wait."

As we drove up to her house, her father was out raking the leaves.

"Dad, Ken just had a fight with his Dad over his mustache. Do you think he can stay in the guest room tonight?"

I guess Judy's parents thought a pre-law student at Columbia was a good catch, so I had to suppress my hormonal excitement as he acquiesced,

"Just for tonight, Ken, but you really need to make up with your dad."

"Thanks, Mr. P."

Judy got me a pillow and a blanket for my night's sojourn in the guest room. We both knew there was no way I would spend the entire night there alone, but we'd have to wait until we heard the snoring from her parents' bedroom before one of us quietly tiptoed to the other's resting place. As it turned out, I could only wait about 45 minutes, because my bladder filled from the several Cokes I had before I went to bed. Hearing no sounds of wakedness in the parental room, I snuck into Judy's room, hoping to find her in a state of nakedness. She was still awake as I climbed beneath her covers, and we immediately started to make out, to fondle each other, to go as close to hitting a home run as we ever had. After about 30 minutes, Judy said, "Ken, we'd better not press our luck. Go on downstairs and I'll see you in the morning."

Reluctantly, I retraced my steps carefully back down the stairs, and went to sleep with visions of breasts and thighs dancing in my head.

Mr. P. came down first in the morning, and found me sound asleep. "Ken, would you like a ride into the city? I could drop you off at Columbia on my way downtown."

This sure was easier than walking to the Penn Central Station in Scarsdale to take the train and then having to come back uptown on the IRT subway. "Sure, that'd be great."

Judy came downstairs in her nightgown and robe. "How'd you sleep, Ken?"

"Fine, Judy. Thanks, Mr. P. for letting me stay over."

"No problem, Ken, just call your dad tonight."

But I was too headstrong to call him that night, and as days passed, neither of us was willing to give in. I know I was aching inside, angry yet hurt, depressed, feeling I was letting my mom down. Was my dad aching? Did he hurt? Did he feel he was letting his first wife down?

Finally, after ten days, Marty called.

"Ken, please call Pop. He's so upset; he doesn't know what to do."

"Marty, he should be calling me. He's the one who screamed at me."

"Ken, please!"

"I'll think about it."

I called Judy. "What should I do? Maybe we should just get an apartment together."

"Ken, I'm still in high school. I don't think that'd go over so good with my parents."

"Well, then promise me that you'll move in with me next year."

"Ken, you know I love you, but how will you live? You're going to school. You can't support yourself."

"I know how to type. I can work as a temp."

"Then we'd never have time to see each other."

"If I was on my own, I'd get a scholarship."

"Ken, it's easier to make up with your dad. It's not like you told him to drop dead. Just do it."

"I don't know. I'll call him after I take my shower."

"Call me right away after you're finished."

Fifteen minutes later, I was on the phone.

"Hi, Lil. Could you put Pop on?"

"I was hoping you'd call."

"Hi, Ken."

"Hi, Pop."

"Listen, Ken, I need you to respect me. Don't you understand that? It's your duty to honor me."

"Sure, Dad, but, I'm not nine anymore. You can't control my life like you used to."

"But I'm paying the bills, don't forget that."

"Look, Pop, I didn't call to argue. I'm sorry if you didn't think I treated you as my parent."

"Ken, how can you go around looking like that? You look like a hippie with that mustache. The next thing I know, you'll be occupying the administration building with SDS."

"Pop, this isn't radical, this is just being myself. I still love you. You don't need to worry about my doing anything stupid." (Or really stupid, I should have said.)

"It's really not that important, Ken, I guess, in the long run of things, as long as you still respect me and remember your mother."

"Don't worry; I'd never do anything to make her ashamed of me."

"Okay, apology accepted. By the way, will you be coming home this weekend to see Judy? You still have some work to do on your bibliography before it goes to press. You need to make some corrections."

"Dad, I've got a big paper due on Monday. I'm not even sure if I'll see Judy." Of course, I didn't tell him that we were meeting in the city to go to the movies on Saturday.

"Well, I'll need you soon."

"I'll work on it."

"Thanks."

"By the way, 'Let's go Mets!' Isn't it great? If we (shouldn't I have said "they") beat the Braves in the playoffs, we'll be in the World Series. What a miracle."

"Maybe we can watch a game together."

"That'd be great. I'll even type a letter for you if they win."

And, of course, the next week the Mets moved closer to the "Miracle" by sweeping the Braves in three straight games. I had come home over the weekend, and, between working for my dad, we had watched together as a family as the Mets came from behind to beat the Braves in slugfests in Atlanta, 9-5 and 11-6. And they came back to New York, needing only one more victory to advance to the World Series. The week before I had gone down to the main New York City Post Office on 34th Street, posted my certified check for two seats at 12:01 a.m., and bingo—four days later two sets of tickets arrived in the mail! Ned and Clark couldn't comprehend my excitement as I got ready to go to the Monday afternoon game at Shea. Judy was at my side, missing her first day of school that year due to "illness." The Mets, behind Nolan Ryan, beat the Braves 7-4, for a sweep. It wasn't so unexpected that the series would end in three games—only that it would be the Mets who were victorious!

Two days later, World Series tickets went on sale at Shea at the ticket windows. I had an exam at 9 a.m., so I couldn't be there on line; but at 11 a.m., I called the stadium and found out that, although games 3 and 4 to be played at Shea were sold out, there were still tickets available for game 5. What this meant was that everyone believed the Mets would be swept in four games by the Orioles, and there was no reason to buy game 5 tickets. But, believing in miracles, I took the subway out to Shea, and with no waiting in line, bought my single ticket. In retrospect, what a fool I was. For the $8 that the ticket cost, I could have had as many as I wanted for what would be the deciding game of that World Series. But little did I, or anyone else, know how it would all end. And, lucky me, that night, when I got back to Columbia, there on the bulletin board was an ad for two tickets for game 4 on October 15, upper deck, at $12 each for $8 tickets. My first experience with a "scalper" went through easily, and I was now the proud owner of tickets for games 4 and 5—my third and fourth World Series games, if the series lasted that long.

I returned home the next weekend, mainly to see Judy, but as she still had to spend some time with her family, I watched at home as Tom Seaver gave up a lead off home run to the Baltimore Orioles' Don Buford. Even though the Orioles had been my team in the '50s and the early '60s, and even though we still owned our ten shares (which would pay a $0.75 dividend per share if the Orioles won the Series), my heart was with my "Miracle" Mets. Becoming a millionaire would have to wait. My integrity as a Mets fan couldn't be bought.

"The Mets are going to lose in four straight. No doubt about it." My dad was ready to give up after the first batter.

I watched with growing despair as Tom Terrific gave up three more runs in the fourth inning, and the Mets went on to lose 4-1. I think the general feeling was that the "miracle" had run its course. But, on Sunday, a 1-1 tie was broken in the ninth inning as the Mets' third-baseman, Ed Charles, "the Glider," doubled and was brought home on a single by second-baseman Al Weis—he of reserve fame in backing up Buddy Harrelson. Ron Taylor saved the game for Jerry Koosman in the ninth inning, and we had hope. We had won one against the mighty Orioles. And it meant there would be that fifth game at Shea, no matter what.

It was back home to New York, with a day off for travel, and game three at Shea. I didn't have tickets, didn't try to get them, as I had two exams that day. This was during the good old era, when the World Series was still played during the day, when people would have to choose between work and the game, when "boys" (aka men) would sneak transistor radios, with earphones carefully hidden, to listen to the games during history class, and teachers (with the exception of Miss Phillips in third-grade) turned the other way in deference to this true national ritual. As I couldn't be there, and because I was taking exams and unable to listen on my radio, I wouldn't see the highlights of the Mets' victories and the two fantastic catches by Tommie Agee in center field until I saw the replays on the evening news.

October 11-14, 1969

It was Mary's last day at work. The girls gave her a going-away party after work at the local watering hole, and presented her with a red Samsonite carry-on bag, into which, unfortunately, she was able to fit all of her clothes. Paul and Reggie had already gone home to their Midwestern towns, to their high school sweethearts, leaving Tammy and Rosa feeling one step above groupies and two steps above prostitutes. But as they drank their way through a bottle of Southern Comfort, Mary could console herself with the fact that Tony was waiting for her in New York City.

She boarded the 9 a.m. flight, settled in, and treated herself to a screwdriver on the plane back east. Arriving at JFK airport around 7 p.m., she hailed a cab at the curb and told the driver, "Take me to the Roosevelt Hotel at the Grand Central Terminal." Then, pulling out her crib notes, she said, "Take me to the Belt Parkway and over the Brooklyn Bridge, then up the FDR until 42nd Street." She had been primed by one of the executives at the bank that New York City cab drivers were notorious for giving out-of towners a "guided tour" of the city, at the passenger's expense, naturally, and without their knowledge, obviously.

As the cabby drove up, the doormen came out and assisted her with her bag, with their hands out in unison. Mary gave them each a quarter. They passed the bag onto the bellhop, who waited patiently while Mary explained to the well-dressed man behind the desk that, although she was wearing a short dress and a low-cut blouse, she had not just walked in from a few blocks away, but, rather, that she was a young actress who had just flown in from California that day, and was, in fact, about to audition with a young actor in Room 517. The bellhop helped her with her luggage and escorted her up the elevator to Tony's room. Tony answered after a couple of knocks. His white, athletic undershirt enhanced his black, glistening muscles. The bellhop gave Tony a long glance, wondering what Tony had that he didn't have. Tony glared back, letting him know what he had that the bellhop didn't.

Despite the jetlag, Mary was ecstatic. They embraced and kissed, making up for the week they were apart. They had room service that first night, with two bottles of champagne, and also the next morning, when they finished the last of the second bottle.

"I've got some good news, Mary. Stan got you a ticket for Wednesday's World Series game."

"You mean, us."

"No, that's the bad news. The team needs me in Puerto Rico by Wednesday. I've got to leave tomorrow."

"You can't leave. I just got here."

"Mary, I'm sorry. I have no choice."

"You prick! You son of a bitch! You got me all the way here, and now you're leaving me. Where do I go, where do I live?"

"Mary, I've paid up this room for you until the end of the month. Then we'll work something out."

"Oh sure, and until then I can always get a job at a bank."

"Or you can come down to San Juan with me. I'll get an apartment."

"That'll go over real big. White chick with black stud."

"Well, suit yourself."

The next day was like winter come early to New York City for the lovebirds. Rather than a long, loving, "let's make every moment count" day, it was a "how soon can we get this over with" day.

While Tony packed and got his passport and Topps baseball card endorsement contract in order, Mary spent the day searching for a job, wandering into several banks.

"We'll let you know."

"Maybe something will open up."

"Josie's due to go out on maternity next month. Call us then."

Mary arrived back in the room around 2 p.m., hoping that maybe she and Tony could have a chance to pull it together before he left—give themselves a chance for the winter.

"Caught an earlier jet plane," said the note attached to the bottle of cabernet. "It's easier this way. Love, Tony."

In an envelope on the desk was a one-way plane ticket to San Juan. "In case you change your mind," was written on the outside.

All Mary could think about was Peter, Paul and Mary's song.

"What a crock of shit," she muttered. "Do you really think I care if 'he'll come back to me again?' "

October 15, 1969

Mary looked out the window as she awakened to the cacophony of New York City. "Who needs an alarm clock in this town," she wondered. Police sirens heralded the mayhem of the metropolis, interrupting the cacophony of cars honking as they inched their way across gridlocked intersections. She saw streams of young people, not the crowd of commuters and secretaries she had seen the day before heading downtown.

"It's Vietnam Moratorium Day," she realized. She wasn't in Florida with her mother, where there would be no peace rally; she wasn't in San Diego with her father, where Balboa Park would be filled with hippies; and she wasn't in Norfolk with her grandparents, where any demonstration against the military would have seemed like treason. She was here in New York City, alone, among strangers. But she was no lonelier than she had been among her extended step-families.

At least here, she thought, she might find her own peace; there was a sense of serenity in her solitude. She thought again of Simon and Garfunkel singing "I am a Rock." But Mary wasn't hiding on an island—and she really wasn't into books and poetry. She had put all the hurt and loss into a black box inside of her, to keep the pain from infiltrating her soul.

She dressed in her jeans and her last clean T-shirt, along with her sandals, using an old yellow and brown striped guitar strap for a belt. She headed downstairs, out the side door, into the sunlight, bringing her rose-colored sunglasses down off her hair to shade her eyes. Instantly, she smelled the aroma from Chock Full o' Nuts. She found herself drawn into the restaurant, the smell as addictive as the smoke of marijuana leaves. She sat at the counter, ordered a black coffee, and, seeing the "staples" the regulars were munching on the counters, added a plain donut. All around her the secretaries of the Fortune 500 companies were coming in, getting their coffees to go along with bags of donuts for their offices.

As she dunked her donut, its crisp outside becoming soggy in an instant, a man, about 25, sat down next to her. He was dressed not in jeans, not in a suit and tie, but in dark chinos and a blue denim work shirt. He smiled at Mary as his coffee and powdered donut were brought to him by the waitress, a chatty, thin, black woman, somewhere between 30 and 50 years of age, who obviously knew his order by heart.

"Thanks, Annie." And then turning towards Mary, he said, "Miss, could you please pass the sugar?"

Mary looked at his face. Was it kindness or politeness or just plain "New Yorkness" that she heard in his voice? "Sure."

"Thanks," and he smiled back as he poured in three teaspoons, stirring all the while.

"Wow! Don't you believe in cavities?"

"Nah. New York City water is fluorinated. No need to worry about that. And I'm too old to get zits."

"You're not that old!"

"No, I'm 26, old enough not to be trusted by your generation. I'm over the hill, ready for the farm."

"What makes you think that I'm so young?"

"Your high school ring on your finger. No one wears those once they're out of college."

"Never finished college."

"Hippie seeing the world?"

"Working class girl from the South, trying to save up some money to graduate."

"Then what're you doing in New York City?"

"I came to meet a friend who sort of deserted me."

"Well, today be a friend of mine. I'm Maurice."

"Mary."

"Nice to meet you, Mary. I work over at the 43rd Street Loews Theater on Broadway. I'm one of the projectionists. Maybe I can get you a job."

"No, I've got experience as a bank teller. I think I've got a lead at the Manufacturers Hanover branch on Madison Avenue."

"Well, look me up if you need a job."

"Well, I gotta go. I think I'm going to go over to the peace rally."

"Hey, that's where I'm off to. I figure Tricky Dick needs to see that it's not all teenage hippies against him. It's also the working class, the vets who've been there."

"You mean you were in 'Nam?"

"Three hundred and ten days in the jungle. But then, who counted?"

"And you survived? In one piece?"

"Except for this shrapnel wound." He raised his pant leg, exposing a ragged 12-inch scar. "And a fuckin' heroin addiction."

"Shit, I'm sorry. Are you still in pain? Are you still fucked up?"

"Yes and no. I still pop Tylenol like they're going out of style. But I kicked the habit while I was in rehab after the VA hospital."

"Well, it's an honor, major, to attend this reception with you," Mary laughed.

"More like corporal, but what the hell."

As they got up to go, Mary reached into her bag. "The tip's on me, in honor of a man who has served his country. My aunt and cousins are in the Navy, out of Norfolk. They'd be proud to meet you."

"I'm not so sure. I've sort of become anti-military. My dad was military, straight laced, three shots of bourbon a night, and now he won't even talk to me, wouldn't even send money when I first got out of rehab. I'm the degenerate of my family—twelfth generation. We came over on the Mayflower, real bluebloods."

They walked out the revolving door, laughing as they got stuck together inside one compartment. They wandered slowly over to Bryant Park, with a whole morning ahead for them to hear about the immorality of the war. There was the potential for a new beginning in an island of strangers—of settling down, with their haunting families far away, allowing their wings to stop flapping in a random pattern of stuttering flight.

They approached the park as the SDS speaker was yelling, "Fuck this." "Hell no, we won't go."

"Who's he to talk?" Mary looked at Maurice. "At least you were there. And I'm glad you got back."

"Jamie told her parents that she was coming with me to this Vietnam War Moratorium thing," Judy said, laughing, as I met her at Grand Central Terminal when the 8:10 arrived from Scarsdale. "But she's just cutting so she can spend the day with George."

"Are they coming with you?" I was a bit disappointed.

"Are you kidding? They'll spend the day in bed at her house."

"We could have done the same," I said, smirking, tentatively.

"Her dad's such a liberal. If he only knew that his daughter was on the pill."

"Well, Jamie better listen to the radio to make sure she knows who's speaking here today," I suggested.

"Nah, I'll call her later. You know, it sure is fun being in her dad's class," Judy joked. "All he ever talks about in his American Literature class is this war. We never talk about Fitzgerald or Steinbeck; although he loves Hemingway and his stories about the Spanish Civil War. Every day, it just takes one comment to get him going."

We were walking towards Bryant Park, along 41st Street, approaching the corner of Fifth Avenue. The throng of protestors was congealing into a crowd. Most were dressed in the fashion of the day—jeans, T-shirts, bandanas, sandals—with long beards or shoulder-length hair. We "almost" fit in, but not quite. Judy was wearing her bellbottoms with a tight fitting white blouse. She was a "mermaid," so to speak—part hippie, soon to believe in almost free love, but still clearly living in the upper class. She glanced around, still with me, and ready to follow me after the Vietnam Moratorium out to Shea Stadium for the World Series game. I really wasn't sure, however, that she wouldn't try to get some other cute guy's phone number.

We could barely hear a black woman speaking about how the 1199 Union was supporting the moratorium.

" . . . if we can make this democracy work first for all Americans, we might not find it necessary to kill people in order to convince them that our way is good for them too."

We passed by the New York Public Library, with its two lions in their reconnaissance position out front, ready to defend their hallowed hall.

"Hey, look!" I yelled. "That's Ralph Ashford, the radical Columbia teacher I was telling you about." All of a sudden, I felt like a fraud. There was Ralph, dressed in his "uniform:" tattered jeans and a Black Panther T-shirt. I was wearing my "faded" but untorn jeans, with Keds sneakers and my Tulane "69" football jersey, which Robin had given me last year, after she had visited that campus. (Our class was the only one that could truly wear "69" without being accused of fornication.)

"Remember my 'Intro to Economics' class that my friend Jon and I lucked into? This teacher, Professor Ashford, who would've thought? A world-class racquetball player on a fast track to a tenured faculty position in economics all of a sudden becomes a radical. And guess what? He's off the tenure track, and this is now his last year on faculty. He knows he's out, so he's fucking with the university. All we need to do is read one book and do a verbal report with him, and he gives us whatever grade we want. Our first A's at Columbia."

"You're paying $3,000 a year for that?"

"Hey, it'll help my GPA for law school."

"Won't they find out? Someone will know."

"It's funny you say that. Jon's friend, Bunny, is in our class, and she's only giving herself a B+. She says, 'When I get to heaven, God will look at an A and say, uh uh, no heaven for you.'"

But for now, Ralph was in his glory. He was speaking with a group of college- age coeds. His long, black "Jew-fro" was clearly a turn-on for these Sarah Lawrence girls who had taken the train down from Westchester to be here. "I bet he's more interested in teaching them about his views personally after the rally," I commented sarcastically.

"I don't know, Ken. He is cute. I'd love to have him as a teacher."

As we were passing by, I'm sure he didn't recognize me from his class. But he did notice Judy. He stopped talking for a minute, then continued. "The South Vietnamese government is merely an agent of the U.S. Imperialist Military Establishment." The girls were hanging on to his every word, susceptible to his impassioned speech about the ultimate victory of the Communist societies. Then his words were thankfully muffled by the chants of "NO MORE WAR" that resonated from the crowds, intermixed with sirens and car horns in the background.

"Judy, I wonder what your father would think if he knew you were so intrigued by him?"

"So, my father knows I'm here today, he has questions about the war also."

"Yeah, but he's a stockbroker—the caretaker of John Kenneth Galbraith's 'Great Society' that I'm reading about now. Who do you think is profiting from this war?'"

We caught the tail end of Roger's polemic. "We need to boycott the establishment, the industrial giants, like DuPont, makers of napalm. They're suppressing the masses."

"PEACE NOW, PEACE NOW, PEACE NOW," rang out from the crowd.

"Like he says, Judy," I said mockingly. "Who do you think is paying for your jeans and shoes? All made by the capitalist society's profits; all made by your dad in his stock trading."

"I never thought of it quite like that. My dad doesn't trample over anyone."

"It's all corporate greed, Judy, even if your father's not directly involved. Why don't you call him and tell him, "Dad, don't sell any more DuPont stock, they're no good. Please get another job, Dad. Come on down to Bryant Park with us."

"You're so full of yourself, Ken. Just fuck off. There's no reason for my dad to give up what he's doing."

"Yeah, then you'd have to give up your car and your clothing allowance." I was beginning to sound like Jay—and about to be alone once again!

"I don't think what my dad does or what I spend makes a difference; no one is dying from his investments."

"You're in your own fantasy world. I still take my step-mom's money from the stock market to pay for my education at Columbia, but at least I feel some guilt about it."

"But not enough to refuse it. If you're so guilty, don't take it and do it right. Get a job slicing meat at Mama Joy's."

Next to us was a student wearing a peace button, pinned next to the Izod "alligator" on her pale green shirt, along with her jeans and penny loafers. It was ambiguity at its greatest—ambivalent feelings toward wealth. "You go to Barnard?" she asked Judy.

"Nah, my boyfriend Ken" pointing at me, "goes to Columbia. I'm still in high school."

"Just look around here," she retorted. "All of these kids cutting classes. I wonder how many are really involved in the protest movement, trying to bring our soldiers back from the jungle. Most of them are going back to their cozy dorm rooms later. It pisses me off."

"Even so," I pleaded, "What a statement—tens of thousands here, thousands more around the country, all peacefully protesting the Vietnam War."

"Hey, Cindy, what's up?"

"Brian, we're just getting into a political discussion. This is Ken; he goes to Columbia, even though I haven't seen him around."

"And this is Judy," I volunteered. "She's hoping to go to Barnard next year."

"Look me up before you come here," Cindy smiled. "It's not all it's cracked up to be."

"Ken just wants me close to him next year. But I'm looking all over the country."

"Look me up when you come here," Brian winked, as Cindy pulled him towards her.

"Shouldn't we get closer to the platform? I want to hear what they say about taking down our government."

Helen Hayes, Julie Harris, Colleen Dewhurst, and Dick Benjamin were introduced on the podium. And then the biggest cheer—for Woody Allen. But all we heard was, "Thank you all for coming today."

"Cindy," I said, perhaps a bit more meekly than I should have, "can't we somehow still love our country without overthrowing our government? This was a civil war long before we got engaged. I mean, we can protest this fucking war without becoming communist."

"And still live in luxury, while our soldiers get killed in Southeast Asia?" Brian retorted.

"Not to mention the Vietnamese soldiers," Cindy added. "They don't even want us there."

"Ken," Brian said sarcastically. "Why don't you go on over and take the place of one of those poor, black soldiers from Mississippi? Die for him."

"I'm not saying it's fair. I don't want either of us to die."

"You guys are so brave," Judy said laughingly. "Both of you with your 2S. You're protected."

"Not for long," Brian scowled. "I'm a senior."

"That didn't stop my best friend's brother. He went to his family doctor up in Scarsdale with an imaginary illness that made him 4F."

"I'm not that wealthy. In Brooklyn, we don't have the choice. It's sort of like abortions—available to the rich or privileged, but not for the rest of the world."

"So, are you telling me if you got me pregnant, I'd have to have your baby?" Cindy was pissed off.

"Just make sure you take your pill every night, and we won't have to worry. Otherwise, just like the Mississippi blacks, you're stuck— either you got to go to war or you got to have the baby."

I started to pull Judy away. I'd had enough of this inquisition.

"Hell no, we won't go." The chant became louder and louder.

We were able to finally inch our way to where we could see Jay's hero, Senator Eugene McCarthy, on the podium, delivering his speech.

As we pushed through the crowd, I thought, "Self protection versus protest. Were we trying to get the rest of our soldiers back, while leaving Vietnam to the Vietnamese, or was I just scared the war wouldn't be over by the time my 2S ended three years later?"

It was almost as if Judy were reading my mind. "Ken, you know my dad was in Italy grenading the Italian fascists. He thinks the protestors should all be sent over there."

"It was easy; he was fighting Hitler and genocide and stopping the Fascists from controlling Europe."

"But aren't the Communists just as interested in taking over the world?"

"Judy, Ho Chi Minh doesn't even want the Chinese in his country."

"My dad says it's not so simple—look at what the North Vietnamese do to the South Vietnamese."

"It's their war, Judy. This isn't about Communism versus Capitalism. This is a war of nationalism."

"Ken, just wait until we lose in Vietnam and the Communists decide to attack us; then we'll be invaded by the Chinese or the Russians. My dad says we've got to fight 'em there to protect the world. It's our duty to the free people!"

"Judy, it was so much easier for your dad. There was no question regarding the moral imperative." I was sounding like one of the protest leaders, speaking in tongues.

Senator Eugene McCarthy was continuing to speak. "We may be in the position . . . in speaking about the government of Germany, that perhaps the government should dissolve the people and get itself another people. Well that seems to be the policy they'd like to have become effective—unhappy with the people, unhappy with protest."

From off to the side, we heard, "Ho-Ho-Ho Chi Minh."

I wasn't quite sure. I hated what we were doing in Vietnam, but, unlike the mentality of Jane Fonda, Ho wasn't my hero either. I just wanted us out of Vietnam, and to let those people have their country have back—and to get our country back.

Instead of remaining silent, I yelled again, "Peace Now!" At least I wasn't a member of the silent majority.

William Sloane Coffin, Yale University's chaplain (not to mention former commencement speaker at Scarsdale High), was stepping up to the mike.

"As you know, the president, the vice-president and the secretary of state have all pleaded with us to close rank behind the president. But that is asking a lot. For how can people close rank behind a leader when they are so far ahead of them. He should push on ahead, a little faster . . . . We must remember that those furthest from the seat of power are often closest to the heart of the truth. The president has said that we have met the enemy and they are ours. But I assume we are here because we have met the enemy—and the enemy is us!

We need to confess that we have intervened massively militarily and unilaterally in the civil affairs of another country. After all, how many Vietnamese fought in our Civil War? Then we need to confess that despite the blood of 44,000 American dead, despite the billions of dollars of aid, despite the heroic labor of many dedicated Americans, we are now supporting a government that is incapable of finding support among its own people. It is a government that has nothing to win and everything to lose at the Paris Peace Talks.

We need to confess . . . that we have rained terror from the sky . . . . But let us be clear that the fault does not lie with the infantrymen, the bomber pilots, the Green Berets . . . violence in its cruelest form is not individual and haphazard but it is bureaucratic, and efficient, antiseptic, and profitable. It is not blue collar, it is not "no" collar, it is white collar. The truly violent ones are not the mugging drug addicts who live in slum tenants but those who live in pentagonal palaces and the leaning tower and other houses of weaponsville. Our nation is being conquered by our own warfare industry.

And so Mr. Nixon, the truth is our authority, not authority our truth! We cannot stand silently by while South Vietnamese people are perse-cuted by a government so rotten that it would fall within a week if it were not propped by American power.

And as for ourselves, we can only say that silence becomes treason when good Americans die bravely in a bad cause. And so we pledge our-selves . . . to recall immediately all of our sons from Vietnam."

The crowd cheered in agreement. No one could have said it better than Reverend Coffin. The rest of the morning could only be anti-climactic, starting with the factual speech of New York's Senator Jacob Javits. He was drowned out by cheers as John Lindsay arrived, our hero (although he certainly was not the hero of the teachers and transit work-ers' unions, or of the residents of Queens, where the previous year streets had remained unplowed for a week during a severe winter blizzard).

Mayor Lindsay had announced his support for the moratorium, and had ordered all of New York City's flags to be flown at half-mast. I was proud that I was volunteering in his campaign for re-election, going door to apartment door to ensure four more years of compassionate govern-ment. He was young, vibrant, handsome, well spoken, and outspoken; and although he came from the "silk stocking" district of the Upper East Side, his heart appeared to be "for the people, and by the people," even if he wasn't "of the people." Here was a man of the government on our side, on the right side, not on Nixon's or the establishment's side. Here was a man we could trust to work to attain our goal through mainstream protest, through anti-war marches and protests, without destruction of lives or property. Here was a man who would wear a black armband with us to protest the war.

He began, "There was a cynic who once said, 'We learn nothing from history except that we learn nothing from history.'"

He reiterated Reverend Coffin's words about the tragedy of the war, the mistakes that were made, the 40,000 brave Americans killed in a war where, instead of pride and victory, there was only destruction and despair, both at home and in Vietnam. He repeated that peaceful protest was, in fact, patriotic; that freedom of speech was what has made our country so great and powerful.

He ended with "We pledge to say no to this war, to say yes to peace and to say yes to the lives of our fighting men. . . ."

The crowd listened with respect to our mayor; no chants disturbed his speech. But the cheers were overwhelming as he left the podium.

As our junior Senator, Charles Goodell, was introduced, I turned to Judy.

"Let's go." We had done our duty. We had honored the movement. "It's 11:30. We need to catch the subway to Shea Stadium—the game begins in 90 minutes!"

As we walked and pushed our way through the crowd, Senator Goodell began speaking. Off to the side were banners saying "Hell no, we won't go;" and along the perimeter were "Black Panthers," their raised black fists juxtaposed with Joyce Kilmer's trees, whose changing, soft autumn colors stood in antithesis to the harshness of the speakers.

Standing on a concrete container surrounding a beautiful oak tree was a screaming rebel, 6' 2", white, with long, dirty-blond hair, shouting to make his sub-protest heard over the senator's amplified voice. "We need to be solid with our brothers," as he embraced the next speaker, one of the Black Panthers, whose brothers were standing off at a distance. As he yelled "Power to the People," the Panthers' distrust came through even as they raised their fists in support. They made little attempt to mask their sense of superiority that this "whitey" was their soldier and legitimized the middle class nature of this protest. After all, he had neglected to add: "Fuck the Pigs!"

I remembered back to the stories at Columbia during the 1968 uprising, when Mark Rudd led SDS into barricading the buildings. "On strike, shut it down," he yelled—upper middle class guilt over the fact that he had grown up safe while the "black brothers" in Harlem and in Vietnam were surrounded by poverty, drugs, diseases, and death. How did Mark Rudd feel when the black students took over their own building and forced him out? Apartheid protests in reverse?

And then the black man came forward, his "Afro" and full beard radicalizing his appearance. I could barely make out what he was saying, getting only about every other word, as Senator Goodell spoke of his promise to get his billed passed to immediately withdraw all troops within the next year. Of course, as every other word or phrase from the Panther was "fuck" or "shit" or "whitey or "the white motherfuckers" or "fuck Nixon," I'm sure I didn't lose much in translation. The rest was lost in cheers and echoes.

But it was scary when he started screaming, "Burn, baby, burn!" with effigies of Nixon in the crowd.

My ambivalence started to penetrate throughout my gut. The phrase "Peace at any cost" brought on new meaning. I wanted peace, I didn't want to go to war, I didn't want to die. But I didn't want to kill people to get there. The ends didn't justify the means. Our society still could be the model for the future. Mark Rudd, the Beatles, and Eldridge Cleaver spoke of "Revolution." I wanted "evolution."

But, then again, I was living in Scarsdale, getting a great education, with a girlfriend at my side who had similar hopes. Judy and I weren't going back to a sixth floor walkup at 116th Street and Lenox Avenue, only four blocks east of where I was going to my Ivy League school but a "million miles away" in most other respects. We weren't getting off at a subway station with the stench of urine and with bent needles infected with bacteria and virus.

We could wait.

I was part of the political scientists, the intellectual liberals, the best and the brightest, working for John Lindsay, the "Great White Hope," to bring the city back together. We were here today, children of wealthy families with a "conscience," alongside the poor minorities—blacks and

Hispanics (and even some whites)—the deprived generation, depraved by drugs, by disease, and by gunshot wounds not just from Vietcong artillery, but also from local police in Newark, Detroit, Watts, and from each other.

I could wait.

But could the black speaker and his family wait?

We left, not completely guilt-free. After all, as far as Judy's principal and teachers knew, we'd be at the protest all day. Lying to our educators wasn't the problem—it was the soldiers lying on the ground in Vietnam that were the problem.

"Ken, shouldn't we stay a little longer?"

"Judy, if we don't leave now, we'll miss the first pitch."

We inched our way out to the edge of the crowd, past the Josephine Shaw Lowell Memorial Fountain.

"Judy, did you know this is the first public monument to a woman in New York City."

"Another obscure fact from 'It's Academic?'" she mocked.

"No, just, you know, 'You've come a long way, baby.'"

I was imagining that everyone was watching us leave, that we were being judged, that we would be called up on the stage for public humiliation—traitors to the cause to be hung in ridicule.

But no one seemed to notice as we walked down the concrete stairs at 42nd and 6th Avenue to catch the #7 IRT—the Flushing Line—to Shea.

A continuing stream of young men and women passed us, unmindful of the rules of the New York City subway system, to stay to the right. They streamed up the stairs, as late in arriving as we were early in departing. Dressed in the "uniform"—ripped jeans, tie-dyed shirts, and sandals—they were glassy-eyed, stoned, high—as in "wrecked." That would explain why they hadn't gotten here earlier. We fought through the surges and at least once rubbed too close to a homeless man who clearly hadn't changed his clothes this month. I wondered what parasite had just crawled into my shirt.

"Stay to the right, Judy." I tried to avoid touching the handrail. Who knew who had recently touched it? As I moved as close to the rail as I could without contaminating myself, I finally understood the rationale behind the graffiti that was written on the subway wall, "Up against the wall, motherfucker."

The stairway was poorly lit; there was gum on the ground, ready to attach like a bloodsucking leech to the unobservant shoe. There was the "*L'odoer de piss et puke*," the new fragrance to replace Chanel #5.

"Breathe through you mouth, Judy."

"That won't help. Do you have any gum?"

"Wait til we get downstairs." At the bottom was a Chicklet machine, but three plungers were stuck. I put a nickel into the only one that was sticking out and pulled—nothing but the clink of my coin. I pulled again. Nothing. I tried kicking the machine. Nothing, nothing. Fuckin' New York City subway!

We were the only ones standing on the eastbound platform of the subterranean environment, the city's bowels of crime, with enemies lurking everywhere behind the pillars and the newspaper stands. While the "Underground" movement remained upstairs at Bryant Park, we went downstairs to go to the World Series. I checked my jeans' pocket—yep, the tickets were still there. I felt their gravitational forces, like Newton's Fifth Law of nature, returning me from "on high" back to Earth, to baseball and apple pie.

"At least we went for a while—we did our part."

"I'd had enough!" Judy said, sympathetically. "Some of those people hadn't taken a shower in weeks."

"I don't think that is a problem for the SDS organizers. You know, the natural look, no deodorant, unshaven armpits."

"And unshaven legs."

"At least for the girls."

"That's the newest rage."

Still, no train came, and no one else came down to the platform. Only the long-term denizen of the station came forth from the shadows to put out their hands, hopeful of a better handout from the soft-hearted liberals. I put—or, rather, dropped—a dime into one of their disease-infested hands, with nails one inch long and filled with dirt. That was enough money for a cup of coffee. Otherwise, I squirmed, trying not to show how uncomfortable I felt. I wouldn't be much of a deterrent to robbery or rape. I kept one hand around Judy and one hand near my pocket, with both eyes roaming around the platform and staring back towards Times Square, waiting for the train to come, to end our isolation, our vulnerability. We were among our dysfunctional family, the crazy uncles, the worthless cousins from the backwoods, so disparate from the sophisticated relatives on the commuter trains rolling into Grand Central Terminal.

"Finally, it's coming," Judy exhaled. The exteriors of the subway cars were spray-painted with decorative graffiti.

As the train approached, we could see the "sardines in the can" packed tightly, with Mets' caps on their heads (at least they still had their "heads," I thought). The tin can may as well have been sealed, because there was no way we were going to get on this train filled with passengers from the Times Square starting block.

"This'll never work, come on, let's go over to the westbound train. We'll get on here and retrace back to Times Square—but at least we'll have seats."

"You mean we're going in the opposite direction we want to go. You're a fool! We should never go backwards!"

Ah, a recurrent theme in this brilliant young narrator's life—knowing, for sure, or at least thinking for sure, that I was right while my partner questioned my intelligence or commitment.

It would have been so easy to have just given in and stayed there, waiting for the next train. After all, if we got on, we would have saved time at the expense of my losing face. And if we didn't get on, wouldn't that prove that I was right? But at the expense of time and missing the first pitch!

I didn't give in. "Follow me."

"You're crazy, Ken."

I pulled Judy up the stairs, and then back down the other side. We only had to wait three minutes for the returning train, which was empty. And two minutes later, we were back at Times Square, one stop back; but the theory of negativity worked: we now had seats as the baseball masses piled on.

Judy's stare said it all. "If you know what's good for you (and your sexual organ), you'd better keep quiet."

Above us, at 43rd Street and Broadway, was the U.S. Army Recruiting Center. What irony—only a block away we'd been patriotically trying to bring our boys home and they were up there patriotically trying to bring our boys to war. We were now the "underground" beneath the military sergeants—sporting crew-cuts, pressed khaki slacks and shirts, neat ties, and nametags in place over their left shirt pockets—who were signing 'em up, enlisting the poor and ragged of New York City to protect our country and the American way.

The subway car filled quickly, and I thought the term "cattle car" seemed particularly apt. As the young men scrambled for seats, knocking over women dressed in their cleaning uniforms on their way to work, the aberrancy of the human race was manifest.

I smiled as I remembered our genetic biology lecture last week. Our attractive female professor, only a few years older than the students she stood in front of—a room of horny, freshman and sophomore boys—had articulated:

"Scientific evidence has shown that when you artificially inseminate cows, there is an increased incidence of genetic mutations."

One of the pre-meds in the front row asked, naively, "What does that prove?"

"It's obvious, sir; If you spare the rod, you spoil the child!"

There was silence, as a few pre-meds took this down verbatim in their notebooks.

Then there was a gradual smattering of laughter from the classroom. A little humor went a long way at Columbia.

But here it was pretty appalling what was happening. Judy and I got up and offered our seats to two women in their 60s with packages from Macy's on their way home to Queens after a morning of shopping.

"Thank you. You're so well-mannered. Your parents must be proud."

We stared at each other and blushed. "If they only knew."

As we stood with our hands holding the steel pole, I got a better look at who was going with us to the game. There was a mixture of businessmen in their ties, some loosened at the collar, with their suit jackets slung over their backs. They were talking to each other about the latest financial deals, speaking quietly under the din of the subway. They brought back memories of old newsreels of the crowds at Ebbets Field in Brooklyn—middle-aged men dressed in suits and ties, their "formal wear," attending a Dodger baseball game in the 1940s. But today's suits varied.

The older men wore dark suits with narrow lapels and baggy trousers with cuffs, along with their white shirts and two-inch wide ties—just like the engineers in Mission Control.

Contrasting with the elder statesmen were the younger businessmen, the "Mod Squad," either salesmen or men working for "liberated" companies. They were adorned with suits fashioned with wide lapels, "colorful" (aka outlandish) ties and wide bellbottoms, and blue and dark orange shirts. Their long hair was still controlled. They were still part of the establishment, trying to make a statement that they were different. But there was an ambivalence about the side of society they were part of— the side that gave them their paycheck, their daily bread, or the "dark side," the side that smoked pot with their friends on weekends after coming back from watching Elliot Gould and Robert Culp and Natalie Wood and Dyan Cannon in "Bob and Carol and Ted and Alice," the original movie about swinging couples in the '60s. They were comfortable with their economic status, but no longer instilled with the values of the 1950s "man in the gray flannel suit" of the Madison Avenue advertising industry.

Much more distracting were the group of boisterous, obnoxious, and infantile ruddy-faced 22-year-old boys, Irish to the core, loaded to the core with a bag with two six-packs of Ballantine beer, the champagne of the champion New York Yankees. They were of the "Ice Age." Their hallucinogen of choice remained hops and malt rather than marijuana. The "now" generation was passing them by. They were dressed in their plain, white T-shirts, stained under the armpits, blue jeans, and white sneakers and white athletic socks, ready to argue with anyone on the train who disagreed with Papal authority—except, of course, in the matter of sex with the pretty ladies.

And finally, there were the middle-aged black women on the train—not the "brothers" or "sister" whom we had just left above ground, but the lower working class, eking out a living so they could escape the slums and give their children a chance. They included the 40-year-old grandmothers who, having raised their children, were now supporting their unwed daughters' children and working two jobs to avoid a life of welfare for their children. This was their stretch limo, their chariot. Only they were in place in the subway—and now their place had been invaded by interlopers, disturbing their mantra, "Gotta get home to fix dinner."

There Judy and I stood, so '60s, so turn of the decade. Judy, with her neatly combed, brown hair, long and straight; and me, with my blond, wavy, unkempt hair growing longer, needing a trim as did my freshly grown mustache. Our jeans were cleaned and pressed. Judy had on sandals she bought over the summer in the Village, and I was wearing my new boots. There we all stood, hands intertwined, black and white, young and old, hangnails and manicured fingers, holding onto the melting pot pole of New York City.

The darkness was transformed into sunlight as we moved farther away from the peace march towards Shea Stadium, our subway car emerging from the dungeon-like underground into the elevated section of the Queens segment of the Flushing Line, with Industry City beneath us. We were blasting off into the urban sky, towards our own moon, astronauts on our own Saturn express. As we traveled into space, we also traveled back through time, back through the time warp of the black hole, traveling back faster than the speed of light, to return to yesteryear, to the previous century in the era of the elevated trains.

As we climbed, the subway wheels squealing, Mars, the Roman god of war, strode through the train. A young black male, with a beard, Afro, and T-shirt emblazoned with "Fuck Whitey," walked by. A loose steel chain served as belt and his jeans were studded with steel crosses. I grabbed Judy's hand and instinctively put my hand on my pocket to protect my tickets and wallet. My middle class suburban stereotype.

Last year, in my English class, "The Black Man in White America," we had spent an entire session discussing the difference between stereotyping and prejudice. As discussed in the 1969 "college dictionary of pure thought and liberal thinking," here was the way to conceive the difference:

Stereotype: If you see a young, white male wearing jeans walking down one side of the street and a black man similarly dressed walking down the other side, what side would you walk on? And would it make a difference whether you were black or white or if you were in New York City or in Selma, Alabama?

Prejudice: You need a partner for your chemistry lab, someone you will be working with in close personal and physical contact. There are two remaining students: 1) a well-dressed black student from the Bronx High School of Science and 2) a white football player recruited only for his skill at throwing a football 60 yards. Who would you pick? Do you really want to get into medical school?

But we had neglected to study reality in that class. This guy walking through the subway really hated white people. And he was armed with a chain. It was only reality to understand that he could be a threat in the right circumstances.

Intellectually, I was not prejudiced. After all, Willie Mays was my favorite baseball player when I was eight years old, along with Eddie Mathews. I only wanted the best—there was no stereotyping in my fantasy league.

But still, I looked up, and then away, hoping to avoid his glare, hoping that he would not choose to take it out on me, hoping this was not the battlefield he had chosen. Were there enough other people around to protect me? So I guess I was just stereotyping!

I found myself looking at the Rheingold Beer Miss Subway poster for October 1969. The August and September posters were still up in various positions on the train. These were the most clean-cut women that could be imagined. Their pictures were the antithesis of my father's *Playboy* centerfolds. These New York City hopefuls had simpler aspirations: "I want to go to college and be a teacher." "I want to marry an executive and raise a family." "I want to be a fashion model." Here was the best and brightest of the lower middle class, with the upper middle class their goal. I couldn't picture these women having sex, except as it was portrayed in the 1950s and early 1960s television shows: behind closed bedroom doors with the lights out and no fragrant candles or pungent smoke, as their husbands—the Ozzie Nelsons, Ward Cleavers and Dick Van Dykes—returned to their respective twin beds after doing the unmentionable. They were dinosaurs, out of place in the forthcoming sexual revolution.

My eyes shifted to Miss September, whose aspiration was to raise a family and have a nice life. She had beautiful, black hair, a small nose, a wide smile, and perfect white complexion. She would make a great wife, I thought.

Then I moved on to Miss August, with aspirations to get married and have three children. She had beautiful black hair, a small nose, a wide smile, and perfect black complexion. She would make a great wife, I thought—for my black classmate at Columbia.

"Culturally repressed," my English teacher at Scarsdale High School would have written on my evaluation.

Judy wasn't interested in Miss Subway. She was searching for Mr. Subway instead. She maneuvered close to one of the executives, whose hand was brushing hers on the pole.

"We just came from the peace march."

Days of innocence still controlled my mind, as I didn't yet understand that Judy and I had met too early in our lives, before she had experienced the full breadth of her sexuality.

"Jamaica, change here for the Long Island Railroad," came over the loudspeaker.

"Well, that's for the hippies," the executive said. "You don't look like you even belonged there."

"You talk like my dad. He thought we were hypocrites, going to the march and then to the World Series."

"Smart man, what does he do?"

"Works as a stockbroker."

"So do I. Where does he work?"

Judy had already lost interest. She didn't need to sleep with her father's protégé. "Barnaby, Jones, and Ebsen."

"Never heard of them."

"Then you must be new," she gloated, seeing that her private joke about television names went right over his head. As she turned away, the stockbroker turned to me.

"If you were really committed, you wouldn't be coming out here—typical fucking liberal. You ever walk through a muddy field with a 40 pound pack on your shoulder during night patrol?"

"96th Street, exit here for the bus to La Guardia Airport," the conductor announced.

I shook my head.

"My little brother is in the Marines and he hates you Commie pinkos. He doesn't feel appreciated. He's putting his ass on the line for the good old U.S. of A. —you're fucking him over."

I blurted, "But we're doing this for him. We want him to come home in one piece. Why should he die in Vietnam, fighting for a corrupt government? Let the Vietnamese have what they want. We can't make them Americans."

"You're so fucking naïve."

Did he really know what the word meant?

"What about all of the South Vietnamese who want democracy? What will happen when the Viet Cong and the Chinese come down and destroy the villages, when the Russian MIGs destroy the cities? Do you think the Commies will have any compassion for those people once they're the dictator?"

"It's their war. They've been fighting it for generations."

"Like hell it is. I'll put my trust in Nixon any day—he's not going to let the Reds take over the world."

"One-hundred-eleventh Street. Next stop, Shea Stadium, World Series," the conductor announced.

"Honey, my grandson's stuck over there," one of the black matrons thankfully interjected. "I want him home. We've got all of our boys over there and we still can't win this war. I want my baby home now."

"We're the United States," the stockbroker was flustered. "We don't lose wars. Who will respect us if we don't finish 'em off?"

"Well, honey, why don't you take your lily white ass and go on over there and take my Gregory's place. He'll be really glad to come home to Grandma."

We glared at the "money man," watching him get red in the face. He started to answer. He should've lied, but he didn't—too Catholic, I guess.

"I can't, I've got a bad knee, football injury."

"Humph."

"Anyway, we may as well just nuke 'em and get it over with."

"Real smart," I answered. "World War III over Vietnam."

"Shea Stadium. Next stop, Willets Point, Flushing. Watch the closing door." The conductor was still doing his job.

"Let's go Mets," the straphangers yelled, as everyone exited.

"Let's go Judy."

"Aye, Aye, Comrade!" she laughed.

We walked down the concrete stairway to the circular platform. There was Shea Stadium. Only six years old and already a storied history—its first World Series. The blue and orange panels, blue for the Brooklyn Dodgers, orange for the New York Manhattan Giants, were now joined in Queens. The five tiers of the stadium, a modern symmetric monstrosity, had the slick look of '60s utilitarianism. No more outdated ballparks with asymmetric foul lines, obstructed view seats, dingy locker rooms. No need for the charm of Fenway Park or Wrigley Field. No, today "The Museum of Modern Stadium" was spruced up for the Series. At least there still was real green grass. And the police were out in full force, riding their horses as if this were Central Park. They were part of Mayor Lindsay's show of security.

We were immersed in a mob of businessmen and young professionals, along with rowdy teens and secretaries in the arms of their sugar daddies.

As we were propelled forward by the wave, I almost fell into a 12-year-old boy who was clinging to his father's arm. I flashed back to my first World Series game with my Cousin Bruce. The memories were still fresh in my mind—memories of pleasure that floated to the top of my teen years.

"I'm sorry," I said, as I brushed by him smiling. "Enjoy the game."

He looked up, frightened by the transformed masses, and then he laughed, looking up to his dad, who nodded.

"Thank you, sir."

His dad looked at me. "It's his first game."

"I know. I remember mine."

As we reached the bottom of the stairs, we walked towards the stadium gate. Norman Rockwell's America was shattered.

"Check it on out, Black Panther Party newspaper." I wasn't going to mess with the guy on the subway's cousin, so I took the leaflet, knowing I would "deep-6" it long before I got home. It would not be a part of my World Series memorabilia. We continued walking toward Gate F, the right field section, and I heard a less threatening voice saying "Check it out, Black Panther Party newspaper." This time it was the "cousin" of the skinny white, college radical with long, dirty-brown hair we had passed at Bryant Park—mainstream U.S.A. transformed into radicalism. He was hardly physically threatening, but he was certainly morally threatening to his parents and to the establishment, this pawn in the black radical movement.

"Come on, Judy."

Finally, we made it past the political hustlers and heard:

"Hey, program here!"

"Hey, Mets' hats here."

Familiar sounds:

"Who needs tickets?"

"Who's selling tickets?"

The scalpers were walking past, speaking furtively. Their eyes were looking out for police and plainclothesmen whose eyes were looking out for scalpers and pickpockets.

I quickly checked my pockets again. I saw that the tickets and my wallet were in place, as I recalled the scene from the movie "Casablanca" where, whenever Peter Lorre passed by, everyone checked his jacket pockets. We made it to the gate and surrendered half of our ticket as we entered through the turnstile into the holy shrine. Here we were at the fourth game of the Series, which was expected to have been the final game of a four-game sweep by the Orioles. Now, however, a reversal of fortunes had occurred, as the Mets were ahead two games to one, on the strength of Agee's spectacular catches and Nolan Ryan's pitching—the same Nolan Ryan who was inexplicably traded away a year later and went on to pitch seven no-hitters. The "Mets curse" of Nolan Ryan was not as significant as the "Red Sox curse" of the Bambino, but to this day the Mets have never had a no-hitter thrown by a pitcher while wearing a Mets' uniform.

I clenched the ticket stubs in one hand, as I held on to Judy's hand tightly, making sure we didn't get separated. My obsessiveness regarding the little pieces of cardboard that guaranteed our seats at this game was only a front for ensuring that Judy would not be befriended by another. After all, I was one of the few fans with an attractive woman in tow. And it was a good thing she looked so good that day, because that was becoming her only attribute.

"Ken, I want a hat."

"I want a soda."

"I want some popcorn."

"Are we really going up to the upper deck?"

When we had our first date two months earlier, she hadn't complained about our seats in the upper deck. It's amazing what we put up with on a first date. Now, as we entered the second stage of our courtship, reality and awareness of faults, along with familiarity, allowed the bitchiness to surface.

"Are you kidding me? You're not taking me all the way up there."

And, "I'm not going with you!"

"Well, you can't very well stay behind."

"Can't we sit down there?"

"Judy, that's the bullpen bench. That's where the Mets' pitchers sit."

"Why couldn't you get us seats there?"

I wasn't sure if she was pulling my chain, especially since Judy was not entirely wrong. Only wild horses or the World Series could get me to overcome my fear of heights and get me up there this day. If my dad had worried about my falling out of the stands at the Polo Grounds back in

1962—protected from the precipice only by two soldiers on weekend leave—he would've had a "cow" with these seats, three rows from the top, three seats in. Only two people were between me and a 200-foot fall into the Mets' bullpen.

"I'm sorry, Judy," I said, realizing there were only eight seats out of 55,000 worse than ours in the entire stadium.

We were there 20 minutes before game time, as the Marine Color Guard came in from center field. The flags were at full mast, as we learned later, due to the servicemen's protest that they would not march unless the flags were restored to their appropriate height.

We finally settled in and watched from deep, high, right field. The Mets took a 1-0 lead in the second inning on a home run by Donn Clendenon. Then we settled in, hoping for more runs for the Mets, hoping for more outs for the Orioles. Tom Terrific was pitching a great game for us, only Judy didn't appreciate the finer points of the 1-0 shutout in progress.

"Ken, can you get me a hot dog, please?"

"You can have my wiener later, if you want."

"No, I want one now—with mustard. And sauerkraut."

"What do you think this is, a Sabrett's hot dog stand?"

Nonetheless, in between innings I carefully put my compulsively scored scorecard down and ran down the stairs, quickly buying two hot dogs and two Cokes from the vendors who were hawking their wares in the crowd, and then running back up the 24 rows to make it back before the first pitch of the next inning.

By the ninth inning, the excitement was draining me, as the Orioles got two men on base. And then Frank Robinson hit a line drive to short right field that Ron Swoboda, the Mets' right fielder, not known for his defensive prowess, caught with a sliding backhand stab that the press would claim was more spectacular than the two catches Tommy Agee had made the night before.

But as the game was now tied, and when it went into extra innings, a terrible dilemma appeared in my mind as I peered into home plate as the Orioles came up to bat in the tenth inning. Judy had to be home by 8 p.m., meaning she would have to be on the 7:20 train at Grand Central. I had planned (i.e., fantasized) that the game would be over by 4 p.m., giving us enough time to go back to my dorm and do a little base-running ourselves, even though I was pretty sure the coach would stop us well before we approached home plate today. I now had a terrible thought. Did I want the game to be over, regardless of who was victorious, regardless of the effect on Mets' history, so I could have 15 minutes of our own game?

Of course, I had no control over the outcome of the game. I did not have the power that Harlan had attributed to me in the past, when I would say, "The Mets are going to win."

"Now you've jinxed them. They're gonna lose." And of course, more often than not, he would be right, even though the stars and the heavens were not mine to coerce.

"Snap out of it, Ken," I muttered to myself. "Don't even think about leaving early, you traitor. You already fucked up the night the Mets clinched in September. Be a man. Judy's not going anywhere."

I stopped daydreaming. "Let's go Mets."

"Let's go Mets," I yelled, the mantra for today.

"Besides, the only home run you'll see today is here at Shea," I realized.

"Let's go Mets," I yelled, on autopilot.

"And don't even think of getting her home late. Her father's probably listening to the game, and you can only blame the subway for so much delay. He may think his daughter is innocent, but don't push your luck too far."

"Lets' go Mets." There's still plenty of time.

It was the bottom of the 10th inning and the game was still tied.

"This is it, Judy. We're gonna win it here, I can feel it."

"Ken, can we leave soon?"

That was music to my ears. Was she thinking what I was she thinking?

"I have to get home. I still have homework."

"No way! We don't leave. For no reason." Especially for homework!

Pete Richert, a "crafty" leftie, came in to pitch for the Orioles. Elrod Hendricks was still behind the plate for the Orioles; Boog Powell was at first base, Davey Johnson at second, Brooks Robinson, the human vacuum cleaner, at third, and Frank Robinson in left field. I mean, how could we even think we could beat these guys?

And then the Mets' first batter, Jerry Grote, hit a shot to the outfield, rounded first base to our cheers, and eased into second base with a double.

"Ken, I have to go to the bathroom."

"Judy, aren't you watching the game? We have the winning run on second base with no one out."

"I have to go."

"Just wait, you're like a little girl. Anything could happen now."

"Okay, one more batter."

Rod Gaspar was sent in to pinch run for Grote at second base, as J.C. Martin, the Mets' left hand hitting reserve catcher, came up to hit. His only duty was to bunt the ball and get Gaspar to third base with one out. As Richert pitched, Boog and Brooks started charging towards the batter, Elrod crouched behind the plate, ready to explode out onto the field to orchestrate the play. J.C. bunted the ball up the first base line, away from Brooks. It was a perfect bunt, near the foul line, and Richert fielded the ball, having only one play.

From deep right field we watched as the sure-footed (aka slow-footed) Martin "streaked" towards first base. We heard the crowd's roar —with a delay due to the speed of sound needing a second to travel the 550 feet to our seats—then saw the ball ricocheting into short right field, as Richert's throw hit J.C. in the back.

"Run, Gaspar, run!" I yelled, as the ball caromed past Davey Johnson and Gaspar crossed home plate.

"We win! We win!" I yelled, as I jumped up and down.

But Earl Weaver, the Orioles' manager, was out arguing with the umpires. He was vehement, yelling, gesticulating, animated, and undoubtedly cursing.

"What's he doing, Ken?"

"I don't know. Maybe he's claiming Martin interfered with the play."

"What will happen then?"

"They'll call him out and send the runner back to second."

"You mean, we didn't win? I have to watch more of this? This game sucks!"

"Shh, just watch." And then, thankfully, I saw Weaver walking off the field, still yelling back at the umpires, kicking at the dirt. But most importantly, the umpires were leaving the field.

"We win! Let's go Mets!"

Even later replays were inconclusive. Was Martin outside the baseline when he was hit? Not that it would matter. Not only is there no crying in baseball, except in Little League and for three generations of Boston Red Sox fans and players, there was also no replay official in baseball; there was no "do over" in the World Series.

"Let's go. We'll never get out of here."

"Judy, I don't think it'll matter. The subway will be jammed anyway."

It was a happy, rowdy crowd in the train on the way back. We were all tired and hoarse as we hung onto the steel straps while the cars returned around the elevated curve, diving into the bowels of New York City. As we hadn't gotten into the train until 4:30 and didn't get back to Grand Central Terminal until 5:24, I knew there was no time for a tryst.

As we surfaced from the underground once again at Grand Central Terminal, I looked at Judy. "Do we have time for a steak at Tad's?"

"Just so I catch the 6:40."

We walked across the street to New York's discount steak chain. For 99 cents you got a rib-eye steak, baked potato, and piece of garlic bread, and for 20 cents more a soda. The steak was cooked to order, not that it took long to charbroil the thin slab of meat. The fat dripped onto the grill, making a succulent sound and smell. We carried our trays to an empty table in the corner. The steak wasn't bad, just a little tough, but nothing like the sirloins Lil served up at home.

"Want some ice cream?"

"No, it's 6:30. I need to get my train."

As we walked back to the platform, I was plaintive. "I was looking forward to some time alone with you at my dorm." I was hoping, without saying it, that this would be the day.

"Sorry, Ken, maybe this weekend."

"Sure." I was unable to hide my disappointment.

"Well, tomorrow night Jamie is taking me to my appointment at Planned Parenthood."

My eyes lit up as I kissed her goodbye. Hey, was that her tongue I felt in my mouth?

I made it back to my dorm just in time to check out the CBS Evening News. Granted, I had to plead with Tex to change the channel from another "Superman" rerun. But there was Walter Cronkite and his legion of reporters, with scenes of the moratorium from all over the United States. I watched as they reported the speeches of Edward Kennedy and John Lindsay supporting the moratorium and Barry Goldwater and Hubert Humphrey railing against the protestors, fearing that Hanoi would take solace. Then came a commercial for Marlboro cigarettes—which would kill and maim more citizens than we lost in Vietnam—followed by Jay's hero, Eugene McCarthy, speaking at Rutgers University, only a few miles from my first house in Highland Park, New Jersey. I was hoping to see myself at the protest, as I searched the crowds. But everyone had long hair and was wearing jeans. And besides, they weren't showing the 40,000 of us who had invaded Bryant Park; instead, they showed the protest at the Trinity Church near Wall Street, along with protests in D.C. and around the United States and Europe.

And then came the last story—the Mets' miraculous victory. Again, as they showed Swoboda's great catch and Martin's mundane bunt, I hoped they would pan up into the right field stands and show Judy and me cheering for our heroes. Imagine, being on CBS news twice in one night!

Ned actually got up around 7 p.m., showered, and then announced that he and a couple of other students from his film class were going to see "The King of Hearts," starring Alan Bates—a movie that had become a cult classic about the inmates of an insane asylum during the First

World War who were more sane than the generals. When he invited me along, I figured, "It can't get any crazier than today's reality!"

Mary missed the World Series game and, instead, went with Maurice to the movie theater. She missed seeing Swoboda's great catch, but she did feel the warm embrace of Maurice that evening, after watching "Midnight Cowboy" four times. They sat to the side in the orchestra for most of the first three showings, far away from the matronly audience (several of whom were so offended and obviously uninformed that this was not just another John Wayne Western that they got up and left during the sex scenes of the matinee performance), and then she joined him in the projection room for the final performance. He romanced her with a plate of fried clams and a milk shake at Howard Johnson's across the street. And even after he had dropped her off at the Roosevelt Hotel—a truly chivalrous gentleman, of Jane Austen's 1890s—and left her in the lobby with a brief kiss on her lips, she was held through the night by his embrace.

October 16, 1969

"Woke up, got out of bed, dragged a comb across my head." The Beatles were so real, I thought, as I was brushing my teeth this morning. I had an 8 a.m. English class that I wanted to cut, but as game 5 of the Series didn't begin until 1:05, I really didn't have any excuse to miss it—not that reading and discussing another short story by O'Henry was going to really further my education.

Ned, on the other hand, didn't need an excuse to miss class. In fact, it wasn't unusual for him to be coming in from his nightly "studies" as I was getting up. His idea of an "all-nighter" with a student body differed dramatically from the rest of the student body. In fact, I had inadvertently experienced his gaiety the previous weekend when, after we had a quick dinner at Tom's Restaurant (future home of Jerry Seinfeld's "corner diner") followed by a few drinks at the West End Bar, Ned had invited me down to the "Village" to hang out. "Hanging out" had actually meant going with him to a club in the West Village (as in the old Meat Market district) in which I experienced my first homosexual dance scene. Even after a few Budweisers, I knew that I didn't want to be groped by a strange man, and so I had left to take the deserted subway home, arriving in a half-stupor back at my dorm at 3 A.M., wallet and body still intact.

But then again, Ned would be the perfect roommate if and when Judy could spend the night with me. We'd have the night alone!

"Ned," I whispered, "today, this is it." He rolled over, totally unexcited about the Mets.

I put my "Let's Go Mets" banner—a white sheet painted with blue letters—out of my latched window, and closed the window on the sheet to keep it in place. That was an idea I had copied from Lisa, my high school "sweetheart," who was advertising her loyalty to the Mets in a similar fashion at Bryn Mawr.

"Shit, Ken, it was great shit last night. We did acid and I'm still tripping. Do you think you could get me into the game? Those blue and orange seats would be like a kaleidoscope."

"Ned, the ticket would be wasted on the wasted you." Baseball wasn't for Ned, not for a bisexual Greek theater major from Regis Catholic High School—not that there was anything wrong with his sexuality as long as I kept my bathrobe on!

"Yeah, but I'd love to be in the men's clubhouse after the game. Champagne, who knows what else popping off."

"Is that all you think about—sex and drugs?" I already knew the answer. "Did you ever get to the Moratorium yesterday?"

"We tried, but after the last joint, it just didn't seem to matter."

"Shit, Ned, if you're against the war, you have to protest. Don't you stand for anything? You're just a fuckin' pothead."

If only my father could hear me now; I really was making up for not using the "s" word or the "f" word while I was growing up. If only my mother heard me now—I shuddered. I knew she'd be shattered. Her memory was fading as a ghost, her influence losing its hold.

"Fuck, if I can't keep from swearing, will I lose her from inside me?" I bemoaned internally.

Ned brought me back to Earth.

"Ken, I was there in mind and spirit, if not in body. Although I'm sure there was plenty of grass there—not that you'd care."

"I just don't want to get busted. How would I know who the undercover cops were? They'd click my picture and bam—end of college and 2S and over to 'Nam. Just what I'm protesting."

"How'd Judy like it? I mean, it wasn't like your suburban, lily-white high school."

"Hey, I had a black kid in my class. And we knew how to protest in Scarsdale. We even played guerrilla warfare during a 20Th Century Revolutions course in summer school. Kids running around the woods, camouflaged, acting like make-believe soldiers. It made *The New York Times* front page. Boys playing men, without the risk. It was real glorification of war."

"Yeah, and how many of your buddies are ever going to enlist or have parents who won't pay for their deferment?"

"Well, we're both 2S, so we should talk."

"Did your dad fight in the war?"

"No, mine was 4F. He had a congenital bad hip. He couldn't even play baseball in high school. It never was a question for him."

"My dad was drafted—fought in the Pacific in WW II. He still has the medals."

"What does he think of this war?"

"We've got to fight them but he still wants me to go to college. But I think he feels guilty about it. His dad didn't want him to go off, to enlist. He wanted him to go to college, become an accountant. But he went anyway. Just like your baseball player, Ted Williams."

"Hey, you know who Ted Williams played for?"

"Just be happy I know he's a baseball player."

"Oh, I forgot, you're not a true American. Don't follow baseball. Boy, Joe McCarthy would've had a field day with you at the Communist hearings in Congress. 'Mr. Darrow, who did Ted Williams play for?' 'I'm afraid I don't know, Senator.' 'You don't know, look him up—you are obviously a Communist pinko—and un-American.' I mean, Ned, you would have been shot as a German spy in WWI—blue eyes, blond hair, they'd have fooled you with, 'Who's the better team, the New York Dodgers or the Brooklyn Yankees?' Boom, blindfolded, shot at dawn."

"You and your baseball—doesn't anything else make a difference to you?"

"Well, not today—but I'm not gonna lose my 2S."

"Boy, would your dad be pissed if that happened."

"Shit, yes. My dad . . . the hypocrisy of his generation. He doesn't want me to go, but he still supports Nixon and the war as long as it's somebody else's kids. Be loyal, don't protest against this great country, but don't send my son! I mean, don't you ever feel guilty that we're here, pontificating about war and about Nietzsche through the night like intellectuals, while those poor guys get their brains blown out in freakin' Vietnam? Except for the Marines, most of who volunteered for this. I mean, no one wants to be there."

"Ken, no wonder they get wasted every chance they get. What kind of fucking war is that? You'd go crazy if you didn't know if the woman or child or old man who comes up to you is the enemy—every minute on the lookout, scared shitless about being blown to hell; or maybe worse, seeing your buddy get blown up next to you. Hey, be wasted or get wasted. I guess it's all the same."

"So, what happens if you fuck up here, Ned? Don't go to classes and get drafted?"

"Easy, Ken, I'll just spread my 'cheeks' for the drill sergeant. That should keep me out."

"What a pleasant thought. Just keep your pecker to yourself. I gotta get to class. Just help me straighten this banner."

"You are a fucking lunatic. They should send you to the Moon. And leave you behind when they take off to return to Earth! That sign comes down tomorrow. They call this the Ivy League?"

"Let's go Mets," I yelled back at him from the hallway.

"You're weird. Don't show your face if they lose. By the way, good luck. Let's go Mets!"

Ned didn't know how much that meant to me—my friend, my crazy, fucking roommate.

I walked across the campus to Hamilton Hall where my freshman English class was being held. I climbed the stairs of this venerable ivy-covered building, where we read Mark Twain and Shakespeare, where we wrote freshman compositions. Forgotten, unknown, or rarely remembered by our freshman class was the fact that this was the site of the initial student occupation in the 1968 protests. There was a semblance of the importance of learning as I sat in class, trying to pay attention to Joe Sanborn, our Instructor in the Department of English (Professor Lionel Trilling he was not), as he discussed plot development in fiction. Joe, as he asked us to call him, sat on the desk. His long, blond hair was neatly combed across his forehead, and he was constantly pushing it out of his eyes with his left hand while his right hand contained his cigarillo. The second-hand- smoke permeated the air. He was adorned in a purple turtleneck and khaki pants, and his short, brown, leather boots were neatly shined.

He droned on and on. How much longer could I stand his drivel? My classmates were gazing out the windows. A few were exploring their newfound academic freedom by poisoning their lungs with the cigarettes that were no longer outlawed in class, now that they were mature college students. My friend Jon sat next to me, wearing his red pajama top that served a dual purpose as a polo shirt, surreptitiously writing on a yellow notebook—probably his Humanities paper due the next day.

I wrote Jon a note: "I'm going to see the Mets today."

"I hope they do better than my Red Sox did two years ago," he scribbled on his pad, tilting it my way. We were reading Joyce's *A Portrait of the Artist as a Young Man,* and my mind was wandering as I listened to Mr. Sanborn (I mean, Joe), hoping for "lightnings of intuition" to help me write the paper; but all I heard was the poem:

"The ivy whines upon the wall

And whines and twines upon the wall."

"Fitting for an Ivy League university," I whispered to Jon.

"And just about as relevant as this class," he said, just a little too loudly, causing Joe to look in his direction. Years later, when I saw the movie "The Paper Chase," I thought of Jon when John Housman speaks to the precocious freshman law student and tells him to call his parents and tell them it is doubtful he'll become a lawyer.

But as Joe droned on about the stream of consciousness of Stephen Dedalus, aka James Joyce, my stream of consciousness remained focused on the World Series. And I realized that anyone who had written about the Miracle Mets a year ago would have been given a "D" for credibility.

I ran back to the dorm after class, quietly opening the door so I wouldn't awaken Ned. Not to worry, he was sound asleep. I laid my book down and proudly placed my blue baseball cap with orange embroidered "NY" on my head. "Proud to be a Mets' fan today."

At the 116th Street IRT station, I picked up copies of *The Daily News* and *The New York Times*. Both had coverage of the Mets' victory, Swoboda's catch, and Martin's base-running acumen, with a photo showing one foot just on the baseline. Sharing space in the papers was the Vietnam protest. *The Times* showed the crowd from behind the podium, with the intellectuals listening to Eugene McCarthy. "There I am—that little speck off to the right," I laughed to myself. If I didn't make it on CBS News last night, maybe I could make it in the tabloids.

There weren't too many people on the subway platform, but a few had Mets' caps. I wondered if they were "merely" fans or if they were lucky enough to also have tickets for today's game. There were no little kids with their dads, though.

The subway "platform voice" announced, "116th Street. Columbia University."

I waited for the doors to open as the train came to a screeching halt. Students arriving for their 10 o'clock classes rushed by. I looked around the car as I got on, and scrambled for a seat as far away from the disheveled, bearded man with his cardboard sign that said "Out of Work. Please help me."

At 96th Street I changed trains as the express rolled in simultaneously. After only a short delay in the tunnel, I was at 42nd Street in ten minutes. I power walked through the corridor to Times Square, and then retraced my steps back down to the Flushing Line.

There were plenty of Mets' fans standing on the platform, despite the fact that a train had just left. It must have been full, I surmised. I looked over at the pretzel booth and saw a middle-aged Indian man take the golden brown twists with coarse white salt on top out of his miniature oven and place them in his warmer; he was ready with a new tray of raw dough with which to repeat the process. This was the culinary specialty of the subway system, the peak of civilization of the dungeon. I looked forward to fresh pretzels, never wanting those that had been sitting under the warming lights for five minutes. I would only buy them if I saw them emerge from the womb while I was waiting.

"Let me have three," I said softly, handing the gentleman a quarter. He barely acknowledged my request, except to pick up the trio with his tongs. His expressionless face made this transaction as impersonal as putting your money into the Chicklet machine—although at least you were guaranteed the product would be delivered.

I ate the first pretzel right there, giving it a minute to cool off, as its warmth literally melted in my mouth. It was crisp on the outside, chewy on the inside, and so fresh and tasty that it didn't need mustard like those famous "Philadelphia pretzels," which need to hide their lack of taste and wooden consistency. This was New York, and we have (notice the present tense) the best. The other two I left in the bag for later at the ballpark, which I preferred to eat instead of the day old pretzels (probably imported from Philadelphia) that were sold and warmed over charcoal outside of the stadium.

As the subway pulled in, I piled into the car, latching onto the steel pole.

"Do you think we're going to win today?" A short, stocky student type with cropped black hair and acne disfiguring his cheeks started up a conversation.

"Hell, yes. We've got Kooz pitching—they've got Cuellar pitching, but he's a lefty, so we'll have Clendonon and Swoboda in the line up."

"I sure hope so. But, still it means Boswell will be on the bench and Al Weis, that weakling, will be playing second base."

"But he's a better defensive player. I mean, defense is what it's all about. Did you see that catch yesterday?"

"No, I was in class."

"Well, I was there. What a play."

"You were lucky. My teacher wouldn't cancel class."

"Oh, for the grand old days of transistor radios smuggled into class."

"Too bad they don't play these games at night. Then everyone could watch," he lamented.

"Yeah, but then we couldn't cut class. It would be the end to a tradition."

"But a night game, with extra innings. How cool would that be— seventh game, everything on the line?"

The future that he saw then has obviously become reality now, with games ending at 12:30 a.m. Eastern Daylight Time. All the East Coast viewers are either asleep or doomed to sleep through work or class the following morning. And don't forget the players, who are bundled up for football weather, in long-sleeve shirts, wearing jackets and gloves, their breath condensing in the 40-degree drizzle.

The trip went fast, probably because I didn't have to be concerned about making Judy a part of the conversation. We talked about who would be the Cy Young Award winner (Tom Seaver was our mutual choice) and Most Valuable Player (I picked Hank Aaron, he picked Cleon Jones, a true hometown choice).

As we got off the train at Shea we parted, colleagues at heart. "Let's go Mets!" he yelled at me, as he walked off toward the left field gate.

"Have a great time," I bellowed, walking towards the first base gate. What I should've said was "Have a great life!"

I was forced towards the turnstiles by the crowd, and held on to my ticket even more possessively than yesterday. I got a free program promoting Sanford Garelick for City Council president (he had come a long way since his days as the police officer who liberated Hamilton Hall from the black students at Columbia University in 1968). There was a notable absence of Black Panthers and war protestors outside today. I doubt they were observing the sanctity of the World Series. They probably realized that the crowd today was too into baseball and the Mets to really care.

My seat was much better on this day—still in the upper deck, but in the 14th row and around first base. I was surrounded by Mets' fans, and had no fear of falling or lack of people to gab with during the game.

The opening ceremony was a brilliant display of the bearing of the colors by the joint military contingent. Shea's flags were at full mast. These were the best and the brightest of the military. After all, they were representing our country's colors; they were the honor guard. Yet they would be sleeping in real beds tonight, with firm mattresses and soft pillows, halfway around the globe from any threat. But their parents could be proud of them; they were serving their country. They didn't run away to Canada, and after the war they would be heroes. They got the respect of the Shea Stadium crowd.

Even the millions of fans who weren't there but saw the game on TV or heard it on radio were drawn in by the emotions of the moment. There would be such hope, despair, celebration, and desperation—all in any one inning. The optimism that we had as the game began quickly faded as the Mets and Jerry Koosman fell behind 3-0 to Frank Robinson and his Orioles.

"Don't count us out yet," I said to the middle-aged executive sitting next to me. "We're not going back to Baltimore."

"I wish I had your confidence. Cuellar is pitching a great game. He looks unhittable."

But in the bottom of the fifth inning, Cuellar's pitch skipped by in the dirt, as Cleon Jones jumped out of the way. Called a ball by the home plate umpire, Jones claimed it had hit him in the foot. It was all for naught until the Mets' manager, Gil Hodges—he of Gil Hodges Night so many years ago—came out to show the ump that the ball had a smudge of shoe polish on it from where it hit Jones. As Cleon took his lead off first base, Donn Clendonon stepped to the plate, and with one swing of the bat his home run brought the Mets to within one run.

We were still behind in the seventh inning, and we talked optimistically, pessimistically, loudly, quietly as Al Weis came up. Al Weis, who had hit just two home runs all season, was playing today only because the regular second baseman, Ken Boswell, had trouble hitting lefties.

"Maybe he can walk," I said to my 'friend.' Then Kooz can sacrifice him to second."

We watched as Cuellar's pitch approached the plate, only to be returned in the opposite direction—a ball hit by Weis probably as hard and as far as he had ever hit one. It looked like batting practice as the ball headed out to the outfield and over the fence. Our own Babe Ruth! No one had ever hit a more important home run.

It was 3-3. We were jumping, yelling, clapping, hugging.

"See, I told you!" My "friend" was turned away from me, cheering with his buddies to his left.

From around the crowd, I heard:

"Al Weis? Who is he?"

"Orioles suck!"

"Let's go Mets!"

It was in the hands of the gods now. The inexplicable force that had propelled us to the Moon and allowed us to return was now about to orbit us to victory.

In the eighth inning, we scored as Cleon Jones slammed a double, followed by a line drive down the left field line by Ron Swoboda. I was standing, screaming, as Don Buford retrieved the ball, but much too late to prevent Jones from scoring the go-ahead run. An error on Jerry Grote's grounder gave us an insurance run.

Only three more outs, and then—we would be World Champions!

In the ninth, Frank Robinson flied out. One down.

Boog Powell followed with a double. Not that his run would count, but now we've lost our cushion.

Brooks Robinson came up, the tying run at the plate. But he hit another fly ball. Two down. Only one more out.

Davey Johnson—yes, the same Davey Johnson who would manage the Mets to our next World Series victory 17 years later—was coming up as the tying run.

We were all standing now—still one out to go—except the jerk behind me.

"Sit down! I can't see!"

I turned to him, incredulous, barking hoarsely, "I've waited eight years for this. I'm not sitting down!"

Eight years of futility, of ninth inning rallies by the other teams, of ninth inning rallies by the Mets falling short. Eight years of losing 26-inning games, of being no-hit, perfect gamed. Eight years of being the "Mutts." Now, I was ready to be saved. Of course, I didn't realize that I was relatively spoiled. Only eight years—nothing compared to the 51 years for the Boston Red Sox, 53 years for the Chicago White Sox, 62 years for the Chicago Cubs. Their fans would have to wait again; they would have to continue to feel the pain, to mourn their loss.

I remembered back to Opening Day, 1962, when my mom had picked us all up from school and we'd met my dad in the city and gone on to the Polo Grounds to watch the Mets lose on a dreary Friday the 13th. I'd been to Gil Hodges Night with my dad—just Dad and myself—watching Rod Kanehl hit a home run off Don Drysdale. And now I was here with my adopted Mets family—strangers in the upper deck—all alone, missing Mom, wishing Dad would still take me to a ballgame.

And as Kooz got ready to pitch, I had to wonder what Davey Johnson was feeling—the last vestige of hope for the Orioles, the team favored to win in a sweep of four games. What an end for his season if he made an out. And then Koozman pitched and Johnson sent a fly ball out to left field. I've learned to watch the fielder rather than the ball, but Cleon Jones was moving back towards the wall. My heart stopped for several beats (just kidding, I didn't need a pacemaker), and then it started up again as he turned to face the plate several feet in front of the warning track. He reached up for the ball, and then fell to his knee as he squeezed the sphere into his glove—the capsule having landed safely on Earth! Mission accomplished!

The celebration began. On the field, the Mets were jumping up and down on one another, hats strewn everywhere. In the stands, we were jumping up and down on one another, hats strewn everywhere. We were family, all 57,397 fans in the stands, along with 25 players, four coaches, and one manager on the field. We were together as the stadium was rocking.

Only the Orioles' 25 players, four coaches, and one manager were leaving the field, collecting their hats, their gear, and heading back into their clubhouse. Their season was over, they were second best, victims of the gods' revenge for their hubris. We had landed on the Moon—our Eagle had landed and returned. And they had crashed and burned into the lunar surface.

The Mets fought their way into their dugout, into their clubhouse, where the champagne corks were popping, the bubbly shampoo was drenching Gil Hodges' crew-cut, and Tom Seaver's neatly cropped hair was being messed up by his teammates' celebration.

The Mets' fans fought their way down onto the field. As we streamed out of the stands, onto the field where our gladiators had slayed the lions, we were screaming, jumping up and down in adoration for our players. We were smiling, laughing, "We did it!" to no one in particular, a cacophony without any distinct conversation between individuals. "We want Tom!" "Let's go Mets!" echoed through the stadium.

I joined the throng of fans trying to run the base paths, stepping on the phantom first base, second base, slowly picking our way through others who were just milling around. As I started towards third, there seemed to be more obstacles in my way than I had ever encountered in a dark movie theater with a high school girlfriend. But as I made it, I realized that, unless I went all the way home, I wouldn't be satisfied. So I weaved my way towards the plate, avoiding collisions with other fans, using others as interference as I headed towards home plate. Home— where it seemed you always wanted to finish, to score a run in baseball, to complete your journey, to experience sexual fulfillment, to rejoin your family in the dugout.

Baseball! "Home Sweet Home."

As I approached the batter's box, there was a hole in the ground. Home plate had been dug up by a fan and snatched away from me.

Shea Stadium was now among the city's homeless. I guess Thomas Wolfe was really right when he wrote, "You can't go home again."

But if I couldn't have been part of the game, at least I was on the field. And if I couldn't be fielding grounders, at least I could be fielding the ground; so I ripped up a piece of the turf for posterity. Thousands of

New Yorkers would return home from Shea that day with their own grass, preserved in plastic bags, where it would dry out over the years; grass that, as it dried, would provide memories that would allow me to float higher than any of Ned's "grass" would get him.

After about 30 minutes, we began to disperse, leaving the field— the fall home of the football New York Jets, now decimated. As we glided towards the subway, no one was in a rush; no one was pushing each other or jostling for position. It was the ultimate anti-New York minute, as the Big Apple slowed down. The trip back to Manhattan was jubilant. As the regular subway riders would get on the train, we would tell them what had happened, sharing the experience.

I didn't have any more classes that afternoon, and I didn't start class until 10 a.m. the next day. I had brought my Calvin and Hobbes monographs with me to read, but, obviously, they were still in my bag, only the World Series program lay open on my lap.

I decided to get off at 42nd Street and Grand Central Terminal and take the train home to Scarsdale. I figured I could see Judy for a while, then go home and celebrate with my dad, and drive back into the city with him in the morning. I got out at the Bryant Park exit and walked up the stairs from the subway back into the sunlight.

The park was relatively empty now, and most of the litter from yesterday's Moratorium was cleaned up by John Lindsay's sanitation crew. Instead of throngs of protestors with angry fists raised, there were crowds of New Yorkers on their way home from work, on their way home to their apartments or suburban split-level homes, on their way home to their pets, their wives, their children, their parents. I went up to the statue of William Cullen Bryant, a bearded man sculpted in a seated position who was overlooking his park. His repose was juxtaposed with the speakers from yesterday's moratorium, who had risen from the platform erected next to him. I read with interest his poem inscribed on the statue's base:

> *"Yet let no empty gust of passion*
> *Find an utterance in thy lay.*
> *A blast that whirls the dust*

Along the howling street and dies away.
But feelings of calm power and mighty sweep
Like currents journeying through the windless deep."

Ralph Ashford or Eugene McCarthy? Abbie Hoffman or Bobby Kennedy? Eldridge Cleaver or Martin Luther King? Who should we follow? Who should our generation follow? I found solace and peace in the words of the park's poet.

I turned away to join the commuters on their way home, each one alone. But today, instead of looking at their watches, hurrying along, many were congregating in the park, being regaled by stories of my fellow spectators from Shea. We were all smiling, New Yorkers spirited together. Even among those who were politically "radicalized," thoughts of the Black Panthers and SDS were shunted "underground" tonight. The thrill of victory certainly beat the agony of defeat.

I made my way to Grand Central carrying my reading material and the morning editions of *The Daily News* and *The New York Times* with pictures of the moratorium crowd, along with photos of Ron Swoboda's catch. As I passed through the historical architectural building, surrounded by its grandeur, I glanced at the evening edition of *The Daily News.*

"CHAMPS."

On the cover was the Shea victory celebration with crowds on the field. And I could imagine that I was one of the specks. As I bought the paper, I now had two editions of *The Daily News* from October 16, 1969. The morning edition showed New Yorkers protesting against DuPont, the makers of the defoliant napalm, in a Bryant Park in full glory with its foliated trees; and the evening edition showed New Yorkers celebrating, as we participated in the exfoliation of Shea Stadium.

I quickly called Lil and told her I would be home for dinner. "No problem, I'll just cook another chicken."

I called Judy and asked if I could see her.

‹ "Sure Ken, but come after 9. I have an appointment, remember?" As if I could forget.

I walked by the Oyster Bar Restaurant. There was a television playing above the bar. And all eyes, from the commuters sitting on the bar stools to those of us standing behind, were watching Walter Cronkite smile as he talked about the Miracle Mets' World Series victory. The lead story, bringing all New Yorkers back together (except maybe the lowly Yankee fans) was the pandemonium on the field and in the clubhouse at Shea Stadium. At least for tonight, the Vietnam Moratorium seemed to be placed on the back burner. As the commercial for Bayer Aspirin came on, it seemed that the pains of the divisiveness that our great city had felt yesterday had now subsided—but, unfortunately, as with the effect of pain-killers on the headaches caused by a brain tumor, the relief was only temporary. Only by removing the cancer, or radiating it, could the suffering be brought to an end.

I had to run to catch the 6:40. The train was packed with commuters. Businessmen, accountants, and insurance executives, along with a smattering of "feminist" businesswomen, were juxtaposed with the society ladies returning from a visit to the Museum of Modern Art or, perhaps, a tryst at the Plaza Hotel. For the business-people, it was their pre-family time, when they could have a drink, read the paper, and decompress from work before they went home—to teenagers in crisis, bored wives or philandering husbands, and, if they were lucky, little kids and dogs greeting them with unconditional love. Some were reading *The Wall Street Journal* (Yankee fans, I guessed), while in the bar car, a middle-aged attorney with graying hair and aviator glasses was holding court, dissecting the World Series game he had watched on the television in his office.

I got several side-glances from the drinking crowd as I wasn't dressed for the "bar." In my bellbottoms jeans and brown and black plaid pea coat, my hair longer and more unruly, I represented the "child" at home about whom they despaired, worrying if "I" would smoke dope, get busted, drop out of college, get drafted, and go to 'Nam. But little did they know that I was tonight's expert, that I had first-hand experience about what had happened today at Shea. As I listened, I could barely contain myself from correcting any misstatements. After all, didn't I have the responsibility to make sure that the truth and nothing but the truth was expounded?

Thirty minutes later, the "gospel son" got off the train in Scarsdale and walked the mile home.

Hope was the first to greet me. I still missed her nightly snuggling, as I always had and always would. She was always there for me (except when someone else had food for her), never complaining about being left behind.

"Hey, Ken, what are you doing here?" Marty asked.

"Just got home from the game. We won!"

"Well, don't expect to stay up late tonight in our bedroom. It's mine now, and I've got a big test tomorrow."

My dad got home at 8:15.

"Ken, what a surprise. Did you see the game on TV?"

"Dad, I was there!"

"Wow."

And I showed him my ticket, my program, my grass—the only kind he had ever seen.

"Let me go to the bathroom and then you can tell me all about it."

"Dinner's ready," Lil yelled several minutes later. The table was set for five—a mom, a dad, and three sons.

And now there were two chickens broiled to perfection, with crispy skins covered with garlic salt and lots of butter. There was enough for everyone; no need to share a chicken breast or wing. And she had thrown in some frozen crinkled French fries—never as good as McDonald's—along with a green salad.

Lil and Richie and Marty listened as I held court, telling my dad exactly what had happened . . . about the shoe polish, about Al Weis' home run. It was an event described over dinner by the 57,000 fans who had attended the game that day. And it was an event described at parties around New York in weeks to come by the "100,000" fans who had "attended" the game.

At 9:30 p.m., I went up to my dad's room. He was lying on his bed next to Lil, in his boxer shorts, white T-shirt. and socks, his old leather hip brace tethered to his back. "I'm going out to see Judy for a while, if that's okay with you. Can I get a ride with you in the morning?"

"Sure. Now I know why you came home!"

Lil laughed.

"Hey, I wanted to share today with you. It all started with our first game at Yankee Stadium, then Opening Day at the Polo Grounds in '62, Opening Day at Shea in '64."

"Don't forget that day at the Polo Grounds when you almost fell out of the stands."

"How could I forget? And the soldiers saved my life, right, Pop?"

"Lil, I didn't even watch the game, I was so nervous."

"I know, Bill."

"Yeh, Dad, but now I'm all grown up. I wish you could've come with me today."

"Bad hip, upper deck—are you trying to cripple me, boy?" He laughed.

"No, Dad. But thanks. See you in the morning. Love you."

I pecked Lil and him on their cheeks and went out to the car.

Mary and Maurice spent their second day together. Maurice picked Mary up from the Roosevelt Hotel around 11 a.m. and took her to that gourmet establishment, Horn and Hardart's. Mary was like a little child as she deposited her quarter and dime into the slots, then put her hand into the little, heated cubicle to take out a ceramic dish filled with macaroni and cheese, golden brown on top and baked to perfection. She had some lima beans, a bit mushy she thought, and then for dessert, for another dime and nickel, a piece of lemon meringue pie. It was not quite as good as MJ's key lime pie, but not bad for a northern joint. It was all washed down with a cup of "java," as it was known in New York City. Maurice had his staple of potato pancakes and applesauce, along with a piece of cherry pie. They finished up their meal and then Mary, again, sat through four more showings of "Midnight Cowboy," the first one down in the audience, in case the manager checked up on Maurice, and the last three with him in the projection room, eating popcorn and holding hands, with just a little bit of making out.

After the evening showing, Maurice took Mary to Sardi's for her first taste of the splendor of the city. They sat next to post-theater goers, including middle-aged couples talking about "Hair" who were thrilled and appalled by the nudity. It was almost 11 p.m. when they took a cab back to Maurice's loft in the West Village.

They sat and talked, burned some incense, and relaxed in each other's arms. Slowly they began to kiss.

"Let's get stoned," he whispered.

"Maurice, try something different tonight. Let's be close without the grass."

And so they experienced the gentleness, the passion, the excitement that loving could provide not censored by drugs or alcohol, allowing each to feel their partner's presence. Her head was spinning, but it was not out of control; it was spiraling around her new man and his developing love for her.

Judy had school the next day and her parents were home, so after telling them about the game, she and I went out to the park, where she showed me her pills and described how they wouldn't take effect for several weeks. That limited us to a brief petting session that night, our sexual desires only partially satisfied.

It was around 11 p.m. when I got home. My parents' light was out, and only the blue haze from the television shone from under their door. I climbed upstairs, where Marty was already asleep. Hope was sitting on his bed, her eyes reflecting the glare from the street light outside my window. CBS News was on—more about Vietnam, more about the Mets.

I got under my covers; the fresh sheets were courtesy of Lil. I whispered, patting my bed, "Come on over, Hope." I watched for a few minutes.

It was ironic. The war in Vietnam would cost us 55,000 soldiers — a sold-out Shea Stadium of young Americans lost over in Southeast Asia.

Hope jumped over to my bed, crawled into my lap, licked my face, and then burrowed her way under the covers, turning herself around and around, as if in reverse orbit, as she curled up in my lap. I felt secure, comforted—as close to Mom as I could be. And then I closed my eyes with her in my arms, home again, hoping for endless sleep.

DUTY TO HONOR ME

October 16, 1999

I rewound *The New York Times* microfilm from 1969. As it returned to January 1st, the tape pulled away from the spindle and started spinning wildly, the whirling noise awakening the student sleeping next to me.

Flash forward with me 30 years, to October 16, 1999. The world was readying itself as we were on the "eve of destruction." Y2K was about to be upon us—annihilation not by cancer from radiation, nor by the now "contained" (at least in the U.S.) Human Immunodeficiency Virus, but, rather by contamination by computer viruses, and now, more imminently, by the possibility that everything would stop, that the world would come to an end, that we would be destroyed by lack of foresight. The simple binary computer switch from 1999 to 2000 caused as much trepidation as the single, red, nuclear button in the president's office. In the '60s, we had feared being blown back into the Middle Ages. But now, in 1999, our trip back would be shorter, only to 1900—but just as devastating, as all power would be shut off, all records up in "smoke."

The political decade of the '60s ended with the Vietnam War in full force and 600,000 American troops still oversees. Nixon talked of peace with honor; Henry Kissinger went to Paris to talk and talk; Ho Chi Minh died; and the South Vietnamese government remained corrupt. Nixon secretly bombed Cambodia, and students across America protested against continuing imperialism. The generation gap widened when, in May of 1970, my first year at Columbia, four students were dead in Ohio —killed at Kent State University by the National Guard during an anti-war protest. Across the country, there was an escalation of anti-war protests, not against any specific university or university activity, but in general against Nixon's handling of the war in Vietnam and Cambodia. And predictably, at Columbia we went "on strike and shut it down," once again during my freshman year, ensuring that I wouldn't have to go into the Mathematics Building to take my calculus final! And, unlike 1968, even the jocks supported the strike!

The next two years went by "quietly," years dedicated to studying and my relationship with Judy. I had been able to hover over all of this controversy, seemingly unscathed, remaining liberal, protesting the war legitimately. I had started as a political science major, assuming a career in law, government, or politics. But I switched to pre-med after becoming aware that senators and congressmen, and, even more so, state and local officials, usually had only a small political impact on a large mass of people. I foresaw a career as an attorney and as a councilman in Tenafly, New Jersey, having an even more negligible impact on an even smaller mass of people. My decision to apply to medical school would ensure that: 1) I would have a large amount of influence on the lives of a more definable set of patients; and 2) the additional four years of 2S draft status would protect me from my lottery number "56." And even though in 1973 the draft no longer loomed over my graduating class, I continued to pursue my goal of medicine, of healing disease, of curing patients with cancer.

In April 1972, the last month of my junior year at Columbia College, the "peace" was broken as I watched from my window in Hartley Hall as the police again were called on by the university administration to clear Hamilton Hall of anti-war protesters. And, boy, was my dad pissed off at the effect any student strike would have on my application to Columbia Medical School!

Later that fall, Nixon and Agnew were re-elected, only to have Agnew soon resign in disgrace because of tax evasion charges from when he lived in Maryland. The Democratic Headquarters in Watergate were broken into by Republican stooges, and the trail led straight to the presidency—as "Deep Throat" leaked the damaging clues. The 18 minutes of missing tape recording from Nixon's White House was the final straw in his downfall. Nixon was disgraced and then, the following summer, while Judy and I were sitting at a campsite in Yellowstone National Park, we watched on a portable black and white television, with a make-shift antenna fashioned out of a metal coat hanger, as he resigned due to his participation in the Watergate cover-up.

I was accepted into Columbia Medical School. I learned medicine at the same time as my patients and I experienced the two-tiered medical system, the loss of dignity of the poor and minority patients lying in 12-bed wards, the beds separated by curtains, while the private patients had their care given in the private or semi-private rooms of the new wing of the hospital.

Vietnam became a secondary battle, and by 1975, as our last troops helicoptered out from the roofs of Saigon buildings, the United States military was out of Vietnam—and as predicted, Saigon would fall to the North Vietnamese. But the world did not come to an end. Democracy was still safe. However, the War was over, Nixon was no longer in the Oval Office, and Gerald Ford, the only president never elected by national ballot, pardoned "Tricky Dick," so the country could get on with its business of making money and healing wounds.

The Vietnam Vets came back to the United States—all except those who died in the jungles or were missing in action or remained in prison camps. Those who came home often did not return to a hero's welcome. There was the shame of having fought in the first war that the United States had lost. There was the stigma of having fought in what many thought was an immoral war. There were no instant jobs, no parades—just months in veterans' hospitals overcoming loss of limbs and loss of minds, combined with drug addiction, Agent Orange toxicity, and the not-yet-identified scourge of post-traumatic stress disorder.

I didn't marry Judy—or, more accurately, she didn't marry me. We were together, off and on, for seven years, losing our virginity with each other. Through our journey together, she would leave at times, choosing to have several relationships with what I considered "bad" boys, forsaking her "good" boyfriend for all others, until she eventually went to grad school and found peace with another "good" guy, an attorney (heaven forbid) from NYU Law School.

My cousin Bruce died in January, 1977, of a burst brain aneurysm at the age of 41—the same age as his favorite cousin, my mom. And as with my mom, he left behind three wonderful boys in their teenage years and a loving spouse. My faith had survived that January evening in 1966—but now, eleven years later, almost to the day, I lost my faith in the all-powerful God. How could this have happened over and over again to such wonderful people!

But now I had both breast cancer and brain aneurysms to cure.

I would date several of Judy's friends through medical school, but eventually I married an Irish Catholic nurse who I had met in the ICU at Roosevelt Hospital in New York. After I finished my fellowship in cardiology on Long Island among the middle and upper class whites of Long Island and the blacks and Puerto Ricans at Queens General Hospital in Jamaica, we made a mutual decision to abandon the city (and the Mets, who were going through a prolonged rebuilding phase) to move to rural New Jersey to practice our professions in the land of farmers and horses.

Nor did Mary marry Ronnie, Maurice or Tony—the red, white, and black boys of America. Instead, she chose to marry a Jewish boy with a hankering for making money as an accountant—and a wandering eye.

Both Mary and I had a child—my Jannie being the "bestest daughter a dad could have." But each of us, finding ourselves unhappy in our marriage, got divorced, making four attorneys rich in the process. We could've written an article for *Cosmopolitan:* "Jewish Men and Catholic Women Gone Wrong."

Mary moved to New York with her son, Jordan, a budding child actor. She did get back together with Tony for five years, and he provided the father figure for Jordan that his own father didn't provide. But as Tony's life as a big league baseball player and coach led to increasing stress, their relationship ended and she became a single mom, supporting a college student.

Lil died in 1986, probably from the breast cancer she had been "cured" of five years before my father married her. She lived long enough to see Michael, her oldest son, along with her three step-sons, become physicians; her two middle children become struggling social

workers; and her baby, Ritchie, a true spirit of the '60s, become a struggling artist in the gentrified Haight-Ashbury section of San Francisco.
My last conversation with her was the day she called to congratulate me
on my passing the Cardiology Boards. At least there was a sense of completion, of letting her know that she had helped me to achieve my goal.

My practice of cardiology matured, as I overcame my fear of making a mistake, of killing a patient. My anxiety with seeing each patient
was at least partially replaced by a sense that, as long as I did my best,
tried my hardest, and didn't cut corners, I would be an asset to them. I
kept Mom inside of me, attempting the miracle of denying that I had left
her behind, trying to make sure she would have been proud of me. So I
became an "esteemed" member of my now suburban community of
Flemington, New Jersey, and the Hunterdon Medical Center. I had the
honor of treating many of our county's veterans of WWII, the Korean
War, and of course, Vietnam, in my practice—and learned about the impact of Post Traumatic Stress Syndrome on heart disease from my care of
one of them.

And in 1994, when the Democratic mayor died (no, she wasn't my
patient, as many people would ask), I was one of the few Democrats in
town even willing to be put on the list of three candidates to replace her.
I guess I was viewed as the least of the three evils by the Republican-
controlled council, who felt that I would only want to "play" at being
mayor and serve out the remaining months until the fall election, when I
would put my political science fantasy behind me and allow the real boys
and girls to take over. Instead, I put my political science fantasy in front
of me, and ran for election myself, helping the Democrats to sweep into
control on the issue of openness during public meetings, and more importantly, on the issue of how to properly finance the rehabilitation of the
sewer system. Ah, the crises of local politics.

Jannie became the "Little Mayor" as my slogan "Mayor Kutscher
Cares," with a red heart and blue background, won the "hearts" of my
electorate.

Jannie played recreation softball and I played out my fantasy in an
over-40 hardball league. We traveled to Iowa to the "Field of Dreams,"
where Jannie and I played catch, father and child. I took her to Shea Sta-

dium to watch the Mets, teaching her that baseball is about being with loved ones.

Back in New York City, Mary was hard at work managing an Ob-Gyn practice in SoHo, supporting Jordan's education at Trinity College in Dublin. Her mom had died in the '80s of an inoperable brain tumor and her father had just died of terminal egotism and old age. Her sister, Katrina, and her step-families were no longer part of her spiritual center of gravity, as Buddhism had brought Mary from orbiting out in the stratosphere back to within herself, where she found peace and understanding with the Dali Lama.

But what brought us, our two planets in orbits, near enough to exert their *gravitational* forces on each other, was not baseball, not space exploration. What brought our two different spirits together was the memory of the Vietnam War.

My goal as mayor was to lead a government and council that worked together, ruling by consensus, playing well together in the sandbox. I enjoyed being mayor. It took about three or four hours per week, mainly in the evening and on weekends, rarely interfering with my cardiology practice, as I learned to delegate well. I brought medicine and government together by passing an ordinance making Flemington the first municipality in New Jersey to make it not only illegal to sell tobacco products to minors but also for minors to possess them—all in the name of cardiac preventive health.

Other than that, I tried to serve as a guiding light for my community, with my most solemn moments during my brief annual speeches at the Memorial Day Parade. Every year I tried to sanctify the sacrifices of our servicemen and women, making the holiday a day of remembrance, not of sales and picnics—nor of a day off for my birthday.

Several years before, my family had gone to a ceremony in upstate New York, where a replica of the Vietnam War Wall was being displayed. So moved were we by this that I had applied to the sponsors to have the Wall come to Flemington. And five months ago, an unexpected cancellation had led us to receive an invitation to jump the two years on the waiting list, if we could accommodate them on this short notice.

My Veteran's Alliance had sprung into action, performing the miracle. They had organized, volunteered, raised money, and worked with our police and parks departments. They had pulled it off. The setting was a secluded park on the edge of Flemington, a football field-sized clearing surrounded by trees. It was a bucolic fall evening.

Earlier that day, Mary's managing doctor, Dena, had received a phone call from her brother, an insurance broker in New Jersey.

"Mary," Dena said while chewing her falafel sandwich during the five-minute lunch break, "my brother asked me to go out tomorrow to somewhere in New Jersey to honor our uncle who died in the Vietnam War."

"What kind of ceremony is it?"

"He said it's a replica of the Vietnam Wall. Your father was military, wasn't he? Do you want to go with me?"

"I don't know. No one in my family died in Vietnam; but I do know my Aunt Kitty's brother-in-law died outside of Danang."

"Do you remember his name?"

"I knew it was a Jacobs or a Jacobson. I'll know it when I see it. There must be a directory."

"Then you'll come? You know I get lost anytime I leave the city."

"Where in New Jersey?"

"Flemington."

"Where is Farmington?"

"Flemington! I don't know. It can't be that far away."

"Go check the Internet and then we'll decide."

Ten minutes later she said, "50 miles southwest."

"Sounds like farm country to me."

"Well, it may be, Mary, but it's right up your alley. They have an outlet center there and Flemington Furs. You know, Joan Hamburg on WOR 710, Rambling with Gambling."

"Why not? That jerk Francois whom I'm renting from is being a real pain in my ass. Let's go."

"Pick me up at 1, so you can go shopping."

"Okay, meet you at Sixth Ave. and 9th Street."

I sat in the front row of speakers at the opening ceremonies as Jannie—now 11 years old, wearing her best pink dress—fidgeted at my side. We were both tired. She had watched me play center field earlier that Sunday morning for my "Over 40" Hunterdon Bucks hardball team, where I had amazed her by slamming a line-drive double and making a backhand catch of a long fly ball.

Janie and I stood up to walk to the podium. It was quite a metamorphosis from the 11-year-old string bean who earlier in the afternoon had been wearing her riding outfit, her brown hair pinned underneath her black helmet, as she cantered her horse, Ben, around and around the indoor ring. She would alternate listening to her instructor telling her to change her leads and smiling at me each time she passed the spot where I was standing. My face wore a mixture of pride and anxiety as she jumped each three-foot railing. I'm sure my expression and inner emotions mimicked those of my dad that one and only time he had watched me as I faced a fastball in my first Little League plate appearance.

As we reached the podium, I whispered to her, telling her how lucky we were to be able to have shared our afternoon together. But what was unspoken was that our lost soldiers wouldn't have this opportunity to enjoy this summer evening. Their families were all congregated, along with the veterans, some in their military dress uniforms, clean shaven, with polished shoes and others in their camouflage fatigues with green berets—more like the image of the soldiers we had seen on Channel 2 during Dan Rather's reports in the '60s. They were reminiscent of the introspective soldier who was interviewed after the walk on the Moon.

That my first wife was not there explained a lot about our family relationship.

That my dad and new step-mom were not there was a function of his infirmity and the difficulty he had walking on rough surfaces. He had remained self-centered in his work, and there was probably yet another journal to be published the next month, "with so little time to complete it." But more importantly I figured there was really no place for my dad here, who, through no fault of his own, was a legitimate 4F during World War II with his severe congenital hip disorder that continued to plague him all of his life. It was as debilitating as most war injuries, and he progressively limped and required a cane. His ambivalence regarding the protests against the war and the role of Columbia University in military research didn't keep him from obtaining a psychiatric colleague's letter regarding medical deferment for one of his students. I was sure that the war was just a distant nightmare for him, to be forgotten. So, as on the nights when he was late for the ceremony for me to receive my Boy Scout badge, when he missed my Little League games, he wasn't there with Jannie and me this night. Let's face it—I had watched him try to be a grandfather as he had awkwardly picked up Jannie when she was an infant. It just didn't seem to come naturally then, and I'm sure it hadn't when I was her age.

That Mom wasn't there—that sort of explained everything for me. Even 15 years of psychotherapy couldn't undo the empty feeling inside.

As I stood in front of all of these people, I had this final thought— my final guilt. What was I doing here?

True, I had initiated the application and received confirmation that Flemington would be honored by having the Moving Wall within its borders. I had pleaded that the Wall be constructed not on an open field on a state highway but, rather, in our Borough Park. But, it was still truly the Veterans' Alliance's project. They had raised the money, made the logistical arrangements, volunteered their time to staff the events, and constructed the Wall—all in memory of their fallen comrades.

As I had formulated my speech, initially I viewed my role as the mayor of the town in which the Wall was erected. I could welcome the audience, and then reiterate the speech I gave on Memorial Day, passing on the respect of our community for the fallen heroes and their families.

I certainly couldn't talk as a veteran, and I felt inadequate and fraudulent as I thought about what to say. I hadn't fought and I hadn't wanted to fight or die. I had protested the war, even if it was to bring our soldiers back home so they wouldn't be listed on this Wall.

But tonight, with these feelings of guilt, of shame in avoiding fighting, I almost felt worse than if I would have been wounded in Vietnam. And there would have been no shame if I had died fighting in Vietnam. My 2S deferment, my medical school enrollment, and the fact that the draft ended before I graduated from college legitimized my non-involvement for everyone except me.

It is shameful that with all of my generation's protests against our government's waging an unjust war, no one in my college class talked about the need to honor those who had died fighting for our country in the fervent hope of preserving democracy. Our generation showed its immaturity, its schizophrenia, its cognitive dissonance, as our hatred of the war was so overwhelming that we couldn't separate the individual men and women who fought and died believing they were protecting our freedom from the leaders who sent them to fight this war. They were merely heeding the call of their government. Whatever anger we had towards Johnson, Nixon, and Westmorland had been inappropriately transferred to these victims of the nationalist, imperialist, fascist, and communist elements of the world—the sins of government passed on to their children.

I began to speak, hoping Jannie would remember the words I was pronouncing slowly and distinctly. I kept the secret to myself that I was hoping to feel some exoneration of my guilt as I spoke to the veterans who my father had not fought next to and who I had allowed to take my place in a war that, in the end, left us without glory. Only bravery and sacrifice were left in the sanctity of their memories.

"Each of us has been asked to limit our remarks to two minutes. This may not seem like a long time, but it is an eternity to a soldier waiting for the enemy to pass by or for the Medivac chopper to arrive. And it is long enough for a loved one to die in a foreign land.

Today reminds me of past Memorial Days, where we have stood with citizens to mourn those who have died in service. Thankfully, there is none of the feeling we often see on that day in which shopping at the mall outweighs the true solemnity of our ceremony. As citizens, we must respect that day as one of great sadness and mourning, along with praise and honor.

Two years ago, when my family visited the Wall in upstate New York, we realized that there was a way to get the community involved in honoring those who have fallen. And through the dedication of the Veteran's Alliance and the employees of our Borough, Flemington is proud to sponsor the Moving Vietnam Wall.

It seems to me that this Wall symbolizes what was wrong and what is right with America.

What was wrong is that our soldiers died in a war that so divided our country. That our generation in protesting the war did it at the expense of neglecting to support our soldiers. What is right is that we can come here today to mourn for those brave men and women who have died and to say goodbye.

What was wrong is that our Vietnam Veterans did not receive the hero's welcome from their country when they returned to the states.

What must be made right is for our generation to honor these brave soldiers, loyal to each other and this country.

What is wrong is that our present generation of students has so little understanding of what our soldiers sacrificed. What will be right is that together, children and parents, soldiers and families, will come to the Wall to learn, to mourn, and to heal. For it is through the tears and love of this generation that we can ensure that our heroes will not be forgotten, not only today, not only on Memorial Day, but everyday."

As Janie and I took our seats, I heard one of the vets say, "Thank you, Mayor, for your words." They had been nice words that seemed sincere, but how come I still felt empty? I looked up at the Wall and the answer was written 55,000 times.

Later, I walked over to the black, multi-paneled memorial, to see if any names were familiar to me, if any acquaintances had the misfortune of being "honored" here. I made a rubbing of the names of the two heroes from Flemington. And I searched for the names of those who had also died so prematurely on January 10, 1966, the same day as my Mom, destroyed by an unseen enemy, leaving behind loving families.

Mothers and sisters and fathers and brothers approached the Wall, wreaths in their hands, laying them at the base of the memorial where their sons and brothers were honored. Not much to leave behind after 35 years of absence; and all so transient in nature, as the Wall would be leaving in five days.

"That was a wonderful speech."

I turned and saw stunning, youthful women with shining white hair. She reminded me of a beautifully matured Betty Sue from my teenage magazine fantasies. As Humphrey Bogart would have said, "There's no way she was from around this town."

"Thank you."

"Your daughter is beautiful. You must be so proud."

"She is my little princess."

"I know, my little prince is now off in college."

"We're so lucky there's no draft now."

"I know, although all of my family were military."

"Are any of them listed here?"

"No, thank heavens. I just drove down from the city with a friend to be with her and her family."

"Oh, I went to school in New York. Do you live there?"

"Where else is there to live up North? I live in the West Village. Where'd you go to school?"

"Columbia College and Med School."

"You're a doctor?"

Pointing to my beeper I said, "Unfortunately."

"I didn't think doctors knew how to make speeches."

"I guess I'm special." I laughed, self mockingly. "By the way, I'm Ken Kutscher."

"No, you are special. I'm Mary, Mary McAuliffe. I'm the office manager at SoHo Gyn and my doctors have no bedside manners."

"Well, it's a pleasure to meet you. Here's my card if your friend ever needs a cardiologist, or if you ever need help with a parking ticket."

"How'd you know? I always need help with those."

"Yeah, I can get them to double the fine."

"Very funny."

"Hey, you'd better get back soon. This town folds up early at night. It's not like you're used to. God, I do miss the city from my college days. So much to do. Here, it's dead."

"Well, thanks for your advice. And thank you for bringing the Wall to New Jersey."

"It sure is different from the last time I was part of an event regarding the Vietnam War in New York. I remember Bryant Park in the city on Moratorium Day in October, 1969."

"You were there? So was I."

"Oh yeah, I remember you. You were the girl with long, dark hair, jeans and a peace T-shirt listening to the speeches."

"Yeah, and you were the guy with long, blond hair, jeans and a peace T-shirt listening to the speeches."

We both laughed.

"It's hard having been there and being here now."

"What do you mean?"

"Like, here are all of the vets who were fighting the war we opposed. They thought we were protesting against them. As far as they're concerned, our generation let them down."

"I don't know about you, but I was just trying to get them home safely."

"Of course, but I also didn't want to die there."

"Mayor, honey, neither did they."

"Hey, Daddy, let's go. I'm hungry."

"Soon, Jannie, I just have to say goodbye to some of the people here."

"I'd better let you go. Here's my card if your wife ever needs a second gyn opinion."

"I doubt she'd listen to me. We're on our own now."

"Sorry to hear that."

"Life goes on."

"Daddy, please. I'm starving." Jannie grabbed my hands in hers and started whirling us around and around, until she got dizzy and fell into my arms.

"Okay. We'll go in a minute. By the way, Jannie, this is Mary. She came all the way down from New York City."

"Hi, Jannie."

"Hello, Mary. I know New York. That's where I go with my mom to the opera."

"Such a cultured young lady."

"Thank you. Dad, let's go."

"Well, doctor mayor, or is it mayor doctor, have a wonderful life."

As we left, Jannie asked, "What's culture?"

A few months later, the veterans celebrated the Vietnam Wall ceremony with a party thanking all concerned. They showed me their appreciation by giving me one of the directional signs and a cube of pictures from the event. It was a small degree of acceptance. And they invited me to join the Marine Corps League.

But what I really wanted was something that the veterans would never be expected to understand—that my protest was against the United States government that sent them to Vietnam, not against them. I wished that I could have replayed for them Reverend Coffin's speech over 40 years ago at Bryant Park, when he said,

"We pledge to say no to this war, to say yes to peace" and then he concluded with: "to say yes to the lives of our fighting men, whose courage in this most tragic conflict goes without saying."

I wanted our veterans to know that I was not a part of the society that had rejected them when they returned home safely, but that I was a doctor, helping my patients with post-traumatic stress disorder.

What I really wanted but could never expect to get, nor deserved to get, was their forgiveness—forgiveness for not being there next to them risking my life, for allowing their colleagues to die instead of me.

What made me so special?

# # # # #

Anyway, these were the events that shaped our lives. Anyone who lived in the '60s experienced and was affected by them—except for those who were either computer geeks or continuously stoned. When the '70s and '80s came around, memories faded. As Annie in "The Field of Dreams" calmly screams at Beulah, the book-burning woman who indignantly claimed she had, indeed, "experienced the sixties,"

"No, I think you had two fifties and moved right into the seventies."

There were those men and women in the United States who were embattled during the '60s—the poor, the blacks, and the other minorities fighting for their lives, fighting a system that kept them "in their places." Their inability to achieve social and economic equality because of racial and economic discrimination led to rioting in the cities, with death and destruction which paralleled the experiences of their brothers and sisters in Vietnam and left scars throughout the nation that are still healing one or two generations later.

For all of us, there are memories that we would like to forget, to wipe off the slate, to remove from our hard drives. Most have adjusted, but PTSD is still rampant amongst those soldiers who have returned home. Some relieve the pain with alcohol, others with pharmaceutical remedies. But as everyone knows from watching Jack Bauer on "24," even data "erased" from a computer can still be retrieved and wreak havoc.

There are also the memories of music, love, and friendship that we want to save to our USB flash drives, to be available to us wherever and whenever we are in need of comfort. And there are the visions of John and Bobby Kennedy, Marilyn Monroe, the men and women who died in Vietnam, and, for me, most of all, my mom—all of whom have died but will remain in our minds as forever young, never being ravaged by old age or arthritis. No matter, each of us has been shaped by our experiences in an individual manner, leaving us vulnerable, powerful, depressed—who we are today.

Each of you, as a reader, has your own story. The stories don't all end happily or with final resolution. Fifty-five thousand soldiers were mourned by their families. Their sons and daughters, husbands and wives, fathers and mothers were left behind in grief, along with a ravaged Vietnam whose population and villages had been destroyed. In addition, thousands of families in America were torn apart as sons deserted to Canada, as daughters protested the war. And on the home front, tens of thousands died of drug overdoses, gunshot wounds, and infections due to IV drug use and sexually transmitted diseases.

It's easy to invoke memories of the '60s. Dress people up with hippie clothes and long hair, play rock 'n' roll songs in the background, and you can capture the spirit of the baby boomers. Or to paraphrase the "voice" in "Field of Dreams," "If you 'film it,' people will reminisce." Dress our veterans in their combat fatigues, their military boots, and weapons, and we should weep. But how many others, like today's teenage boys, will glorify war and death on their GameBoys, with the sanctity of life, of heroism, lost by the push of the replay button. As real as the blood looks, there is no permanent "dying" in video games.

Well, this book is just what we needed, another coming-of-age memoir by a middle-upper class spoiled white boy! I promise that the historical background is accurate. And I apologize to any of my friends or family for any discrepancies between your memories and mine. But as with *The Catcher in the Rye*, J.D. Salinger's tale of a teen in rebellion, published in the year of my birth, my individual story pales when compared to the suffering of the impoverished in America and the soldiers abroad. Like most of the 99% of my generation who were never featured on the CBS Evening News, Mary and I don't consider ourselves heroes or villains. But we did believe in our ideals.

And so I've written a "history" of the world that was around me, of the coming-of-age of a generation living through the Cold War, space exploration, the civil rights movement and the tragedy of the Vietnam War. It is a remembrance of who and what we left behind—our loved ones, our innocence, our inner cities, and the souls of those who fought for what they believed to be the forces of the greater good.

Well, as Walter Cronkite would have said, "And that's the way it is." I've written enough so that maybe I'll understand my parents better. I can only hope that Jannie will understand me a bit better, that her own memoir will be softer and less traumatic. But I doubt it; coming-of-age isn't that simple!

June 8, 2001, 10 p.m.

It was almost two years since the Moving Vietnam Wall, and Mary and I had been married for two months. Our divergent pasts had led to a convergence of inner souls, a sense that we were now one, a completed unit. Maybe we were able to heal each other, to fill the empty spaces our childhoods had left us with. But although I finally found someone I could love without fearing that she would leave me, to say that Jannie easily accepted another woman in my life would be an understatement. But we were all trying our best.

When we got home that night from the library, Jannie headed straight for the computer.

"Jannie, you have to read some of the book first, then take notes, then make an outline, and then you can write the paper."

"Dad, let me do it myself."

"Jannie, you'll never get it all done by tomorrow. Why'd you wait so long?"

"Ken, come on downstairs. Let her do it herself."

As I trudged down the stairs, I glanced back at Jannie, who was almost in tears.

"I'll be watching the Mets."

Five minutes later, just as the bases were loaded and Mike Piazza was coming up, I heard, "Dad, please help me get started."

"Okay." I raced up the stairs in my imaginary "Superdad" cape. "Take some notes. Here's the thesis."

"First things first, Dad. Tell me again. How did it end?"

"Well, the U.S. was wrong, there were no dominoes. It turned out that the Vietnamese were much more of a national unity than they were a Communist country. When China invaded them in the late 1970s, trying to take them over, the Chinese were beaten back, just like the Americans."

"So what's the thesis?"

"Maybe that there was a lasting heritage of our war in Southeast Asia. If the Vietnamese were going to fight so hard to keep the United States out, they sure as heck weren't going to give in to the Chinese."

"That's a great ending, Dad. Now, how do I begin?"

I gave her four or five headings, and she started taking notes, distracting herself by rolling her 6-sided pencil on the desk, watching the #2 come out on top.

"Jannie," Mary called up, "Do you want something to drink? Can I get you anything else? Maybe you need a break? Can I help you with your typing?"

"Sure, thanks, Mary. I'd like a Citrus Cooler."

I ran down and brought it back up for her. "Looks like you're doing a good job."

"Thanks, Dad."

I looked over her shoulder and read her "research dissertation."

"Maybe you want to switch sentences here—put that one first."

"Dad, let me do it my way!"

"You sure?"

"Daaad!"

"Well, just make sure you get some sleep."

"Don't worry, Dad."

Mary and I went into our bedroom to watch the news and the "Seinfeld" episode about the "Soup Nazi." We turned out the lights. I glanced at the picture of my mom on the bureau, along with one of me lifting Jannie when she was a seven-year-old flower girl.

It was now 11:35. "Jannie, how are you doing?"

"I'm tired, Dad. Just a few more minutes and then I'll get up early in the morning to finish it." It sounded like an old recording from my teen years. "Is it okay if I don't practice my Torah reading tonight?"

"I won't tell the rabbi if you don't."

"Thanks, Dad."

"Love ya, Jan-Jan."

"Love ya lots."

At 3 a.m., the phone rang. It was the Emergency Room physician describing a middle-aged woman with chest pain. I shook myself awake, trying to relieve myself from the recurrent nightmare from which I had been awakened. I was back in college, woefully behind in my reading, totally unprepared for an exam, with a paper due the next morning, and the date for dropping a course had passed two days earlier. I tried to get dressed as quietly as I could.

"Are you okay, honey?"

"No, honey, a 45-year-old woman with chest pain."

"That's awfully young."

"I know, I think she has pericarditis, fluid around her heart."

"Why?"

"They said she had breast cancer."

"When will you be back home? I'll wait up for you. You know how much I hate it when you leave in the middle of the night."

"Honey, please try to get back to sleep. You have to take the bus into the city in the morning."

"I love you, I'll be here. Call me if you need me."

I tiptoed into the bathroom, bypassing Jannie's room where she was sound asleep in her bed, curled up with her stuffed bear and Zen, our Shih Tzu puppy.

I went downstairs, putting on my coat and getting ready to go out the back door. I came back upstairs with a glass of water for Mary. "I'll be home as soon as I can. Luv ya."

As I drove off to the hospital, I remembered my first patient with breast cancer during my internship. Hope (that was really her name) was a Native American, aged 41, who was dying of breast cancer at Roosevelt Hospital. I had taken care of her during the initial stages of her cancer, but now she was on a different floor with a different set of doctors caring for her. Over the loudspeaker came the ominous announcement, "Code 444, Winston 4, Room 405." I had visited Hope at least twice during the past week, and I knew that this was her room. I also knew that her time had come, that she wanted no heroics, and that she had no close family in New York.

I ran to her room as she lay gasping for air, her sunken cheeks pale as a ghost, her body gaunt from the effect of the tumor on her body, with a naso-gastric tube through her nose to relieve the pain of intestinal ob-struction. As her regular nurse arrived, she quickly protected Hope from trauma of CRP by assuring us she had DNR orders.

The other interns moved back to their rounds, their medical skills no longer needed. But I continued to sit with her, holding her in my arms as she gradually lapsed into a coma, stopped breathing, and was no longer in pain as her heart stopped beating. Hope had passed not down the white tunnel with my mom but up into her great hunting grounds in the sky.

This was the first time, and it has remained the only time, that I have sat with a patient and held her while she died. There were incalcu-lable odds that Hope would have the same name that we had given to the dog we had adopted when my mother had died. But a 41-year-old woman with breast cancer—it was as if Mom had come back down from heaven to give me a chance to hold her as she had died, to be with her one more time.

I am not a believer in mysticism, in parapsychology, or in reincarna-tion, but who else could it have been? But then Hope was dead, and I was again alone.

As I entered Hunterdon's Emergency Room, wondering if this patient would need an emergency procedure to prolong her life, I pondered how many doctors had gone into medicine to reclaim the past, to protect a parent, to cure their disease and keep them alive. Me . . . maybe I had gone into medicine to reclaim the past, to protect a parent, to finally be with them when they died.

Thankfully for this lovely woman, it turned out to be a false alarm, just a minor muscular pain which could be treated with aspirin. She wouldn't need emergency surgery after all. I drove home in a daze, fa-tigued. I turned on my CD soundtrack of the movie "Armageddon." Aerosmith was singing:

> *"I could stay awake just to hear you breathing*
> *Watch you smile while you are sleeping*
> *While far away and dreaming*
> *I could spend my life in this sweet surrender*

I could stay lost in this moment forever
Every moment I spend with you is a moment I treasure.
Don't want to close my eyes
Don't want to fall asleep
'Coz I'd miss you baby
And I don't wanna miss a thing."

I saw the blue light from the television on in our bedroom. I climbed the stairs and walked into our bedroom.

"Is everything alright?"

"Yeah, she'll be okay."

I changed out of my clothes and crawled under the covers.

"Luv ya, honey. Get some sleep."

Zen walked into the bedroom, checking out what was going on. He jumped onto the bed and curled up next to me as I curled around Mary.

I lay in bed, my eyes getting acclimated to the dark. This was as close as I could get to the 1960s. Parent/child/dog—all at home, cuddling together. My "home" could be a three- bedroom Victorian house with two bathrooms and a two-car garage, or it could be a cardiac floor with patients hooked up to monitors as we attempted to mend their broken hearts, just as long as Mary and Jannie (and Zen) were there with me to keep me whole.

As I closed my eyes, I wondered whether I wanted to stay awake so I could treasure every moment. Or did I want to go to sleep and hope that time would be suspended, that my mom could stay alive, that Jannie would never grow up, that Zen would never get frail, and that Mary and I could hold each other forever?

It was 4:30 a.m. and I had to get up in two hours. I was exhausted and fell asleep.

At 6:30, the alarm went off. And still the Beatles on Q104.3:

"Woke up, fell out of bed
Dragged a comb across my head.
Found my way downstairs and drank a cup"

Jannie was back at work, typing frantically. Four words correct, then a correction—her fingers pecked away at the keyboard.

I furtively looked over her shoulder.

"Hanoi is spelled with an "i.""

"I know, Dad. I haven't done spell-check yet."

I looked at my watch.

"Gotta go. I've got ten patients to round on before office hours."

I poked my head back into our bedroom. Mary was barely awake.

"Bye, honey."

The Beatles beckoned:

"Looking up, I noticed I was late
Found my coat and grabbed my hat."

As I started out the backdoor, I had second thoughts:

"I found my way upstairs."
Somebody spoke."

"Bye, Dad, luv ya."

"Bye Jannie. See you later. Luv ya, Don't miss the bus."

"Bye, honey. Luv ya."

"Bye, honey. Luv ya."

Stereo love messages, a veritable philharmonia to my ears.

I walked out my back door. It was beginning to pour, a torrential rainstorm. As I stepped out onto the porch, I felt the loss of the protection of my home. As scary as the thought of nuclear war had been in 1962, our homemade bomb shelter was there to keep my family together as a unit. There was room for me with my mom and dad, Harlan and Marty, and Fuzzer. But, on this morning, I had to depart my shelter, all alone, to go to work, leaving Jannie and Mary and Zen as unprotected as I now felt. The umbrella I unfolded kept the raindrops from falling on my head, but that was about it. How would they or I get through the day? I thought about Jannie's Torah reading for her Bat Mitzvah from "The Book of Numbers."

"May the Lord bless you and keep you.

May the Lord make his face shine upon you and be gracious unto you.

May the lord lift up his countenance upon you and give your peace"

I haven't believed in an all-powerful God ever since Mom and Cousin Bruce died so early. But I have come to hope that there is a God who is all-loving and is there to comfort us and help guide us through our lives.

I started singing with my mom as she sat in our dining room playing her organ:

"When you walk through a storm
Hold your head up high
And don't be afraid of the dark.
At the end of the storm
Is a golden sky
And the sweet silver song of the lark.
Walk on through the wind,
Walk on through the rain,
Though your dreams be tossed and blown.
Walk on, walk on with hope in your heart
And you'll never walk alone!
You'll never walk alone."

EPILOGUE

November 5, 2008, 1:15 a.m.

Oh how my dad and I had fought 40 years ago over the protests at Grant Park during the 1968 Democratic Convention. I was anti-war and he was really pro-establishment rather than pro-war. He had become more conservative as he grew older, eschewing his own 1950s civil rights activism at the dental convention in Miami and Adlai Stevenson's social liberalism for the 1970s and '80s conservatism of Nixon, Reagan, and the Bushes.

So, as I smiled to myself at Jannie's text message, *"Obama rules! Everyone says hi! Luv 2 u and Mary! Jannie,"* I wondered what my conversation would have been like with my dad tonight. But it had been over a year since my dad passed away at the age of 84, while he was recovering from what was supposed to be a benign vascular procedure. We had all been assured that it would be an overnight stay for a simple kidney artery stent to control his blood pressure. However, immobility due to his hip had led to complications, and he had ended up in a rehabilitation center a few blocks from his apartment in Riverdale, New York. He had maintained his mental faculties, and even while he was lying in bed after a day of exercises and physical therapy, he still continued to compile a list of new projects for his foundation, which was now 40 years in existence.

The last day I had seen him was Mother's Day, two weeks before he died, May 30, 2007. I had brought him a delicacy that was not served at the center—Chinese food. And we then watched the Mets, not on a premium cable channel, but on the old Channel 11, as they squeaked out a victory. That was my last visit—and his last Chinese meal and Mets' victory! And, as I had always done in the 41 years since my mom died, I kissed him goodbye and said "I love you," in case there might not be a next time.

Two days after he had died, Mary and I sat with DJ, the funeral director, at Fisher's Funeral Home on Main Street, Flemington. The day before, we had given DJ a copy of my dad's curriculum vitae so that he could write an obituary for the local papers. The resume was 23 pages long, documenting all of his schooling, all of his degrees and academic appointments, all of the books and journals he had edited, and all of the symposia he had organized.

As I glanced around the office, I noticed a folded American flag on the desk. DJ then showed us the final draft he had sent in to the papers, which included an entry that was absent from my dad's printed CV.

"He also served as a 2nd Lt. in the MARINE CORPS RESERVES from 1943 to 1947."

My dad, despite his congenital hip problem, had been in the military during WWII as a dentist! Through all of our battles, he never divulged his secret. He had done his patriotic duty, while I (granted, maintaining my 2S status had been with his overwhelming encouragement!) had not. And why he remained a "closet" veteran is just the final piece about my father that he took with him to his grave, forever to remain unknown to his family.

But he was a "veteran" and all of his sons were not.

He had served his country and I had not.

What made me so special?

And six days from tonight, on November 11, 2008, Veteran's Day, it will be with great pride that I will fulfill "my duty to honor him."